Life Is a Game

Life Is a Game

DJ CON

iUniverse, Inc.
Bloomington

LIFE IS A GAME

iUniverse books may be ordered through booksellers or by contacting:

iUniverse
1663 Liberty Drive
Bloomington, IN 47403
www.iuniverse.com
1-800-Authors (1-800-288-4677)

ISBN: 978-1-4759-5939-0 (sc)
ISBN: 978-1-4759-5938-3 (hc)
ISBN: 978-1-4759-5937-6 (ebk)

Library of Congress Control Number: 2012921227

Printed in the United States of America

iUniverse rev. date: 11/08/2012

Contents

Introduction

Life is a game.
I honestly believe we have two choices in life:

1) to be unconsciously played
or
2) to be consciously a player!

To be played or to be a player . . .
That is the question.
This is my gift to you . . .
The choice is yours!

This book consists of short stories and experiences that life has given me, which have invited me to have an open mind, to see past many illusions, and to experience many truths that were once beyond my own comprehension. The purpose of this book is for me to pass on those experiences in written form and also invite you to explore some interesting topics. I hope you too will see through many of life's illusions on the path to awakening.

I have delved into certain subjects of the unknown, the supernatural, and whatever life gave me an opportunity to experience. I started doing all of this first as an interest and then as a topic for my side of the argument, but as the story went on, I felt I needed to continue in order to help people. As this intense life kept playing out, I continued on in the belief that I could give people back to themselves after I broke free from many of life's controls that are out there.

I am writing this book due to the experiences that life has given me, in order to give you, the reader, lifelong lessons that you can apply to each day of your life, so that you have the gift that life gave me whilst you're still young and want to live a great life.

After you read this book, I believe that you will see that each person has guidance. You will understand that the universe does not care whether you want a pleasant outcome to your situation or a not-so-pleasant outcome; either way, the universe accepts it as your point of attraction and matches it.

I also believe that due to the step-by-step experiences that life gave me, you too will be able to understand the concept of timelessness and that we always live in the present.

It is now at the end of 2012, and I need to finish this book and get it published. In recent years, I have jumped off the Sydney Harbour Bridge and survived, I have tried to electrocute myself in a bathtub and survived, and there have been many planned but failed attempts of suicide and many years of wanting out of the game of life. The reason for all of this was because I was set up. I could not see this till afterwards, but my own deeper self, my subconscious mind, set me up. There was no way that I could continue on in life without surrendering and watching the light at the end of the tunnel switch itself off.

After taking this interesting journey, and after surrendering to life itself, I have understood the true meaning of life being a game due to surrendering and awakening. I became connected to my subconscious mind, I became my deeper self, I walked around not in my head, but in the awareness of the knowing within, I became my subconscious mind, aware fully in the present. I know that time is an illusion. I can clearly see from both perspectives of how it is an illusion and how many people believe it is real and cannot comprehend that it is an illusion. Time is a mind illusion, and once a person's energy steps out of the mind and connects with the rest of its energy, that person becomes aware of truths that once seemed impossible to comprehend.

I lived a life that consisted of highs and lows, which is what life is about; everything is relative to the next. But these highs and lows over the years went from good mood, bad mood, to a spiritual awakening, suicidal depression. After questioning life many times and getting no positive help, only more help to set me on a path of complete destruction, I felt that I had no choice but to give up and to get out of the game. It was then, the moment I tried to electrocute myself, that all the thoughts in my mind froze and a new awareness was awakened. But this lasted only a day or so, and then I became lost in my mind again and made another crazy suicide attempt. This got every cell in my body to stand to attention; it finally brought me to the next level, awake in my subconscious mind, aware of so many amazing truths, and living with a natural happiness within. During this period, I tried to find out why all this happened and how I got from A to B, so that I could pass on the missing link that clearly was missing.

I looked at numerology, the science of numbers; I also examined birth charts. You name it, I checked it out, and then, looking at the overall picture, I could see what was going on. I was driven to an awareness that the mind cannot handle, questions that I had about infinity and mind illusions. After reaching such mental highs, in the world of the relative, I also hit such mental lows. Once I kept expanding my mind to try and understand new concepts, new ideas, that were coming from inspiration within, the elastic band got stretched, and when it came back on itself, I found myself imprisoned in my own mind, unable to escape, constantly looking at any events in the worst-case scenario. The highs got higher and the lows got lower until there was no escape from this emotional roller coaster. I had to give up, I had to give in, and in doing so, I expanded my consciousness from the mind perspective to the subconscious perspective. I crossed a bridge within.

I wish to thank all the people in this book, for playing their part in my life—without them this book would be meaningless, but because of them, this book holds many meanings and truths. This is a true story, although names and locations have been changed to protect the identity of those involved in this book.

Experience begins within. Everything in this book works off states of mind, connections, and experiences, just what life is all about. This book is not intended to be about me as a person, it is intended to be about the experiences that I have had, in order to show you what life has shown me.

CHAPTER ONE

The Game Of Life

The game is here to be played. When we really connect with the source—on a deep level—we see this game. We see it is a game when we get a feeling, a glimpse, a moment that we belong to something profoundly deeper than what we perceive. We then know we are part of a foundation that brings all of this game to existence. When we know that we "come from" and "go back to" the source, we then see that life is our own experience of evolution. When we connect with, even become, this energy, we then see the creation as it really is—a game.

Between states of mind, thoughts on top of thoughts, re-creating and re-creating our reality.

All we need to know are the rules of life, universal rules and laws, the mechanics of our world, and then we prove to ourselves that life is really a game and then we all find out what we are here for, and we become the players that we potentially are. The aim of the game is to understand one's self—find out why we are here and to justify our existence.

SPIRITUAL EXPERIENCE

Here I am. I am on a bridge—it is the Sydney Harbour Bridge in Australia. I am walking over this bridge for the first time, and I am just at the start of it now. As I am on this bridge, I realise that it seems like forever since I have experienced this feeling, if I ever did. Finally I have made it somewhere, not just because I just landed on the far side of the world a few days ago, but because I have found peace of mind; something is waking up inside of me as I am walking across this bridge. My mind is so clear, and I am becoming aware that I am separate from my mind also. I'm feeling peace and tranquillity, and I am so awake all over my body, where my body feels like it's becoming so alive.

As I keep walking, realisations are coming from deep within and in a strange but also familiar awareness that lets me see that I am not separate from anything—I am fully connected with everything.

I have had glimpses and short connections to these feelings throughout my life, which is where I strived to be, but I can see now that I was just too close to everything to even see anything the way it is.

I am awake, and it is very funny, amazing, and overwhelming for me, as my whole life passes before my eyes but now with an awakened perspective on each event. I see it all: how, what, where, when, and why all this was happening to me. All my experiences are seeping up through my body as energy, entering my mind, where all is analysed as my mind becomes the computer and tool that it is and I become the watcher, as I have woken up within and see it all before my mind's eye.

Each and every event that once stood in confusion, all the madness my mind was experiencing because it was full up, is all becoming so clear now and everything is slotting in place, thus leaving me with a great natural insight, in depth, full of ecstasy, awareness, and well-being.

I see now why each person has come into my life when they did and what part they have played in my life—in my game. I see my whole life as a game that we play, where I once believed it to be the real reality, but now I see each person had played their part perfectly to get me to experience all I needed to experience and also to give me perfect understanding in so many things that I would have never understood. It's my world and my game, and I can't have negative feelings towards anyone now as I see it all, it's all perfect, and now I just have to let each one of those people walk their own paths in life.

I am trying to write all this down as I am walking across this bridge. I am not even halfway across the bridge yet and a lifetime of events and experiences has been revealed to me. My mind is like a computer, processing all this data. I am going deeper into myself, I am expanding too, I am becoming aware of myself, not just my body and my life, but all this energy and aura that my body is housed into. I am walking faster and faster, and my energy is vibrating faster, and I am becoming more awake. They say your whole life flashes before your eyes when you are about to die, but I don't think I am dying, I am becoming alive. I was asleep my whole life, I was unconscious, and now—this is so amazing and clear.

This bridge is the path I am walking on, the harbour is revealing something to me, and the sky above. As I, myself, my energy vibrates faster, I can see life in a totally different perspective, as everything goes deeper and expands at the same time, I can see and feel what is in the sky above me and the water below me; it holds the same essence that is also in me. All of this essence is connecting with me, or me with it, as this same energy stuff is vibrating at the same level. I am so connected. I almost feel that I am going to burst into a complete ecstasy of awareness.

I see it all, nothing is what it seems, and it is impossible to see all this as clear as I see now when living in your mind, as that is the illusion that keeps us from the truth. Searching for answers outside ourselves and not finding them because the only way to find all the answers is inside us, and it is only when we are at this place of awareness that the reflection outside ourselves becomes clear and so different. It all works on levels, and I am racing through all these levels, connecting to different realties as I go deeper and deeper.

Nothing really matters, and living in our minds allows us to just see the tip of the iceberg. When we start to become that iceberg, not just the peak, we see the world in different perspectives, and the more we become the whole iceberg, the more we see the truth, even become the truth; it's all in us, we just have to become it.

I make it up to the centre of the bridge now, and I stop and look over the edge. I feel that I am the happiest man in the world, and there is nothing material that gives me that happiness. The happiness is coming from this essence that I am becoming, and the more essence I feel I become, the more open and clear and aware I am.

I connect deeper and deeper, I have no recollection of time, and at this moment I see that it is an illusion, another mind illusion. I can't even put into words what I am seeing or feeling here. I am seeing and knowing through my feelings, my energy within, and my mind is letting me see that which I am feeling. I am now connecting to the energy that is all around us; it is still unseen to me, but I feel and know it is here, and this energy knows I am awake as we connect on this vibration. I'm realising that all of this energy around is what influences us in life, we are not completely separate from everything and everyone, we are all connected on this core level. All we become or do derives from that. I see how it works, how every material thing has an essence inside of it and all around it, and once we become completely connected to this essence, we can change it and manipulate it, for it is the same stuff that is in us, which we are. I see how it all works.

I believe what is happening here is that I am having an in-depth spiritual experience, to say the least. How far and deep does this go is what I want to know? If I follow this, will I ever come back to pass this missing link onwards? This missing link in this bridge from the material world to the spiritual awakened world cannot be comprehended from one side of the polarity to the other. The links must be explained also, the experiences that lead to this experience and more.

I am still on this bridge, I am walking again. It is almost like technology, like the Internet, where I am streaming in information. I am picking up on things that I have never read, studied, come across, or even heard of before, not even knowing it exists till I attract the experience to back up this information. For example, a month later, I met a person who once had an interest in religion, got baptised at the age of thirty-three, and could even speak tongues. That was the language I was hearing in part of this experience. This sort of stuff, I feel, is way out of my league, nor would I even intervene in this, but this energy attraction I am on, as my energy changes, I am attracting outside energy, information. I am magnetising truth beyond my own comprehension!

I am not a very educated person, and I am a slow learner in many ways. Up to this point here, I read two books in my life; one was in school, and the other I never finished. My education is coming from my experiences, so it may be slow education, but it is education that becomes me, I become it as I experience it, it is a part of me, and I am evolving. After this experience I had a lot of thinking to do, but I couldn't quite get back to this awareness, as my energy became limited again, back into my mind. That's another story.

Something happened to me on that bridge—the Sydney Harbour Bridge. In that experience, I felt more at home than I'd ever felt before. I connected to one of the deepest essences that the world has to offer, and I realised that there was no limit to this adeptness or expansion that one could go; it seemed infinite, not like our minds understand that something must start somewhere and stop somewhere. That mind illusion fades away once one enters this depth of awareness—infinity is the truth and incomprehensible to our stop-and-start minds.

The only way for me to pass on the missing links to you is by telling my story, where your experiences can connect with my experiences.

We all have these aspects in common; we can all experience this and much more, and we all have the "good" and "bad" experiences in our lives, only in this awareness, I see that the bad ones now don't seem bad at all. I was just too close to see and judged them as bad, for only because of this badness has come this relative greatness. So all is what it is.

We're just living different lives with different stories, but our experiences connect on the same levels, the same feelings, only our stories may be a little different. Our states of mind, how we react to certain events, we all have these experiences. We can get imprisoned in our own minds—rarely we can find the freedom of our minds. We have the stress, the worry, our highs and lows, all through creating our reality on many different levels.

For our thinking creates our emotions, which is our energy in motion, and with the laws of attraction, our world becomes reality; in many levels, what you think—you become.

I remember imagining all of Australia whilst my life was limited and my world was small at home. I remember picturing a world open to possibilities and so much open space and freedom, a place where I would have a real clear mind and sense of peace surrounded by an amazing landscape and oceans of water and great beaches.

This is what I constantly pictured from where I was in Ireland, these were the happy thoughts in my mind that made me feel so good. But what was happening for me here was much more than what my mind could possibly think of, create, or comprehend, as what I am experiencing was out of mind and onto a deeper awareness. This experience was being magnified so much more than what I could have imagined.

So welcome to the game. I will tell you my story, and hopefully you can walk across your own bridge from unconsciousness to consciousness, and perhaps even from consciousness to subconsciousness, whenever you feel the moment is right for you. Let the game begin!

I HAD A VISION—I HAD A DREAM

I had a vision that set me on an unstoppable path. This vision became the most influential experience of my life, as it has influenced every decision I have made since that experience.

I was driving at the time and was playing music as I drove. I became so relaxed, and it was like my awareness was tapping in between two worlds. Then I saw another world or another time was coming into my reality; a beautiful lady was dressed in white and standing on the edge of a cliff. As I drove closer, I experienced something that has been a question in my mind since, beyond logic and rationality; I questioned the existence of time and even free will, and this had the greatest impact on my life from that moment onwards.

Then with a series of thoughts, feelings, and visual clips, my reality became this:

I am standing on a beach located over 14,000 kilometres away, the other side of the world, first looking out to the ocean. I am in my thirties and have my own family beside me, consisting of three kids, two boys and a girl and a beautiful partner. We are very happy, and I am feeling complete within. I've never felt this good before; I finally made it; I'm a happy, self-made man with a family of my own, and this is where I belong, free of restrictions and existing here, on the beach, looking out to the ocean, open space, open mind, clarity, peace, achievement, in a moment of how I envision life should be.

The feeling was amazing, what life should feel like, and this experience was where I felt I belonged. This moment seemed to last forever, and when it was over, I was back to my reality, stopped in my car, not driving anywhere, just as if life had paused or perhaps I had just stopped in my tracks for a good five minutes. I felt like I just lost it all in a moment; questions arose in my mind as to why I was back here. First I was lost and confused as to what happened, always questioning this experience throughout life, but I also knew within I need to rush through life to get back to the happiness and clarity of my thirties. That's where I belonged in life, and I needed to do whatever I had to do just to get back there and to fully live that life, being very happy and very comfortable.

CHAPTER TWO

Numerology and Astrology

Towards the end of my story, after I finally got it altogether, I came across some amazing people who have put most of their time into some very interesting subjects. I decided to see if they knew anything about me without me letting them know anything, apart from my date of birth and the place I was born. To my amazement, these people were able to tell me so much about my influences and my life and my world. This information amazed me greatly, and I remember saying to myself, *If I had of known this ten years prior, things could have been a lot easier,* but I then realised it was only when I became aware of the truth within me that it was then attracted to me—my inner world reflecting my outer world. But if none of this information has been ever known to you, the reader, at the end of the book I will explain how it all works, and you will open up doors within and attract that information in your world.

NUMEROLOGY

One of the subjects is numerology, the science of numbers, and it is so amazingly accurate. Each number holds in it a different meaning. All numbers can be brought down to their primary state, from number 1 to number 9 (in addition to numbers 11 and 22 and, in some cases, 33). A person's life can be explained to them in a matter of minutes as to how they may be driven in life or inspired. The pinpoints of where great changes could happen in their lives, and each and every year can be explained as to how it would individuality affect that person. All of this is from the science of numbers, and all information is derived from a person's birth date. The thing about numbers is, they are in sequence with the game of life itself and with us—as numbers are infinite and so we are too.

If there ever was a moment of total transformation, it is the moment of your birth. In that instant, you stepped through a door in time to a new reality—the reality of human life. The most important number in your numerology chart is based on the date of your birth, the moment when the curtain goes up in your life. Even at that moment, you were a person with your own unique character, as unique as your own DNA. Everything that is you, existed in potential, much like a play that is about to begin. Your entire life exists as a potential that has been prepared for. You have ultimate freedom to do with your life as you like, either to fulfil its potential completely or to make some smaller version of yourself. It all depends on your effort and commitment. You make the decisions to fulfil, to whatever extent, the potential life that exists within you. That is your choice. In this sense, the possible you is implicit during the moment of your birth. The Life Path number gives you a broad outline of the opportunities, challenges, and lessons you will encounter in this lifetime. Your Life Path is the road you are travelling. It reveals the opportunities and challenges you will face in life. Your Life Path number is the single most important information available in your personal chart.

The following numerology report was explained to me (my Life Path number is a 16/7):

"You are a searcher and seeker of the truth." Also, I have a clear and compelling sense of myself as a spiritual being. As a result of this, my Life Path is devoted to investigations into the unknown and finding the answers to the mysteries of life. It tells me that I am well-equipped to handle my task, that I possess a fine mind, that I am an analytical thinker, and that I am capable of great concentration and theoretical insight. It indicates that I enjoy research and putting the pieces of a puzzle together; once I have enough pieces in place, I am capable of highly creative insight and practical solutions to problems.

This report is about twenty pages long. After I read it, I found the opening statement highly interesting: "May great awareness of who you are support greater happiness and success in your life."

ASTROLOGY

The other subject is the heart and soul of astrology.

With your date of birth and place of birth, an astrology birth chart can be printed out that explains so much about your influences, traits, and characteristics. Your birth chart outlines what was going on at the start of it all. There is a lot that is not understood, but at the moment of your birth, you can determine what was in the skies and what influenced you, or better still, it is a reflection of who you are and who you could be. The stars that shine upon you at the moment of birth are connected with you.

This is how a game can be entered, at the start of the game, the moment of birth, the essence of life from all around—projected into you. All that is in your heavens, from your place in the universe, is your first reflection of all that is within you. Each of these stars, where they are in the sky, from your perspective at birth, all play an influence on you; to you, it is you, radiated outwards—as above—so below.

I will display some of my birth chart here. This will also give you an insight into what to expect when reading this book; it gives you a heads-up as to what direction we are going with this. The chart was done by a man named Tom, who has been doing this for approximately thirty years, first as a hobby and now a career.

Tom said, "Okay, D.J., I'm going to talk to you about your chart here. I thought I'd put it on audio tape for you. Mercury represents the way we communicate, the mind, the telepathic apparatus, and your Mercury is in the sign of Cancer. So you think like a Cancer mind, unlike a Gemini; you were born in the sign Gemini, which gives you highly developed intuitive abilities, and you are especially very in touch with your feelings. If you're ever upset in any kind of way, you're not going to be thinking very clearly, so it is always best to still the mind—meditation is a good thing for you, that is when your insights come there the most. You also have a very intuitive mind that doesn't have to depend on logic, because you get answers in a whole. You also have the planet Uranus there, and the planet Uranus is in a very good aspect or angle to Mercury, which gives you this great ability to have flashes of insight; these hunches, these leaps of faith come to you that are very accurate. You have the mind of an inventor, by the way, if you ever want to get into inventing things. Besides that, you also have the planet Pluto, which means you think in terms of great depth; you go to the core of issues. You know, you're not afraid to just penetrate to the core, and that can connote great intuitive abilities and physic abilities on a Mental Plane.

"Now on the Emotional Plane, you have Moon in Virgo; the Moon represents the way we feel, and that's in the sign Virgo. That in itself is not very intuitive, but you also have the planet Saturn and you have the planet Neptune, and Neptune gives great spirituality, incredible sensitivity. You know, one of your challenges in life is that you're so sensitive and you've got to learn when to turn it off—because you could be around people and feel really good and if you walk into this party and somebody's angry or pissed off, you'll walk out and be angry and pissed off. It's not coming from you, so you have to learn really strong boundaries with other people, especially if you get into this kind of work, that you protect yourself."

"Now, your sensitivity is just so profound as far as being able to get psychic consciousness and feelings from others. So that's Moon and Neptune also. Now the Moon and Neptune and Saturn are in the third house, the house of communication, so it's really important for you to communicate this. Now you have natural creative ability, you have great charisma, mate, like you challenge it, you just test it out. You have Venus and Mars in a tough, really good aspect—it's dynamic—it gives you great charm. You also have Leo North Node, which means you are here to express yourself, to believe in yourself, to get into your creativity, you're here to develop a sense of self, to develop an ego; ego's not a bad word for you.

"Now looking back in your childhood, you had a very difficult path. You did not have an easy childhood, and you are learning to believe in yourself, you are learning to develop your own self-esteem. You like control, and people see you as very strong, but inside at times, the sense of confidence is not there, but you don't let anybody else see that. But it's important for you—you will be a self-made man, and nobody will ever be able to take that away from you."

"All right, looking back a few years too—you really have gone through tremendous change here in the last few years. You have gone through hell in the last four to five years, you really have gone to the depths of hell, mate, but you're out of it now and it gets better."

"Anger has always being a challenge for you—because you're so sensitive, you picked up a lot of your parents' anger when you were young, or anger within the family. It was either held in or was averted but you picked it up, so learn to come to terms with this powerful force called anger. It's not a negative thing, because once you accept it as a positive and acknowledge it—okay, I got a part of me and it's really pissed off—then the energy can be rechanneled into the way you want to do it, a positive aspect, and one of your positive aspects here is your work. You have the ability to encourage others, and that's because you have a lot of bleeping courage, ha ha, okay, a lot of courage, so you have the ability to encourage—to give that courage to other people. So, this thing with anger, okay, really important, you know—whew. Years ago you would have been pretty dynamic with this. You are like me—you have a tendency to hold in your anger, and we hold it in, and we think we're cool, and we don't even know when we're angry until something triggers it, and we can have tremendous explosions. And if not, if you don't let it out, that's even worse because you are holding it in at times, so it's important to reconcile, to see anger as your friend. It's your power, it's your ability to encourage others."

"You need to focus on how you can use this incredible energy to support others in reaching their dreams. Now you also are a very multifaceted person, your Venus is in Gemini, so you can do many different things, you certainly have communication ability, the writing skills are going to be really good for you."

"You have been going through tremendous transformation emotionally your whole lifetime, and so you have a lot to pull from. So your biggest asset is that incredible mind of yours, it's an intuitive mind. It leads you in the right direction. The biggest challenge is to work with the energy of anger, also to work with the vulnerability, because you are so sensitive, you see, Saturn moon gives great sensitivity too. You'll be a really good teacher and a really good healer; you have what's called Chiron, a planet that is in the tenth house which shows healing abilities. But Neptune, which is the planet of great spirituality, is very favourable in your chart here. Anything to do with Tai Chi or movement would be excellent for you to integrate that power of anger in a very positive way.

"As far as your psychic abilities go, yes, you have it in spades, and the key for you to opening up your psychic abilities is your amazing emotional nature, by coming to terms with it and opening up to your feelings. Hope that helps you. Again, you need to communicate this and express yourself fully, and every day you're here on the earth, your self-esteem will get stronger and stronger. I'm going to see if I can record this on to a CD now and send it off for you."

CHAPTER THREE

The Mystery of Life

I always felt that something mysterious was keeping itself secret from me—it was a secret I needed to know. I was born in Ireland but raised everywhere, and I have educated myself through experience. I am writing this book for whoever attracts it into their lives, hoping that I can help some people out there who may be going through some of the same experiences I did. Some of my friends died as young men due to various reasons, and I can't help but think that if I knew then what I know now, I could have helped them out, perhaps even prevented some of the madness and sadness I have seen. I'm writing this book to help people by shedding light on certain subjects. I also want to help them understand certain experiences that are either not known or just not discussed, in order for them to live a more fulfilled life. This knowledge is only gained by experience, so I don't want them to spend their lives finding this stuff out like I did. But once one of us does it for all of us, my life too will be fulfilled.

Certain things have happened in my life, things that I would either hear, see, or feel myself, and although I would ask for these things to be explained, no one could answer me. I got many half answers, which frustrated me with the lack of information, and the answers didn't add up for me. I then realised that I needed to experience whatever the topic was in order to fully comprehend and understand it. Any frustration became a creative, driving force for me to do so.

With the unknown and the unsolved issues that came into my life, I first questioned it from the non-experienced perspective, where I could not get the answers, and then I would bring the experience into my life and fully understand it, one experience after the next. Here are my stories. Experience begins within, and if you don't go within, you go without.

But no matter what, the game will go on!

I have been on an emotional roller coaster my whole life. What I mean by this is, I have gone through so many different types of emotions, so many experiences, and I am only getting them altogether now. Throughout all these changes, I have attracted in my world some very clear, consistent reoccurrences that have been a reflection of these energy changes—these states of emotion. The things I have been thinking of and the things going on inside of me have been a clear reflection of what was happening in my outer world, my life. This is one thing that I will demonstrate in this book, amongst many other amazing truths that I found out whilst on this journey.

MY EARLY YEARS

The first four years of our lives, we stay in our comfort zone. As children we learn from our parents; our parents are our teachers. From birth till four years old, we do most of our learning in life. Much of how we perceive the world to be is created in these four years of our lives. We do most of our learning even before we go to school. The other 20 percent or so is learned from the age of four till about thirty-five years old, and then that's it. People will find it extremely difficult to move out of this comfort zone, which is how they perceive the world to be.

I don't recall much of what happened in my first four years of life, but what Tom said in his reading made a lot of sense. Due to my sensitivity, I picked up a lot of anger energy within my family. It must have being inverted most of the time, and it may not have been a huge amount of anger, but with the sensitivity I was born with, this energy was passed onto me. Our house was under construction when I was born, and this went on for the first two years of my life. I do, however, recall when I was four and five that I became creative, building wooden carts from wood, nails, hammers, and handsaws. I had a lot of energy in me, and this became my outlet.

When I was seven years old, I walked over to the front door and opened it; it was windy outside, and when a gust of wind came in through the door, I took a deep breath and seemed to wake up within myself. Something deep and strong inside me woke up, and then my mind began to race. I had amazing thoughts and realisations, giving me great understanding to how life was for me and all. The understanding I received was that life itself is a game, and the way it works is through experiences, through cycles, levels, and we always exist playing this game, whether we are awake playing or sleep walking. We have been here before, we're always alive in one form or another. I could see that on the outside I was seven years old, but within me, I was a spirit that never died, and I felt that I had so many experiences behind me already, I was a player and I just woke up to my game.

I realised then that my game was about having this knowledge and never forgetting it, but to confirm to myself that what I knew here was true and to prove this life was a game. It sure was one big breath of fresh air.

It wasn't long before I wondered if I had a wild imagination or if this experience was really real. This I had to find out, slowly but surely.

According to Numerology, Ruling number 7 people like me go inward for the first time at seven years old, and we seem to process some sort of inbuilt spiritual wisdom. The truth of this, we will have to see for ourselves.

I lived a normal sort of life as we all do, if there is such a thing as normality. The only difference that there may have been with me, was that I downloaded everything in my reality on two levels. One was how we all go through life amazed at new things and new friends and learning, and the other was on a deeper level, constantly looking for connections, ways in which I can find a core rule, a core influence or law that brings all of this to play, searching to see where life itself derives from, seeing life from the perspective of being awake, also trying to prove to myself that looking at life from this perspective is actually a more real way of life. Or do I have a wild imagination? I am looking for a truer sense of life that leaves us feeling fulfilled, and I am trying to really understand the game of it all.

As I got a little older, I did wild things with my friends: I lived on the edge and got natural highs by climbing hills, trees, and buildings, and with just one slip, it could have been game over for me.

I was constantly trying to wake up again from my mind that was constantly thinking and holding me captive. These extremes in my life woke me up, they brought something to my life, where I wouldn't be lost in my own mind with thinking. This daredevil carrying on is what a lot of us do in order to get it altogether, to get into the moment and be awake like never before. What are we searching for? Was it something that is so real, that's only been experienced by a few? Why did we want it? Was it because it let us feel so alive, real, connected, where we can do anything? I enjoyed racing motorbikes, and all I did it for was to reach this feeling, to get out of the negative anxious feeling and out of my mind and connected with myself. Each time I raced, I got my fix and could handle my world again, from school situations to work life, having friends, and having fun. I became at ease, relaxed, and connected with it all. Without these fixes, I was unconnected and uneasy.

SIXTH SENSE

There was a sense that somehow opened up whilst I became so relaxed, an inbuilt sense that we all have but seldom use. This is known as our sixth sense, and it bypasses all logic and lets us see a bigger picture that not even time gets in the way of it.

We all have our five senses—touch, smell, taste, hear, and sight. Without these senses, we would have no choice but to awaken other senses within us. Sometimes when a person loses one of those senses, they develop another one, like having awareness or intuition. Each of us experiences life on four different levels: with our physical body, our mental faculty, our emotional makeup, and our intuition. Each of these areas has a specific means of perceiving information. The physical body is capable of touch, taste, pleasure, and pain. It provides us with a sense of the physical world.

The mental body, like the emotional and intuitive natures, perceives the invisible worlds. Our minds deal with the world of thought. The heart, of course, is preoccupied exclusively with the world of emotion.

Our feelings teach us many things about ourselves and about others. Finally, we have the capacity for direct contact with the higher realms by way of intuition. Intuitive insight comes in a flash. It is not rational—that is the world of the mental plane—but it comes as if it were placed at the doorstep of our minds. Intuition, therefore, bypasses all effort.

These four faculties exist in all of us. But we usually only depend on one or two of them for the bulk of our knowledge. Some of us are possessed by our senses, while others live almost exclusively in our hearts or minds.

Have you ever heard the phone ring, or the door knock, and you just knew who it was straight away, even if you haven't even heard from that person for a long time?

Have you ever just picked up on the sense that someone is watching you, even though you cannot see them?

Have you ever sensed trouble was coming and you just stuck around, just to see if this sense was correct and it was?

This sixth sense is known to most people. So, somehow for me, that sixth sense was intensified—I was born like this.

In later years, I searched to find out why was I like this.

I didn't find out why I was like this, but I found out that I have great sensitivity, that even when I am around a person for a while, I feel what they feel, sometimes is anxiousness and I try to get away from it, but in younger years, I couldn't and it becomes me after a while. If I'm around a person who feels exhausted tired, soon enough it will get me and I'll have to go for a nap somewhere, which is very unlike me. If I am working with someone who is highly emotional, that energy gets into me, if totally fuels me, I can use that energy to write a book, but I don't like the feeling at all, and if I don't rid that energy, I get sick, I cough up that energy, whilst lying on the side of a park, choking and coughing up blood. I pick up on people's energy, and I could not switch that off. I am not sure if you can imagine how difficult that has made my life at times, but it does mean that this should be an interesting story for you. Secrets are often uncovered due to this sensitivity. I feel it all and have felt it all.

When I was a child, I picked up on people's feelings, and then after a while, I noticed that I would sense when someone close was in trouble or something bad was about to happen to them. When I was a teenager, I got in trouble with the police quite a bit, as I had a lot of energy and didn't have many desirable outlets, so I became destructive at times. I always sensed when the police were coming after me or calling to the house. Whenever they knocked on the door, I knew not to answer. To me, it felt like trouble.

It wasn't long after that when I sensed a new event, just out of the blue. I could see it in my mind's eye; my sixth sense was giving me this information. I could see in my mind that my parents were going to break up and that my father was going to leave the house. There were no arguments or unpleasantness in the house at the time, so none of this made sense to me. I did not mention it to anyone; I just stayed connected to this inner knowing, amazed by where it came from, as it grew stronger and more intense. I questioned everything about this event in my mind—how, why, when—and rationally thinking, it just didn't make sense to me. Soon enough, in a few weeks, my parents had a big argument. Emotions were high, and the next day, my father said that he was moving out for a while. He never came back, although I always stayed in touch with him and he is a great bloke. My parents just wanted to go their separate ways. We all have this gift of knowing within; it is a sense that most of us don't use or have been taught not to use by religious zealots over the generations, but we all have it.

A few years after that, I was out having fun and enjoying life when the sixth sense feeling kicked in, and I knew someone close was going to die soon. This is what entered my mind, and I tried to shake it off. This knowing within kept coming back and getting stronger and stronger, until there was no denying that someone close was going to die. This intense feeling continued for about six weeks, growing stronger and stronger. I did not get the information on who was going to die; I only knew that it was going to be big. My mind tried to understand this; without ruling out the possibility of insanity, my mind tried to guess who would die. I became very stressed, thinking it would be a family member, and I panicked each time someone was not home before midnight. I asked life to tell me who it would be so that I could help and stop it. I received no information of that kind; I only knew that this was a big thing and it was going to happen soon.

For a couple of days, I completely shut down; I could not talk to people anymore, could not have any interaction with the outside world, could not even relate to family members. I became completely isolated, as this sixth sense seemed to have taken over my body and mind and was still powerful, letting me know the same information. I was powerless to stop it.

Then a very good friend of mine called Mikey came to my house, looking for me; he was concerned about my behaviour, and after humouring me for a while, he convinced me to go for a beer in the local. We went, and after I had two beers, I felt I was coming back to normal. I felt good again; I could not believe it, as it had been so long since I'd felt that good. I then suggested to my friend that we head out to a club and party all night.

After we were on our way, we heard that another friend of ours called Cairan had been killed on the motorway after being hit by a car. I didn't believe it and still forced my friend to go to the club. When we got there, more and more people told us that our friend had just died.

I was confused that night; how could I feel so good just when someone close had died? I was in mixed emotions all night. Soon enough I worked it out that when my friend died, the sixth sense within switched off. All of this clicked into place when I was at the funeral, because that's what I was feeling, something really big. The whole town was at the funeral, thousands of people, and the feeling at the funeral of loss and sadness was the same feeling that I was feeling before. Six weeks before that funeral, I had the same feeling within from this sixth sense.

The sixth sense, the intuition, the gut feeling, the feeling deep in your bones lets you know when something is about to happen. Not once in my life has this feeling ever been incorrect.

Have you ever sensed that someone was in trouble—perhaps even someone thousands of kilometres away? You ring and ask, "Are you okay?" and the person says, "No, how did you know?" This sixth sense does not get restricted by distance. It happens in an instant and is full of information, unlike your other senses that you could spend so much of your time and still not get close to the truth.

We all have the sixth sense, on one level or another. Developing that sixth sense could be the way forward.

MYSTERIOUS LIFE

When I was growing up, I couldn't help but notice that life was showing me things. My father, Arthur, didn't make any time to help me with things. Whenever I tried to build something out of wood in the garden, he would take it all away and say that it was rubbish. But I could see that these putdowns were making me strive to be better. The things he said to me deeply affected me; I could have blocked them but decided to take them on board. Many conversations were had between people, but even when they were having their conversations, there were certain parts that stood out for me, certain parts that I chose to take in (or my subconscious mind chose to take in), and the moment the information entered my mind, it was analysed automatically on a deep level. Other times, music would be playing on the radio, and certain words of certain songs really seemed to connect with me. Actually, due to this mysterious happening, I began to match certain songs and lyrics to certain experiences I had. I needed to live my life, as we all do, but also I needed to do a lot of deep thinking, understand many mysteries and experiences, and therefore having a song to match that experience let me move on to the next experience without having to keep it all written down or clogged up in my mind. I connected with the song that was playing, and that experience became my memory. The experience, the truths in it, how I saw it to be, and the wisdom received were all reduced to a song that came into my reality at those moments. At the end of my game, life brought all those songs to me, which activated a memory trace, and I would relive that experience again, this time putting it on paper. One of the songs, for example, was "Open Your Mind," which I related to these mysterious ways of life. The lyrics include this line: "Wait till the end of time," and I felt that was something to wait for, time standing still or the end of time.

I believe that all of us do connect to certain songs, and I feel that life (or whatever substance that holds life together) seems to be connecting with us on different levels. There seems to be something unseen or on the other side that is in synchronisation with our evolvement, our growing up. This was my connection with life, and this is what I searched for: to understand and to find out what was really happening behind the scenes. We react to certain statements made by people, and that's what makes a part of us grow—the part of us that needs to develop. It's almost like opposites attracting. Or someone can come into our life and their personality gets us to develop ours, where we were not like that before; this opposite attracting was very interesting.

ENERGY DROVE ME ON MY PATH

I believe that due to my sensitivity as a child, I picked up a lot of energy. It was like a certain part of me that was angry, but this energy could be used to do many things. I just needed to be active and creative in order to release it or burn it out. Whatever was passed onto me, between inverted anger, strong emotions, or some form of negativity, I was around this energy for a long time. I could feel it, and although I didn't like it, it wasn't long before I called it my own.

I could constantly feel this energy; it was always there in our house. I often ended up in hospital with stomach pains. There was no escape from this, and the only thing that I could do was to be able to take it, to be able to live with it within me, to be able to accept myself with half of me full of negativity.

This had to happen to me, and this energy drove me through many different experiences, until it was partly released. I spent my whole life trying to relax this energy and keep it at ease. This energy became a part of me, and each time I went near high emotional people, this energy was intensified. Also, my energy attracted the same like energy out there, and that often led to problems.

As I was growing up, I became magnetised to situations; kids my age who had this energy in them became magnetised to me. I constantly tried to suppress this energy, and I would attract people who wanted to fight me or do things to bring this energy in me to the surface. They wouldn't even know why they would do this on a logical level of thinking; it just felt right for them when they were around me. Energy and energy attractions became a clear understanding at a young age. When I was able to use this energy usefully, I could burn it off and become balanced and at ease, and I didn't attract other anger energies to me.

There were only so many ways to release this energy as a child, and there were many times when I attracted angry people, angry groups, and even angry authorities. I would take in all these events on two levels; the logical one didn't make much sense, but the deeper connections did make sense. Energy, we learnt in school, can neither be created nor destroyed but only change form, from one form to the next. No matter how hard I would try to keep this energy suppressed within me, circumstances were attracted to me in order to bring this energy to the surface. Different things triggered off this energy in me: some places, certain lighting, and some people in certain situations. I would do my best to not let this energy come to the surface, as I didn't feel good with it and had no outlet for it. I could have gone into fighting, but it just wasn't for me. I was really secretly out to help people, not to fight with people, so I wouldn't fight people when they confronted me due to this energy attraction.

This energy was kept within, and it was only at certain times in my life where I could release it. When I was young, it was playing with friends; when I was a little older, I raced motorbikes. I did a lot of cycling each day when I finished school, as school used to make me very uneasy. School would leave my energy unbalanced, uneasy, and it filled me up inside where I wouldn't feel hungry. Many times I couldn't eat. As time went on during the school years, I constantly needed to feel at ease. I did this by listening to music and cycling to other towns to meet friends. I had lots of good times in the start of my teenage years, but after time went on, the negativity started to build up in me. It started to take over, as there became too much build up. When the summer was over and the winter was coming in, this energy would build up. I became a different person, and all the friends that I used to have so much fun with, I didn't hang out with them any more, as I was changing from the fun-loving character I once was.

As time went on and I was in my last few years of school, I started to develop an ulcer in my chest area, as this energy in me was not being released anymore. This soon developed into internal bleeding and blood loss. School made me feel very uneasy, and the main thing that seemed to agitate this energy in me was the unnatural lighting inside the school. Somehow it just was not good for a person like me with a sensitive nature.

FOCUSING ENERGY

I had this huge ball of energy in me. Whatever I decided to do with this energy, I could do. For example, I could work very hard and get jobs done very quickly. I could also analyse situations or think deeply by using this energy. I could be creative or destructive when I wanted to be. But I needed to use this energy or else I couldn't rest. The thing

I noticed with this energy in me was whenever I focused on a certain part of my body, the energy went there. This ball of energy could be passed around my body to any part, and it gave me lots of strength. One time I decided to focus on my leg and send that energy there, as I was just trying to relax the rest of my body. The energy went there and my leg started to turn red and very hot; it was almost as if my leg had been very sunburnt. I found this to be amazing. The controller of this energy was my mind, what I focused on, and it was as simple as that.

When you place your attention somewhere in your body, you can feel that it's not just your perception that is focused there. Something else is happening. Energy is displaced to that area. It is possible to measure this: the temperature of the spot you focus your attention on will rise. The Chinese say that "chi follows yi," where "yi" is the mind or intention/attention. Energy is converted from one form to another, but it is never created or destroyed.

Between your mind and your thoughts, you can use your mind for the tool that it is by focusing on a part of your body. As energy is put there, the temperature rises. To build up your muscles in the gym, focus on that muscle whilst doing the workout, energy is put there, thus increasing the muscle there. So with a relationship or an event, focus energy on that, the way you want it to be; energy is put there with your intention also. With a relationship, put the energy in, do the work, and relax, it will come to you. Chase and never catch or resist, and it will persist.

If you keep thinking about your fears, you put energy there and you attract the same thing that you fear. What you resist, persists, because you draw that very experience to you, until you overcome it, and then you no longer fear it. Or else you just don't think about it, don't send the energy there, and don't attract it. You may call this cheating in the game of life, but really you are just starting to understand the rules of life.

VIBRATIONAL ENERGY

On more important realisations, this energy has helped me to delve deep into understanding. At a young age, I saw life as a game; this was when I was awake within myself, when this energy was burnt off. When

I connected with life and my mind was at ease, I would clearly see that life is a game. So I am constantly taking in, searching for information in order for me to prove this to me. This is my greatest interest, and most hours of every day (if not all hours), this is what's going on in my head.

So there I was, fourteen years old, and my friends and I were outside on a summer's day. We were listening to music on the radio. Music was always a stimulator for my mind, so a constant supply of music kept my mind and thoughts entertained and at ease, and then inspiration arose from within or from my subconscious mind when I was in this deep awareness.

I was searching for a connection, going into deep thought. I needed to see past the illusion of life, and the only way I could was to work out how the game works, and then I could see clearer. I spent years searching for a connection, and then it just came to me, a foundation on which I could build all my philosophy.

The music was pumping out of the radio; I could see it in my mind's eye and clearly feel the vibrations it was making. In this deep thought, my mind flickered through all my connections, and I realised that music was a sound carried on vibrations, along with life and all that is in it. Everything vibrates, and everything in life has in it, holds, or is made up of a vibration, which is energy.

The music and the vibrations are one with each other, and it's the vibration that we are hearing, as we too are made up of energy that vibrates. This is a core truth for me, vibrations, different speeds and different pitches, all vibrations, and this is our connection. Sound is the most obvious of all vibration energies. We all hear and feel the vibration of sound. Radio stations are made up of a frequency that vibrates. Light itself and all its colours are made up of vibration energy. All matter, whether rock or earth, can vibrate, creating earthquakes. A train can move past a building, and the vibrations can be felt in the bricks. Everything vibrates to a precise frequency, and this is one of the core essences of this game as we know it. There is even a way of healing people, called vibration healing, and this is how it works: when the c string of a harp or piano is struck, all the other octave strings of c begin to vibrate. They are in resonance with one another. The different parts of our physical, emotional, mental, and spiritual being resonate to various frequencies of vibration. This energy vibration therapy gently invites stuck energy to move or vibrate again; if energy is overstimulated, it is invited to explore stillness. Over time, this is the experience of not only health and vitality, but expansion, transformation of consciousness, and eventually transcendence.

DEEP THINKING

Sometime later, I got back into my philosophical thinking; I wondered, what are the rules in this game, if there are any, and what are the illusions, if anything is real at all? I got time away from all influences, and I was able to get at one with myself and continue to capture my deep thinking, searching for answers.

I was working with a lad named Steve, who was a philosophical thinker. On the last day we worked together, he was racing around on some machinery, and he stopped and looked at me and said, "Nothing matters, nothing matters." He was so happy with what he had worked out, and this changed his own character. He spent his whole time working things out in his head while he was speeding around, and everything was racing in his world, and at the end of it, he came out with "Nothing matters." I thought about this for a minute and figured it was a state of philosophy that I had not reached or understood. What he worked out made him so happy, and soon after that, he stopped working there.

These were the people and the circumstance that I would attract in my life when I was searching for answers. I sure was relaxed and happy, and it was my time out to take things deep in understanding again. I started to see things in my mind's eye; as I became connected to my emotional energy, I could see events before they were happening—things that were about my life or affected me.

I could not work out how I could see things in the future, and I couldn't just settle it with a gift of some sort. I needed to know how these things worked. I realised that my mind was like some sort of computer; what I took on board to be worked out constantly stayed in my mind, working away. It was like a series of programmes running in my mind.

I began to think that all we are is the mind, and everything else is illusion. I kept this thought on board and imagined how it could work;

I then created a mental picture about what we are. It was just a series of brains or minds all placed on the ground, one after the other, and they were all connected. Where everything is in the mind, the use of our legs and arms and all that we see and hear is all created in this mind, and I was left with the question, if this is so, who then is running the show? So what's really going on, I thought whilst I drove around. Colour is not a real thing, I was sure of it, as it only exists from the light reflecting off the objects into our eyes, and our eyes are a sense built into the mind, where we all perceive the same colourful objects, as we are all connected—something connects us all.

The colour is not real; the sun, when it shines its light, gives everything colour, but without the light, there is no colour. The main point that I'm making here is that if we were blind, we wouldn't see colour, and the only way we see it is through our eyes. So we are just minds living in this illusion. But then where did these minds come from? Or else we are spirits inhabiting this mind, and when we are, we see these colours and hear these sounds, as this mind is a tool for us to inhabit and see the world in this game. I believe that we are slowly finding the workings of a game here.

THOUGHTS

When I was in school, there were some classes that I was comfortable in and other classes I was not. I was either highly intense or I would search for peace of mind and become so chilled. There was no balance at all. In one class, I was so chilled that I would sit in the back, where I could see everyone but no one could see me. I looked up and saw energy coming from everyone's mind, like circles or rings over their heads, so close together and getting so wide. Once, it was two feet high; half the class had these energy rings running into each other, and as they reached the ceiling, all the rings ran into each other.

This was what they were thinking. Their thoughts went upwards in rings, and everyone's ring was connected by the time it hit the ceiling.

What was this collective energy or consciousness doing? How does it work? I was not sure at that time, but I said to myself, *Don't forget this, you're onto it.* It was something I saw, and it was quite easy for me to remember things I saw. Vibrations and thoughts were the workings of the game. These findings were so important for me, and I was on the way to working everything out.

A couple of years later, I began to question about where I was getting my realisations from, as my mind was not giving them to me; the more I thought about it, the more confused I became and the further away I got. I realised that only when I stopped thinking for a split moment could I let the information in, for example, when I drove and listened to music. My mind was on a sort of auto-pilot and something inside me let me see the truth. So I questioned this and wondered how many thoughts our minds had in a day? If we could switch these thoughts off, we could let in the very information that we were searching for in the first place.

This game was becoming intriguing. I requested a direction as I was tapping in between my mind and my spirit and I had no answer for these questions. Then it happened; I heard on the radio, out of the blue, a show on science discovery information, and it said, "Every person has on average 50,000 thoughts in any one given day." It was amazing, hard to believe, that this just came on the radio. It was as though I was getting connected to this spirit side of life, streaming and downloading information.

This can happen to us all; often when we turn on the radio, the words of a song are directly in contact with what we need to hear. We almost feel that the song was written for us. On a technical level, this is the source of energy, the mystical spirit that is made up of intelligence, vibration energy that is communicating with us through radio, television, people, and many other ways.

Thoughts and vibration energy became the core workings of the game and factual truths for me to begin to experience and explain this game. There is something that brings these into play, but for now, we know that they are the core foundations in order to bring this game into existence. Thoughts when focused on a part of the body, an event, or any matter in our world place energy in that area, and the circle gets complete because the thoughts themselves are made up of energy, a vibration of energy. Everything derives from these two truths. I felt that I finally found a foundation for my game to begin.

I decided to look up "thoughts" on the Internet. Here are some quotes on this subject:

> *"Great men are they who see that spiritual thought is stronger than any material force, that thoughts rule the world."*
>
> Ralph Waldo Emerson.

> *"Thoughts are free and subject to no rule. On them rests the freedom of man, and they tower above the light of nature . . . create a new heaven, a new firmament, a new source of energy from which new arts flow."*
>
> Paracelsus.

> *"Men fear thought as they fear nothing else on earth—more than ruin, more even than death . . . Thought is subversive and revolutionary, destructive and terrible, thought is merciless to privilege, established institutions and comfortable habit. Thought looks into the pit of hell and is not afraid. Thought is great and swift and free, the light of the world, and the chief glory of man."*
>
> Bertrand Russell.

THE GUN STORY

Here is a crazy story that happened around this time, and even though I created it all, I still needed to analyse it. Here's what happened:

I had a few stories that I felt I needed to get off my chest in order to confirm what was going on. But I couldn't trust many people with these stories; better still, I didn't think that certain people could possibly understand. So I had one friend who I was going to share a few things with, but I first decided to tell him something that wasn't true in order to see if he could keep a secret.

It was the summer time, coming up to May/June, and I was out drinking with my friend, J.J. I then told him, "I have a gun, it's up the field."

He said, "Are you're kidding me?"

So I said, "I was shooting it earlier, and there is some power in it; when I pull the trigger, it throws back my shoulder." I did the actions of my shoulder getting pushed back as I was pretending to pull the trigger. Then I said, "Hey, don't tell anyone, will you?"

J.J. said, "Oh no, I won't."

I didn't think he could keep a secret like that, but it was up to him.

A half hour later, a crew of J.J.'s mates came around for a drink. I later looked over and there was J.J., pretending to shoot a gun with his arm and shoulder getting thrown back, exactly what I had shown him. So I realised that I couldn't tell him anything that was real for me, but he still remained a good friend. After I had a few drinks, I went up to another friend's place, and when I left there and walked up the field to see who was around, I saw Sean, one of J.J.'s friends, and he said, "You okay, D.J.?" And he showed concern after J.J.'s story.

"Yes, I'm fine, Sean," I said, "I'm just going to check on that gun, hid it in a good spot, you know."

I probably didn't look my best at the time, sometimes feeling like I did want to shoot myself, which in turn made all this so real.

Sean was concerned and said, "Don't do anything stupid, D.J.; see you later on."

The seeds were planted for whatever was next; all of this windup just seemed to feel right, and I just went with what felt right. We all went out that night and ended up in a house party. People were all over the house, sitting down, talking, and standing up, and I just got the urge to leave. I left and started walking home, which was four kilometres away. Then I saw a group of lads coming towards me. I started to run, and I think they began running after me, but I was gone. When I was halfway home, a car pulled up.

J.J. jumped out and said, "What are you doing? I was looking for you."

I got into the car. The owner of the house was driving; I thought they were going to give me a lift home, but they brought me back to the house party. I didn't feel comfortable in those house parties, particularly in this one, because I didn't know anyone. I couldn't believe I was back there again, and as soon as J.J. went into the kitchen, I left again. As I made it to the front door, there was a lad standing at the door and he stopped me. He showed me a kid's machine gun he had in his hand and said, "Hey, D.J., you off again? It's dangerous out there, you'll need this." He handed me the gun.

"Cheers, mate," I said and ran off.

So I went for my jog again with my plastic machine gun, and about halfway home again, a car came towards me. It slowed down and stopped ahead. It was about 3AM; I didn't know who it was, nor did I want to find out. I looked for an escape, and to my right was a gate and an open field; the rest of the road was lined with bushes and trees. As the car stopped, I ran to the gate, jumped it, and ran down the field.

Sean and another friend got out of the car; he recognised me and shouted, "Hey, D.J.! It's me, Sean! Are you all right? Come back."

I laughed and came back up. As I made it to the gate, I hopped over, and Sean said, "What are you doing out here? Where are you going? Were you at the house party?"

I replied, "Yes, I was at the house party, but I'm tired now. I'm real tired now." As I stood in the road, Sean's friend watched as I dropped to my knees, put the gun to my head, and shouted, "Three, two . . . ," and as I was getting to "one," Sean shouted, "No!" whilst running towards me. He stopped, put his hands up to cover himself, and looked away, as he couldn't let himself see what he believed was happening.

As I shouted "One," I dropped the gun and laughed very hard as I saw Sean's actions. I laughed very hard as I realised the perfection in this windup; we were all connected, this mysterious chain that links one thing to another.

Sean's friend said, "What's going on?"

He was real angry as he ran over and picked up the toy gun.

He said, "It's only plastic," and threw it in the bushes.

Sean was in shock and said, "No way."

I said whilst laughing, "My gun, that's my gun."

I went to get it, but it was in the middle of the bushes. Sean's friend said, "Come on, Sean, we're going." They drove off and told everyone at the house party. It was funny for everyone then, particularly me.

From this windup and many others, I always felt life was a game, but who was controlling it? Who was making all of it perfect? I was just playing it. Every windup had truth involved in it. When I met Sean on the road and had the machine gun, there was truth involved in that joke, as I looked the part because I did want to shoot myself in the head at times. I was just known as a joker and a windup merchant in my spare time, but on my own time, I was searching for fulfillment and analysed every situation.

I thought that gun up; I mentally put it out there. Also by thinking about it, I created that energy in myself and thus attracted the very thing that I was thinking about (a gun as a joke—a toy gun).

Sean, who seemed very concerned since he first heard the story, had been thinking about it all day and magnetised himself to the situation at hand, and I just followed it through. It's all thoughts and energy that create and attract these events, and whoever it affects the most, or thinks about it the most, draws that energy to them, draws themselves to these situations.

CREATING THROUGH SPEECH

A lot of times, we create by speaking it. We notice this more when we do it jokingly. By saying things many times that are funny but are not true, often times those things actually happen, and then that joke becomes reality. I guess it's like the boy who cried wolf. He joked around too many times, and wound up too many people, and they didn't want to be fooled again, so the next time he cried wolf, it wasn't a joke but they ignored him. But I started to see the deeper meaning of that story; apart from the obvious, you shouldn't joke like that, but his story telling actually manifested and attracted the wolf to him; it became his reality. That's what I see after lots of joking myself.

CANARY ISLAND STORY

I am always attracting control and authority, even when I am on holidays.

This I need to develop within, it's like a hole that I keep falling into because it needs to be filled by me. In a sense it is energy; opposite attracts. It is like an emptiness in me that needs to be developed.

A few friends and I went to the Canary Islands, and it was an interesting holiday. We were all split up in small groups, and my small group included a friend named Skipper. When we landed at the airport, I said, "Let's rent a car and we can put our bags in it and drive around afterwards to find the rest of the lads."

We rented the car on Skipper's licence. It was a yellow sports car. We drove around looking for our friends but couldn't find them. I knew where they would be but couldn't quite find the area. My mind was in a haze over there. I was just one street away but I didn't find it that night.

We decided to go for a drink but we were in a dodgy area around the centre, where all the gangs hung out; the majority of them were robbing tourists all the time. We went to Ministry of Sound nightclub, which was down in a complex from the main road. I liked the way the area was set up, and the club looked good, but most of the people were dodgy around there. We went out drinking, and somewhere along the line we lost each other. A few hours later, I came across our car and got into it. I figured I would drive around to see if I could find Skipper. But I couldn't, so I drove around the back of the main road, where it was completely deserted. I drove the car hard and released the energy that I had built up from airports, travel, and so on; after driving and with the sun gone down, only then was I thinking clearly again. After I drove around the back road, I continued to search for Skipper again, as he had nowhere to sleep or stay; it was important that I find him.

When I took the corner onto the main road, the police were there. They asked me to pull over, and I stopped over on the footpath area. There was an area there where two or three cars could fit on the side of the road. They asked me to step out of the car, and I did. They then searched the car, which was full of our clothes and bags, so that took them a while.

Then they asked for my driver's licence, and I said it was in my bag. At this stage, there was me and my car, one police car, and two police officers at that time. Then they radioed in another police car. I wasn't sure what it was about, but I think it was to see about the company who owned the car. That police car arrived, and two other police officers came on the scene. There were four police officers and me. They were all checking out the car and going through our bags. They asked was I drinking, and I said I had one earlier on, but that was it. I laughed out loud then, as I was looking at the situation I was in and was summing up my choices. I looked behind me, and over the wall was a thirty-foot drop to an open field with unlimited escape. I realised it was an option but first I waited to see what happened next.

Another police car drove past, and they didn't have much to do, so they pulled over to see what was going on. There was me and six police officers. I was just watching all of this and thought it was very funny; as the minutes went on, the more snookered I was becoming. The two new cops were just having a laugh at me; they asked me a few questions, and we began talking. They thought I was funny, and there was not much hostility at all. The first cop asked the other two if they had a breathalyser with them, but they didn't have one. I looked over the wall again, and although it was still an option, there was concrete down below, and I was sure to injure myself.

The new chilled-out cops radioed in another crew with a breathalyser, and soon enough, they too arrived on the scene. Before I knew it—there was my good self, Skipper's rented car, four other police cars, and eight cops there, and at this point I was wondering if there were any more left in the police station. I sure was the centre of attention and fairly trapped. They asked me if I was I had no more than one drink, and I said, "Well, maybe I had two but not much more than that."

Out came the breathalyser, and I had to blow into the bag. I said I was very short of breath and could only breathe a small amount. They knew I was joking and figured I was somewhat drunk when I was laughing to myself. There was some stalling, and eventually I had to blow into it. I did first and missed, and the coppers began laughing and showing me how it was done. I then blew into it, the bag filled up halfway, and I failed straight away. This they all thought was quite funny, and they asked for my licence, and I had to find it in my bag.

I found my passport and put it in my pocket, I then found my licence and took it out; it was in its clear plastic cover, but also there was a picture of some topless girl that was handed out as a flyer beforehand. I said, "Look, that's me there," as I placed my hands on my chest, and they all started laughing. They thought I was the funniest man and decided to let me off the hook on condition that I left the car there. I said, "Thanks very much, it was nice to meet you all," and I left.

I realised that I was in a very tricky situation there, and it could have gone either way. The way I turned it into a sort of a joke, clearly with a sense of humour about the whole drama, this seemed to ease the situation. If I had stood there, all drunk and guilty and hanging my head in shame, they would have taken me away and let a judge deal with me. Also because I have no control in my life, I live in a freedom way where I am searching to be connected with the source, to be at one with life on a constant basis—there is a part of me that is missing that needs to be developed, and this uncontrolled part of me, as opposites attract, attracts control and authority (police, in this circumstance).

I walked down the road and looked back a few times at the area where the car was to get a mental picture, so I could find the car the next day. I walked on and on, and I then realised how far I actually was away from the centre. I was getting near the centre where I lost Skipper but I was becoming tired. There were concrete benches all the way along, so I lay down there.

Someone walking past told me, "If you fall asleep there, you will be robbed," and I said, "I know." I was going to take off my shoes and all I had in my pockets and hide it in the ditch beside me, but I then thought that I might wake up and not remember, so I just fell asleep. I was just so tired then and finally comfortable.

A little while later, a girl woke me up and said, "This is your passport, I found it up the road, and your driver's licence was on the far side of the road."

I got up and said, "Thank you so much." I had indeed been robbed, and they took everything on me, all I had in my pockets. I got up and had a mental picture in my head of the gangs down in the centre.

I started to go down to the centre to meet them; I was bleeped off and wanted to get my stuff back, so off I went, fixed in my head of just getting my belongings.

When I got to the centre, I was ready for action. I couldn't believe what was going on in front of me: Skipper was fighting two lads, who were throwing bottles at him. Skipper was dodging the bottles and still trying to get the lads at the same time. Then there were too many bottles, and Skipper backed off and then the lads ran off.

I said, "Hey, Skipper, you got robbed too?"

Skipper said, "I just woke up with them in my pockets, unbelievable."

I said, "I know some of these thieves have my money, and my chain around my neck is gone, but I don't know which one of them has it."

"Where's the car?" asked Skipper.

I said, "Oh the car, yeah, well, I went looking for you in it, and the police stopped me; it's back up the road somewhere. I know where it is, but I just don't know how to get there any more. It was on the same road where I woke up, but I ran down here and don't even know where I woke up."

"D.J., all our stuff is in that car," said Skipper.

"We will find it, I'll remember soon enough where it is," I said.

We then went off looking, and I went in the completely wrong direction, but what I did find was this mysterious centre where the lads were staying, the same place Skipper was beginning to think was a myth.

"Excellent," I said, "the lads will be up here somewhere."

As we walked up, I met Gar and John, and they were just laughing when they saw us. Gar told us where the lads were staying, so we went up and met everyone. They were all on top form, drinking and laughing and messing. Skipper and I got cleaned up there, and John gave me a loan of a T-shirt to wear. I told the lads that I lost the car with all our clothes in it, and they asked, "What do you mean, you lost it?"

So Skipper and I made up a story about driving it into the sea, and we were lucky to get out of it, but we were hoping the tide would go out and we might be able to see it. Everyone knew about this car in not much time at all. We got something to eat and went off looking for that car; two days later, we found it in a tow-truck compound.

We had to pay to get it out. The rental car owner came and took the car back, and we got our stuff and dropped it off in our friend's apartment. There was good fun, lots of drinking, and many stories exchanged between us all. The nightlife was good, and the pubs and clubs were enjoyable. But there was so much energy that I was picking up on, I was getting uneasy and needed to be away from crowded places. I didn't really have an outlet for this energy.

One particular night we went out, there were so many of us and everyone was drunk, but I wasn't and found it very difficult to get back into that relaxed frame of mind. I left the pub and went walking down towards the centre. I was getting frustrated with myself about always being the way I was, where I felt that I could handle this way of life when I was on work mode at home, constantly picking up on energy, but this was my holiday, and I was not happy having to be like this—needing to be away from people, feeling trapped, as if my mind was caught in a mesh with an unclear perspective. I find it difficult to separate my thoughts from my emotions, so when I have a build-up of this energy, my mind too becomes unclear. I was going downhill mentally, as if there was a constant cloud in my mind. As I got near the centre, I met one friend and he said, "Where are you going D.J.? All the lads are up here."

I said, "I'm just going down to the centre for a while, I'll be back up soon."

So off I went, and when I got down there, I sat down on a wall that was like one big tree pot, and inside it were wallets thrown there from people like me who were robbed. I picked up one of the wallets and was thinking to myself about how much of a rough place this is and how bad it is with the entire tourist industry getting robbed.

I began to realise what I needed as a solution to the problem I was having here. I put it together clear in my mind and it went like this:

I need out of this madness, as it's just full on all the time. I don't want to sleep, as I would lose my clear frame of mind, and when I do sleep, it takes me so long to get it back. I need to get away from everywhere just to think clearly, I need out of the game.

This was my request, and I could mentally picture a dark place outside all influences where I could relax and think. This was the only clear thought I could get together in order for me to get out of the game and think clearly again. Meditation may have been good for me but I never got into it. I sat there for approximately two minutes, and then a police car drove up and stopped. They saw me sitting beside a lot of wallets and called me over. I looked at them from this unclear frame of mind that I was in, and all I could see was more problems. I said to myself, *Bleep these lads, I'm out of here.*

I ran and they chased me. They didn't know why I was running, only that I must be guilty of something, but I was only running to get away from these lads, as I didn't speak their lingo. I ran down to the centre complex, and I stood up on the wall. Down below were escalators leading to the complex below. It was at least a thirty-foot drop to the ground. I stood there for a second and realised if I jumped, I would break my two legs for sure and then they would just catch me anyway, so I turned around. They were coming for me and I was getting snookered. There was one lane to my left, and I ran for it to get away. It was a dead end, and they caught me. I struggled to get back out to the open, where people could see me, as I didn't trust these police. I had heard a story of a guy getting raped over there by some Spaniards. This was going through my mind, and I made sure I was out in the open before I stopped trying to get away. They gave me a beating with their fists and batons and then put me in the car. They brought me to the police station. They put me in a cell and locked me up for a while. Then they brought me back in to speak to the sergeant. I asked the sergeant if he would contact my friends to let them know where I was, as they were looking for me. He told me that they already did that.

He asked me what was I doing and I said, "I was doing nothing, and your friends beat me up."

He said, "What?" and I said, "Your *ami* [as I was trying to say "friends" in French] beat me up." With that, he punched me in the side of the head, and I was completely deaf in one ear. I was put back into the cell.

Sometime later, a solicitor came along and asked to speak with me.

I was brought out by the two cops and sat down at a table in front of the solicitor. I was covered in my own blood, and my ear was streaming with fluid.

I wasn't a pretty sight to see. The solicitor looked very concerned about me, and I looked at the two coppers who were standing right behind me. I realised that I could not say anything about getting out of this madhouse, as after the conversation, I would be back in the cell and beaten up. I was thinking if I was bad enough, they would have killed me, and I would just be another missing tourist on the list that nobody finds. So the first thing the solicitor asked was, "Are you okay?" I nodded. She said, "Who did this to you?"

I said, "I was fighting some Spanish lad down in the centre, and these good police officers here came along and broke it up."

The solicitor looked at me in disbelief and said, "Really?"

I replied, "Yes, that's what happened," and that was it. I was taken back to my cell. I knew that my life depended very much on what I said, so I lied about what happened.

There was nothing in my cell, no windows or seats or anything; I did not know whether it was daytime or night. The police came over after the solicitor left and said, "You good boy, you smart kid, would you like a cigarette?"

"Yes," I said. He gave me some cigarettes, and I realised I had made the best decision with what I told the solicitor. I was safe then in my own solitude. I was completely closed off from everyone and everywhere.

I then realised that where I am now is what I was requesting.

I was mentally putting it out there with all the energy I had, thinking it over and over again that I needed to be out of this game, to be out of this environment, to be in a dark place somewhere, away from all influences, just so I can get my frame of mind back together. I requested this timeout, and I guess in a strange sense, I got what I asked for, out of the whole lot. The power of thought is not to be underestimated.

First I was sitting on that wall, and I knew where I needed to be, having no idea how to get from point A to point B, and then it happened. Whether I ran or not, it would have happened. I sent it out there and that dark room was magnetised to me. Life just filled in the missing pieces for me to end up in that dark room—away from it all. How does it work or why does it work? These are good questions. When I was in that room, when I fell asleep—I could see that mysterious girl on the hill in my awaked dream, standing there looking at me. I woke up and wondered, did she answer my request? Did she put me there? Am I being looked after by some mysterious power, and if so—is this what they call looking after?

So the ending of that story went like this: Another policeman came into the station, and he laughed and told the sergeant, "This is the funny man that we were telling you about the other night."

I was on my own and could think clearly; I was beaten up, but for once I could relax. I was locked up in that cell for forty hours, and then I had to go to court. There was one other lad in a cell that was two cells down from me. He was from Ireland too, and he told me that they picked him up in the centre after some girl pointed him out. The girl's things went missing on the beach, and she thought he had stolen them, but he was just in the wrong place at the wrong time. We were both innocent people, and we both went to court the same time. It was different from the Irish courts; there was no audience, only one big table with what appeared to be six judges, but three or four of them were solicitors. The two of us sat down for our court hearing. The solicitor explained in Spanish that I had been fighting and the other lad had been taken in for stealing, but he was pleading innocent. I thought at the time this was really something, two innocent lads whose families may never see them again, and what had we done? Only go down to the centre. We were told by the judge that we were free to go and that we were not to come back to the Canary Islands again.

I was so glad to get out of there; the other lad and I left. I was very weak and limping, and we went to his apartment to get a drink of water. His mate had flown home without him, and his parents were planning to pick him up at the airport, but he had missed his flight. I, however, had two hours left before my flight took off, and I began walking back to where we were staying. After walking for an hour, I just wanted to lay down on those concrete seats, but I wasn't going to do that again and kept moving. Then I heard a friend laughing so much and saying, "That's my T-shirt; what has happened to it? Where were you? The flight's going in a half an hour, the lads are out looking for you. We thought you got lucky with some girl but you didn't, did you?"

"The cops locked me up, did they not tell you? They told me that they notified you all, clearly they did not," I said.

I told them about the other lad and said that it looked like he would be selling flyers for $10 a day on the street for a year to get a flight home.

BEATEN UP, THOUGHTS AND ENERGY

A month or so later, I was back in the routine of working life, doing carpentry work. I needed to get a trade, which would help me work and travel and live in Australia. But this way of life was really getting me down; it was a constant routine, working with the same people, no time out, and stuck indoors. Between the unnatural lighting, the dust, people's energy and no music, I was letting that anger energy rise up in me, and that was affecting my state of mind. I was sinking into a sort of sadness. I couldn't seem to get out of this state of mind, even on the weekends. When I was finished work, I was still getting lost in my own mind, and this happened to me a lot. My mind was constantly thinking about the job situation that I was stuck in, how I felt about the job and every person there and all the confinements in my life. I needed to be my own boss and have my own freedom, but I had to go through this phase first.

One night, I thought I needed to just get into a fight or something to release this energy and knock myself into an awakened mind again instead of staying in this haze and constant cloud.

I was looking for solutions for my problem, but all I could come up with was that I needed to get into a fight or something along those lines. So one Friday night, I went out with some friends to the local inn. I was in there for a short while, and then another friend wanted to go somewhere else, so we left. We went up to a different pub, where she wanted to see someone, and when we left, she asked me if I was going back to the first inn, and I said, "I don't think I will."

I walked her back to the inn, and when we got there, four lads came out. One of them asked me if he could have the can of beer I was drinking, and I said, "Get your own."

The girl walked into the inn, and I decided to go back in. As I got to the door, one of the lads put his foot on the door to stop me; I knew I was in trouble with these lads, who were just looking for a fight after being thrown out of the inn. They were from a different area and started to gang up on me. I knew what was happening so I went after the lad who was blocking the door. I grabbed him and pushed him over; the two of us fell back, and I pushed his head against the wall. His mates were coming for me, and they started laying in the kicks and punches. I just tried to cover myself as I got such a kicking. As I was laying there, the man who worked in the local inn stuck his head out and looked at me. He could see the four lads giving me a beating, but he just closed the door. I thought he was going into get others to help, but he just locked the door.

This went on for quite a while, until a friend came over from the taxi rank. He broke up the fight and helped me up and said, "D.J., are you all right? I didn't know who it was on the ground, I just saw that it was going on for too long and came over."

The lads started fighting with every person who passed by on the street. Everyone that came walking past got a beating from them. It was just unbelievable. I left after that and went home. I cleaned myself up and went to bed. The next day, I went to work, and then I realised how bad I was. I had two black eyes and was unable to work. I had to go back home.

The next day, I was on the bus and saw a lad who knew the rowdy group that had beaten me. I said to him, "Look what your mates did to me, what is their problem?"

He said, "Yeah, that's all they came up for was a fight, one of them got New Rock shoes just for giving a kicking, and they were telling me about all the fights they were in." He started to chuckle but then said, "I don't mean to be laughing, it was just funny the way they were telling me what happened. One of them said that the only injury he got was from the first lad he fought, who cracked his head off the wall. I guess that was you?"

I said, "Yes, that's all I could do when he stopped me from entering the pub. I knew they were looking for fights and just got the lad who stopped me and lay down then, trying to protect myself.

The fact is, I sent out strong thoughts, with a needfull intent behind it, intention/attention on an event and the energy follows. I felt I deserved or needed a beating, and I kept thinking this over and over again in my mind. I eventually got just what I asked for, just what I mentally saw as the solution to my problem and sent that thought out there. This has happened on a few occasions, expressing how I was feeling, and it didn't ever put me good. My inner world just became a reflection of my outer world. Within, so without.

There was one occasion where I was still thinking the same way and attracted a beating that I felt I needed as a reflection of what I was feeling within. I was with a group of friends, and someone ran over and stole one of the girls' bags. I chased after him to get it back and ended up running into a group of people, who were together with the thief. They gave me a beating for about ten minutes, kicking me up and down the road. I had to go to three different hospitals afterwards; I had broken ribs and a broken cheek bone, and the doctor told me that I could lose my eye. I am a quick healer and I survived to live another tale. There were a few other cases where this happened in my younger years where I did not think it up or feel very negative, I just had a whole load of anger energy within me, kept down in me.

As kids, we used to go to a club that was organised by some older people for us to have something to do. It was a good idea and it was good fun. Sometimes we would all get on a bus and travel to other areas; one night we all went to a nightclub. When we got there, another group from the town were there too, and one lad tried to pick a fight with one of my friends. I got up and said, "Lads, leave it out, we don't want any trouble."

After that, the lad went off and told his mates about me, and everywhere I looked there were some lads looking over at me, real angry and full on eye contact. One of the older people who organised our group came over to me to tell me to watch out, that there could be a big fight on the way out. As we were leaving, a whole group of angry lads came after me. I stood there just looking at them for a moment until the older lad grabbed me and said, "Get on the bus."

I got on the bus, and these lads outside were like animals, banging on the windows, shouting at me, saying that they wanted to kill me, and so on. We left and went back to where we were staying. Later that night, some people were on our roof, and when I went outside, all those lads were standing around on different roofs on top of our accommodation. They really wanted to get me and only me, and everyone knew this. We just went back inside, and when the next day came, all was back to normal.

After many of these occurrences, I could see that whatever was in me was driving people crazy. It was as though the anger body of energy that was in me was making any anger in them arise to the surface, and they wanted to get me as they felt that their anger was something to do with me—which it was but not logically understood. This anger energy in me was attracting this in my life, and I could not tackle this situation as it would be suicide; I could merely observe that which was happening.

Soon enough I decided to stop taking these trips, as I seemed to be the downfall in the enjoyable times for the rest of our group. I felt sad about this but still thought that life must have other plans for me. My world was getting smaller the longer I was experiencing life.

CHAPTER FOUR

Sensitivity

THE BAD POINTS

You see, there are different things that really affect my energy, really affect me as a person. For example, sometimes lights will drive me crazy; they make me feel very uneasy and very unbalanced. I do not have to be in this situation for long, but the longer I am, the more uneasy I will get. Having this sensitivity lets me feel a lot of things, a lot of energies and a lot of people. There are good feelings and bad feelings. The bad feelings are not really bad, it's just I judge them bad as I don't feel the way I want to feel. Many things affect me. I'll tell you about one example.

Some days, I go to sleep early and wake up and shower and eat and feel great. Then I'll go to the shops, perhaps to buy some clothes, and when I enter the shops I feel okay. But the lights in the shop can seriously affect my energy. I'll continue shopping and trying on clothes, and after being exposed to these lights for a long time, between half hour and one hour, I feel weak in the stomach, nauseous, and heated; I become completely off balance. If I stay in this shop and continue shopping, then I start to feel twitches through my body and a twitch through the top of my head, which feels like a mild electric shock running through my head and into my forehead. At this stage, I'm more anxious, uneasy, and I need to get away from these lights. Then I'll leave and when I get outside, I feel tired and drained and still unbalanced. Then I'll eat something small to get myself together, perhaps smoke also, and even drink alcohol at times to relax this energy and put myself back in a harmonious state of being. This has always happened to me throughout my life.

I used to go on buses, and they had the same lights on them. I would start to feel uneasy and get a burning sensation on my neck and face and sick in the stomach. After getting off the bus, I would enjoy life with my friends wherever we went, but I would leave them later on and go our separate ways as I wouldn't want to get back on the bus. The whole day I'd be on good form after I balanced my energy from getting off the bus, and we would all have fun and I wouldn't want them to see me completely uneasy and uptight and full of tension on the way back on the bus, so I would just put myself through it on my own and that was easier done.

I have exposed myself in this environment for a long time, and each day, I feel sick and tired and far from the balanced state of being that I should feel. When exposed for too long, I feel very uneasy, uptight, and stressed. Then with a constant exposure to this energy that is building up and not released, it starts to burn out the inside of my body. I developed an ulcer and eventually began coughing up blood.

The whole time I lived in Ireland, I needed to deal with many energies or lights that affected me a great deal, and it was impossible to deal with it. It's like having an allergy to something. But there are no tablets for my condition. So staying at a place that has this affect on me means that I cannot be happy, and the only way to find balance is to abuse my body to kill off this energy and feel balanced again. The whole time I was in school, I had to try to relax and to fight this. If I went with it, my body would be shaking, my energy unbalanced, and my mind getting shocks through it. When I finally got out of school, I was happy for a while, as I was working away and didn't experience many of those conditions. But when I went back to do carpentry work, I often had lunch in these places, and any time I worked in an office, this was my main problem and I was very angry with the way my life was, struggling with this uneasiness, due to the lights.

I feel that it is the unnatural lighting that does it; florescent lights constantly flicker on and off, they do not always stay on like the sun—natural lightning. Our eyes and nervous system don't allow us to see this flickering because they go on and off so quickly on a constant basis. This flickering also happens with televisions. When I take in this energy from the lights, my body energy becomes negative, my mind connects to my energy, and I think negatively, and it completes a circle. I would be mentally sinking and would need to break free eventually or I would be sleep walking in a negative mind.

I tried almost everything, from drinking lots of water to drinking alcohol, from smoking to not eating, but nothing solved the problem; this energy filled me up, I didn't even need food. This energy was a driving force for life, and these experiences that the future held for me gave me no rest.

This would be one of the main reasons as to why I would want to beat myself up and hurt myself at times. It was a way of releasing this energy.

MANIFESTING BUT NOT IN THE BEST WAY

When I was almost sixteen years old, people were organising small birthday parties for me. I was going steady with a girl named Sue. There was always a lot of people at Sue's place, and I could barely handle staying in there, never mind to be the centre of attention for my birthday.

This energy in me made me seem like a shy person. It was the uneasiness to be the centre of attention that triggered off this energy in me. I was panicking all that week coming up to my birthday, the more I thought about being the centre of attention, particularly in an environment with florescent lights where I would feel sick anyway. I would rather skip the day and continue on in life.

So I needed something to happen; I couldn't come up with an excuse myself to dodge everyone that day, as people would then be offended or feel that I had more important friends to spend my day with. This would create all sorts of misunderstandings.

I thought about this for a while and then sent it out there; I asked life for something to happen. I put all my energy into the intention of "I need a solution to this, a way where I am unable to be at this party—I need something to happen so that nobody feels rejected but also leaving me with no choice—that I won't be able to go to any party."

When I sent it out there, it was either by talking aloud or by creating a clear thought in my mind and releasing it out there, by focusing and by sending it out to the essence of life, something that you believe in, something that you know is out there. For me, I know there is something because I can feel something. I can feel the stillness and the peace, the wisdom, and the comfort when I connect with it on this level, looking for guidance.

Something happened a day later. Something got my attention whilst I was at a job doing some work. I saw a clear plastic bag with some jewellery in it; it looked like it had been tossed aside, of no importance. As I picked it up, it didn't look real, but Sue's birthday was coming up, and I thought that I could give it to her.

I took the jewellery home and put it in a box. That night I went to Sue's house; whilst we were talking, I got a phone call saying that the police were at my house and wished to talk to me.

I went home, and the police had searched my room and said that they knew I had the jewellery. Apparently it was worth a lot of money and they wanted to give it back to the owner. I was shocked and said, "I am very sorry, I didn't think that it was worth anything. Of course, here it is." I took the bag out of the box and handed it over. I was told to come around to the station tomorrow to meet with the owner and my boss, who was the owner's friend, to see if they wanted to press charges.

The next day was my birthday, and I spent it at the police station; I had no choice in the matter. I met my boss and the owner, tried to explain, but they didn't seem interested. They just seemed very disappointed, that was the main feeling I got. I felt bad that I took it, I felt bad that those people would think that I was a thief. Also Sue had friends and family around at her house for a party for me, and I couldn't get out of the police station for the day. I couldn't help but think that something worked, something went my way. No one around me in my life could possible see why I would be happy with this outcome; it wouldn't make any sense, but to me, it was perfect. I could see what I asked for and what I got. It was not how I would have planned this getaway, but I didn't have a plan, I just sent out this need to not be at my party, and this is what happened. No charges were put against me by the owner, but the police did take me to court.

A month or so later, another party came up. I was enjoying my life, racing motorbikes and having fun outdoors. My energy was always burnt out from racing the bikes, and I was always cool, calm, and at ease. I was relaxed and happy, but for me to go to really busy places, getting on buses, bright lights, all of these things would activate this energy body in me, and I would then become a different person, so uneasy and sick and full up of energy. I wouldn't be happy, and people would see that. I needed not to go to the party. I needed something to happen again and didn't have an excuse. Sue told her friends that I said I was not going, and all her friends approached me, looking at me as if I thought I was too good to go or that I didn't want to be seen with Sue. So all of this nonsense started to happen and be talked about. Then it happened, I got word from the police that my court date was on the same date as the party. I showed Sue the paperwork and sat her down, saying that I didn't want to mention the court date as she was upset the last time, but this was the reason I could not go. I was saved again. Really, I shouldn't have had a girlfriend, as nothing was ever going to last with me. I was an impossible child, really.

That's what happened: court cropped up about six times in total, and then one day, I saw what this was doing to my family. They had to take time off work, and it was affecting everyone. I requested, "Could this all be blown over with and in the past," and soon enough it was over with, no charges and all in the past.

I believe that we create our own future—I believe that we know this when we are doing it, but when we look back in the past to see what happened, we call ourselves "unlucky" or "lucky." But if we need something to happen at certain times in our lives and it happens, we love it but pretend that we don't. Over so many stories and throughout life, the end conclusion may become confusing, as there are so many theories to what happened. But at the time, I believe we know, that we send out, we ask for, we even create events and reasons why and we draw to us circumstances that get us out of that situation. So never have regrets, because at the time, what you did was exactly what you wanted.

Some people may thank their higher power for these happenings, but there is an explanation for all happenings, and the evolution of our own spirit lets us get closer to the truth.

WAKING UP GIFTS

Sue and I stayed together through the summer, but when the dark evenings came in and the sun was no longer out, our relationship faded away. But there was one particular story that I never did get the chance to make proper sense of, but maybe it will be cleared up now.

Sue got a new job in a pizza shop, and it was a family business. But there were two other lads who were working there, and they were not part of the family. These two Italian lads were named Moe and Ronald. Moe was small in height and was a real nice bloke; he also seemed quiet or shy. Ronald was quite tall, he must have been about thirty years old, and he took a fancy to Sue. Sue told me that Ronald acted really strange around her sometimes, and one night he asked her for a kiss. I called up each night after work then to collect her and to just be there for her. She was getting worried about his behaviour. One night when we were outside, Sue kissed me; Ronald was looking at the two of us and did not seem too impressed. Sue was my girlfriend, and I should have been the one who was not impressed at his carrying on. I figured he was a strange one all right and that was it all forgotten about until . . .

Sue came back to my place, and after her mother came over to collect Sue later on that night, I went to sleep. Sometime later, I was woken up by screaming. There was such an amount of screaming going on in the house, and all the hairs stood up on my arms. My first thought was, "This is because of me."

This was all I felt inside me. I ran down and saw my mother, who looked so scared. She said, "There was a man in the house, a man is in the house and he ran downstairs." I tried to calm her down, as she wasn't making sense, she was just screaming. She told me that he said he wanted to rape her, and she felt she couldn't scream at all, and as soon as he walked to the door, she started screaming and he ran. She said she was going to call the police, and I said, "No point at all calling them, they won't do anything."

She said, "Sure I have to, D.J., it's a break-in."

I ran outside; I could see this man's face in my mind, and for some reason I was quite confident he ran to the right.

I ran to the right and down into the town. I realised he could have gone any direction after that, so I ran down to the pub and asked some people I knew, "Did anyone come running down this way?" They said no, and I ran back up to the lane. I had a strong feeling he went that way.

I ran up the lane and up to the top of the road, and at that point I strongly felt he was going through the fields. I could see him running through the fields in my mind so clear, almost like I could physically feel the long grass at my legs. The first direction was just to put me off. The fields were at the top of my road and turning right outside the house; running and then going back across the fields was not a rational thing to do, as he would be going around in a circle.

When I got back to the house, the police were there. They asked all sorts of questions, and when my mother tried to describe the man, her description fit with my mental picture. I could see him in the dark in my mind, and I just knew he did it because of me. The feeling was of a pure violation of our place of rest, our home. Imagine having your house as your home, and then whilst you're asleep, some stranger comes into your house and threatens to rape your mother. I thought to myself, *It was all to do with the screams, and it wouldn't make any sense if he was really thinking about rape.* I did not have any idea about what I could have done to have this in return, but I would have placed all I owned as a bet on it was all to do with me.

When she started screaming so loud, it rattled my mind, as I was asleep, and it put shivers all through my body. It was the most unpleasant experience, which left a new feeling in me, a feeling that my own security had just been violated. I said, "Tell me what he did. I don't think he was ever going to rape you, I think it was all built up and he would have said anything just to get you to start screaming."

She said, "Well, he came in, and I thought it was your brother for a minute, but then he stood there with a scarf around his head. He came over and then walked back to the door and kept checking the door. He asked where the video recorder and the television were. I don't know why he was asking these questions, as they're all downstairs. He kept coming back and saying something, but I couldn't hear him, and then he went back to the door. I was so afraid that when I wanted to scream, it would not come out; this has always been my fear. He came over again and sat on the bed and said that he wanted to rape me and do things to me, and when he went back over to the door that time, I just screamed as much as I could."

I knew what happened, and I knew it was all to get her to scream, and I knew he ran down the road, up the lane, and across the fields, but I didn't know who it was or why. I could mentally picture his face in my mind in the dark, and when she told me his description, it matched perfectly. What she told me confirmed what I saw. I knew what he was up to, and she confirmed it by telling me what he said and did. I was up all the rest of the night, trying to work it out.

She said, "Sue must have left the front door open when she left, sure, how else could he get in?"

I rang Sue's house up and asked if she left the door open, as someone broke in and threatened my mother. She didn't say yes or no, but I didn't believe he came in the front door. I checked out the back, and the small window was off the latch. The police didn't even check around the house at all. My mother said, "I thought the police would have investigated the house."

I said, "I told you there is no point in ringing them, as they won't do anything for us at all. All they are going to do is protect the person when I find out who it is."

Sue rang back up and said, "I'm so sorry, D.J., but I don't think I left it open at all."

I said, "I know, Sue, I'm sure he came in the window, it was just that the front door was wide open when June saw him running down the stairs."

The police brought my brother Jonsey around to the police station, as my mother said the person who broke in had a thin face like him. He was not in the house at the time, so the police questioned him, indicating that he was on drugs or wanted a drink and all this sort of nonsense.

That morning I was outside the house, standing at the pillar, and it was clear to me I needed to work this out. Then Ronald, the man from the pizza shop, came walking down through the estate. He looked at me with a smirk, and I just stared back at him.

That's it, it was him, I'm sure it's him, I thought to myself. I went around the lane to see if I could find my mother's red coat, which was missing from the cloakroom. It was the only thing that was missing. The television and video were not even touched. The red coat was around in a garden in the lane. It was just thrown into a garden, and this was confirmation of all I could see. I knew he went up the fields but wondered where else he went. I walked up the lane, which led out to the estate around from us. It was a dead end there, as there was a lane in front of me and houses on either side. It must be one of those houses, I thought, as he didn't go down the lane. I knew these things but could not explain how I knew. All that was said and found were all confirmation of what I was seeing in my mind clearly.

When I got back home, Sue came over.

I explained that it was definitely Ronald that did it, and Sue said, "I know he is strange and all, but this is just a bit much, don't you think?"

I went into the house, where the window was off the latch, and there was a footprint on the sink and the floor. It was roughly a size ten, and it was from a pair of Caterpillar boots. I said, "Sue, are you in work tonight?"

"Yes," she said.

"Right, can you check out to see if Ronald is wearing these boots? I'm sure it's him and I'll bet anything he has these boots on. Now don't say anything at all, just have a look at his boots for me please, can you do that?" I asked.

"Yes, I will and I'll tell you later," she said.

Sue came back down after work and said, "He does have those boots on, and they are big, just like the footprint."

I was getting worked up at this stage and couldn't relax at all. I knew it was him; why were the police asking ridiculous questions to Jonsey around there? What a joke this was becoming. I described Ronald to my mother and said, "This man works in the pizza shop with Sue and fancies her. He broke in because of me; he did it to get at me. I know this is all just hard to understand but I know he did it; he is like that in the head."

I told my father the same thing, and Arthur suggested that he and June go up for a slice of pizza. We both explained to June not to go crazy in the shop, just see if she recognised him. June and Arthur went up and everyone acted normal, and they got some pizza while June had a look at him, and then they left.

When they came out, I asked, "Well?"

June said, "It could be him, all right. I'm not sure as it was dark, and he had that scarf over his face. He has a thin face like I saw, but I am not 100 percent sure, D.J."

So my mother told the police, and they said they would check it out. I asked Sue to find out where Ronald was living. She asked Moe and he said that Ronald lived in a flat in the next estate. This was exactly where the field ran out; I knew it. And the flat was the house on the corner beside the lane. It was a family house, and he was renting out a room there.

The police came back and said, "It wasn't any of those lads up there; we play cards with them after they close the pizza shop some nights."

I was really building up a rage inside of me at this time. I knew who it was, and the cops were defending him at this stage.

"Mom," I said, "don't bring the coppers into anything again, as now if I get him, I'll be one who gets arrested. I know it's him."

Sue left her job then, as she realised it was him too. I went up there every day after that and just stood at the counter, watching him. Other workers came over to ask what would I like, and I said, "Nothing please, I don't want anything."

I watched him constantly for about two hours each night, waiting for him just to say it was him. I was cracking up at this stage; I was snookered in all directions. I would get arrested if anything happened to Ronald. A serious frustration grew within me. My mother got over it very shortly afterwards, and she was just fine. The screams were still going through my mind. I had visions of myself taking a gun and going after him. Whenever I got really angry, guns came to mind. None of the gun visions ever happened, but I sure was thinking them.

I kept going into the shop and everyone knew something was seriously up, but Ronald acted cool and didn't say anything at all. He just worked away as if I wasn't there. I was bothering everyone else at this stage, and that was all good. I felt something better happen soon. I walked out and saw Ronald's car. His car window was open a little, and I pushed it down, then turned it sideways, and took it out all together. I also took his road tax disk. I walked around the corner and threw the stuff into the ditch and left. The next day, I was walking home from school. Just as I came to my estate, I got this strange feeling that some lads were about to pull me into a black van. It seemed so real to me, and I turned around but nobody was there. I kept getting this feeling and I tried to think, what I could have done to have someone pull me into a van? What is it all about? It played on me and I thought I'm going somewhat mad.

I didn't walk down to the town again for a while after that. Each time I went out, I walked up my estate road and jumped the wall up by my friend's house. I walked along there, which led past the football field, a road that was parallel to the main street of the town. I did this for a few days. One day, a friend from school came over to see me. He lived in this area and he was a bit concerned about me.

He said, "Hey, D.J. What's going on? I know it's none of my business but I just want to give you some advice. Ronald came up to my garage to get his car fixed, he said his window was broken out and his tax disk was taken too; he thinks you did it."

"I did," I said.

"Well D.J., I think Ronald and Moe are sound lads, but I've only known them a short while, and now there are four Italian lads driving around in a big black car looking for you, asking people have they seen D.J. around anywhere. They asked me earlier on. These lads are like the Mafia; they look like real serious people, so I just want to let you know. Just be careful, mate, I don't think you know who you're messing with."

"Cheers," I said. "Don't worry about it, but thanks for that, mate."

I walked all the way through the estate and then walked back down towards the pizza shop, which was not far from the village entrance. I walked into the pizza shop and stood at my usual spot at the counter. watching the usual suspect at hand for about an hour. I knew I was getting to him real slowly, but he still did not say anything. Moe went out for a cigarette and I went out with him. He was acting really nervous, but I was cool, calm, and collected at this stage.

I thought to myself, *I'm born for this hard man crap as playing with these boys feels good.* Moe then said that he had nothing to do with Ronald, and the only connection they had was that they started working at the same time. Moe said that he didn't know what was going on but Ronald was acting really strange lately. He added that Ronald was very good at karate and fighting, and I should be careful with him. Moe, I felt, was a nice lad, and I was glad to hear that he was not really good friends with Ronald.

As I walked down to the village, I met Jonsey and said, "I know it's that bloke in the pizza shop; I'm going to get him soon, I don't care."

Jonsey went up that way with people from the town, and he was hanging around outside the pizza shop. He went in and started saying things to Ronald, but nothing much happened. I left it for a while, and about one week later, I walked into the pizza shop and there was nobody there, only me and Ronald.

I said, "Tell me something . . ."

Ronald said, "What you want to know?"

I said, "Did you break into my house?"

"Yes I did," said Ronald.

Then I said, "That's fine, that's all I wanted to know."

I walked out and saw Jonsey down in the town. I said, "Hey, bro, what did I tell you? I just went into the pizza shop and asked Ronald did he break into my house, and he said he did; told you it was him."

Jonsey didn't say anything to me but between the break-in and him getting interrogated over it, I'm sure he was not too happy. The next day I heard that he went up to the pizza shop with a big branch and started smashing it down on the counter. Ronald came out and the two of them were fighting on the ground. After that, Ronald no longer worked in the pizza shop, as the bosses knew something was up and let him go. I didn't ever see him again.

What was that all about? For some reason, life felt that it was time that I felt a new feeling, lived for a new experience. I had no idea why that happened, only that the moment it did, I knew it was because of me, but I didn't know who or why or any important information.

The moment this event happened, it felt like it was meant to happen, there was a deep reason for it, and it was more to do with me than anyone else in the house. What it did was create a new depth to me, a new feeling, a new defeat in a sense, a violation, then rage, and then trying to play Ronald at his own game, but it also opened up a gift in me. As this event happened and I was asleep, I woke up and my surroundings were very intense; a lot was happening, new feelings and clear thoughts. I see that this gift would not open in me on a quiet relaxing day—it took an intense, heart thumping, shocked, screaming experience from the moment that I woke up to get this new connection to wake up within me. I guess a main point of this story is that some gifts wake up within us, under situations like this one, where one believes that rape, murder, even life-and-death situations could be actually happening.

All I know is, nobody got any good out of that happening, only that I found out that I'm connected to something, that I can see things before they happen and whilst they are happening, even when I'm not there.

I can see that this man came into my life to mess with me, this event seemed to affect me more than it did my mother. She seemed just fine a short while later and forgot about it soon after that. Events and happenings affect us all in different ways. Perhaps, on a deep level, this was just about me developing intuition and connections.

THE DEATH OF MY FRIEND JAKE

Does dying really kill us? Here is the story about Jake. He and I used to go to school together, along with about fifty others, and we were all friends. Anyways, this happened after school years, I was working away driving machines and got this flash in my mind, like watching a trailer of a movie. I saw myself driving around on this red motorbike and this was how it all started for me.

I heard an advertisement on the radio for a moped, and I got it in my head that I was going to get a moped and drive around on it.

I mentally put it out there, I even tried to borrow money off my boss in order to buy one, but it was too much money. He said, "I've never seen so much money before in my life." This was a funny point to make but I understood clearly. So I didn't do much after that about the bike, only by letting the system know that I wanted it, by mentally putting it out there, expanding that thought. It was on my mind, soon to be in my energy, and soon it was attracted to me.

Later, I met Jake as I was walking back home from work through an estate. Jake asked me if I would like to buy his bike from him; it was a red moped. I said, "Yes, mate, I would like to."

At this stage, it was very new and he was asking a lot of money for it. After he bought it, he realised he had some money problems and needed to sell it.

I really liked the bike and said, "I do not have all the money for it now, but maybe in time I will get the money together."

I met Jake again after Christmas; he had crashed the bike over the holiday season. He asked me if I would still like to buy it, as he had dropped the price due to the crash. He told me how much he wanted. I said, "That will be great, Jake, you must be stuck for dollars."

Jake called around to my house with the papers and gave me the bike. I gave him some of the money then, and later I rang him up to pay him the rest of the money. We trusted each other, we were mates, and he gave me his bike for cheap enough and let me get the money when I could. So I had the red bike, and I drove all around everywhere on that bike, from job to job and town to town, catching up with friends. It was great. I loved it, I had a radio attached to the bike, and the music was always pumping away. The little things in life made me so happy.

After a short while, I was working away at a carpentry job, and this strange feeling came over me. This never happened before—this was all new to me. I don't know where it came from, but it was like I knew someone was going die soon. I didn't particularly like this thinking, this knowing was deep within me, but I started to know it, to acknowledge it, as I could feel it in a distance. This probably doesn't make much sense, but it's like when you know something is going to happen, you just know it from deep within you, and then it happens. Well, in this case, I could feel this was going to happen; this feeling grew strong, but I had no idea who was going to die. I tried to shake this feeling off a few times and continued on with my work and life. But this feeling kept taking over me, and I knew someone was going to die soon. I started to accept that but wanted to know who it was so I could stop it before it happened.

As time went on, this feeling grew stronger. I began working with a lad named Mike; he was just the best fun, and I thoroughly enjoyed working with him. We were to go on a job in the city at that time, and we did some work in a theatre. Whilst we were in there working away, I noticed how nice the place looked. At the end wall was a whole section done in lights of different colours; it was almost like the stained glass in a church. It looked very expensive.

We had our radio playing, and a song came on the radio called "Viva Forever" by the Spice Girls. I was not a particular fan of the Spice Girls, but the song really got ahold of me in ways very difficult to describe. When it came on, I went from my unclear thinking to a very clear state of mind. Something within me just connected to this song; there was noise in the theatre from other people working and there were other distractions, but nothing came in the way between me and this song that was being played.

I left the theatre at lunchtime and walked around town. I still could not get rid of the feeling that someone close was going to die, but I also could not think with all the people around. This was how things were for approximately two months, only the feeling grew stronger. At this stage, I was becoming very uneasy and couldn't get rid of this feeling. So I went to a place on my own and said, "Who is going to die? This is just so strong, it must be a family member; who is going to die?"

I wasn't sure who I was talking to, and no one replied either. I guess I was asking myself in a clear mind, but I got no answers. I couldn't do much about anything, as I was becoming worse. I closed myself off from everyone over the next few weeks and just tried to get some fixed point of knowing what was going on. I knew this was going to be a great loss. I was thinking it was going to be a family member, as the feeling was just so strong. I closed myself off from people and just tried to keep an eye on my family.

My mate Tommy called down to me a few times and asked, "Are you coming out to play?"

He sure was funny but I said, "I can't today, I'm losing it."

Tommy knew me, and though it may have appeared to others that I was on drugs the way I was looking like I was lost in my own mind, I wasn't taking drugs. I was lost in my own mind, and Tommy knew it. This intensity went on for about five days, where I didn't sleep and ate very little. I was actually thinking about taking my own life, as this unknown connection was so strong. Then Tommy called up again; it was the weekend and he asked was I coming out. I wasn't sure whether to or not, and Tommy talked me into going out. We went for a drink in the local and then we had a few more, and to my amazement I started to come around. We went from one pub to the next, and I felt like the world had been lifted off my shoulders. I couldn't believe how free and normal I started to feel; it had been so long since I felt that way.

I wondered what was happening to me for so long, and then I didn't care. I felt good, so good that I said, "Let's go to the club dancing."

Tommy said, "All right then, let's do it."

We left the pub and saw a girl outside that we knew. She told us that she heard someone was killed on the dual carriageway. Tommy then started feeling bad, but I said, "Come on, forget about it, it's probably just some made-up rumour."

We took a taxi to the club and went in. When we got inside the club, some people told us that Jake had just been killed on the dual carriageway. I just walked away but knew what had happened. The second Jake died, the connection was broken, and I was myself again.

Tommy came over and said, "Ah, I just feel so bad inside, I can't stay up here and drink. Jake is after dying, so many people just told me."

I walked across the dance floor, and a really beautiful looking girl stopped me and started slow dancing with me. I said, "I just came up here and my . . ."

She put her finger over my mouth and said, "Don't say anything, just dance with me."

I danced with her, she came out of nowhere and gave me some comfort, and then she went. What a mysterious girl she was.

The next day I went up to the pub, and everyone was there, all the people I was in school with and all of Jake's mates. I grew up with all of them, and they were all crying over Jake's death. We had the jukebox playing, and I just stood looking at everyone; all the girls were really upset, and the lads were trying to be their tough selves after just losing their best mate. We all stayed up there drinking all day. I was still coming to terms with what had happened and realised that I had my grief for Jake before he died, and everyone else was after he died. I was just pissed off at life for not giving me the chance to stop his death, as I questioned the fact that I knew someone was going to die. Why be given a gift where one cannot change the outcome?

Jake's funeral came up soon after that, and everyone went. This was it, this was what I knew, something really big and really strong. This was what I was feeling, the loss of a young man in the area; everyone was at the funeral. I was feeling the energy of the whole area before it happened. I was feeling the complete loss of someone who died so young, the feeling of that day at the funeral. I wasn't thinking and drove down the road on my moped, which had been Jake's moped. All our friends were looking at me as if I was Jake. They were so used to him driving around on the bike. I thought about bringing the bike down to the church, as some friends brought things to put up on the altar, but I decided not to for the attention it would cause.

Jake was nineteen years old when he died; the whole area was at the funeral. When I arrived at the funeral, I stood at the main entrance, and someone said, "There's something about D.J. and Jake, but I don't know what it is."

It was so sad. A lady walked up and put a rose on his coffin. I stood there on my own and couldn't help but shed a few tears, which rolled down my cheeks. I knew someone was going to die and couldn't stop it; that's where the real hurt was. Two girls who were great friends of Jake's brought a radio onto the altar and played a few songs that Jake really liked. The first song that was played was "Viva Forever" by the Spice Girls.

What was that all about? A gift turned into a curse? At this point I don't really know why all this happened, only that it happened to me and to Jake. To me, it was as though he somehow knew he was going to die, whether conscious of it or not, perhaps deep within he knew. This was his favourite song, "Viva Forever," where he will always be eternally young, wherever he may be. Jake's statement was "Forever Young."

He didn't want to get old or grow up, and he'll stay young in his heaven forever.

This story continues. I couldn't get Jake out of my mind. At one stage I thought I saw him, but it was just someone who looked like him. I said to the girl that I was walking with, "I just saw Jake up the road there," and the girl said, "I know, I know." she knew that it was hard to let go of a friend. But it went on; what was happening for me was, I could feel Jake around just like I could feel anyone else around, especially when high energy people were around and feeling emotional. But my sensitivity is so profound, if someone is standing beside me in a bar, sometimes all of a sudden I feel like I need to go to the bathroom. I wonder what has come over me and it gets intense. Then the other person says, "I'll be back in a few minutes, really need to use the bathroom." They go and I start to feel better, and within a few minutes, I don't need to go to the bathroom, as that feeling was not even coming from me. I laugh to myself how this is. I notice all of this so much clearer in later years, as at these stages, I was picking up on lots of energies and feelings everywhere, but a lot of the time, I was not sure what was going on.

It is all to do with the feelings, and these things cannot really be understood by the scientific mind. One day I was at work and felt that Jake was there. I could feel his presence there much more clear than anyone else, for some reason unknown to me. His energy was huge, strong, I could feel it all over the bottom section of the work area. I feel the energy of Jake come into the building and hanging around for a few hours. There was a small party going on, as someone was leaving work, and I clearly felt that Jake was there. This happened on a few occasions, and it just seemed so strange to me. In previous years, my mind would have been uneasy if someone told me that spirits or ghosts were around. But when I am feeling it for myself, it is a good feeling, a great feeling, and it can bring so much ease and comfort into one's life.

A month passed, and there was another memorial service for Jake. So many friends turned up, and I was there too. I looked around at all his other friends crying and so sad over Jake's passing, and I wanted to tell everyone that Jake was still around and that they could even talk to him if they wished, but as I thought about what I was going to say, I didn't go any further for fear of people thinking I was crazy.

I was constantly in two frames of mind for that whole month. One was telling all our friends, and the other was keeping quiet. I guess Jake wanted me to tell everyone but my mind kicked in and I just couldn't.

I did however tell one friend there; I said, "Jake is here also," and my friend looked at me with a strange look. I said, "I can feel it, it's clear."

That friend of mine didn't say anything. The energy here was so intensified, and to my amazement, I couldn't understand why no one else knew he was there. I was thinking about getting up on the stage and explaining this, as I felt so clear about what Jake wanted on this day. Then his mother got up, and she was so happy to see all the friends he had. She didn't know about all of his friends, and during her speech she said, "I know Jake is here with us today, and I can feel him here, so listen up, Jake, look at the amount of friends you have here with you tonight, you have really brought happiness to all the people here."

Then she read out something that was on a card that was picked for his funeral, and it went something like this: "Death is nothing at all—I have only slipped away into the next room. Whatever we were to each other we should still remain the same. Call me by my old familiar name and speak to me in the easy way which you always used. Laugh as we always laughed at the little jokes we enjoyed together. Play, smile, think of me and let my name be the household word that it always was. Life means all that it ever meant. It is the same as it ever was; there is absolutely unbroken continuity. Why should I be out of your mind because I am out of your sight? I am but waiting for you, for an interval, somewhere very near just around the corner. All is well. Nothing has past; nothing is lost. One brief moment and all will be as it was before—only better, infinitely happier and forever—we will all be one together with Christ."

I figured if that didn't do it, what could? Jake was there, I knew he was, and so did others. What can I say, only death is really not the end as felt by me, nor is it a sad place to be, for Jake was happy and always laughing and all he really wanted was for his friends to stop crying and realise that he was still around and not going anywhere else.

The whole feeling that I get is that Jake is outside the game, Jake is the watcher of our game, he is happy and content, his part in the play, the drama, the on-stage part he played is over, and I believe that he experienced and achieved that which he set out to do.

The game must go on, and the sad thing is all us players don't even know what part we are to play to complete our lives. It doesn't really matter at what age a person dies, but I think it matters more whether the person lived whilst they were alive or not.

FORTUNE-TELLER

A friend of mine named Annie was interested in fortune-tellers, and on certain occasions, she got one to come around to her house, and whoever was in the house could take turns going into the sitting room with her. One day I went into the room with this fortune-teller named Shelly; I didn't give her any information about me apart from my name. She started to talk to me about Jake, how he was still around. This confirmed to me what I already knew. She said that Jake was laughing at my other friend who had worn a suit to work. This friend sure was funny, and he only wore a suit after Jake died, just for work.

Shelly then said that someone I knew was showing her something. She said, "I'll just tell you what I am being shown here; you are up in your room in the house, it's where the attic is converted, yes?"

"Yes," I replied.

"And the light is on and you're standing there and you get this feeling—you know something is wrong downstairs, and you quickly go down the ladder and down the stairs to the kitchen, and there you saw a fire, coming from the cooker. That was your grandmother who got your attention, and she is shaking her head at your mother, she thinks it was a very careless thing to do."

I was not sure what to say; I just said, "Okay, thank you for that." And then I asked, "What is going on here, how does all this work for you?"

Shelly said, "People who have died just come to me whenever they want me to pass on a message to people like you."

Annie asked was Shelly any good and I replied, "I think so, let me think about it." I believed Shelly, she didn't know me. There was a possibility that someone told her about Jake, that he died, and there was a very slight chance that someone mentioned that I thought he was still around, but I didn't believe that. My mind is just sticking to facts here, I had to prove this to myself. There was not much chance that if someone did mention anything about me and Jake, they also knew about the friend wearing the suit too. This was very unlikely. But then we get to the part where I was in the attic and got this strong feeling around me; I looked around but no one was there, then this feeling told me that something was wrong downstairs, and I went down really quickly. The cooker was on fire. This really did happen, and I didn't tell this to anyone.

No one heard anything about that—there was only me upstairs and me at the fire. The more I worked out all possibilities, the more I began to feel sane. I was shocked at first when Shelly said these things. I was also shocked when they were happening to me. But after all this, I felt sane and knew that somehow, this was actually happening. It was an interesting conversation, and it was strange how it happened. I needed some sort of clarification of events before I started to think that I was going crazy, and this clarification came my way.

SPIRITS WITH A PHD

One day Annie was telling me a story about this person she came across. Annie had a back problem, which was caused by a car accident. She tried everything to fix it but still had problems with her back. Then one day she met a girl who claimed to call spirits into the room who were doctors and nurses; she said that they could help her. I thought this was really something. Annie was up for trying anything, and she went down to this girl's place. She later came back and told me what had happened. She told me that she lay down, and the girl called the spirits into the room, then her arm was picked up and then her leg, and after a while she did a complete spin whilst lying on her back.

"Hold on now," I said. "Before you tell me anymore, this is so out there, can you tell this girl that I have a back problem too and could she fix it for me?"

Annie told this girl that I also had a back problem and asked if I could meet up with her. The appointment was made, and a few days later I went down and told Annie to come and watch. Not that she needed to at all; it was me who needed to experience this. We were all in the room and I was lying on a bed. The girl called the spirits into the room and said, "They are checking it out now." Then I felt someone's hands massaging my feet, and I honestly thought it was Annie messing with me, but when I looked down, there was no one there.

"Annie, look at my feet," I said. "They're getting massaged."

She did look and my feet were moving, and it sure wasn't me doing it, which Annie knew. Then the girl said, "They want you to turn over onto your back, as they are not too concerned about your back right now. There is a bigger problem somewhere else, so turn over please."

This big energy body that I had inside of me, which I kept in my chest and often made me bleed inside, all of this was kept secret until this moment. Then she said, "They have their hands on your chest and they're indicating to me that the problem you have here is just too big for them to fix, there is too much energy here, and you're bleeding in the inside. You need to get this fixed somewhere before you get your back fixed; it is important, you know?"

That was my secret energy body that I got when growing up and had throughout the years, but it was a secret, as I felt everything happens for a reason and that it should just be played out until I work it out. I knew I was bleeding on the inside. What that girl was doing there was real; somehow it was all real. Annie suggested that I go to the hospital, but I explained that I was fine, it would be okay. I disliked hospitals, the bright florescent lights affected my energy and made this energy body in me pump, making me uneasy and sick and completely off balance, not the harmonious way of life that I constantly strived for. The other reason was the long wait in the hospital; I had little patience and felt that the hospital only dealt with surface problems or x-rays, not energy that was in me.

I had developed an ulcer over the years, and there was a lot of internal bleeding inside my body, but I knew what was activating it. I did have the energy there, but that could be used every day on a constant basis. It was a lot to do with school, when I couldn't burn that energy up, and school just did it for me between lights, stagnant energy, and I was shy too, so I always felt very uncomfortable. Then this ulcer I developed in my chest area started to bleed, and I began to cough up blood each time I felt all this energy building up. I would cough up blood every couple of weeks, and then I would feel okay for a while. I knew this lifestyle couldn't last, but I didn't see many other choices. The only choice I could see coming was to finish school and start physically working and become a free man. At this stage, I was out of school, but I was back in confined places with unnatural lights and environments that affected my whole energy.

MANIFESTO—I REALISED WHAT I NEEDED

There were times where I realised that I if could mentally see a way out, a new way of feeling good, I would follow that idea and bring that into my world. But I couldn't picture a way out for me. I needed help to get out, to be away from home and life as I knew it. I remember thinking of options, and I got an idea into my head of what I needed in my life. I could see that if we feel like we are victims, all we need to really do is change our thinking and attract a new way of life. I tested my theory out, and this is what I thought: *I need to meet some girl, someone who is older than me and has her own house and doesn't live in our area,* and then I thought about the house and how relaxing it felt being there as it was made out of timber, it was away from other houses with a nice view, and she had incense burning in the house, and it was all so relaxing.

I was trying out new things—I tried to mentally see what I needed in my life instead of what I didn't need. But I was left with a question: how do I bring this into my life? I thought it up, I clearly thought of every detail, and then I envisioned it and held onto that frame of mind where my thinking changed my emotions. I started to feel how good it would be, and then I just let it all go.

Later that week, I was at a nightclub with friends and completely connected with this older girl who was very good looking. I was dancing in a joking way, and when I looked up, she was standing there watching me. From my perspective, she completely stood out, looking very nice and very attractive, and I felt connected with her energy, but also I was thinking she was way too good for me, but I went over to her all the same, and we danced and joked and had a great night.

I went back to school that week and was still thinking about my problems and how to escape them. This girl got my number from one of my friends and rang me at home and wanted to meet up. I wasn't sure who she was; it was like I was in two minds these days, one mind was trapped where I was looking for inspiration, as opposed to the negative way I was thinking, and that night, I had connected with a gift from life that was sent to me or brought to me or attracted to me on an energy level.

She was ten years older than me, and as we were talking, I had a flashback of the nightclub and remembered her. I pretended that I was working the following day and not in school, as I felt I needed to portray I was older than I was. Anyways, the Christmas holidays came up soon, and she kept asking to meet me. So I said to her one day, "I can move into your house and you will see more of me than you might like."

I was joking when I said it, but she said, "Okay," and there was no school, so I followed suit.

I stayed there on and off over the two-week holidays, living in this house that was made of timber, all of it was timber, inside and out. It was up on top of a hill, away from other houses, with a great view; the feeling was great, the lighting was so nice, my energy felt so calm there, and there was even incense going in the house.

I needed to pause and remember, as this environment and this beautiful, smart girl felt vaguely familiar. I then recalled this was what I was dreaming about, this was what I could see as an outlet to my problems, a huge benefit to my well-being. She lived up a hill, away from everyone. It was as though my prayers had been answered, but who was I praying to and how did all of this work?

At the end of the Christmas, any sort of relationship we had feathered away. I'm not sure what she was thinking, but I knew I couldn't keep this up and be back in school too. We just went our separate ways.

The point of this story is, I didn't even need to set my mind in a direction and to physically follow suit on that frame of thought. I just needed to mentally get it together and focus on what I needed, every detail that appealed to me, and then see it in my mind, even feel it as my energy changed, and then I just snapped out of this, what later felt like a daydream, and I let it go. The opportunity then came to me and I knew there was something mystical about the connection at the nightclub, but I couldn't quite get my head around it at that time. I went with what was drawing me to the situation without any thinking or contemplating. This reality was magnetised to me. I just needed to go with the flow, and that I did.

Is life really that simple?

ACUPUNCTURE—POINTS AND CONNECTIONS

I had a lot of back trouble and went down to Nancy's, a Chinese clinic. I called in and asked for help as I was unable to do any more physical work. She was great to me and took me in and started to work on my back. I explained that I had no money to pay but that I was a carpenter by trade; I asked if I could pay after I got my back fixed and made some money.

Nancy said, "I would like a small deck done out the back of my house; if I can fix your back, I'll just deduct the cost to your charge if you would like to do that."

I said, "Nancy, if you fix my back for me, I will gladly do your deck for nothing. If I am able to work after you're finished with me, I would be delighted to repay you by building a deck for you."

Nancy started working on my back by placing needles into acupuncture points in my muscles, relaxing the muscles and then trying to correct the problem. My back was all knotted up; she had her work cut out for her. She had needles all down my back, and I could feel the tension going and my back becoming more relaxed. Then Nancy took the needles out, placed both her hands on my back, and said, "Breathe out." When I did this, she placed pressure on my vertebrae, thus crunching it back into position.

For approximately four years, four of my vertebrae had been out of place. I forgot what it felt like to be able to stand up perfectly straight.

After she fixed me up, I could not do anything for two weeks as the vertebrae had been out for so long, but after the two weeks, the muscles began to grow back onto the spine and vertebrae in its correct position. I became a new man. I bought the lumber for Nancy's deck, got it delivered up, and built a deck for her behind her house. She was delighted and insisted on giving me some money for it.

One would think a hospital would know these things but sadly they don't deal with things like vertebrae or energy. People should not have to go through the pain that I went through because of lack of knowledge. Acupuncture has been used in China for thousands of years; the Chinese are very smart when it comes to the body and energy, and they sure know a lot of stuff. Nancy was Irish and studied Chinese medicine for many years, earning many degrees. She Nancy was (and still is, of course) brilliant. She leant me a book on acupuncture; every organ in the body is connected to another point in the body. By placing a needle in the point, it vibrates it and makes the healing process quicker for the organ it is connected to. There are hundreds of points, and many things can be done.

I decided to check this out and asked if she could stop me from smoking. She said, "That's no problem at all, I can stop you with five pins, but you have to want to give up yourself."

"Okay," I said, "get the pins out and let's see how this works."

Nancy carefully placed five tiny pins on my left ear. The pins were approximately three millimetres long and had a flat, circular head; the point was so sharp that it was difficult to feel it going in. She then put five very small stickers on the pins to keep them in place.

So I was all ready to experience this; I had a problem with understanding how the will power one worked, but off I went. I told my family what I had got done. They were interested but reckoned I was crazy, as they just couldn't see me not smoking. I was off them for a short while, and then I wanted one. I took a drag of a cigarette and it tasted just terrible. I really hated them. Even if people were smoking around me, I had to move away from them. After some time I could feel the toxins building up in my face, like poison just underneath my skin. When I was in the pub, sitting at a table with some friends, they were all smoking, and I explained that they couldn't smoke around me, so they blew it in a different direction, but that didn't help. So when they put their cigarettes in the ashtray, I grabbed it and broke each one up and said, "It's about time you all gave up anyway." They thought I was crazy for getting it done but we all had a laugh, and I experienced what I set out to try and understand.

The smoke was building up in the pubs, and it was making me sick. I just couldn't stay in the pubs any more. I saw Nancy and she asked me, "How are you getting on?"

I said, "It sure does work but I can't even go into the pubs any more, I can't go anywhere where people are smoking."

Nancy laughed and said, "Sure that's good for you, keep you out of the pubs as well, that's a bonus."

After a while, I began to understand how it worked. There are points all over our bodies. Each one is connected to a different organ in the body, sometimes points in different areas are connected to the same organs in the body. When a pin is placed in the point, or when this point is massaged, it gets to vibrate at a faster pace. The organ it is connected to also vibrates at a faster pace, increasing the health of the organ, increasing the healing aspect. The pin arouses the point, speeding up the vibrations and also speeding up the recovery and vitality for the organ.

In my smoking situation—these points were vibrating at a faster rate, thus healing the organ by the vibration and the healing process, and the poisoning cigarettes process just didn't go hand in hand; they did not mix. My body was coughing up any toxins whilst I was on this acupuncture process. I then had enough of this experience, took the pins out, soon enough I was smoking again and moved onto the next unknown that I didn't understand.

ACCIDENT BY MANIFESTO

The job I was working at was really getting to me at one stage. I was working away but was feeling very trapped again, all the routine of a job starting from seven in the morning and working till five or six o'clock. I couldn't relax in the place, and the more I couldn't relax, the more attention I seemed to be getting, and that's what was really getting to me. I felt trapped with no time out at all. I thought to myself quite clearly, *I need out of this place, I could do with a week off from here; how am I going to pull this off, how will I get myself out of here? One week off would be perfect.*

Then, in the same two minutes of time, I went to put my newly sharpened chisel on the table but was holding it by the sharp end. I went to place it on the table as the bell went for lunch; the head of the chisel hit the table instead of going over the table, and as my hand went forward, the sharp end went straight through my hand, cutting my palm open. I looked at it and thought, *This is amazing, I'm going to have to get stitches, and it sure is nasty but looks like I'm going off for maybe a week.* One of the workers came over and saw it; the safety officer came over and the foreman just said, "D.J. is very unlucky at times, that could happen to anyone. He's just unlucky, yes, that's it, isn't it?"

The worker said, "Yes, he just seems to be unlucky with accidents."

I left the job, drove to the doctor's on my bike, and got stitched up. It was a bad cut and I had to get six or seven stitches.

The doctor asked, "Would you like an anaesthetic?" and I said, "No thanks." I was so full of stress-like energy which was like a strong negative force, and I needed to balance out all that was in me. The feeling of pain was releasing the negativity within me; it was almost like the outward pain connected to the inward energy and created a balance where I felt at ease afterwards.

I realised that something was really going on with what I was mentally sending out there; I was connecting with something deep within or something outside me. I requested a way out and a solution happened.

I needed to be very careful about what I sent out there, as it just might happen. I thought up very clearly that I wanted out for a week, and how could this happen for me? And something happened by accident for me which left me with the break I wanted. I understood that I requested something to happen, and it was I who had the accident. but I did not do it intentionally; it felt like it happened to me but how could it happen to me?

I was left with wondering how this worked.

Sending out this way of thinking, really focusing on something and mentally sending it out there to a higher power or to the source of life, or to what it is you believe in—I'm sending this out to whatever I feel is making this game work. I guess it's a little like when people say a prayer at a church, once they believe in something and send out that thought, their answer could come into their life. There is most definitely something going on, something that is mystical, unseen to the eye, something that seems like it is everything as it knows everything. This unknown I am still discovering.

The trick I realised is to request the circumstance the way you want it to happen, as otherwise, just sending this thought out, this request out, with all your energy, really needing it to happen, could happen just like this. Not everyone would be happy having pain or injury inflicted on themselves.

TO CREATE ON THIS LEVEL

The way it works for me is—I'll tell you a story. I needed something to come into my life, as I needed a change of circumstances. It was more of a situation that I needed to work out in my favour, there was no plan B.

One of my friends was asking me if I would come out for a party on the weekend, and I said that I needed to sort this thing out. He said, "You have done all that you can do."

I said, "Just let me focus, let me see it through."

He didn't understand me at first but later he did. I would keep my focus on the situation and not lose it. After a short while, circumstances were coming into my life which were shaping that situation.

I was not sure how to get the situation to come to me, I only knew that if I could see it in my mind over and over again, it would soon happen.

So different things happened in my life that were like jigsaw puzzles of that situation coming together, and soon enough it all came together, worked out perfectly just as the mind, the tool we use for creation, held that picture. The same frame of mind, the same thoughts over and over again, and then, manifestation.

My friend saw how my life worked and couldn't understand it until I said, "Just let me focus on this."

Soon enough, he did the same thing and it worked for him. I could see that he moved up a notch, to a new level of awareness, but still this was something most people could not comprehend.

CONNECTING WITH NEGATIVITY

There was not much chance of my life going real smoothly any more, as there was this burning energy in me that constantly needed burning out. There were so many things that drove this energy and me to be always on the go, high energy, negative energy, feeling sick, bleeding ulcer. At this stage, I was becoming concerned about my health, thinking that if this exploding energy in me kept happening to me, I would be an old man before my time, if I even lived to reach old age. My main priority was to keep this energy down, not have it activated in any way. But over the years, I was getting myself snookered after having a bad experience here and there; soon enough there were not many places I could go or many things I could do. My world was becoming limited.

But life seemed to have other plans for me, and the moment I realised this was when I was walking down the road past the church—I got this feeling that what the church stands for and what I stand for were heading in opposite directions. It felt like there were two different energies, the church holding in it a pure energy and I the opposite. The church was not a place where I belonged. I could feel the difference, and it was like chalk and cheese, oil and water; these energies just didn't mix.

The reason I was walking down the road was because I had lost my bank card and applied for a new one. I received a new bank card, with a new pin number. I went down to use it and as I was there, I took out my pin number. I began to key it in on the keypad and the keypad lit up to me—I keyed in my number, which was an upside-down cross. Everything stopped for a moment; I looked at the upside-down cross and said, with a feeling of recognition, "I'm becoming someone, but who am I going to be? The devil?"

I felt the upside-down cross symbolised the opposite of Christ.

I realised that I was on my way to experience all the negativity and to become it.

CHAPTER FIVE

False Enlightenment

When I was nineteen years old, things changed for me. I was reaching the peak of my teenage years, and many other things were happening. We all have our underlying core beliefs, and my beliefs were confused at this time. There were two reasons for this. When I was about twelve years old, I could foresee my future so clearly; I saw a darkness that was coming at nineteen years old. I could see this darkness, and to me it was to be the end of my life or the end of life as I knew it. I honestly believed that I was going to die.

But then there was another foreseen event that I could see that led me to have hope and to believe that there was a life after this darkness. Someone really mystical was to come into my life, and I could see that their name started with "A." It felt like mystical, even magical, healing; perhaps I would die and this would happen afterwards, as having this in real life didn't make much sense to me. So when I reached nineteen, these visions were my mind's thoughts.

I could see that the darkness was coming, and I knew it so clearly. I spent many nights just staying awake to get the most out of this life that I felt was going to end soon. All I could see from a young age to this point was that it was going to get dark, and I couldn't really see past that blackness, so I figured I would soon be dead.

On my birthday, I was in my room; I believed that this was my last year, and I thought that I was so close to working everything out, but the darkness was coming. I believed I was so close to beating the system and understanding life's illusions; if I could only have more time.

Moby was on the radio, singing in the background, "I had to close down everything, had to close down my mind." People were coming into my life, and they were saying negative things, complaining about others, and all of it was making my blood boil. Lots of these circumstances were coming into my life at these times. Not much was positive, and there was not much positive energy inside of me.

My whole energy was changing; I was becoming more intense, more awake, but also more negative, angry inside. This anger energy was seeping up in me, and I didn't have any time to listen to complaints anymore, as it was fuelling me. I was on an energy change again; sharpness and anger were all too easily activated in my life at these times, and I knew I needed to get away. I knew it would happen by one of two ways: Either the energy change in my world, in me, would drive me away from where I was, as none of us could connect with each other, or I would be attracted to new friends on this same energy. The choice I had by having this knowledge was realising this: leave and wait for the attraction of a new group of people or stay and fall out with all those in my life.

Survival against the blackness was a main priority. Some friends came into my life and insisted that I go with them and meet some people. So I did just that and started to hang around in Manorville. I was down there with a whole new crew of people.

I felt I could become whoever I wanted to be with all new faces down there. I needed to express this energy that built up in me, and I could appear to be a tough guy down there; it didn't look out of place to anyone, as they did not know me. I had one or two mates that I knew, and the rest I just started to know. We went to a few house parties that Christmas; these were wild parties, and people came from everywhere. Two of the people I knew very well and one of them went back to be with his family for Christmas.

There was a lad named Earl who lived there; he had scars all over his face but seemed okay. There was another lad named Ro; he was from Yorkshire and was a classic. He spoke in a Yorkshire accent and told funny stories; he had a lot of intelligence. He was educated and worked as a tree surgeon, which I thought was funny. We lived in a rooming house, and some of the lads were Irish and some of them were English. When it came to Christmas time, we all started to live it up. We went out drinking one night and continued a house party all night, and then I was only getting warmed up. I was with new people on a new scene and came across as very confident in myself. It was just like all this energy in me, this person I was becoming, on this strong powerful negative energy vibe. I attracted all these people on this same vibration. We were one big bubble of energy, and I felt at home with this energy change in my life.

I stayed awake searching in my mind for the peace, to capture the perfect moment, the slowing down of thoughts after burning off that energy that drove my mind wild, and when I got it, I didn't let it go. It was a crystal clear frame of mind as opposed to the hazy mind I had lived in before. Once I started to burn off some of this endless energy, by staying awake and going to different places, constantly on the move, I was able to connect with this, find peace of mind and keep it. That's when I was 100 percent on the ball. The longer I stayed awake, the sharper I became.

I was awake all the time, out at parties and pubs, and each one of those people I felt were creating my new character. I was becoming someone who could relate to all of them, and with my own energy in me, I was so awake all the time. Each day and night I was down there, and whenever I took a taxi back to the house, the driver would not go there because the house was so wild; I had to give the address of the house next door in order to get there. The house was a party house; my old friends thought it was a dodgy place and didn't feel comfortable around the lads or in the place, but I was in my element. I would drive back on my bike to my house and spend some time up there until midnight, and then I would go back to Manorville.

What was happening for me was due to releasing some of my high energy. I found peace of mind, a fixed place, and with all these new characters, I was becoming one of them. The day went past, then the night, then the day and then the night. It was just one day for me with no sleep; I was fixed in a mental frame of mind and becoming quicker and quicker each day.

Each time one of the lads said, "What happened last night?" I would tell them to the finest detail, as it was only a short time ago for me. I did this for four days and then started slowing down; I wasn't as quick on my bike, and if I fell asleep, I would have to start all over again. This year it was very important for me to stay conscious, as in my mind it was going to be my last year. Christmas Day came and I went home for dinner. I was very tired as we sat there at the table, and I needed to keep on moving in order to stay awake. I ate my dinner and nearly fell asleep halfway through it.

After staying awake for four days, I noticed that some of the lads were taking drugs. I ended up getting a bag of speed off Earl and tried it. I was back on track again, completely awake.

All the negative energy in me and frustrations and the powerful force was coming out to the surface in me, which left me feeling quite strong and alive and very awake. I would get cleaned up in the house and kept moving on my mission of staying awake. I had music playing all the time. I noticed that the longer I stayed awake, I couldn't listen to too much talking any more. Some pervious friends were giving out that I was not around, and when they started I was gone. I just played the Stereo MCs song with the words, "I'm going get myself connected." And I knew that I was searching for the connection, between my mind, body, the emotion, and the spirit, knowing that this connection was a strong force by having it altogether.

I was good fun to be with, but I was also a reflection of all I had around me. I was sharp, strong, also quick with answers, and I found myself to be completely in my element.

The people I was with were taking drugs; one occasion, I was out with John and Joe, and we were just hanging around having a laugh. Joe had some ecstasy with him that he was to give to a friend of his. The police came along and wanted to search us. Joe objected to the search and was taken off to the station. The next thing I heard was Joe was laughing in hospital. Then we found out what happened in between.

Joe said, "They brought me to the police station and had all my belongings on the counter. There was one copper behind the counter and the other copper was filling out the charge sheet. He was charging me for possession of ten ecstasies. The coppers were doing their own thing for one second; they both had their heads down, and the ecstasy were just sitting there on the counter. So I grabbed them and threw them into my mouth. I was trying to chew them real quietly, and the copper doing the charge sheet turned around to look at the items I had. He looked at the counter and then looked at me. Then he asked the other copper, 'Where are the tablets?' The other copper shrugged his shoulders, and then he came for me. He knew I had them in my mouth and threw me up against the wall; he grabbed me by the neck and said, 'Spit them out.' I swallowed them, the whole lot, and said, 'They're gone.' The copper then asked, 'What have you got to say for yourself?'

and I said, 'Can I have a glass of water?' He gave me a punch in the stomach and then they realised they better bring me to hospital to get pumped. So here I am, after getting the best buzz of my life."

Taking that many ecstasy could kill anybody, but Joe didn't care; he had no great respect for his own life at all. There was something about Joe, the way he perceived the world to be, the way he felt all the time that led him to not give two bleeps about his own life. I could see the connection between us—there was something in us that we could not overcome, and we both had this attitude towards life.

The decks were played all the time in Manorville, and I was happy there. I fit in with everyone down there. Then I recognised one lad who arrived on the scene. I had a mental flashback of standing outside the disco when I was sixteen years old, just before I got beat up by six lads. He was the first lad I ran into, and when I put my fists up, someone behind me cracked me over the head. I saw him and I told one of the girls I was with, "That bloke who just walked in there gave me one bad hiding over three years ago, but now I'm bigger than him." The girl talked me out of going back in; I stopped and thought, *I'm going to play this my way.*

By staying awake for so long, everything was coming together. It was one big long day for D.J. I was attracting characters from my past that were on this anger level of energy, I was seeing things clearly. I also could tap into my gift about seeing events that were to come into my life, and I was happy staying awake. I felt that I was getting closer to life's mystery, and so awake I stayed. I asked the people in the house who this lad was, and they told me he was Col, a dangerous man. I was ready for a fight with him but first I introduced myself. He had a few scars across his face and looked dodgy, but so did I. I figured it was about time we cleared it up between us; he had no idea who I was. People began to tell me stories about others who messed with his family; one lad was pulled into a van and a shotgun was put into his mouth. They made their point that his was a family not to mess with.

We all went out drinking in the pub together, and I just sat at the table in front of Col. I could mentally see guns coming my way. With all my thinking about them for years, the peak of that was coming, my time was coming for the choice of whether I really did want to get involved with guns or was I just contemplating, thinking about thinking?

We were sitting in the pub, and to my amazement, after a few pints, Col starting shaking his head and saying to me, "I am a bad man, I have done so many bad things, real bad things."

I said, "Okay, go on."

He said, "I'm a real bad person," and he started to sob away to himself.

To my amazement, I rubbed my eyes and was saying to myself, *This is a very dangerous man; I'm here to confront him about our incident, and he is making some sort of a confession to me. Who does he think he is talking to? No one else can hear our conversation, he is only talking to me here; what's going on?*

He seemed to feel so bad, and between that and his sobbing, I decided to let it go without saying who I was and why I was sitting at the table nor about me letting it go. All of that was just for me, and I could see he was so bad because he was hurting so bad. We became mates, and no one ever became the wiser.

I stayed awake for a very long time over that Christmas. I had my bike and I had at least three houses to call into in a sort of roundabout as time went on. I did have to keep dabbling in speed in order to do so. Each time a party was finished in one town and people were falling asleep, I went on to Manorville, day and night; I loved it. One night, I was in Manorville with Earl and a few others, and I began to find out what Earl was like behind the look he portrayed. He had heaps of astrology books in his room. I asked him, "Is there really truth in all that astrology?" and he said, "Yes, there sure is, D.J., but you've got to know what you're dealing with." That was interesting, as I didn't figure him to be that sort of person.

I met a girl through a friend down there, and she fit right in with this group of energy. Sometime after Christmas, at the end of January, I heard that this girl climbed on top of the motorway bridge and jumped off it to kill herself. When she landed, she broke her legs and ended up in hospital. She had a death wish. She was taking hard drugs and trying to kill herself because of something. There are no effects without causes. What I am saying here is there is a reason why people take drugs, some energy within, an unseen pain. The point is, if you rid the emotional pain of the body and the surface issue, there's no need to take drugs.

But this was the relative opposite of what we were all portraying. Each and every one of us had this dark side in us, and we were constantly jumping from both polarities throughout life. Guns and fighting back against all I perceived the world to be was the direction I was going in.

I could see it clearly in my mind that guns were coming my way, and we were about to be one bad group of lads. Out of all of us lads, there was energy, like energy attracts like energy, all of us dangerous characters were all attracted to each other. I was heading for a point of no return. I could see what we were all getting into. I could see guns and trouble, only we were to cause the trouble. I kept getting these visions of what was to come, and at these times, it just felt right, and it was a pleasure to let go of my frustrated old life. In one vision, there was a young man that was attempting to do something bad to our group; we came after him later on, when I was the ring leader, and put a gun to his head. I could feel the strong anger that I had towards him in this vision, and whether I pulled the trigger or not was still to be played out.

One night, we were in the pub and Earl began to talk about this one lad who was acting like he was going to try and bleep the lads over. As we were sitting in the pub, the Queen song "Bohemian Rhapsody" came on the jukebox: "Mama, I've just killed a man, I put a gun against his head, pulled the trigger, now he's dead. Life has just begun and now I've gone and thrown it all away."

I kept getting more speed off Earl, and I said to him, "It is got to be pure, not mixed with anything, it doesn't matter how small it is, it's just got to be pure, okay?" He asked me what I was doing with it. I told him so many of my mates wanted it, and he said, "Just as long as you're not taking it by yourself." But I did take it all by myself; anytime I felt tired, I just licked my finger and put it in my mouth and got the kick I needed.

I used to listen to a lot of vocal trance music, and there was a song that kept playing on the radio, as if there was some mystical aspect to it trying to speak to me. It was like some spirit was watching out for me and singing a message to me. It was a nice thought, but there was no way that I could be sure of this. I was not sure whether the drugs I was taking were having this affect on me, but the words went something like this: "Turn it around now baby—spend more time with me, you have gone too far—turn it around now." This song always came on when I listened to this station on the radio. There seemed to be some mystical force in life that was telling me to stop this, but why would I want to stop anything? I felt that the more I was awake, the closer I was getting to some truths. I felt inspired on a mystical level but on a physical level and emotional level, anger was all too quickly accessible.

People were moving out of the house and into a new place, which had five bedrooms. One character, named Domo, seemed like a nice lad but there was something to him; he was in deep thought a lot. One night, after I was drinking down there, he said to me, "I'm going to tell you something I haven't told anyone really before, only really close mates. I'm a born again Christian. What really happened was, when Christ was up on his cross after getting crucified, I was there. I was on a cross behind him. This really happened and it was me who was there at that time. Don't tell anyone about this but it is true."

I wasn't sure how to take Domo after that one. I told one of the lads, and they said that Domo had told all the lads the same thing. There was a Carman song out then that went like this: "Who's in the house? Jesus is in the house," and we changed it to, "Who's in the house? Domo is in the house." It did relax the atmosphere, and Domo didn't seem to mind at all; it was all good fun. Domo seemed pretty much completely sane otherwise, but who really knows anyway?

I was in my house just listening to some music, and Tommy called to the door. Tommy had been down in the pub and was pretty drunk. So I brought him in, and he began to tell me a story. He was funny but I could only listen to so much. My mind was ready to receive a good, short, to-the-point, funny story, and Tommy was telling a long, drunken story which would probably not come to the end in our lifetimes. After ten minutes (maybe only two) of this, I left and went upstairs, and when I came back down, Tommy was still talking; he hadn't gotten much further than where I left him. So I grabbed him, carted him out to the hallway, opened the door, threw him out onto the street, and said, "Don't call back in here again."

My behaviour was shocking, but this was what was happening to me with all this lack of sleep I was going through. I was afraid to sleep and lose all I knew. I didn't think too much about this, as I figured Tommy would forgive me soon enough (if he ever remembered).

After staying awake for twelve or thirteen nights, it seemed that each and every person was draining my energy. Talking was draining me, and if there was any sort of a problem at all, I just couldn't handle that. A friend called around and said, "All the girls are going to the nightclub; do you want to go? You can do it, one more night, hey?"

"No problem, I said. "Just give me a second." We took some speed and were back on track.

We went up and had a good time, but at the end of it, I knew I had to sleep that night. I went home but had this energy in me that I couldn't release, so I closed the door, walked back to the other door, and put my fist through nine panes of glass, one after the other. I just couldn't cope with anything and needed to release the energy within me. I just needed to sleep at this stage, as I could not release this energy from me. I went without sleep for thirteen days, nearly two weeks. Two weeks I think is the max for any man. I experienced what I set out to experience.

I went back down to Manorville a few days later and told the lads in the house how long I stayed awake for; there were three of us who did it for the whole Christmas. Two of them signed themselves into a mad house after staying awake fourteen nights. One of them wouldn't admit it at first but that's what happened. They signed themselves into a mental institution and finally fell asleep; the institution had a look at them the next day, and they were fine. They were asked to leave the place. There is such a thin line between sanity and insanity. At the time I loved the whole lot of it and wanted to stay that way forever in the one clear long day. It was a long day with thirteen nights. They say that drugs can be a pathway to spirituality, and perhaps this is so, but this is a false enlightenment.

GYPSY PSYCHIC

I went to Annie's house after Christmas, and there was a mystical lady there who did insightful readings in the sitting room. Everyone said that she was very impressive. Jane, Annie's sister, was there, and she said, "Hey, D.J., this girl is very good, would you like to go in instead of me? I am next but I've seen her before. You should go in, hey?"

I said, "Are you sure, Jane? I might do that."

Jane said, "Do, D.J., really you should."

I said, "Jane, you're a star, thanks a lot. I'll see how it goes."

I noticed there was a van outside the house before I went in, and the driver had no one in the passenger seat, only a few kids in the back. He gave me the impression he was a Gypsy man. I went in to see the girl, who said, "I thought someone else was coming in, but it does not matter."

I sat down on the armchair there, and we began talking. She was about forty-five years old. She got me to take a few cards from the deck and placed them on the table. She turned the cards over and began to tell me things about me and my life. She told me that I was a king, as one of the cards I took was the King.

I said, "Will you stop? I'm no king."

She said, "Even look at the way you're sitting on the armchair, just like the picture in the card. But you worry too much, really much, you shouldn't worry at all." She put the cards down and began to talk to me without any cards or crystal ball; it was a one-on-one conversation. She had this conversation with me, explaining events that had taken place and all that I was doing, where I was hanging around in Manorville, just as if she was beside me during my whole time over Christmas. And no one knew where I was over Christmas, as I was everywhere on my own and with everyone. She told me a list of things:

One of them was very important; she said, "You are hanging around with a group of lads in Manorville, and it may be all fun at the moment, but they're into things, guns and that, and I think you know this, but it just hasn't got that far yet. Soon enough, a lad down there with a scar on his face is going to ask you to get involved with them and what they're doing. If you do get involved, and I think you know what I'm talking about here, if you do, you will get into something and you may not ever get out of it. If you say no when he asks you, you can go on and live your life."

I said, "What will my life be like if I say no? Will I make it to the top, will it be the best?"

She said, "Your life will be okay, but if you say yes to the question, you won't be able to get out of what you get into; if you say no, you will have an okay life. Do you understand?"

"Yes I do," I replied.

She said, "There is a boy in your workplace named Dick, and he is getting to you, but don't hit him."

I said, "I'm going to burst him," and she said, "That is what he wants, that is what he likes; just forget about him, as it isn't worth it." Then she told me about Jake, and it just confirmed all I knew. She also told me about a lad named Phil: "He is having a conversation right now to his wife about you. Check it out," she said. "You will find all of this information accurate and true."

I said, "Thank you very much for all this."

She said, "Just remember, you have the choice with those lads; you got to say no, D.J."

The simplicity of words, the "yes" and the "no," created a huge difference in the future for me; what would it be?

This person came into my life at this very important moment, or more to the point, I came into their life, purely by accident, at this very important time when I was at these crossroads in my life. Why did we meet?

Was it for her to tell me to say no? That's what it sounded like to me.

Was it a pure coincidence that we met at this time? I don't believe in coincidence any more—I used to but now I believe it's a copout for not understanding life's mysterious ways. We were brought together, that mysterious lady and I, for reasons that are fairly clear, but the workings, yet again, are not yet fully understood. How does this work? Who is controlling this game? Was it Jake who did it? Was it just life's way of saying, "You brought it to a peak, now let it go; the experience is over now before it's too late"? Do I have free choice in life? I now believe so because this girl came into my life to tell me to say no—many songs came on the radio singing words that seemed as if they were wrote just for me, many sayings that really spoke to me on many levels. So I believe we must have choice, or all of this wouldn't need to happen.

How does it all work? That is my greatest interest.

STILL HAVE CHOICE

I went back down to Manorville and called into the house. I went into the sitting room. There was only Earl sitting there on the couch, and then I was sitting there on the chair.

Earl said, "How are you doing, D.J.?"

I said, "I'm doing great, mate, thanks."

He said, "Hey, D.J., we know you now, and we all had a great time this Christmas; would you like to know what we really do behind all these house parties? Would you like to be a part of it?"

I paused for a moment, and then I said, "No, mate, not for me."

Earl was shocked, as that was not the way he thought it would go, but that's all the information he gave. He respected me and was happy enough asking me to be part of the gang. I would have said yes, only that mystical lady had come into my life and explained so much to me. I would have said yes, as all I had to do was reflect on my life, not even that; my mind was full up of all that was happening, and there were no enjoyable moments. It was just high anxious feeling, beatings, frustration, no clear thinking. All I had to do was weigh up the pros and cons. A life of negativity or else a life of, don't mess with us dangerous bleepers and perhaps creating negative events.

I left soon after that and said, "Nice talking to you, mate, talk to you again."

Earl said, "Okay, D.J., catch you later."

I was back in work soon, and I had all of the mystical lady's conversation in my mind all the time. I decided to talk to someone about it, and it turned out to be Phil. Phil said to me, "Oh, what were you doing all Christmas? You have that look in your eye and it's dangerous; don't tell me you don't, because I have seen it before."

Phil didn't give me any more abuse then, as he sometimes really bleeped me off. I noticed that when some people saw me, they backed off from me, feared me in ways. That's who I was becoming, I was feared by people I knew and got on with.

My father backed off from me over that Christmas, and that felt okay because I wasn't a nice person and I was glad that I was not in his company. There was one stage where my mother said something and I replied, "Enough of this!" She made a face that was hard to describe, but it had a hint of fear in it. Our house cat hissed at me and walked away. Our cat and I were falling out! There it was, people who loved and cared for me were becoming afraid of me. I questioned myself, would I rather be loved or feared? I would rather be loved would be my choice.

So Phil and I had a chat. I explained to him about the mystical lady and a few things that she said. Phil tried to be open minded about it, but he didn't believe in any of that. He then said to me, "I was talking to my wife about you the other day, just over you cutting your hand and coming in drunk and . . ."

I said, "That lady told me that. She told me that there was a lad named Phil who was talking to his wife about me at that particular time, no joking."

I also told him, "She told me about a lad at my job who was out to provoke me and for me not to hit him. I was going to hit him until she told me that it is what he wants, so I'm just letting it go."

Phil understood about the lad at work, but he thought I was winding him up about the conversation he had with his wife. But the way it worked, I forgot about the mystical lady telling me about Phil talking to his wife, nor did I ever think it was this Phil, until he said it to me. Phil explained to me that he had gotten hypnotised before, when he was about twenty-five years old. His wife got him to do it to quit smoking, and he didn't ever smoke again. He agreed that there was a lot out there that he didn't know but he couldn't believe that someone would know that he had a conversation with his wife about me.

SUM UP THE CRAZY

There was a change of energy in me, the anger energy in me was not held deep within me anymore. It was gradually coming to the surface in me. Energy attraction was what was happening; I was magnetising a new group of friends on the same energy level. They were all portraying a fun existence; they told many witty stories but there was also a mysterious dark side to them. One big energy bubble we were, all vibrating at the same speed. I now understand them all, as I became one of them. The mind was a tool; I was sending out thoughts of guns and expressing my negative life, and that was magnetised to me.

The mystical lady—my spirit or some other spirit—was getting me to stop as I had experienced enough and next phase was coming up. Life was directing me, but define life. Spirit was directing me, but explain that one to me. Who was the spirit? I was guided back to my path, but who was doing it? How could they do it so perfectly? Something tapped into me, into the radio, the music, the mystical lady, the girl in the house that gave me the turn to see the lady—something that can get into us all or manipulate us all. Questions, always questions, always in my mind; once they entered my mind, they would not leave until the answer was there, till the mystery was solved, no matter how long it took or what I had to go through.

STAYING AWAKE

I tried to see past the controls in life—the illusions and the ways we must live, the way we live: work most days and sleep most nights. Each weekend, young people would drink and party and rarely ever connect with life's illusions behind the scenes. I needed to get deep within, stay mentally awake to understand life's mysteries. I had to stay awake for my new and final, last chance of getting it all together. As I wanted to find the answers before the blackness came. I stayed awake, and awake I stayed. Night fell; all the people were asleep but not me. Daytime, then night, then daytime again. I became more aware of the essence of life, more connected the longer I stayed awake with life. My spirit fully held in the game without any sleep or unconsciousness, awake becoming the Awakened One. I monitored myself throughout; I took speed, and they say drugs are a gateway to the spirit world, and that's what I felt too. I reached awakened highs that I never did before and learned so much. But the body we inhabit must comply with life's rules, the rules of the game. Or this rule breaking high will become its relative opposite, the crashing low.

I moved back home, and after some time I began sinking again. I was thinking about everything in work, about Jake and how it was all possible and how it all worked. How could the lady tell me such exact information? She could see all that was happening for me. Was life mapped out? I had a choice, though, with my situation in Manorville, so therefore there was a choice of endings. After Christmas, it could have gone either way, but then again she came into my life so I would make the correct choice in the long run. I could not see who was controlling me. Was Jake helping me out? I didn't think so, too much work involved, so who or what was controlling all of this? She was spot on about Phil talking to his wife, and she was spot on about other little things. How did it all work? I needed to work it all out. What was Jake doing? Was he just chilling and laughing at us all? What did he think about where he was? Clearly he was not in a sad place; where was he?

How could I feel him around sometimes? He was here where we are, but we just couldn't see or hear each other; I somehow could feel him just like I could feel anyone else around me. I didn't know the answers, just heaps of questions, and I was closing down possibilities, ruling out maybes, and searching for truths.

NEGATIVE ENERGY INTENSIFIED

I tried to continue on with life, but life was not finished with my negative and anger energy experience. The energy in me was a heavy burden. This energy I could keep down at times when I burned it out, by cycling or racing bikes or doing dangerous things that could damage my body or end my life. But the things that got this energy going was when I was in company with people and we were not doing anything, stagnant energy times, sitting down for dinner, watching television, anything like that. The bright lights would really heat up my body, and this would activate that energy or add to it each time. The buses, school, and the jobs with those lights were a constant build-up. A build-up of this energy became very unhealthy. I got worse as I got older, or maybe life just became more difficult where friends were evolving, experiencing, and growing up but I wasn't. I was stuck with this burden.

When this energy rose up in me, my mind and thoughts raced and became hazy. At times, I became a prisoner held captive by my own mind. When I got out of school, my whole body was knotted up with this energy in me, and I began to develop an ulcer in my chest area. When I was working, I was offered some night work, and I went for that straight away. I felt great doing night work. I started to see that I was comfortable with the energy at night; I liked working in more or less dark environments, which did not expose myself to too much heat and light. I would stay awake all night and do the night shift, then I would stay awake all day; the daytime then became easier as my energy was burnt out or close to being burnt out. I had enough energy to work, it was just that I didn't have too much energy anymore and felt calm and relaxed.

When I was exposed to the lights, the energy grew. I became sad with a hazy mind and uneasy feeling, but in dimmed lights, or in a pub area with this relaxed lighting, I became happy, even confident and relaxed. Over the years, between all of this energy getting intensified by either emotional people, circumstances, or lights and static energy, this energy grew and became massive. Coughing up blood became a regular occurrence. Then it still grew and grew, and it became massive. Parts of me felt happy when things went wrong and disasters happened and negativity became manifested in reality. This was who I was becoming, and I couldn't believe that a huge part of me felt this way. I would then send out thoughts that I needed to be beaten up rather than beat up someone else. That I saw the illusion, the reflection of life, and if I wished for bad on others, really somewhere I wanted it on myself.

Solutions were for me to get beaten up, and I attracted them. This energy in me wanted me to be miserable, to be alone, and to suffer. I had to keep moving and getting time to myself in order to keep this energy under some sort of control. If I stopped working or doing things that didn't keep this energy burnt out or kept it down, then the energy would take over my mind. I would be corrupted mentally and head for a depression. Half of me was forcing the other half to be awake and fight for serious awakenness beyond this corruption of negativity. I had to keep moving or just sleep; I couldn't watch television, had to stay focused to keep it down, couldn't relax, and didn't know how to anyways. I couldn't even sit in a car as a passenger and wait in traffic. I had to get out of the car and walk, and if the traffic moved, I could get back in the car. I needed a constant supply of music to keep my mind stimulated, so that the energy would not seep up in me.

Music, inspiration, open spaces, and movement were what I had to have at a constant basis or else I was no good. And when no good, I would be no good for hours or days or weeks, until music or inspiration or good energy came my way and woke me up again, I had to break free, as I needed that clear mind again.

Eventually this energy became so great and so massive, I became like a monster within but still tried to keep the energy below my face, from the neck down. This negative low frequency energy was like a parasite in my energy field. It was fuelling my mind, and when bad things happened, this energy was satisfied. This energy was feeding off my negative thoughts as my negative thoughts changed my energy in motion to negativity, and this parasite that got me to believe we were one fed off the mind that it was fuelling. This was a vicious circle.

My sensitivity would even be heightened, and I would feel that there was an energy coming from the church, that my energy at these moments and that purer energy the church represented were so distant from each other. I couldn't even walk in the same area as a church—I became the opposite of what good stood for as I connected with this negativity.

This energy was passed onto me, and because I was closing off with everyone, it was winning, and therefore I was connecting with it. Eventually I wanted to kill this monster. Reaching the madness of this negative insanity consisted of this. You could think that I had lost all levels of sanity here, and you may be correct in that thinking. I realised that this entity was separate from myself and that it must die before it killed me, but killing this oversized negative parasite meant nearly killing myself. I even considered getting a gun and shooting myself, once in each foot, leg, and arm, and the final bullet to the head was the wild card yet to be played out. I wanted to kill this negative energy, and six bullets may have done it. But if it didn't, the one to the head would kill us both. This was the peak of the negativity—the upside-down cross experience. Luckily for me, Earl sensed that I was suicidal and would not give me his gun.

I did not rid this negativity, but after experiencing it to the full, I could see that it was a separate entity and that it was feeding off me, and it was winning. It nearly won by destroying me. Eventually I calmed down, monitored my thoughts, and stayed away from places that made me feel trapped or think negatively. We need to get rid of negative energy and bad spirits, but how do we do that? This is a good question. How can we completely rid this negativity of all levels? Hopefully we will find out on my travels and experiences.

This energy in the deepest sense of the game is a covering of the positive energy. It is the nothing that is taking over, covering over the something, the emptiness as opposed to the fullness. It is like when the moon covers the sun in an eclipse. The nothing is eating away at the something, and both are relative terms derived from the mystic. There is a way to get rid of this negativity, which I will get into later on in the story, but it also causes us to get rid of many of life's illusion.

MY DEPRESSION

I started to slowly get really depressed. This depression was taking over my mind, and I was afraid. Staying indoors at work seemed to make it worse, as I was trapped; the lunch break with people made me worse, as it was too hard to focus on anything else apart from this depression. Being at home also made it worse—many times, it felt like a de-charging place, rather than a re-charging place, and I'm sure that session over Christmas was not helping the effects. I needed a timeout period, but life went on, and I was not ready to continue on. This was my world, a black cloud was coming in, I was changing, and no one understood. Any conversations I had with friends just led them to believe I was losing the plot.

I played a CD by Moby all the time, and I sang along to one of his songs, changing the words myself to, "Oh Lordy, my troubles so hard, nobody knows my troubles with God."

These were troubles that could not be helped—I was on a cycle in life to find out the unknown, and it could not be stopped. My troubles were so hard, as there was no help for me or this cause; it just all had to be experienced.

GOING DEAF

I started going deaf around this time; there was too much noise in my life, and I was sinking into this deep thinking. I just wanted to block out people's talking and noise and things I thought that were said about me and what people were thinking about me. Everything that was in my outward surroundings was just noise, no truth or anything worth listening to, and I just tried to block it all out so I could find the truth within. I actually started going deaf; I couldn't hear people when I tried to. It was amazing; the doctor actually checked me out and confirmed that I was going deaf. Everyone learned that I was hard of hearing and going deaf. There was talk that my deafness could be hereditary; I was young and didn't particularly believe in that answer, but it was a possibility. The truth is, I thought about my world, the noise outside myself, all that was happening, and I had no control over anything. I chose to block everything out and just keep a few good songs in my mind, to keep me happy and sane, and it worked. Then, as we often forget things, the core thought was created and I actually went deaf and forgot about what I was thinking beforehand. I couldn't get back to hearing clearly. It was amazing. My hearing is perfect now, but it sure wasn't at that stage of my life, as I had things on my mind that required thinking about, and my mind was full of things that were not worked out. It was like a programme running in my mind that required a lot of energy; depression does require a lot of energy, and I went deaf. I chose to.

I was up and down like a yo-yo, acting out that I was fine and keeping my depression hidden. For me it was like out of the twenty-four hours in the day, eight were for sleep, and when I got up, I was thinking depressed thoughts until I left the house. Then I was okay until I went to work. I was getting quite depressed at work, and when I left at six o'clock, it was dark when I was heading back home. I was saving my energy for pretending to be just fine when I needed to. But I was really getting overruled by this depression. Then the evenings started getting brighter, but my mind was getting darker. I spent all my time in work all week, thinking about how I would get through the weekend and that I couldn't handle the sessions any more, but I also couldn't not go out, as I would lose all my friends. This went on for a while until I got sick of this; I kept on high levels of anxiety and deep levels of depression. Monday was my best day, as I had somehow got through the weekend and still had all my friends. Thursday and Friday were becoming the worst days, as I was thinking of ways to avoid going out. So all my previous lows, house and work, were becoming the high points in my life. I sure was sinking. I told my parents about what was happening to me; they were worried about me and suggested that I should go on Prozac.

I asked Arthur, my father, what was happening to me, and he said, "I once talked to a specialist who explained that depression is caused by the cells in the brain. There are white cells and red blood cells. What happens when one gets depressed is the whites are taking over the reds."

And that was it, the white cells were taking over the reds, and that was that; we'll give you a good send-off when you finally do take your own life, was how I interpreted it. I went up to the doctor and asked him to give me some Prozac. He said, "It must be the drugs you young lads are doing."

I said, "It is not, it is something else, it's going on too long, and I think it is best that I take the Prozac."

I remember that just trying to say that was so hard, the emotion behind the words were emotional. People who are depressed find it so hard to ask for help, and it becomes one lonely world. I took the Prozac for a while. I told a friend in work, and he explained that he too went on them at one stage after his father died. His father worked his whole life for himself and the family, and it was only when he owned the house and made money that he died, and my work friend was so frustrated and torn up over this. He explained that Prozac just altered the way he looked at life and left him feeling like he was on drugs, which he was. I observed what it did to me; it took away the depression for a short while, leaving me mellow in ways and altered my vision from a depressed haze to a clearer, enhanced colour. This went on for a while, and then I just stopped taking them.

I figured that whatever my life was about, I knew one thing for sure: it was about having certain experiences and taking them to the breaking point, the point, if crossed, that was the point of no return. I could see that life and the game and the experiences were my teacher. Some people go to college and take a course in this and that, but for me, this was my college; these hard-core experiences were the greatest teacher for me. I needed to know things by experiencing them, and this was how it was to be done.

I stopped taking Prozac and decided to just take what was coming to me full on. I didn't want anything to alter what I was to go through, and this depression sure came on intensely. What I was thinking, I was creating, and as I was sinking in my own mind into this depression, all I could think was that I was going to lose everything in my world and I needed to stop it all. I had to fight for survival.

I left my job after pleading insanity; only joking, these parts are hard to remember, as this black depression stays as a memory. I just left work and said I had enough. Before I left, Phil said, "You'll be dead before you're twenty."

I had the high energy and looked like I had been drinking for forty years and that I had completely abused myself. Energy and state of mind were the most destructive thing. A health centre opened up in our area with a swimming pool and a gym. I joined the gym and began fighting for my survival. I ran on one of the machines and just kept running. They set the speed of the run at 25 KMPH, and it was all to do with how long they lasted. One friend did it for twenty-five minutes, and another did it for twenty-seven minutes, so I got involved. I did over thirty minutes of this, and the lads were amazed, as they played football and I didn't. It was all to do with a focus point for me, as I was actually fighting for survival to get through this madness I was going through. The next day, my legs were quite sore after the run; it was a shock to my body.

In this state of mind, people find it difficult to get out of bed and have a shower; people find it difficult to care for themselves. I could feel it, I was going down in a spiral created in my mind; each thought was leading to the next thought, and none were positive. Each thought was energy, and remember, like energy attracts like energy. Each thought was attracting the same type of thought, and when the mind was filling up with these like minded thoughts, sleeping was the only thing I felt was keeping me alive. When I woke up from my dream state of being and into my depressed mind, I would think about everything again, and my mind was becoming trained to do this. Each thought was still attracting each thought, only after time went on, after this was happening so much, it was becoming life itself, and the memories of any happiness were fading away. Memories, energy, thoughts were all really energy, and they were all attracted to each other. It was one depressed circle. Having the negative energy suppressed like this was the power to send this depression to a deep level.

All our minds then try to think of the way forward. The way forward in this case was to the depths, the core of the depression. It's like being buried alive in a coffin when you're asleep, and when you wake up, you try and get out to the freedom six feet above you. The depression was like being put into a coffin upside down, lying on your chest. So when you try to break free and climb out, you're in fact going deeper to the core of the earth.

As was seen during the Christmas session, I tended to take things to the max; I did the same with this depression. I took it to its core, and it's a state of mind. I was losing weight on my body and was heading for a place so alone. I pictured in my head what it was like to die and where would I go to. I would have previously thought I would be in the same place with the other lads who died throughout the years, and it would be all right. But in this state of mind, afterlife too was a place on its own, so alone in pure blackness and wanting nothing else only that.

One night, I woke up, went down to the bathroom, had a shower, and got dressed. I saw JJ, who was putting on his deodorant, ready for a big night out. He looked so fresh and happy. I said, "I wish I was like you, the only thing that is keeping me alive is the sleep."

He said, "It's just the drugs, D.J."

I went back into my room then. My mother saw what I was like; she asked me if I was still on the Prozac, and I said, "Just on and off."

She recommended that I go back on them, and I did try them again, but it was too late. They were not doing anything for me then; I was gone past the stage of the Prozac sandwiches.

I came downstairs and my brother Jonsey was watching television. I sat down on the couch beside him and shed a few tears. I said, "I cannot live like this much longer, it is just dark in my mind. I don't think it will last forever, but I'm really coming to the stage now where I can't hack it any more. I have a strange, distant feeling inside me that my life will be great in the future, but I can't do this any more. I can't even last another two weeks; I might just have to go."

Jonsey saw our father later on that day and told him all that I said. Arthur drove up to the house and asked to talk to me.

He said, "Don't get angry at Jonsey, but he told me all that you said, as he is very concerned about you. Come on and we'll go for a drink."

I got in the car and we went to the pub for a drink. Beer and cigarettes were not my idea of a cure for my dis-ease. But that's all Arthur did with any problem. This was not a good idea for me. I left the pub and began walking home. I made it to the graveyard at the top of the road and went in. I saw Jake's grave and walked over and said, "I can't do this any more, it won't be long before I'm in this graveyard. I give myself a week max."

I left and walked home in the dark, hoping a car would just run me over, but unfortunately (I felt at that time), the cars all avoided me.

After I stopped taking Prozac, it came to me. I got some inspiration, and to be completely honest, I could see that the deeper that I went into this depression, the opposite experience would have to happen some day. The further that I went into this darkness, the more light I would experience at some stage, as we live in a world of relativity. So I didn't fight the depression. I realised this and stopped the Prozac again straight away, saying, "Bring it on," and on it came and soon to be fully understood by me. It's dark!

My mother was worried about me, and one day I left my bedroom door locked and then went out, and when I came back, the door was kicked in. My mother explained that she had been worried and got my brother to kick it in, just in case I did something. She was picturing the worst-case scenario, thinking that I could have hung myself in there. I felt so sorry for her to think that way, but I guess she was not far off my thinking.

After a short period of time, I woke up to the situation that I was in and realised that I just wanted to die for so long now, and that I was doing things to end my life, so I got myself together and accepted that I was going to take my own life. I thought about it for a long time and could see it was the only way out. All of my previous dreams about doing good things that I wanted to do, I accepted that they were not going to happen. I went home and went to bed. I realised that sleeping was the only thing keeping me alive, and as soon as I woke up, I was back in the mind of depression. I decided to end my life, but then I met up with Nancy from the acupuncture clinic again. She knew I was stressed and insisted on helping. She took me in the clinic and placed fifty or so pins in my head. I looked like *Hellraiser* (the movie). She then said, "Okay, I'm going to make a tape for you, and I want you to listen to it. I'm going to get you through this, so you just wait till I have that tape made and see how you feel after that."

Nancy gave me some pills to help me chill out, and the following day she gave me the tape. I went home and played that tape in my room; it was a sort of meditation tape. Nancy was talking on it, taking me from the high mental thinking from the core of a depression to a chilled-out state of mind.

The radio was playing REM's "Everybody Hurts," but hold on, just hold on. After I hit the depth of this depression, I got what I needed to get: to understand this experience. I took it to that thin line again, but this time it was life and death instead of sanity and insanity. When I listened to Nancy's tape, it slowed my racing mind down, and I was able to get clear parts in my mind again. In this new frame of mind, I asked for a new experience to come forth into my world, and I said to the game and myself, "I choose to love life. I have not experienced that before; life owes me that experience, and this is what I am choosing now."

Whilst I was heading into this depression, I attracted others in my environment who also were in this frame of mind. I didn't attract them as friends or for company in my life, but they were close in my surrounding and environment. Depression is not a sociable frame of mind, but the energy attraction doesn't fail to exist. I knew someone who took their own life after many years of going in and out of this depression. They took their own life and left their kids behind, clearly feeling that they had no choice. I felt so sad, knowing that I couldn't help.

I knew what I was getting into with this depression, but reaching its core and understanding became a main priority for me, due to many stories of people that I knew or came into contact with. And when I was pulled out of this depression, I learned that Nancy, the person who pulled me out of it, had lost a loved one to the same situation I had been in. I went back up to Nancy's place to thank her for saving my life by changing my state of mind. Nancy had gotten some really bad news. Her child had taken their own life. How connected and sad was that? I felt that life had chosen me to survive this; another very sad story but yet another driving force for me to continue on. A life saved and a life lost, and mine was saved.

DEPRESSION EXPLAINED

Depression can be caused by a bad experience that one has to deal with or think about. Each word a person hears about themselves shapes their energy; abuse can cause depression. The false high of drugs can cause depression; a false high creates its opposite, the low. Depression is high among people who live in the north, any place that can get dark for quite a long time. Some of those countries can stay dark for weeks, and those people require the most Prozac. The sun and light give energy; darkness can cause depression, for depression is the darkness. Giving up on life, having no hope in life, also causes depression. Many things can cause depression.

Depression is having a thought about a certain thing and "de-pressing" that thought. To have a bad experience, create thoughts about that experience and see life in a different way. When we have an experience, there are a series of thoughts in our mind to understand and comprehend that experience; this happens instantly and we call this our truth. When we start to think negatively about an experience, we look at things in a different way. With this thinking, we change the emotion in our bodies from the way it was to the feeling that matches this frame of mind. Our emotions are our energy in motion, and what causes this motion is the way we are thinking. When we feel this way, it affects how we look through our minds at different experiences that are happening along the way: working, playing, and spending time with people. When we feel this way, we do not want to be part of their lives, as we do not want them to know we feel this way, nor can we see ourselves enjoying things that we once did. We start to close off from different experiences, from different events, and then after we do that, a series of thoughts is created on that experience. We mentally see, due to these last actions, that we can't do this or that anymore, that the choices we just made become our truth. We believe that something is wrong with us and that because we didn't follow an event through or didn't go out for a drink with friends that particular night, we start to think that the way we feel is who we are becoming. We avoid these good times because we do not want others to see us sad and miserable, and also because we do not wish to have these good experiences turn into bad ones. We then look back on these events and see that we are closing ourselves off from many things. We don't know how to explain why we were not there at certain times, and then we just don't have the energy to explain or confront the problems, as all of our energy is going to the state of mind we are in, these thoughts, this thinking.

Soon enough all the doors are closed in our lives, in our world, and we mentally become locked in a small room, and that becomes our reality too. Due to these experiences and this frame of mind, even if we were to die, we wouldn't even want to meet up with other people who may have passed away, as we are not well at this stage and have created a world of loneliness and being closed off, whilst still in this frame of mind.

Depression is a state of mind, and throughout this story we may just find out that nearly everything is a state of mind on one level or another. We may think a certain way, due to a bad experience, which may not have even been bad, it was just that it didn't go as we thought it would go. We judge that in a negative way, blaming others or ourselves. If we enter this frame of mind, we will attract other thoughts, other events that have the same judgmental outlook and other memories. Then we have created a frame of mind, all these thoughts, as that is what they are, are all attracted to each other, and our energy, which is us, goes around our mind, moving from one thought to the next, giving it energy. This energy we give to our minds and thoughts puts our energy in motion, and we feel that thought expressed into an emotion. When we put all of our energy on a certain thought (or even most of our energy on certain thought), we attract by law of attraction, energy attracting like energy. We attract that very experience to us. When we experience this experience, we have a series of thoughts to explain what just happened, and then not only have we this frame of mind, we also have this belief system created. We now believe in something that we attracted to us in the first place; we now believe that we are destined for failure, for sadness, for negative experiences, for bad karma (I'll get back to bad karma later on).

Our thoughts create our emotion, which then attracts, and our belief system takes us to a new level of our understanding, which may not be entirely correct or in our best interest. But we then become seriously fixed in this frame of mind, and we need to change that, if we want to change our lives, our experiences, and our world. But if we want to believe we are destined to die at these times, we may just bring that into our reality.

Depression is a thought process, and children can copy their parents from birth to the age of four, when children make up their model of the world. This frame of mind is picked up off the parent; children know what the parent is thinking, what frame of mind that the parent is in. They copy this, this frame of mind; this thought becomes their root thought, and then the rest of their thinking is built upon this root thought. The child will continue throughout life and not even know why their minds keep going back to this sort of depression. When they are in this frame of mind, they will see that they always were in this depression. When they are in a different frame of mind, the depressed thoughts are just a vague memory, but they are still there in the programmed mind and in the memory, but the understanding is not comprehended.

This child will have to confront this root thought that they picked up, these depressed frames of mind, at some stage in their life, as it keeps reoccurring. This usually happens after they have a life of good times and sad times, and they start to question this sadness. They delve into this depression, this frame of mind that keeps happening in their minds, like a tape recorder, playing over and over again throughout their lives. Once they delve into this frame of mind, question it and try to find why it is happening, the person puts their energy into these thoughts, they feed the very thing that they want to stop in order to find out where it starts from, where it came from.

After all this energy is placed in this thinking, going round and round through all these thoughts, the energy in the mind gets deeper and deeper, searching for the core. Then their world becomes scary, the depth of this frame of mind is hard to reverse, it's a scary way to be.

Life as we know it cannot be handled. We are looking at life from a perspective that we are now in, and others are just not on the same level. We cannot handle life or anything, as all energy is in this frame of mind.

We search for the core, to beat this once and for all, and I did this.

I tried to go to the core of this frame of mind. I penetrated deep down to try see though the illusion of it, but I found that there was no end to this. When I did it, the thoughts and the depth seemed to be killing my body. The emotion created in this depth of depression was feeding the negativity in me and was destroying the inside of my body. The energy was building up in me as I tried to go deep, and I began to bleed on the inside and cough up blood to release this energy build-up. I didn't care too much about my body at this stage, as I cared more about understanding this depression and escaping it at some stage.

Then after racing through thoughts in this spiral and penetrating to the core, I came to a place where there were no more thoughts, there was just pure darkness, like outer space itself, a place all on my own, completely separated from all people and all of the material world, a place so alone, so separate, and completely detached from all of existence. This was it, the core of a depression. This becomes the point of no return. It is as though the person wants this nothingness to be theirs, but that is only because the person is so deep in this frame of mind, the person knows no other way of being. What is this depression? Depression is everything we are not. It is a complete separation from the whole oneness that we really are.

SOLUTION TO DEPRESSION

There is a solution to depression, an easy, effective, natural solution. It is only by knowing how it works that you can see the illusion, the mechanics, and the simplicity of it all. The harder you try to think and search to get out of this depression, the further you go into it. Thoughts need to be reversed, and a new frame of mind needs to be born again. You can now see how the frame of mind works, and that is by placing your energy on those thoughts and expanding them, attracting more and bringing in memories and filling up your mind with these thoughts creating this frame of mind.

Your mind is not you. Your mind is a tool for you to use. You are not your mind, but you are the energy that feeds your mind. To stop living in this frame of mind, you need to stop placing your energy there. To do this, you need to avoid these negative thoughts by not placing your energy there, you need to go within, connect with who you are, your energy, your very being of existence.

You need to connect with who you know you are and to stop supplying energy to the mind, to switch off the supply. This may sound complicated, but it's very easily done. All you need to do is see the truth. Placing your energy on a thought gives it life. Thoughts come and go in your mind. You just let them come and go and pass through. If you analyse that thought, you hold onto it until it serves you the purpose that you intended to hold onto it for. But if you do not want it, don't feed it your energy, don't give it life, and in a matter of seconds it will die out, for no one or nothing is giving it energy to make it into something. The thoughts are there, they are everywhere, and nothing existed without it first starting as a thought.

It is when you place your energy on that thought, you magnify it, and you make it into something, as it had no life of its own. The thought just is what it is. You give it life, and it can kill you, a slow painful, sad, tormenting, isolated, lonely, destructive, unpleasant, slow death.

The choice is ours. We have tools to work with, and we have laws to follow in the game. We are the energy, and the tool we have to work with is our mind. We can become captive of these thoughts, or we can become the "watcher" of these thoughts. When you become the watcher, you then remove the supply of energy to these thoughts, and in this consciousness, you can watch these thoughts die out, therefore breaking a state of mind that you once believed controlled you. By feeding thoughts that come and go in your mind, you give them life and they in turn change your emotions, your energy in motion, and your experience, which you expressed. It all completes a circle. You can experience, then you can have the thoughts on that experience, and then you create your emotion from those thoughts. The laws you have to follow are, you are housed in a body, you have to use your mind to create your world, and certain states of mind will deteriorate your body.

When I worked this out later on in my experiences, I was just very amazed at how simple it really is. I was also so overwhelmed by what I had put myself through; I could have just stopped it in a moment. But I then realised that I wouldn't have this story to pass on in the hope to help some people out there, and we would all be experiencing what our minds are easily capable of. But in saying that, some experiences just went a little too far, and I just wished that I had the answers to stop it. But the game must go on, and later we may see some serious, self-inflicted insanity in order to seek out a very important truth.

CHAPTER SIX

Loving Life

Once I got over the depression and decided to love life, many good things did happen for me; my mind was changed from before, and I was open to new ideas. But the negative energy was still in me, and I needed to keep moving, keep changing my environment to keep on top, to keep up with what life was dishing out at me. I had to stay in synchronisation with life, and it was a full-time job, but still there were many things that were attracted to me; this energy was still in me.

Before I was to start off in college for my final phase as a carpenter, my father asked if I would like to visit him in Spain for a holiday, as he bought a holiday home there and stayed there quite a lot. Arthur, my father said I could bring with me a friend if I wished.

I said, "Fred hasn't been off the island yet, can I bring him?"

Arthur said, "Yes, okay, Fred's sound."

So Fred organised his passport and we flew to Spain. As we were sitting on the plane, I said, "Now this is just a chill-out holiday; Arthur is in his new place so we'll be on good behaviour and check out the beach, the women, the lifestyle, and the good weather."

Fred said, "That's just cool with me, D.J. I can't wait for this."

We met my father in the airport, and he had his sleeves all rolled up and his hair done up and a makeup tattoo on his arm with a couple of earrings. He sure did look the part, we didn't even recognise him. He just did this for fun. Arthur is a great laugh and a gent of a man.

We got back to my father's place and had a few beers, and then he wanted to go to bed and suggested that we do that too. But I was picking up all that energy from the airport and flight, and I needed to get rid of it or to burn it off. This is what I always have to do.

The conflict had started—not so much in a verbal way, but the energy changed for both of us. I needed to burn off the energy that I picked up at the airport and on the plane. By me going against my father's plans, his energy was heightened—he was now more stressed than before. We could not be around each other in this environment. He would make me much worse than I am, and by me not respecting his plans, I would make him much worse than he is. We needed to separate, and this was only within the first few hours of arriving there.

Off we went; I couldn't understand my father's problem (the story of our lives), and he said the same about me. Fred and I went down to the pub, and Fred was in his element. It was great; Fred was amazed at how warm it was at night and how sunny it was during the day and all the differences compared to home. We had a look around the place, we had a few drinks, and all was great. I was happy, as this was a new experience, and I could think clearly again with an open mind in Spain, apart from the difference between my father and me. But I left all that was in my mind about home, at home. I was a new man yet again. We went back to my father's about four o'clock in the morning and went to bed.

The next morning, my father got up and went to the beach and chilled out. He was always trying to just chill out instead of understanding himself, learning why he has the hot energy body in him or what he was going through emotionally. Chilling out was all he could do to fight his own high energy. When we had a few drinks, I was up for trying anything apart from the beer, as I needed to rule out any causes of my ulcer. Drinking is a huge Irish way of life, and every country in the world knows this, apart from the Irish, as if you are born in Ireland, drinking is a way of life and anything apart from full on supping and partying just seems not correct.

Fred and I got up and got something to eat, and my father had left a note to say where he was. We went down to the beach to find him. There was a bar in the background, and it was all nicely done up in timber and looked nice on the beach. There was also a music system set up there, tape decks, a CD player, and two big speakers. *What a life here,* I thought: houses were going for much less than half the price at home, with a swimming pool in the back garden. It was a short walk to the beach, the views, the amazing weather, and a timber bar in the background hooked up to speakers, ready for action. With the simplicity of life over there, one could work doing anything really. My apprenticeship was the only thing keeping me at home.

I went over to the bar and spoke to the barman. I said, "Are you planning on getting that system singing or does it need a break from last night?" and he said, "Na, it's been quiet over here for a while and we had not much use for it. You can play some music if you like."

I said, "What have you got?" and he replied, "I have a collection of CDs here, a lot of it's oldies stuff, a few techno CDs, so help yourself."

I said, "If I brought down some CDs later, could I play them? What time will you be open till here?"

The barman said, "You come down with your music, play whatever you like, it doesn't matter what time of the night you come down, once I see you and people want drinks, I will open the bar."

I was just putting together a plan of an ending to a night in my head, thinking that if Fred and I met up with a few girls, we could have a beach party all organised. So we went over to my father and his crew. Arthur recommended a Spanish drink called *sangria*. I said, "I don't like wine," and he said, "No, it's not wine."

So I tried it and it was nice enough. It didn't taste too strong at all; it was like a fruit drink, but it did have a high percentage of alcohol in it. My father loved it, and everyone there drank it. Fred and I were like curious children looking at the effects of this sangria drink. We had a chat and a laugh and all the rest. Arthur asked Fred about his leg; it was only really when Fred had his shoes off that the difference in his legs was noticeable; he had to hop and struggle walking. Arthur came across as interested and all that was good. Fred explained that he once jumped over a wall, not knowing that there was a thirty-foot drop on the other side of it, and he hurt himself very badly. The communication was fantastic between them, and I sat there saying nothing but I was still in the conversation anyway. I was amazed at how civil the conversation was going, and I was thinking to myself that maybe it was just me that had a problem at times, but I guess it was all the unexplained energy that I take on board that caused the problems.

After a few hours, to my amazement, my father got up, took off his top, and ran down to the sea in his shorts. He went for a swim in the sea. This was a side of my father I had not seen before; in one way,

I was very surprised, and in the other sense, I was happy that he could have his little outbursts and run off to the sea like a child. It was like the life in him just wanted to leap out of him. I thought it was good stuff, being alive, feeling alive and not just stressed most of the time.

But after he had his swim, my father came walking back up the beach. He came over to me, grabbed a towel for himself, and said, "I hate being out of control." And that was it there, that's what it was all about. His own feeling inside was kept down by his controlling mind. He also looked at me and said, "I'm afraid to be out of control."

I couldn't believe it, it was all so clear. Everything was crystal clear. It was the first real time we really connected from father to son. It was just us two, and the truth arrived. I thought then that sangria was a good drink. It wiped all the nonsense out of all the rubbish and served up a good, clean, one-line portion of truth. "Control" was the key word, just one word instead of the lifetime of conflict and misunderstanding. Sangria pushed my father's button, and he told me the truth. There was a bond there in that moment, a truth, an understanding.

My whole existence is about breaking free of controls and restrictions and all the influences that life has on me. I need to break through it all to find the core controller of it all, the source of life. Control by any person or any group or any of life's illusions is like a cloud in my mind, I feel trapped and seriously lose respect for the person placing the control on me. As I see everyone as equal, mutual respect for everyone, and if someone is pretending to be my friend but is placing control on me, this nonsense mentality where the person feels that they are above me or have one over on me drives me to break that control and remove myself from that person in all ways. This has happened with some friends and, unfortunately, my father at times. I have seen control come in many ways: physical, mental, emotional, entrapment, and spiritual (if you class religion as a form of spirituality). Controlling people is the opposite of having respect for people.

Then I said, "Right, Fred, come on, let's go for a few drinks."

Fred and I left the sangria crew down there and went out to explore. We went to the pub, and after a few hours a Spanish lad came along, selling some goods.

I said, "Ah, here's the lucky man."

Fred said, "Lucky? What do you mean?"

I replied, "He has a collection of ten pence lucky bags; he'll try and sell them for one hundred Euros first. Haggling is the way forward with this bloke."

The Spanish lad came over and Fred started talking to him. He picked up his accent from meeting so many Irish people, and he really did have the accent to a T; he sounded like a Spanish Irishman, and everyone talked about him. He was selling these squeaky Muppet toys and showed us how they worked. He placed the puppet over his hand, and when he squeezed the ball inside, the puppet went "squeak" whilst its six-inch tongue came rolling out of its mouth. It was a classic and after a long session of haggling, we ending up buying six of these puppets each. The madness had begun, and it started off with a squeak.

A few kids came into the pub, and Fred and I hid the toys whilst letting off a few squeaks here and there. We ordered drinks, and once we started on that stuff, there was no end to it. We went from pub to pub and met lots of people and had a great laugh. At the end of this night, somewhere along the way, we met two girls, and either one of the girls took Fred's money or he was charged 100,000 pesetas instead of 1,000 for a drink. I think one of the bar staff cleaned Fred out of it whilst he was getting the rounds in, as the girl knew he hadn't a clue about pesetas. A thousand pesetas was a fiver for us, and I told Fred, "Just throw a decimal point in and half the money," but thinking on holidays was not Fred's way. He was cleaned out in between going from one pub to the next.

But it was all right; he was bleeped off for a minute until I said, "Look, don't worry about it, I have money. I'll just buy the drinks, you should have given me your money. The currency is very different here. I just have the knack of it. I have enough money for us so we'll be sound."

I just bought all the drinks from then on, and it was a pleasure as Fred was a classic. He was a very harmless character, so innocent like a child when he away on holidays and so funny. I can't even write this story without laughing. Fred was just like a character out of the *Life of Brian* film. He was so full of life, so curious about everything about Spain, and he was such a buzzer, creating me the same. I sure was on top form, from a holiday in Spain, away from life at home and the sunny days.

Fred and I met so many people over there who were all living in this small town. We went back to the apartment to get showered and cleaned up, and I chatted with my father, who was trying to control everything and everyone. He wanted me to just sit down and watch some television and rest, and then we would go out later on. He had all of these plans that just left me with the feeling of restrictions and control. There was not much sense of freedom with Arthur, and the way he was carrying on was really affecting my energy, my nature, and I needed to get away from him. This was sad but true. We should have compromised but we were two opposites in many ways.

Fred and I went out and found a place that was playing music and serving drinks. Whilst we were having the fun, I said to Fred, "Wait here and I'll be back in a second."

I went outside and got was sick; the ulcer was acting up, and I knew that I needed to stay away from any more energy. I had too much energy in me, creeping up all the time. My worried thoughts were making it bigger, and adding my father's emotional energy was enough to trigger off an ulcer attack. After I went outside and vomited, releasing the build-up of blood, I took one of my ulcer tablets and went back into Fred. We were back on form; Fred was worried about me and my ulcer, but I felt much better getting out of the house and being free to do my own thing. The drink didn't help the ulcer, but that wasn't the cause of it. The ulcer wasn't in my stomach; it was up in my windpipe, where one feels heartburn. It was all this energy in me, in my chest; if not burned out, there was internal bleeding, and then I had to release it. Each worried thought at home made it cringe up as well, so clearly that it couldn't be denied. Energy and thoughts were my problem.

Fred and I drank lots of bottles, and when we left that place and walked down the road, I sat down somewhere, as I was feeling burnt out. We must have fallen asleep, for some time later, Fred and I woke up in someone's garden.

Fred looked at me and said, "Where are we?"

I said, "We're at Joe's house" (referring to a house in Ireland; the area looked the same).

Fred said, "Where do I live then?"

I said, "You live up there and I live down here."

We both got up and walked off in our separate directions. I thought I was walking down through the estate at home and was trying to remember how I ended up asleep in the garden. A few minutes later, Fred turned around and shouted, "We're in Spain, D.J., we're in Spain, not at home!"

It was incredible to see that we were both walking home, oblivious to where we were, all from that bottled drink. Fred came running back down to me, and we went straight to the pub. It was so funny and we still had our squeaky toys with us; off we went to liven up the town with a squeak here and there.

Close to the end of that drunken night, we went to cross the road from one pub to the next. It was a very dangerous road, where cars and trucks came past at over 100 KMPH. There was no bridge, and there were always a few drunks trying to get across. I went walking across and was looking in the direction where the cars usually come from, but we were in Spain and they were coming from the opposite direction.

As I was halfway across one side of the road, Fred shouted my name at the top of his voice.

I looked to my right and there was a truck coming towards me at top speed. He was so close, and I turned around and ran.

I was only three steps away from safety, but it was so close. As I dove for the grass, the truck hit my right foot. It spun me around, and I landed about ten yards down the road. The driver didn't even stop. Fred came running over; he just couldn't believe it and asked, "Can you walk?"

I said, "My foot got smashed out of it. Leave me lying down for a minute; that was so close."

Just then, a car stopped across the road. Fred said, "There is a few lads getting out of a car across the road; you better get up, D.J., I don't know what they want."

I thought Fred was acting a little paranoid and figured they must have seen what happened and were coming over to help. But Fred was right, they were coming over to rob us. There were four of them, and when they came over, they tried to search our pockets. Fred started to fight with one of them, putting his fingers in his eyes and throwing him onto the ground. The other three were on top of me. My foot was in pain and I couldn't walk on it, but I was getting strength from the frustration of dealing with these vultures. One lad grabbed the chains around my neck, and I grabbed his hand and didn't let him go.

As he tried to get away, I pulled myself up off the ground. I saw a car coming and held him out on the road. I stood there looking at him and said, "You vulture, we're both going to die but at least I'll see you die first," and I held him out in front of the speeding car.

The car swerved and dodged us; his mates ran off, and he broke away from me whilst shouting, "You crazy man, you crazy man."

As he was running off, I picked up this huge scaffolding bar and started to swing it around to hit the lad and get my chains back. However, I hit something behind me, looked around, and saw Fred drop to the ground. Poor Fred, I sure did crack Fred one across the jaw, and there was a trickle of blood running down the side of his head.

I stopped the madness and asked Fred, "Are you all right?"

He got up and said, "Yes, just about; are you?"

I said, "Right, come on, I'm going to get these lads."

It was when the lad stole my chains that I really became angry, and the pain of my foot was just put off. It was crazy, I was lying on the ground after just surviving being hit by a truck, only to get attacked and robbed by some locals. The world is a mad place, full of attackers. We went down after the lads but couldn't find them. There were four of them, but they were afraid of us after what we were trying to do to them, and we couldn't catch them anywhere. So we went to the pub and had a few drinks there, and it was becoming morning time, so I saw a hiding spot under a pool table. I climbed under the table and fell asleep for a few hours. Each time we crossed the road after that, we had an arm around each other's shoulder and looked in opposite directions, conferring every second about any movements on the road.

We went back to my father's to get cleaned up; everyone was at the beach, so we went back out. I really was unable to handle any stress from my father. It was hard being around him without thinking that perhaps he felt I was doing my own thing. He was worried, stressed; I was not able to take any more.

Okay, imagine that the world we live in is a matrix of energy, and same energy attracts and opposites attract too. What was happening out there, I believe, was to do with the energy within me. I was attracting circumstances that did not kill me but brought me close to dying. This was how this negative parasite in me got its fuel; events that create anxious or even fearful thoughts, from the speeding truck or the intense, angry thoughts from the attackers, gave the parasite its fuel, and then it was dormant till the next feed. If I was around other people who had this energy also, I took more in, and this happened in a moment, and I needed to get away and then try and burn it off to be normal again. If I sat still, the energy seriously affected my thinking and my mind would go crazy or I would go into a sort of depression again. But when I moved and went somewhere, I attracted events that could be near to death experiences, crazy things. Once that was over, the energy was then relaxed again. I felt that the ideal situation would be to rid this energy once and for all, but I didn't know how and if I could do it for me, I would do it for everyone. This negative energy was attracting bad circumstances. I don't believe in coincidences. I see that if I just have enough experiences and am still alive, someday I will work it all out.

That night I didn't want to go back home, as I liked staying outside; the energy outside was so calm and relaxed, thus making me the same.

I went down to the beach, and there was a load of resting chairs there all stacked one on top of the other, chained together. I said, "Right, Fred, I'll sleep up here," and Fred said, "Yeah, you do that. I'm going to dig a hole and cover myself in the sand to keep warm."

I climbed the resting chairs, and Fred buried himself in the sand to keep warm. My father came down and said, "Would you not just come home, D.J.?"

I said, "It's nice out here, why do you always want to be at home?"

He said, "Would you look at Fred, burying himself in the sand to keep warm."

Arthur and I were laughing over Fred, he sure was funny, and this eased our tension. We went home with my father and all was good that night.

The next day we went out again drinking. We met two girls, and I was telling them about the bar down on the beach with the music system ready for action if they wanted to come down. We all got a taxi down, and Fred and I were getting drunk at this stage. We bought a jug of sangria, and we were fairly drunk after that. The girls left us there, and we were on our own. We drank the rest of the sangria, it sure was some powerful stuff, and then we headed home. It took a lot of drink to get me drunk like that; I was always on high energy around people, and I sure could handle a good drinking session. We left and started walking up the steps to the main road. The road was about fifty feet above the beach. Fred was talking away the whole way up the steps, and when we got to the top, I fell over onto the wall and Fred kept walking. He was so drunk that he thought I was beside him all the way on his travels, but I didn't make it two feet past the top step.

When I woke up, it was morning; I sure did wake up in some strange places and situations. I opened my eyes and was sliding down the slope of a cliff. I looked in front of me and there was at least a thirty-foot drop in front of me. All that talk about Fred and his fall off a thirty-foot drop; now I was in the same situation. I started sliding and just couldn't believe it. I had one second to try and work out how I ended up there. In the same second, I had to ask life for a second chance, and in the next second, I decided I better save myself, as time was running out. I looked to my right as I was sliding, and there was a tree beside me. It was more like a twig than a tree, but I grabbed it, as it was my only hope. The tree crumpled up like an ash of a cigarette in my hands, and off the edge I went.

I was hoping I would wake up again just before I hit the ground, to realise it was only a dream, but no such luck there. I landed on the sand, and my legs got a shock, but they were still intact. I looked out to the sea and the sky, and even in my own thoughts, I was speechless.

I was alive, on my own and on the beach. I checked my pockets, but my wallet was gone. All the things I had in my pocket had fallen out on the cliff as I was sliding down the slope. I walked along the beach with a good feeling, a sense of peace, and my surroundings were a paradise. I then saw a bar on its own on the beach, and it sure was paradise then. I walked up to the mysterious bar and asked for a pint. I had no money and just sat down and relaxed whilst drinking away. I remember thinking that if only life was just that simple: wake up, fall off a cliff, go for a walk, find a bar, and chill out over a pint. One moment you think you're going to die, and the next you're in paradise, the simplicity of life instead of all the madness that was the norm for me.

Just then my father and Fred came over to me.

My father said, "Come on, D.J., I think it's about time you came back to the apartment. Fred is a little upset, I don't know what happened to him."

I said, "Fred, what happened to you?"

Fred said, "I was walking along talking to you and then a car pulled up, it was more of those Spaniards again, and I turned around to you but you weren't there. They got out and tried to rob me, but I explained that I didn't have any money whatsoever. They drove me off to the beach and threw me out of the car."

I said, "Well, I woke up at the top of that cliff and fell off; come on and I'll show you."

We walked up the steps again, and when I got to the top, I said, "Look, there's my wallet and cards."

I climbed slowly down the slope while my father held me, and I got my stuff and then we left. My father was worried about us when we left before, and everywhere he went looking for us, people told him that we were there with a load of squeaky toys, entertaining the place. He was stressed out, which I couldn't handle, but sadly I was influencing that too. We were very different, my father rthur and I, yet similar in many ways too. He loved having fun, and we asked Fred if he still had his squeaky toy, and Fred took him out. The tongue was gone, and we thought that was so funny. Someone must have come over to Fred and said, "Hey, show me that squeaky for a minute," and pulled the tongue out so he wouldn't squeak anymore and gave him back.

That night Fred stayed in the apartment, and Arthur's friend and I went into town so he could say good-bye to a few people. This girl came over to me in the pub and told me that everyone there knew me. She said to me, "You and your friend Fred, you are something else. I have never known anyone to come here for such a short time; you're only here for a week and everyone everywhere knows you two; everyone is talking about you with your squeaky and your stories. You two are the talk of the town."

I was well behaved on the last night and didn't recognise anyone, since I was sober. Everyone was smiling anyways, we put smiles on people's faces and that was a good thing; we were entertainers.

When we got back home, after a few days of recovery we were back on our messing form, having fun everywhere. I couldn't help but notice that whilst I was on my messing way of life all around this time, I attracted other jokers. Many friends came my way and couldn't understand where I had been all the years beforehand, after they saw all the messing and the way Fred and I were all up for a laugh. I thought the same about these people. But I guess it was just at that point in our lives, we all connected on a complete messing vibration. Lots of fun was to be had and many fun stories were made.

We used to all dress up on certain occasions, and one Christmas, I went out and bought twenty Santa suits and gave them out to the whole crew. Those Santa suits were worn by all our friends over the Christmas period. There were Santas all over the place. Everyone had so much fun, different pub owners asked us to hang around for the kids, and many people in the area had many laughs over us. We had the best fun ever. This whole time put smiles on everyone's faces including our own. After choosing to love life, many opportunities came my way, and we all fulfilled those opportunities and attracted each other on this very funny vibration. This enjoyable time in our lives was fulfilled, and a book in itself could be written about the carrying on, but that's not what this book is about.

I NEEDED MONEY AND ATTRACTED IT IN MANY WAYS

I kept thinking of ways where I could get myself a lot of money together, and I felt that this money would sort my life out perfectly. I think we all think the same way. I tried to play the lotto a few times and hoped of winning, but it just didn't seem realistic that I would win. I thought about if I did win, would I still be continuing on my journey that life had planned out for me? If I won that much, would it change my whole path in life, whatever that may be? I think it would. I then realised that for me, life would not give this to me, as it would probably do more harm than good. I still needed money, though, and I began to think of smaller amounts, just enough to get me out of my life at present and get myself to Australia, where I felt my life's path would continue.

So I kept projecting this out, trying to bring this winning into my reality on a mystical sort of level, and things happened. The brother of a friend of mine came home from the United States and told me about a company that was only starting off, and if you bought shares in it, it would triple at least. We hear these stories all the time but for me, I could see this on a connection level, this opportunity was attracted to me, it was my answer, and I needed to go with it. I tried to get the money to put into it from various places, but no one I approached about it would lend me the money.

Finally, I couldn't get money to put into it, but I told various people, including a coworker, that I put ten thousand pounds in it, just to see how this would have ended out. Each week my coworker came into work and was amazed that I was so informed about shares. He informed me once a week that my money was going up and up; one day he came in and said, "I saw that company on the stock market last night, the one where you put all that money in, and it has gone up now to 3.5 times the amount of money, 350 percent!"

I then told him I didn't really put the money on it, I did try to but couldn't get it together, and I had a feeling that if I did, I would have come out very much on top. I lost out on that one. I tested it though all the same, and I saw that I asked for a sum of money, something around twenty thousand, and the opportunity came my way but I didn't follow it through. But I could feel the connection at the time that this was real and this was my gift from life, just as I asked.

Time went on, and after each intense experience, I felt that I needed out, and I needed money to get out. When I was hanging around with the dodgy crew in Manorville, a friend of mine asked if I wanted to get involved in a fool-proof money-making robbery. It was a job another group were going to do, and my friend decided to take it on himself with a few of his dodgy mates. He asked me if I was interested and explained that it was fool-proof; there was no way of getting caught. I told him that it sounded good but I couldn't do things like that. I thought about it; just one job and then get out of it, but it wasn't really me. My friend did do the job with some other lads, and they got caught and he got locked up for armed robbery. Nothing is fool-proof, everything is a chance. I was attracting many strange ways of making money, and then it occurred to me that I really needed to focus on specific ways of receiving money. The lotto was just too far fetched for me, as I couldn't believe that I could win it, as I couldn't fit it in with the rest of my belief system. You cannot manipulate your own mind.

Then I realised that the more detail I put into this payment to me, the better it would work for me, just the way I wanted it to. As I was thinking of ways to do this, I couldn't help but notice that there were many people in my environment who where getting claims for injuries, and after that happened a few times, I thought to myself that would be the way to go. I already had injuries, and the more I thought about this, the more realistic it became in my mind. So I pictured it in my mind: a back accident. As I was thinking about receiving a large sum of money, I thought a claim would be the best way, and a claim for my back would be perfect. This thinking went on for a while, and then I saw it in my mind, a clear picture like a video clip of an accident, or better still, like a clear déjà vu. I saw a big white van crashing into me on a main road as I was driving, and that was to be my claim as I was injured. I didn't care about getting injured, I just wanted the money.

Some time later, perhaps three weeks later, I was driving down the motorway in my van with Fran, a coworker, in the passenger seat. I had forgotten all about this claim idea. We were going from one job to the next. As we were driving, the cars were slowing down to a halt near an exit, and then the cars were speeding up again. There were so many cars on the road. I said to Fran, "Is your belt on? Someone is going to crash into us."

Fran said, "Yes it is, what makes you think that?"

I said, "There is a lad in a white van behind me, and I just have a feeling, so I'll cross over to the other lane."

I crossed over to the other lane to get away from the driver behind me, and he crossed over then as well. The cars in the front slowed down and I slowed down, and the lad in the van ploughed into us. He was going so fast, I don't know what he was thinking, as he should have been able to see the traffic ahead. He crashed into the back of my van so hard that if Fran hadn't had his seat belt on, he would have gone through the window. We sat there for a minute; even though I was half expecting this, I was still in some shock.

I got out and the van driver said, "Ah man, I so sorry about this." His van was completely smashed up in the front. Then he said, "Are you all right? Is someone else in the van with you? Are they all right?"

I said, "I just got some knock on my back; you really sent us flying there. I saw you coming; could you not see everyone slowing down?"

He said, "I was just rushing as I need to be somewhere. It's a company van, so if you have any injuries you should get them checked out and claim if you need to. They are well insured, and I've quit my job anyway, so no worries there." We swapped over details and then I drove off.

I rang my boss and told him the story. As I was driving back to the workshop, my back did feel like there was a layer of tar over it. It felt like pains from a bad flu, but it was the injury I had foreseen.

I went to a doctor, and he checked out my back and recorded the injuries. The injuries I had beforehand were all fixed up by Nancy, and there was no need for me to confuse the situation with that. I got the van checked out and priced for damage at the car dealers. I found a solicitor and gave him all the details, and then there was an appointment for me to meet up with the van driver's insurance doctor. I met up with him and he assessed me with all the movements he wanted me to do, and after he did a thorough check on my back, he reckoned I was clearly injured from the crash.

The van was assessed for damage, and two thousand Euros were handed over to fix it up. It had a kink in the frame underneath the van. I showed my friend who I bought the van off and said, "Do you remember when I bought the van off you, the doors on the back didn't line up properly, and one of them had to be lifted up in order to close it?"

He said, "Yes."

I said, "Check it out now." My friend checked out the doors, and they were perfect, they both lined up perfectly and closed perfectly. The crash had fixed the doors up; it was amazing.

I got a feeling of someone watching me after that claim went in. Lots of people get a feeling of someone watching them when they are watched by someone. And I couldn't think why I was watched by someone. It played on my mind for a while, until over a year later when I had to meet up in court with the other insurance company. They said that they were watching what I was doing, and it all seemed legit and they paid out. I received just over ten thousand Euros.

I think about this now and don't feel that it was a scam in anyway. But if we can manifest like this, could we also pass a law that we can't? I am out to work out the workings of life, the rules if there are any, and how to play life, as it is a game. I tried out something and manifested that money in my reality. It worked. I thought of a way where I would receive money, a way that was realistic and did not consist of any crime. I did have a back injury, and although it was fixed, I didn't mind another one, as I felt that I could get it fixed easy enough and it would be just a fraction of the pain that I did receive for many years before. I then tried to picture that crash, and then it happened. I could see it all in my mind.

I knew then that I was onto something. I locked something into my life, a incident that once I could see it happen in my mind, it was not long before that would happen. The way to guarantee that is, you just keep having that in your mind, over and over again, exactly how you want it, and manifestation! The crash happened and the man told me to claim—it was all handed to me there. How does it get so perfect?

Did life feel sorry for me and give it to me? I did say thank you to life and thank you for giving this to me. But as time went on, I started to see that what I was onto was the rules of life, it was the recipe for bringing things into your life. Everything was working off what I put in my mind and how much energy I put in that. I planted a seed in my mind, I let it grow, I nurtured it, just as you would plant a tree, only instead of water, I give it my energy, by placing my energy on that seed.

The workings of this next part can get complex—how did this seed become that crash? Was it because it wais in my mind? Did my thoughts change my energy to the emotion that was on the same vibration of this crash and I magnetised it to me? Or was it just nature: plant a seed and watch it grow?

Either way, we were onto something good here. The game will go on!

Does this happening just prosper me or does life itself bring three things manifesting together and make something happen to us all involved?

When something happens, each person involved has drawn themselves to that happening on one level or another. It's always a trade-off, and that we will see as life unravels itself.

MY ESCAPE

It was December, and life was good fun. But I secretly needed to get away. I felt claustrophobic, as I did for a long time. Everywhere I turned, I was getting controlled. In the house where I lived, there was entrapment and emotional control. In my family life, there was mental and moral pressure control. Morals, as in what I should and should not do based on one man's definition of morals, all influenced the outcome to go his way, of course. There were many good friends around too, but this sly, sneaky carrying on was diminishing my power, leaving me trapped every direction I turned, and breaking my spirit.

I still had my mind on Australia, and although it was not my time to go just yet, I could not wait to go. Moving from one experience to the next was perfect for me; it felt so right. It felt like my energy and life were in synchronisation with one another. Routine and stagnant energy were not for me. My energy was bursting as I realised what was happening around me, and I needed to move on. I decided that I would have a good Christmas first, and then I would go to Scotland and England. But I needed a reason to go or else everyone would get involved and wonder why and ask why, and I needed a solution for that. I needed a solution to get these controllers off my case. I was not happy where I was anymore; leaving was my survival, it was the mental fix I needed for inspiration. Staying meant control would get me; my mind would switch off and depression would return, particularly after December and heading into January. It's always a sad time after the Christmas high. This I needed to avoid. I couldn't think of an efficient escape route that would suit everyone; any that came to mind would hurt someone, so I asked life to give me an escape route, and this is what happened.

I had a good friend called Faye who loved to go out for parties with myself and my friends, she was good fun.

On Christmas Eve, I text messaged Faye and asked, "You want to go to the nightclub?"

Faye texted back, "Sounds good."

I had had a few drinks but I was not drunk; I was frustrated over a previous encounter with a friend and needed to relax myself before I exploded. I took a few deep breaths, calmed myself down, and picked up Faye, and we drove to the nightclub. We went in and the bottles were going for one pound a bottle. The thing was one would have to get ten bottles for ten pounds, and that was done. We had the fun as we danced around to the song, "Dancing in the Moonlight."

Faye was great fun, and then when we were leaving, a big fight broke out just outside the nightclub. It was a full on row and I said, "Let's just get out of here, away from all this."

Faye said, "Why don't we get a taxi and go?"

The police arrived and there was a lot of police outside and still many fights going on. I said, "Sure, I'll get my van out of here, because

I'll come back tomorrow and it will be smashed up. Jump in and we'll get out of here."

I reversed back and just as I hit my brakes, I also hit something behind me. I looked in the mirror and it was just the bumper of a car, so I drove off quickly just to get out of there quickly. The police were behind me as they were not far away from us at all; they heard this little bang and as I drove off, they too drove after me. I just saw trouble, fights, van will be wrecked, police, need to get away from all this. I left and as I took the corner, I saw in my mirror the police car coming after me. I went around the corner and the lights were red, so I stopped.

The police car pulled up right beside me, and he asked me to get out of the car. I was completely on the ball then, I just slipped up not seeing that car behind me. I wasn't acting drunk by any means. I was hyper and awake from the bottles and dancing.

I explained to the copper that I just wanted to get the van out of there because of the fights. He drove the van to the police station and I had to go in the police car. We went to the police station and it was just me, the copper, and a few other coppers in the station.

He said, "Will you blow into the bag please?"

I said, "It's Christmas, do I get an extended limit?"

He laughed and I blew into it. He asked my name and I said, "D.J."

The sergeant then said, "Are you any relation to Jonsey?"

I said, "Jonsey eh? Oh yeah, he's a first cousin of mine, what was he up to?"

Even though Jonsey is my brother, I didn't want any paper work going to my family house.

I was asked where I lived and I gave the address where I was staying, not our family house. The other copper was in the background, checking up all my details on the computer, and he said, "How come your van is registered in the same house as Jonsey?"

I said, "Ah yeah, that's my aunt's house."

"Lock him up," was the next line, and I said, "Come on lads, it's Christmas time, I have to do my Santa rounds tonight, don't put me in a padded cell, for the love of God."

They laughed and said, "We just need to find out who you are, as nothing is matching up."

I was locked up in a cell. Faye was in the waiting room. There were two people in the cells either side of me. One was asking me to tell his girlfriend that it was all her fault that they were in there, and she was asking me to tell her boyfriend that she was going to kill him when they got out.

I then shouted out to the coppers, "Hey, I'm guilty for drink driving, I should be in a sane drunk cell with drinkers, not a nut house with lunatics. You got to let me out of this institution."

The coppers thought I was funny and let me out and actually apologized for locking me up. I was free to go and I was to pick up my keys the next day. Faye and I left, and we laughed and joked about it all.

The next day I woke up and thought away to myself. I then realised that what happened the night before was my reason for leaving; I couldn't have made it up, as there were witnesses there. I later saw Fred and told him the story, and Fred thought about the police and what I did and what trouble I was in. He knew I didn't have to leave or go on the run. He knew the coppers wouldn't call on my door for at least eight months with a summons, and he also knew that I was creating my own getaway for whatever unknown reason. But this story I stuck with. It was my getaway story, and there were witnesses to see it happen too. I saw it as perfect, although there would be some sort of a court case the following year, I could deal with that when it came up.

I bought a car off a friend of mine called Paddy, and he was asking me all sorts of questions about why I was leaving. I mentioned the police trouble, but he wasn't buying into that. After I bought the car and said that I would catch up with him again sometime, he said to me, "D.J., you're running from yourself. You are running from yourself."

Was he right? Was that what I was doing? I had to find out. I left, got in my car, and got onto the ferry to England. I stayed in the UK for three months; I had one friend over there that I met the previous year, and it was no problem staying in his place for some time. I also travelled around and had a friend from home over there too, so I was okay with accommodations. I worked in Glasgow for a while, and after a couple of months, I went to Amsterdam on a holiday, where I met up with some friends from home. There were many laughs to be had, my world was made smaller with associates, travel was at a high, and I became a healthy person by getting away.

STRANGE DREAM OR STRANGE REALITY

There was one occasion where something very strange happened, and I couldn't really make sense of it. I had a lighter that was a fake gun that I bought in Glasgow; it looked just like a gun, and I left it in my car. I went to bed one night and had a dream. It was as clear as anything during the day. I was standing there looking at two people who just broke into my car. One broke the window and they both searched the car for stuff I owned. One opened the compartment in between the seats and took my camera. He also opened the dash compartment and pulled out the papers to see if there was anything else in there. The other lad put his hand under the seat, took out the gun, and said, "Look at this mad Irishman." He was referring to the gun and knew I was Irish because the car had Irish registration. When he had the gun, he said, "Right, let's get out of here."

I woke up in a sweat and said to myself, "Bloody hell, it was only a dream."

I got up, put my clothes on, and went out to my car. The window was broken, the camera was gone. The papers from the dash were on the floor, and I checked for the gun. It was gone. I got a shiver through me, a flashback of the lad who took the gun. It was freaky. I needed to work it out; a dream is a dream. How was this possible? I was there beside them, how was I there? Maybe I was looking out the window last night before I went to bed and I saw them then. I wasn't looking out the window, and how could I see them so clearly? I could even see their faces, see their clothes, and knew what he said. Oh, how was this possible? I knew it happened, but how could it be? They took my gun and my camera.

I went back into the house, told the flatmates my car was broken into, and asked what happened last night. The lad in the house said, "We had a few drinks and you went to bed at twelve, can you not remember?"

I said, "Yeah, I thought that all right."

It was an experience for me and not understood yet nor explainable at these moments. So it was just another event that was stuck into my mind that needed to be worked out and understood. It sure was freaky. An unexplained happening but could very well be explained as the story goes on.

THE BRIDGE

Faye came over to see me in England, and we went out one night to the pub and then to a club. Faye was dancing and tried to get me into it, but I found it very difficult at first. England for me was not a very enjoyable experience, I just needed to get away and stay away from home life to stay alive and sane and away from controls and restrictions. It seemed to be a big deal going away, there was a lot of talk about me, and my family were worried about me. The police story got out of hand, and people were concerned. Perhaps I could have done things a little different, but I just needed to get away.

Anyway, we had an interesting night that night. After the club, we walked back through Newcastle. We saw a newly built bridge called the Millennium Bridge. It was right beside the Newcastle upon Tyne Bridge. I said to Faye, "Wouldn't it be good to climb that to the top and get John to take a picture and use it as a postcard?"

Faye said, "You wouldn't be able to climb that bridge."

The bridge was one hundred feet high over the river. There were huge cables that sprung up from that to the Millennium Bridge.

I said, "Sure, I'll have a go and see, then I'll slide down and we can do it again, maybe tomorrow night."

I started climbing up this cable, and I sure was some height over the water, but it wasn't a problem. When I was about halfway up, I looked over to my right. There was a very small car coming in the distance, but it was blocked off from getting to us.

I shouted to Faye, "Who's that in the car?"

Faye said, "I don't know, it's so far away, I can't make out." Then we saw these lads dressed in blue running from the car towards us.

I said, "I think they're running in our direction."

As they got closer, Faye said, "Is it the police?"

I said, "It sure is, run."

Faye said, "What about you, will you get down from there?"

I said, "Run now, will you, run as fast as you can. I'll catch up with you."

Faye ran away, and the police came along this road over towards me. I slid all the way down the rope and started running after Faye. It was a full on chase for about five minutes, and then I caught up with Faye.

She came to a wall and couldn't get over it, and she said, "I won't make it, you run."

I said, "Can't go without you, we've got to try."

As I was giving Faye a lift up onto the wall, the police came running at us. They grabbed me and put my arm up behind my back, and I burst out laughing and said, "We give up, you can all relax now. What did we do to upset you all?"

The copper said, "It's an offence to climb the bridge; we were sitting in the police station watching the screens from the cameras and we saw you climbing, so we came down."

I said, "It's only a bridge, what's the huge deal?"

The copper said, "There was a young lad who climbed it last week, he got to the top and jumped off; he died, so we can't have that happening again."

We were taken to the police station and questioned, cautioned, and released. It was about four in the morning when I was climbing the bridge, and we got back to John's place about eight in the morning. We met John and I said, "Ah, there's never a dull moment."

John said, "I don't even want to know what you two got up to."

Faye told me all about home and what was going on. I was away from all of that carrying on at that stage. I had been gone three months and was finding ways to be happy and content within myself. I was listening to Faye and although I was saying, "Go on, then what happened?" I didn't really want to hear all this.

She said to me, "I'm not sure why you have the friends you have, as one of them is just talking about you so much to everyone, really talking bad about you to all the lads in the pub. Why you have him as a friend, I will not ever understand."

I couldn't understand why this friend was like that. Like, he knew me, knew I needed to get away from people, and I introduced him to many new friends for himself, and this was my repayment. I was getting worked up again, and all I wanted to do was relax my energy. Faye flew back home; after talking to her and understanding what it was like at home, I realised that I should go back, fix it all up, and then I could leave in peace. I realised leaving things the way they were just wouldn't do. I was trying to make my way over to Australia, and I just couldn't do with all the misunderstandings left behind. I got a ticket on the boat and drove home.

When I made it back, a lot of people were not too happy about me going away. I could feel the vibes from some friends, and my father was anxious the whole time, which also led to some problems and a lack of communication. My mother and Jonsey were just happy to see me. They commented on how healthy I looked as opposed to when I left, and I explained that I just needed to go away and that I felt much better now, so all was good there. I would imagine that a person my age should just be able to get away without so many controls and interferences, but I guess that can be impossible with some people with controlling natures.

WORK LIFE

I was offered jobs in many places but turned them down; I felt that I owed it to myself to stay away from crowded places, needed to stay somewhat healthy, and having a constant group of people in my environment was the opposite of what I needed. I needed space and pretty much to be left alone. I liked a bit of socialising but only at weekends or in the evenings. Working outdoors, connecting with nature and life and music, helped me recharge myself.

Don't underestimate the power of manifestation, and try not to forget what was manifested in the first place. We are all the creators of our own lives in many different levels. I was just thinking about and requesting (realising what I needed) how I could work someplace away from everyone and of course out in the open with music as well.

It then came my way once I knew in my mind what I needed—I attracted that very thing. Fred was doing some work on a new park and building going up in the area. He brought me up to have a look at it, and the place was amazing. It was completely closed off from the rest of the world, hidden off the main road behind stone walls. There were hundreds of acres there, and we didn't ever see the four corners of the place. I didn't ever even see two sides of the place, and I drove around the area a lot. It was a great place. I worked there for a while, the weather was great, and I was away from everyone without people, feelings, and thoughts, and I had the radio blasting out the tunes. It was amazing and perfect for me.

I used a sledge hammer to take off the top of the wall. I worked and worked and worked on it. My mind was just full up with frustration, negative thoughts from me being me, not being able to talk to a group of people, me being me looking guilty for things I have not done as I become so full of energy. Me being me in the outside world having bad events attracted to me because I'm taking in others' energy and many other controls and influences that I had no control of or could not change myself.

I had no problem working at all, I didn't get tired from swinging a sledge, I was releasing all the energy, and there was no end to it. I got the wall finished in less than half the agreed time. I focused on work and money and cash jobs, and it was all coming my way.

HEAVEN AND HELL

My grandmother died around this time; she was a nana and a half, and I was delighted to have known her for as long as I did. She was a champion of champions to me anyways. All the times she came over to our house, she would stay in my room, and she always got my place at the table. Each time she thanked me, and each time I said, "It's a pleasure to have you over, Nana." I was happy that I spent so many good times with my grandmother, and I was not greatly sad that she died, I was more happy that she had a good long life. I felt that she would also be happy getting back with her beloved husband that died many years before.

But something else also happened at the same time. I had a friend who tried to end her life, due to her own family problems and issues. She was close to dying but was saved at the end. This affected me a great deal, and the more I thought about what if she died, the more I was getting lost in my own mind, living in a state of mind that didn't need to be. Because of my own deep intense thinking, I started to experience my own hell. I finally went to hell; it's a state of mind.

I went to my loving Nana's funeral but was unable to speak at all; I just stood there at the funeral, looking like a man who was drugged up on morphine. I was just living in my mind, imagining that it was my friend in the coffin getting put into the hole, and all the people at the funeral would have been looking at me, as we were good friends at one stage. I guess I kind off took myself out of that friendship due to various confusing reasons (negativity clearly being one reason). I was in a state of mind where I really wanted to be there for my mother, as Nana was her mother, but I was really in hell myself and was hoping someone would just put me in a hole.

Whilst I was at the funeral, I got the sense of feeling that Nana was still around, and even though my mother was crying, I wanted to comfort her and tell her that Nana was still around and not to be upset, as she was happy now. But I was numb in my body; all that was in my mind. The haze of worry had my body limp, and I was unable to do or say anything.

I then realised that I was in hell standing beside my brother Jonsey, who was here on earth, and I could feel my Nana so clearly around us, although she was in heaven. Three different dimensions, one could call it at that funeral. We were all there, and only Nana, I think, had the perspective of the full view on things. Hell is a state of mind, heaven is the afterlife, and earth is the present moment.

PRAYER

After my grandmother died, we went to the church for the Mass. I really felt Nana's presence around me, and I looked up and could faintly see her standing with her husband.

I decided to talk to her and said a prayer.

It went like this: "Nana, I feel you around me, I want to ask you to help get me off the hook with the court case I have coming up. I'm not asking selfishly at all, it's just that if they lock me up, I will choose to die. If I die, my mother I feel wouldn't be able to cope, and the family could fall apart. So what I'm asking here, I guess, is I'm asking for a second chance for the good of all. Hope you can hear me, Nana; love you lots, miss you dearly, and I wish you well."

Prayers were not really my thing. But it was a life-and-death situation, and I knew she was still around us all; for me there was no question about that. Knowing Nana was around I would class as the positive point of my sensitive nature, and for me there didn't seem to be too many positive points to my nature. However, I did know things, and that was my truth. I knew she was there, and I wanted to tell my mother not to be upset because there was no need to cry. Nana was a great person and great fun, she was happy back with her husband, she was there to help and watch over us, and the only problem that I could see at hand was that my mother and her siblings were so upset. That was the only real problem, so I felt anyways.

COURT

One day I heard a politician on the television, and he said, "A man is to be measured by his actions throughout his life and not just his last action." It was the first time I felt that a politician actually spoke some truth; amazingly, he also made some sense.

Off I went to court. My father went with me, and we had a father-son bonding time. I was prepared and ready to get locked up. I was planning on the worst and thinking that my game could slowly come to an end after this day. The solicitor I had came over and said, "I was talking to the police there and I'm sorry to say but it is not looking good, I think it will be a lockup situation. But we can call for the case again after a few weeks and there are other options at hand but it's not looking good."

I said to my father, "Okay, the solicitor thinks I'll get locked up. I want to go to Australia, and if I have to do any time for this, I'll not be able to leave. So the question from me is, if they decide to lock me up, there will be a bail fee of £1,800. Could you pay that money to get me out? I can leave for Australia in the morning and post you back the money. Can you do that for me, Arthur?"

My father thought about it and then said, "Yes, I could do that, I could bail you out."

That was it there, I had a father who would help me. He was the main man who did love me and would do anything for my safety; we just didn't understand each other. My father was actually there for me when it came to the crunch. That moment there meant more to me than anything else. My whole life I was led to believe that he was out to get me in many ways, and I was angry at him a lot. He was angry at me at a stage, and there it was brought to the experience of "You're going down, D.J., but your daddy is going to set you free." We cooped up this master plan in the back of the courtroom. My father had great respect for the police, and it was a fine line about whether he would stick with the law or help set me free.

My case was called up, and I stood there before the court. The courtroom was full of people. There were a lot of "pikeys" (gypsies) with a lot of cash in their pockets, ready to bail their brothers and mates out of court. The bail money was changed from £1,800 to £3,600. My odds were not looking good; my father was okay with £1,800, but there was no way he loved me as much as £3,600. I wouldn't even ask that question for fear of rejection.

The solicitor previously told us that it all really depended on the judge of the day. If it was the judge whose niece had been killed by a drunk driver, then I would be well bleeped. The courtroom was full. My charges were read out, and they sure did sound nasty: drink driving, two hit-and-run charges (that was what it was called, I really just hit the bumper of the other car and drove off, so that was counted as two hit-and-runs), and failure to produce my tax, insurance, and driver's licence. Six charges I was up for. They were read out, and as terrible as it all sounded, all the people in the courtroom looked at me in shock as if to say, "You're going to hell, boy-o."

The lad next to me kept calling my name; he knew me, and it looked as though we were well aquainted. I couldn't hear the judge talking to me, so I just turned to the lad and said, "Shut up."

The judge then asked me, "Had you insurance and tax at the time?"

I said, "Yes I did, Your Honour."

The judge said, "Why didn't you hand your details into the police station?"

I said, "I called down a couple of times but I finished work at six o'clock and the police station was closed on both occasions." It was all going reasonable well, there were no comments about getting the handcuffs and chains out.

The judge then said to the police officer, "Has this lad any other previous convictions?"

The copper said, "Yes he does, Your Honour, he already had his licence taken off him in another county; he lost it for two years, and there was a motorbike chase by the police when he was sixteen."

I couldn't believe it, I thought I was to be judged on my charges at hand, not have this old stuff dug up. The judge looked at me and said, "Are you working, Mr D.J.?"

I said, "Well, sometimes, Your Honour. I have a back injury, and I work when I can."

He said, "Okay, let's forget about the previous incident and the two years, we'll make it a ban for four years from today. As you are not working, we'll leave the fine as £50 for no licence, £50 for not producing insurance, £50 for not producing tax, and £600 for drink driving; case dismissed."

The court came to a standstill; it was an amazing moment. The lad who went up before me had gotten locked up for a lot less. Everything appeared to go against me, my solicitor, the coppers, but the judge shocked them all and let me off the hook. It really was incredible. I went outside and the solicitor came out. He was more nervous than me, and he was sure when the coppers read out the previous convictions that I was a goner. I thanked him for his help and gave him the money I had for him.

The copper came out and said, "You did very well there, D.J., congratulations. But remember this, just because the damage of the other person's car was not mentioned in court, you still have to pay for it. There is £1,000 to be paid for that car, and it's very important that you pay that."

The copper and I shook hands and left it at that. The copper saw the whole lot as a sort of game; once we were outside the courtroom, he was talking to me as if we were behind the scenes. Whereas in the courtroom, it was a sort of battle between words and who would say what next, and I seemed to have won within reason; the judge was the complete controller.

I left then with my father, and he said, "You have learnt your lesson now, haven't you? You won't need to get in trouble again, will you?"

This conversation started to annoy me, as the only reason I got in trouble in the first place was because people refused to leave me alone; they filled me with negativity, and trouble was the outcome. I was in deep thought here, trying to piece together all the parts of the puzzle. I said, "Do you know what just happened there?"

He said, "Yes I do."

I said, "What happened then?"

"You lost your licence for four years and got a fine."

I got into my father's car and turned on the radio to put on some background music. I said, "Why did that happen? How come I got let go? How come the lad before me got locked up for doing less?"

My father only said, "That is my radio in my car; when you get your own car you can put on what station you want to put on.

Arthur then put on some talk show, and I couldn't even think properly. Now I felt like I was being controlled; the chat show on the radio stopped my mind from functioning and stopped this potentially great conversation we could be having, only it came to an end due to immaturity and negative energy on both our parts now.

That was the most amazing experience I had, and some amazing things happened in that courtroom, stuff I would have liked to share with my father and understand it myself. He and I were having a sad, wasteful, uninteresting, childish, ridiculous disagreement in the car. I wanted to get out of the car and walk home, as a happy and free man.

We made it home, and my father said, "Fancy going for a pint?"

I said, "No thank you, I don't wish to drink today. I just want to be by myself, thanks. I'll see you again."

All I wanted was to feel and share the essence of this victory, and he and I were not on the same level. I wasn't going to say that my grandmother sorted that one out for me, but it would have been nice to know what happened from both our points of view. I felt that I just couldn't share the freedom buzz with anyone. My most amazing fantastic times were celebrated on my own, as no one else seemed to be on the same programme I was on. It was the second chance for me, and there was no way I was going out to get drunk that day and forget what really happened and live back in a mind of such mundane unconsciousness. It was time to really wake up for me and to take that second chance to the full.

I went to a quiet place and thanked Nana for her help on the matter at hand, and I felt a shiver though my body as I saw the event in my mind. What I could see was, as the charges were getting read out, the judge was making up his mind, and it wasn't good, and then Nana, or the spirit world or some mysterious essence in life, changed his thinking and he was dazed for a moment and then he said what he said. It was amazing—prayers I guess really do work. People who have passed away can help us and make things happen for us if we ask.

TWO DAYS LATER

Sunday morning there was knock on the door. I opened it and it was the insurance man. He said to me, "There is a man claiming £1,000 against the insurance you have with us over some crash he claims happened last Christmas Eve. Is there any truth in this?"

I said, "Oh yes, that's correct, I was in court two days ago for it."

He said, "This was a long time ago; how come you didn't let us know?"

I said, "I just went to England after it happened and let it go. I only tipped his bumper on the car and didn't think there was any damage."

The man said, "We have no problem paying that, as long as it really happened."

I said, "Yeah, that would be great if you could, it was only a bumper crash so there can't be any claims in for injuries; the £1,000 must have come from an assessor; that was the only damage."

The man said, "We'll look after that for you, if you could just give us your licence so I can write down the details."

I said, "Oh, the court took it off me; sorry about that, sure it must be on file in the office."

He said, "I work in a different part of the insurance company, so we don't deal with each other. I need to check up on everything myself."

I said, "Well, if you want to contact the court, that's an option."

He said, "It's okay, just wanted to let you know we'll sort out that £1,000."

I didn't ever show my licence to my insurance; I was not even going to ask them to pay for the damage but they came to me and insisted on paying, so it was happy days. I then met my father and we went over to Head the Ball's Pub, as Jonsey and a few others were over there. I told my father, "I made £1,000 today. I actual got off paying the car I crashed into, which was better as I didn't have to pay £1,000. I'll get the drinks today. I have been blessed.

My father and I were driving over to head the ball's pub and something came up about phones. He said, "I would never lose my phone." I said, "Be careful there, you wouldn't want to say never. I said that once and lost my keys." We got out of the car and went into the pub. We were having a drink and he turned around to me and said, "I don't know what I did with my phone." I said, "check the car." He went out and checked the car and came back in; it was really gone. It was amazing, and he said to me, "Did you take it, messing with me?" I said, "No, Arthur, I couldn't do that, my phone means so much to me. No." I went outside and helped him look under his seat and around the place. Then I figured he must have dropped it on the ground. Some kids were playing in the area, and I asked them if they saw a phone at all. They helped me look for it but said they knew nothing about it. It was incredible; the phone was not ever found. All his numbers and details of so many friends were all lost. He had to get a new phone off his insurance and start all over again keying in names and details.

Every time I hear someone saying "Never," they get proven wrong, and it's nothing to do with me. We live in a universal system, the game of life, Never does not exist! Never say never!

PRAYERS AND SENDING THOUGHTS OUT

When you send thoughts out, the more detailed the better. It's really not that difficult, and this is the core of all existence. Manifestation in reality!

Now, there are two aspects of creation in our world, in our reality and lives. One is thoughts and the other derives from thoughts.

We are continually sending out waves of energy, sending out messages from ourselves. We send out thoughts for events and materialistic needs that we have. But dealing with other people, it works differently. It is all to do with our thinking, but it's more to do with what our thinking creates and how it magnetises our energy to that person.

How it all works is, it is a natural law based on like energy attracts like energy. When I think of love, sending out loving thoughts, trying to manifest that in my reality, it works at times. What makes it work is keeping that frame of mind. Why? Well, because your thoughts are creating your emotions—energy in motion. And whatever you think, your emotions will be the same in that moment. So when you have love mentally and send out this love and keep this frame of mind, you create this energy in yourself that attracts someone else on this same vibration of energy, someone else who is also looking for love.

I could see that all the priests, each on their own, say prayers and ask for something, and it is granted. Is it just a few of us, chosen ones? No, certainly not. It is just our beliefs that stop us. Changing our beliefs gives us the key to this creating. We have a belief, and my mission at this stage of the game was to find out who or what grants us our own requests. All religions have strong beliefs, but I see that it's my mind, heart, and soul creating reality, for I have to think it up before anything happens. How does it work? I have to find out.

I told a man about reflections and what my theory was, and he said, "Amazing, and as the saying goes that I once faintly heard, one step closer to the source, creates two steps deeper into the self."

I'm completely onto it but I need more inspiration and experience. I'm going to work out the mind and analyse the self; inward observation is the key to all the answers. We all create, most people think up, ask for, manifest, wish for, things that suit their feeling. For example, a person might complain about something to fulfil their mood, and they do a good job of it too. But after a period of this, they get sick of this and move onto something else. Change mood by changing thinking, addressing issues. Then create what you really want—consciously. Negative is unconscious, and positive is more of an awakened state, where all positive energy derives from is very conscious.

Positive and negative energy are relative energies derived from something that is neither, something that is neutral, something that the mind cannot comprehend. Everything so far has been a state of mind. Once I stayed focused on money and getting out, it all came my way. One night, I went out to socialise, and when I came back, I was so full up with negativity over talking to a certain friend. I went behind my house and shouted at the sky, "What is all of this about? I don't need this, this is not for me, I have had enough of this, and I want to move on. Set me free from this pointless negativity."

People who wait for things to happen, on their own, can wait their whole lives, as everything first derives from a thought, a request; ask and then play. Sometimes it's just a little hard to stay focused in a busy country. I was heading for freedom and the answers would come then. I had to cut out my world, everything and everyone, but there's always the exception of the rule, and that's family and close friends. But i had to keep going; i was so close, and once i worked it all out, i could help so many people and prevent so many lives from being wasted, and better still, stop people from wishing to be dead. My game must go on.

THERE WAS A GOOD FEELING AROUND ME

I could feel that there was a good feeling around me, an influence, an energy that seemed to be around my life at this time. I couldn't really say anything definite at this particular moment as to what it was, but I felt that there was an unseen energy that I had not ever felt before which was hanging around me, giving me the feeling that everything was going to be just fine. There was a change in things for me; all the good things that were happening for me pointed in the direction of Australia.

I went into the city. It was all a haze for me, walking around the city, as it was so busy. Faye told me about this place to call into, where this lady did Tarot card readings. I went there and had a chat. I asked her was I going to die soon, and she said, "No, you're going to have a great life, and you will live for a long time."

I found this hard to believe to start off with, as I could hardly remember what it was like to want to live and feel like I wanted to live. She told me that I was going to go to Australia. I asked her, "Who came into my life recently?"

She did her cards or something and came back with an answer. "An angel," she replied.

I said, "Do I know her?"

She replied, "No, but she's here to help you. There is a whole angel world out there, you know?"

I said, "Who's the main character?"

She said, "Michael Archangel. He was once a warrior but after he died, he chose to help people."

Afterwards I went home; Robbie Williams was on the television, singing his songs, "Strong" and "I'm Loving Angels Instead." He was singing away on MTV, and I came in and said, "Fair play to you, Robbie; angels are definitely the way forward. I am loving them too."

There was a good feeling around all that year. It's hard to describe (to the mind), but anytime I was on my own, I felt great and many good things were happening for me. Things were going well, but they were going well in the direction of Australia, not to stay at home. One day, I went out to a pub and club in the city with friends, and afterwards I got mugged. All my gold chains were stolen, and my wrist got broken in the beating. I wasn't expecting that to happen, but like I say the things that were happening for me at home were driving me away, and many good things were happening about going away. Someone told me that they worked in a flight centre and could get me cheap tickets anywhere. That was how everything was working out for me; nothing was holding me back.

DREAM ABOUT GOING

Even in my dreams this was happening as well as in my life. One night, I had a dream that was so clear. I was in Australia and standing at the edge of a cliff. I looked up and had a hang glider in my hands. I was about to take off, out to the blue sea and sky, away from the influences. There was only blue freedom in front of me, and the ocean was so wide with no land that I could see; I could even see the curve of the earth. Just before I took off, I decided to look behind me to see where I was. I turned around and there was a green park that was very flat and at the side of it were a few houses. I looked closely at one of the houses; it was crystal clear and I knew where I was. The feeling was great, I was free of all the bleeps in my life, and it sure felt good. I then went to take off and I woke up. I classed the dream as a message that freedom awaited me in Australia.

DREAM ABOUT STAYING

I had another dream: I was working away and a huge concrete slab that was over my head fell down. A crane was moving it from one place to another, and when it was over me, the chain broke. The concrete slab fell on me and I died. I woke up in a sweat with my heart racing. I was alive, it was only a dream, but I was to move on and not stay behind to find out if it would come true. I later realised in Australia that each time I had a dream about dying or going to die, it was just about another chapter in my life. It was not really about dying but more so for me to move on to a new chapter. I also learned in Australia that unfortunately this dream became reality for some young worker in the same area where I worked.

MY FRIENDS AND MY LEAVING

Steven who was a friend of Fred and I said, "What are you going to do in Australia?"

And I said, "You really want to know?"

Steven said, "Hit me with it."

I said, "I'm going to work out all about how the mind works and find the truth."

Steven looked at me and said, "The mind, hey? Like mind games and stuff, that's what you're at, is it?"

I said, "I'm not out to play people, I'm just going to work out how it all works. I'll give you all the findings once I find out."

Then Steven said, "Yeah, know what? You could write a book about all you have done so far with all your messing."

I said, "Thanks Steven, keep in touch, yeah."

On the last night, I had a party, and Danny, my good friend and school buddy, came up to me and handed me an address to go to in Australia. He said that his sister stayed there and really enjoyed it. It was a clear moment; Kirribilli was the name of the town, and it seemed so important to me.

My father didn't seem to want me to go away. It was more of an emotional feeling than him being happy for me. This energy that was building up in him was also getting passed onto me. It was not his fault at all; there were just some issues between us. This energy was then in me, and I left the party and became really emotional due to this energy intake.

It was driving my mind wild with thoughts. I was so frustrated that I had to take this in; why couldn't I just be left to go in peace, particularly after my coming back from England to make everything nice and peaceful? I knew how my father felt, and if I made him feel like that for a moment, I would be better off out of his life. But maybe that was the reason why he felt like that, because I was going out of his life and away from any control. Either way, I would die if I kept taking in energy on that level; it would kill me. There was only so much blood one man could release before there was not much left. This emotion stayed with me as it was unreleased, and it became energy in me, just as if he was coming with me.

The thing about energy is, it can cause us to evolve, to make changes in our lives. It's there for a reason. For example, there are so many people taking tablets to relieve stress, and stress is considered as a very bad thing. But if one understands science, one knows a simple fact about an ice cube. If an ice cube is put under stress, it will evolve into something else—water. It will make a change. Having emotional energy in one's self will cause one to make a change in one's self and perhaps one's surroundings. For me, all that energy gave me the strength to get out of the big black bubble I lived in at home, and I made a change.

I had a good party; many great friends came over, it was good fun, and apart from my father and I, the energy felt great. I reflected back on my life, and after looking at all the good friends I had, there were no regrets at all. This place made me who I was, and I loved it for that. But the things that were happening at home were taking me downhill, and the good things that were happening were to get me to go to Australia. For example, on the last night, we were doing some joking around, and I slipped a disc in my back that I later got fixed up in Australia. Also my wrist was broken from the mugging, and I didn't get around to fixing that up. When I got my wrist x-rayed, the nurse in the hospital looked at me in amazement and said, "How can you continue on like this? The bone was broken, and because you continued to work, the broken bone has grounded itself down to a half inch gap between what is two bones now." I was trying to detach myself from my body, as it all felt in pain, and I lived in my mentality about Australia, which was a happy space in my mind.

The next morning when I got up, U2 was singing "Walk On," and I left for the airport and got my cheap plane ticket, business class too, for a very small price. I could feel the energy change coming about, and it was going to be happy days for me.

CHAPTER SEVEN

New Life

I landed in San Francisco, which was halfway around the world, and I would have to get a second plane to get to Australia, so I decided to stay in San Francisco for a few days before continuing the journey and I was just so amazed at the place and the freedom, and it was all just great. There were lads playing the saxophone on the street, singing the blues, and I just loved it. There was an amazing feeling of freedom, and I was so happy. It was hard to describe what I could see, but I was heading to the opposite place from where I was mentally and emotionally coming from, from hell to heaven, from negativity to a positive experience. I became very happy as all restrictions faded away, and I was completely free. All the problems that I felt were previously caused by me were all fixed up. I could not fix up other people's problems, nor could I take responsibility for them. But I cleared my mind by balancing out all issues that were in my mind. It's our mind's thoughts that rule us, our state of mind. If we feel or think that we have done something wrong, we will hurt ourselves or create misfortune on ourselves to balance that out.

I balanced everything out, and my mind became free and open to a future of possibilities. I saw it so clearly that I was heading to an opposite world, to where I felt I was coming from, from an emptiness of existence to a filling up of existence. As the racing thoughts in my mind ceased to exist in these moments, my mind was not blocked in any way but clearly open to receive the perfection of this next energy change that I was entering. I looked so healthy and free, no more coughing up blood or looking like a big ball of negative energy.

I was staying near pier 39. There were lads out playing and singing the blues music, and it was just brilliant. I was really in my element. I fully loved it all.

Pink was singing on the radio, "Going to California to resurrect my soul."

To resurrect my soul was what I felt I was getting myself into, and it sure was about time.

I went for a walk; I walked from pier 1 to pier 39, and when I looked out to the ocean, I could feel so clearly that some spiritual energy was with me. Not just some soul, but I was sure my grandmother was with me, as the feeling was so clear. I said nothing all the way, but when I finished the walk, I stopped and said, "That walk's for you, Nana." My grandmother loved walking along the pier in Ireland, and she did it a lot. I felt that I was getting looked after by someone. I felt my grandmother's presence around me. I also felt someone else's presence around me, and although I could have bet my life that there was some spirit with me, I still was not 100 percent sure who it was. After I walked along the piers, I got a feeling cut straight through me, and all the hairs on my neck stood up. All the hairs on my arms and the back of head stood up too. It was my grandmother; there was no question about it. This was just so amazing and a great truth for me to find out and experience.

My grandmother was around me then; I didn't know why she was, only I figured that she wanted a holiday in San Francisco. I knew she was there, and I knew that she knew I knew, but I didn't know anything more, only that it all felt great. Even now as I reflect back on this moment, I get a shiver through my back as a taste of the experience of that moment. It was like she walked right through me, giving me a hug or something; my grandmother was there, looking after and out for me. Not only was she a classic all the time that I knew her, she still insisted on staying a classic, even coming on a holiday with me. What a great spirit.

I didn't know whether my grandmother became an angel or a spiritual guide of some sort or whether she was just having fun on the other side. I did know, though, that those who have died and are still around are having lots more fun than those who are grieving over them. The grieving is our choice; they don't want that carrying on, and my grandmother always wanted us to be happy and always will want that. Jake was the same as well; he always seemed to be laughing on the other side. But to be honest, death is not the end for these people at all, but still I had no definite answers or exact ideas about what it was like for them. The only absolute definite I had was that it was real and they were there, around, the same place as us, only we do not see. We only feel if we are sensitive, of course. It was all very amazing.

My energy was changing yet again, only this time it was changing from negative to positive, changing from the closed-up, blocked-up energy I had before to its opposite. This time when I had full on energy, it was good energy. I did not wish to sleep much or sit down and relax (not that I ever really did), but it was a great feeling, full of life in me. I could notice things about myself so clearly. I needed to eliminate all that was making me feel uneasy. Any chance I got, I would be outside. I was messing and having fun on the streets with a friend who came over for a few days, but once I got on a bus, I was just be uptight and quiet. The energy body in me would creep up when these situations would trigger it off. I needed to be on the move, outside and free from the lights, the closed uptight areas. I just needed to be outside, and I was in my element, listening to the black lads playing the saxophone on the streets. The way it really was for me at home, I realised that I eliminated so much out of my life. I couldn't take in any more negativity, and towards the end, I had myself pretty much closed off. Everywhere seemed to attract the energy body in me and raise it to the surface, where the bleeding was caused, apart from the freedom of mind and energy places, outdoors, music, sun, travel, and freedom.

The Golden Gate Bridge in San Francisco was built in 1937. This bridge opened up a deep part of me, and it holds a deep significance that I cannot yet fully understand. There was a connection of some sort that my mind cannot comprehend, but something inside me knew that this connection existed. It was all about the bridge, whatever that really means.

Everything about San Francisco was amazing, and the entire black dudes singing the blues was just incredible. I loved the place and fully connected with it, in these moments of my adventures.

SYDNEY

I left California and flew to Australia. The plane landed in Sydney, I got my bag, and I was wheeling it outside the airport. I had a broken wrist and a slipped disc in my back; luckily my bag had wheels, as I couldn't carry it. I realised there that I was the happiest man alive, and I had the feeling that I was in heaven. A taxi pulled up, and I asked the driver for a lift. He said, "The queue is over there."

I said, "Sure, no one will know."

He said, "Quickly then, throw your bags in the boot."

I said, "You got to give me a hand, I can't lift it, I have done my back in."

He loaded his taxi with my gear and off we went. I pulled out the piece of paper that said, "Kirribilli." I showed it to the taxi driver, but he didn't know where it was.

I asked him, "Where are you from?"

He said, "South Wales." I looked at him; he was no more Welsh than I was Polish.

I said, "You have got to be kidding me; sure, you can't even speak English, never mind Welsh."

He said, "Look at my licence: South Wales."

I said, "So you don't know where Kirribilli is?"

He said, "No. Where would you like to go?"

I said, "Drop me off at Sydney Harbour."

He pulled up at a few hotels in an area called Darling Harbour and charged me thirty dollars. I said, "You're dead right, you know what I'm going to do? I'm going to get a taxi next week, pick people up and drop them off here no matter where they ask to go, and I'll charge them a fortune. I'm going to be a taxi driver and I'm from south Ireland."

That just shows how naïve I was about Australia. I didn't know anything really about the place. Sydney is in New South Wales, a huge state. I thought the taxi driver was having me on. I stayed there one night and the next day, I went to Kirribilli and stayed at a lodge.

I walked through the city and found a market called Paddy's Market. I bought some souvenirs, which I posted home. I went to a pub called Cheers, where everybody knows your name and are always glad you came. I met a girl who was working behind the bar and she said, "What part of Ireland are you from?"

I told her where, and she told me where she was from; to my amazement, it was the same small town that my grandmother was from. We got chatting, and she reckoned she knew my cousins; realisations were coming in that the world is a small place.

She filled me in on what Sydney was like and where the good places to go were. We became friends and it was happy days.

Having sessions with groups of people would have me intensely on the edge; all I was trying to do was head for the direction that left me feeling fantastic. She invited me to go out with her friends, but I turned her down. In fact, I said, "That would be great," but didn't make any attempt to carry it through.

I walked all around Sydney for the best part of that week. I was getting a feel of the place and realised so many things. The main thing I realised was that I was halfway to my goal; I made it to Australia, and in a strange sense it felt like I was home. Home at home didn't feel like a home for me. Home for me felt like that amazing experience I had when I was seventeen, where I futuristically saw myself on the east coast of Australia, on the beach with my beautiful partner and our three kids, that was my home, and I seemed to be halfway there. The way my life was for me, when I was young, I was seeing and experiencing tastes of events that had not yet happened. When I was a little older, all I saw and felt became reality. When I was seventeen, I saw what was to be my home, and the feeling was complete within. My life was a sort of game where I had a goal, which was the ending of a huge part in my life, not even a chapter but a whole book. I was playing life backwards compared to everyone else (probably not correct to say everyone else, but definitely backwards to most people I met in my life). I saw the goal at hand, got a good taste of the experience, and it was only a matter of getting from where I was to there. Which was really the feeling of complete emptiness within to complete fullness within.

GRANDMOTHER KNOWING I OWE HER ONE

I heard that my mother was still very sad over her mother dying, and I decided to tell her what was happening as I was just past the stage of knowing my grandmother was around me. I could feel what my grandmother wanted, as this happened before with Jake and I didn't follow it through. I told my mother that her mother was still around and that she was with me in San Francisco and was now in Australia.

She said, "Really?"

I explained, "Really, June, (I tended to call my mother and father by their real names). I wanted to tell you, the day the funeral was on, not to cry, as she is still around and that she can even help you more now than she could have before."

I remembered this clearly as I was walking across Hyde Park, which is in the north centre of Sydney. Whilst I was telling my mother, I was infested in my grandmother's presence, all around me, passing through me; it was surreal.

My mother replied, "Are you taking drugs, D.J.?"

I said, "I am not at all." I then said, as my grandmother was just passing through me, I cried whilst walking along over many reasons. One was because it was impossible to deny what was happening, and it was frustrating as well. The other was my grandmother was with me, and I couldn't understand why she was with me, only perhaps for me to let my mother know. I was getting frustrated with the conversation, as my grandmother was practically walking through me, cutting through me deep within and back out the far side and comforting me with such an amazing feeling.

I then text messaged my mother and said, "Will you, for the love of God, just LET your mother show you that she is there. She is around, just LET her show you."

That was the end of that; I didn't expect her to understand, but I had to tell her, not just because her mother was practically putting me in this position but I didn't want her to be sad and lonely about all that had happened. I needed her to know for her own well-being. Less than a week later, she got back to me and said that she now believed; she was not sure how it was all happening, but she believed now as her mother visited her in her room when she was asleep. It happened in her dreams, but she said it was so real. She explained that she was not sure what was happening but she felt so much happier now. She would keep an open mind in the future.

SYDNEY HARBOUR BRIDGE

I was walking out of Sydney towards the Harbour Bridge. I could feel what was about to happen as I was coming close to the bridge, and it was going to be really good.

Just before I entered the bridge, I sent this text message to my father: "Who says there is no such thing as Majick, I'm going to shake the hand of the Creator and live to tell the tale, this will be the most amazing magical experience there is."

By the time I entered the bridge, I was on a "spiritual experience."

I really woke up to life and my surroundings, which I explained at the start of the book, but here we are now, and I'll explain exactly what was happening to me in this amazing experience. As I walked towards the bridge, I felt that what I was about to experience was very deep and that I would even connect with the real deepest essence where all of life derived from.

As I started to walk along the bridge, I started to move deeper into myself; I really began to wake up, as my energy was vibrating with this frequency. My mind was thinking and seeing in synchronisation with this energy. First of all, my whole life flashed before my eyes, and I could quickly see each experience that I went through. Seeing it from this perspective, I could understand it—the real reasons why things were happening—energy attraction and opposites attracting, where all the people in my life were either on the same frequency as me or completely the opposite, and the opposite was making me grow as an individual and driving me to understand what it was that I was experiencing.

For me it was truly enlightening, but this was all happening so quickly, I did not get any time to reflect on any of this.

As I was coming up close to halfway across the bridge, more amazing things happened. I went deep into this searching for the creator and to shake the hand of the creator of all. Everything became alive in my surroundings. There was a life force in everything: the bridge, the inlet to the sea became massive, and a ship that was coming in was so alive. I was completely connected with everything. I could see that life was all a game, just like I always thought, only this time I really woke up to this clearness. The blue sky, the blue sea, the air, the ship, the Opera House, Kirribilli, everything became very much alive, as I too was becoming so alive. There was a vibration of energy that kept it all that way, and as my energy was changing, I was tapping into the different frequencies around me, first connecting fully with the material world and then connecting with the unseen energy that was out there. I stopped walking halfway across the bridge and . . . words cannot describe.

I was lost for words as I woke up from how I perceived reality, to an inspiring awareness, so deep and so real. I had my camera and took a few pictures of the amazing evening on this bridge, trying to capture this experience. There were open spaces; everything was clear and so amazing that first I thought this just can't be real—until I realised that this was realer than how we perceive real. There I was, on the centre of the Sydney Harbour Bridge, and I had woken up from a dream-like state and entered the realest part of existence. The deepest part of my spirit had woken up. How we perceived reality consists of labels and names and words and judgments of everything and everyone. This awakening bypassed all these illusions, and I was so awake. I looked at the harbour and the sky—it was all alive. There was essence in it all. The ship was coming in my direction, and it too was alive with a vibrating spiritual essence. Everything was crystal clear. I was after coming home to myself. This inward awakening had left the reflection in the outer world so clear. My outer world was alive and awake. I saw it all so clearly, and this clearness was a reflection of my inner world. I did not wish to ever leave this reality, as it was the realest reality that I had ever entered.

I was halfway across this bridge, and when I penetrated to the core of this experience, as I found it hard to separate my feelings from my thoughts, my mind was racing through so much amazing understanding, and the core was, we are this essence, the source is us, just as I was connected to this adeptness. As I was connected, I realised so many things as if I was downloading information from the source of life itself. I could see that there was no place called hell, or any of the other bad places that the church taught us. It was all here on earth, and the closest thing to hell was the bad experiences and the separation of self from this connection. I could see that we, not our minds but we, the essence in us. were the creators of it all and that we were the source and the source was us. The source was life and we were life. We were all the same essence. My spirit held in it the same essence as the source did, we were all one. I could see that we as a whole created the whole game for us to become a part of and to play it.

I could see all the tragic events that were happening in the world, and sometimes we may think, why does our creator let these things happen? It was all created by us. I realised that we had the free choice and free will to create any form of lives for ourselves, but that we were creating on a subconscious level and most of the times we were unaware of this and we created our own lives for us to experience all that we wished to experience.

I could see and feel that there was a spiritual energy around me, looking after me and making things happen in my life, and I could see that we were the source and we just chose to forget ourselves in order to make life so real, but it was really a game. I realised that where we really come from does not have the entire colour, all the good and bad, the entire positive and negative and all the relatives and all the illusions that we perceived as real life.

Also I realised that all of everything that happened in the world was created by us, not just we are the complete creators of our own lives, but all of us together were creating the changes in the whole world, the storms and natural disasters and all of it, was created by us as we all together were raising our vibrations—we were changing the energy in all that exists.

I was completely connected with the only really real essence that existed.

Tom stated in my astrology that I was not afraid to just perpetrate to the core. In this case, this essence was the core, the highest, the deepest one could go, the spiritual experience.

One of the most important realisations was that the creator, the source of it all, was nothing like what the church made it to be, like a human being with anger issues and to fear the creator. The source did not have human qualities, it was the essence that gave life to human qualities, it was a sort of energy that was so powerful, and its main emotion was love, yet this energy was not really comprehendible to the mind. One had to look from their heart or spirit in order to see this. One had to look from the same stuff that it was, in order to see it, to connect with it. There was only one source, that's why it's called the source; I could clearly see that it was one big ball of energy, vibration energy, and not just that but pure intelligence of vibration energy that was in everything, everywhere. My mind started to flicker back to history and to see if anyone had this truth understood at all. I thought of ancient Rome and the Greeks and how they had a "god of this" and a "god of that"; it seemed to me as all amazingly true, for there was and is energy in everything, in us, in the water, the ocean, the air, the sky, the trees, the ship, and the Opera House, manifested with a spiritual essence, and that was what we all were. We all were the most amazing thing there was, we were really the creators disconnected from our own being and looking at life and the world though our mind's eye, amazed by it all. What a game. I just couldn't believe the understanding I was experiencing and receiving. The church at home was putting all the older generation under control by fear and guilt. Like to fear this source was really nonexistent, for this creator was a legend and not to be feared but to be loved. The church obviously knew what they were doing, which was control; so many do it and use so many different types of tools to do it with; guilt is a main culprit.

I got so inspired and could see it all, a perspective from where this source was looking from. We the people were creating everything and then using our creator as a copout, and all the source was doing was just manifested in everything. The source was life and life was the source.

I then started to tap into how the game existed, as I thought about how we could only have one life when there have been hundreds of generations so far; where have we been for all of that? Then my spirit showed me how it was working, that we were an energy of some form always existing, for it was impossible for us not to exist. This energy, which was us, was manifested in the material world following the rules of the game, where everything worked in cycles and death/rebirth was one of the biggest cycles. As we were this essence—our body died and we continued on to the mystic side of life and also connected with the source and also picked a life again to play for the next great experience that our spirit needed to experience. It may sound crazy to hear that we have many lives and have lived before. It's perhaps easier to understand this if it was scientifically proven or even logically proven. Here it is: all of life and existence is proven by the simple fact that energy is neither created nor destroyed but simply changes form. All energy, which includes us people, really is our energy—our pureness—"us" was never created nor will ever be destroyed but will always exist and has always existed. Love it! We live, life after life, and play the game, and no matter what, we will always exist and always have existed.

I started to see that I was in what I would call heaven, as this awakening was really so important to me, and I became so alive also. What a game, that I could see of evolution, of working it all out, of experiences, and how it works is: "The source loves a tryer but blesses a player!"

As I was still halfway on the bridge—as my energy was vibrating at different speeds—I started to not only connect with the source of life but also spirits that were around as well. I could feel lots of light waves of energy, all on a different frequency from our frequency, but life was giving me this amazing experience where my frequency and vibrations were changing, thus having me connect with life's mysteries. Everyone has guidance looking out for them, was what I got out of that. I was listening to the radio, and so many amazing songs were getting played, and all of them I related to in this energy awareness, and all were part of my great buzz. This one was perfect to how I was feeling and thinking in this moment, such a perfect connection: a song by Train called "Calling all Angels."

The place was infested with spirits, angels, energy, and music. It felt like I was nearly being welcomed home or welcomed to a new home; hard to explain but I entered the awareness of what can only be understood as heaven. What I mean by heaven is an awareness that we can reach that leaves us fully awakened and enlightened and with the realisation that you know the kingdom is within you. I tapped into a very deep part of the self—this inward awakening reflected as my outer world.

It was almost like I had the gift to see and feel this entire world; it was incredible, my whole energy was changing, changing through emotional states of energy. It was as if I stepped through the doors of natural ecstasy, and I was just so there. Let me explain this.

As I was changing through this energy in motion stage, I was seeing through illusions that were on my level. When we see the world, we see it through our minds, we don't even see it clearly, as our minds have a series of thoughts coming and going at all times, for the thoughts and the time are connected completely. When the deeper part of the self comes into play—when you become this self—you look and cannot help looking but look at the world in a different way, as you are looking from a different position. When you look from this position, the like energy out there which is unseen by the clear sense is somehow more seen now; it is more felt, and you begin to see clearer with your feeling and knowing more so than your eyes. Even though it may not be seen by the lens, nevertheless, you know it is there on the same level that you are. The truths of the world are all lingering all around us always, as the same truths are in us always, and it is only a matter of tuning into this by going deeper into the self and having a spiritual awakening by expanding and increasing our vibrations. As the self goes deeper and deeper, you feel as if you are going higher and higher to higher states of awareness to a complete expansion of your own consciousness that was always there but you were not connected with—thus have the feeling and knowing that you are coming home to yourself.

Then with these angels in your world—which to me, I always realised that there has to be an unseen energy influence that runs the show behind the scenes—this interventional energy I now had a huge reason to believe was this world of angels and spirits. This was amazing and I didn't think that I could come so close to tapping into this energy influence. But the deeper I went into the self—the higher my consciousness—the faster my energy vibrated; the connections of this world all became connected with me. I was looking in an outward observation, and my whole world was just constantly changing. The actual core truth of all of this was, the vibrations of my energy were getting faster and expanding at a rapid pace.

At one level, I mentally saw a debate about beliefs from a material perspective and awakened perspective. The next level, I made a rapid shift and tuned into this language that my conscious mind had no understanding of, but where I was now, in my subconsciousness mind, I seemed to know it—this was a sacred language that the deep soul understood, and I fully connected with it on this level. Then, as I felt these angels around me, one so clear in particular, I felt I penetrated to the core of this, but it was just happening to me.

This next level that I fully tuned into for a few moments hit me clearly, and I saw it all as I saw the whole angel world with my spirit, my knowing within. Spirits everywhere, all around the bridge and all over the city, people's guides and the energy influence made reality in my world. The view I had of everything changed; the clouds, the sky, and the harbour had a deep essence of comfort and purity. All I ever did really see in the sky and water was just the surface from my mind's perspective, which was nothing compared to what was really there. This was so real and it was really there, but I had to stay on this energy shift to be in tune with it all, this level of conscious, the deeper me. I saw it all, first I felt like crying with joy and happiness, but quickly I moved on. Vibrations were going higher but really more intensified. First I looked at this world in amazement as I went through this journey of racing through to the deepest core of my spirit.

First I was lost but then I was found. I was finding me at a rapid pace, and then this spirit world looked at me and I turned to the harbour. I was radiant at this stage, fully connected with all the truths and inspirations as I went higher and higher, energy vibrating faster and faster. Then I did it, I connected with the all of everything. The essence of the sky burst through to infinity; everything was enhanced and manifested in this moment. I became the essence—I was this essence, we were this intelligent vibration energy, all of us were, and I was fully connected with this pure intelligence of vibration energy. This pure intelligence of vibration energy was no longer a separation of myself, of my spinning with thoughts mind, it was me—it was us. This same energy was in us.

Then I saw the water—the water held in it this intelligence of vibration energy. It too was vibrating. I was me, I was the energy, I was this water, all of this essence that created what we perceived was all the same essence that was in us and that I have become. I took a thought, not from my little mind but from this deep self, from this energy of intelligence. It came up through me, it was me, and it rose up, entered into my mind and left my mind heading for the water. It was a thought, a crystal clear thought arising from the deepest part of my spirit. My spirit created it as my spirit was intelligent vibration energy just like the essence of life and all that was in it, all at different levels of energy—different vibrations. This spirit created a pure thought—I created this thought, and this spirit world watched as I was about to manipulate energy. At this moment here, I just started laughing as natural highs just could not get better than this. I was lost—we were all lost, but I became found, and that was how it was done. I didn't manipulate anything myself but I believe that I tapped into the mechanics of how this manipulation was done.

I started to walk on to the rest of the bridge. But what was happening here was, I was receiving mental clips, movie slides, clear images in my mind, that were produced or created by the emotional changes within me and around me. A lot of things were happening, very educational and extremely inspirational, but they weren't really happening. They merely were manifested in my mind and reality, for example—the language.

As I began walking again, I was so inspired, the spirit was vibrating at different speeds, so many feelings were coming in, and this was connected to my mind as my mind was racing. I could see in my mind what I was connecting to in my spirit. I knew so much in these moments and "inspiration" is not deep enough a word to express the sacred deepness and bliss I entered.

This story was far from over, though. Then, as I continued to walk over the rest of the bridge, I started to see future occurrences. I could see visual clips running through my mind, and to me I felt like I was seeing the future, one clip after the next. I saw a debate between my father and me, a debate from the material outlook to trying to prove the spiritual way of life, a debate between mind and spirit.

I saw myself standing on a bridge after I climbed it and then I was about to jump off this bridge. I didn't see myself actually jumping off it, but I was base jumping with a parachute. Then I saw the illusion of time as I made a breakthrough from the mind to the subconscious mind. I saw that time stopped. Then I saw that I was even out of my body at one stage, completely aware that I was existing as a spirit, looking at my body behind me, asleep. I began to think and try and make sense of what I saw, and I was creating some explanations in my mind about this. One was that this must be when I die—this foreseen future looked crazy.

And then I saw that someone wrote a book about this entire story which passed on this link to others. I saw my whole future before my very eyes, and my life was a life lived for the benefit of all, a sort of divine life; as crazy as it looked, I was privileged to live it.

I then saw that I met the spirits that were my guidance in this period; one was an angel, the other was my grandmother, and there was an older man who also played a part in guiding me in life. I felt that I knew him from somewhere but I just couldn't recall when or where. With my thinking mind as I was in this spiritual awakening, I used my mind to make sense of this, putting the puzzles together, and I thought that I died—left my body—and met these spirits and someone wrote a story about the whole lot.

I was at the end of the bridge now, and I didn't see how I was going to get out of life—alive. This bridge was very significant, as the whole point of walking across the bridge brought me from average thinking to a complete awakening, where the sky burst into infinity! All illusions were seen through. I was not even halfway across the bridge and my whole life passed before my eyes, changing my whole view on my existence. Even the illusion of time stopped. A new language was downloaded. Then I was part of it all, or better still, I was at one with the energy that was in all. This bridge was the whole book, the whole life experiences in these moments, including angels and spirits.

Then I saw that this story was far from over, as my father's energy was in me, and this part of me needed the proof of all that just happened, as it could not even be comprehended by the rational mind, as it involved a deeper look at it all. The game must go on. Truths were found—the awareness had been experienced, but the mechanics of this were still not understood, and that I needed to find out. The bridge was like a dream reality. All thoughts and feelings and visual clips, but none of it was materialised. This was what the bridge was all about, but now I needed to experience that and express that in a step-by-step manner. So I began to analyse what was happening from my father's perspective, as he became the part of me that would say, "It is a good imagination you have, D.J." He was the part of me that forced the other part of me to keep questioning things and try to prove things to myself. But there was much more to it; it was all to do with the feeling, and I could see with the knowing, within which nobody seemed to see, but it was all here. The question was can I have this experience in a material aspect instead of just the spiritual side? That's where we started to prove things to the Arthur side of me. We will continue on.

I was going through all these emotional stages—receiving the greatest education called experience. I felt that if I were to continue on, there would be a point of no return, and I made the decision that I needed to come back; whether the decision was made by spirit before I made it or whether I made it, I needed to come back to get everyone on to this level of energy, as we were all for one and one for all, we were all of all that exists. This was the intensity of my spiritual experience, the most sacred of sacred experiences that I ever delved into. I tried to take with me all of the realisations and all of the truths that fully connected with me as I went through this phase. But after I did come back, I began to question everything from my mind again, which was the middle man between the inspiration of intelligent vibration energy and the experience, and I needed intense focus to be able to write it all down—what actually happened and all truths I received and realisations I encountered. Life's illusions I will get to later on; this game was far from finished yet. The Arthur side of me needed the proof or more factual evidence from the D.J. side of me, in order to even entertain all of this that happened. I was torn apart trying to understand it all. But what I did hold onto and didn't let go of was, "We are this pure intelligent vibration energy" and "The source loves a tryer but blesses a player."

Also, an angel world really exists, and the water, the purest essence of life, the water holds in it the most profound purity. Drinking water is the key to raising the vibrations of the self. But even the lakes and harbours are truly inspirational; the surface holds in it a reflection of how we perceive the world—we can see the reflection of the clouds and sky by looking at it. It's a surface observation, and once you see through that surface, you can see the depth and purity of your own deep self in the reflection, for it makes the breakthrough of your own self. You need the stillness of the self to even see this profound energy. It's fully amazing and infinite, just like the essence of life—infinite. The water is also like the source of life made material, for when you split an ocean in half, you have two sources, half again, you have more sources, still the same source though, and when you divide this water up to many partials, even drops, it still holds in it the same purity, the same essence, even though it has been separated an infinite number of times. The water is like the source materialised, where it doesn't matter how many times you split the water up or the source up, you still have the essence that will always exist as one form or another, whether the water heats up and changes form from liquid to steam, rises up into the air, and becomes a drop of water again.

This spiritual awakening is the real existence of life, and we as a collective consciousness have not yet broke the surface of it. There is so much to become, to see, to experience, to feel, to manifest, and to create. We are a deprived species until we do this. We owe it to ourselves to make this breakthrough some day. Then our world turns to gold and radiates the real essence of life and the source. The essence of all is intelligent vibration energy, and all you perceive as real life is on your level of energy. It is very hard to change that level of energy, as the people around us are on the same level of energy. Therefore, the only way we can make everlasting change is by taking us all together—a complete shift in consciousness. If we can ever do this someday, we will look back and see that our old level of consciousness, our old level of energy, and our past was the craziest reality that ever did exist.

THE LODGE

After that intense experience was over, my life continued on, but I was still tapping in and out of the mystic side of life. In the lodge in Kirribilli, I had my own balcony, which was part of my room. Having the balcony was great for me, as I could sit out there and chill. I bought a notebook and wrote so many things down about energy and how it works. All the information I wrote down in the book was very important to me, as there had never been a time like that moment for me to write down exactly what was making my energy intense. However, in the near future I got rid of that book plus other information, due to a change that happened, as I gradually left the mystic side of life and entered my mind's endless thoughts.

So there I was, chilling out on the balcony, having a cigarette, and I felt someone around me. I looked beside me, and no one was there, but the feeling was clear. I didn't know who it was. My heart raced a little, but I was not frightened. The air was still (no wind), and then there came a breeze of air, and the cigarette went out of the ashtray, over the balcony, and fell three floors below. I was not happy with this and said aloud, "I'm not impressed." I knew someone was there and they were playing with me, but I had no idea who it was. I knew for sure that I was not on my own. Beforehand, I knew my grandmother was there in Australia, but this wasn't her this time. I knew someone was playing with me and was getting my attention by knocking off the cigarette I just lit up for myself. So I left it be for a while. I wasn't sure why I was in Kirribilli, only that I was just following the directions that were given to me. I felt a sense of great peace and comfort in Kirribilli.

After I got a timeout from all the energy influences in my life, I thought that I made it somewhere good and that there were to be no more ulcer tablets or high energy or the intensity of life that I was living. I was emotional for a moment as I tried to release all I went through. Then I was able to eat food, some really nice meals that I got from a shop called Spit Roast. I would eat them out in the fresh air on my own; it must have been the first time I was able to enjoy a meal and eat it all; it was great, eating healthy and being free was so amazing for me. I felt that I was bogged down and held captive for so long by all the negative waves everywhere, and it was all killing me. This was my break after seven intense years of negative energy, bleeding on the inside, and dying. Then I became a free man.

After that, I bought a car from another traveler and drove all around Sydney, just going with the flow, not knowing where I was going.

The weather was fantastic: clear blue skies and the sun was shining. I drove out of the city and followed the traffic on the road. The cars were moving fast, and I also had to move fast. I wanted to get on a road away from the traffic, and I saw a turn and took it. I drove up there and all the way around the coastal edge. The area I was in was called Vacluse; it was an expensive area to live in. As I came around the corner, I could see the sea and just how clear and massive it was.

DREAM MADE REALITY

I decided to pull over and go for a walk, as I just felt the urge to get out of the car. There was a sign on the side of the road reading, "15 Minute Cliff Walk," so I thought that was a good idea. I got out and went for a walk on the cliff beside the sea.

I walked for approximately five minutes; the whole place just seemed so familiar. I had to say to myself, *I was not in Australia before, what is going on?* I think the best way to explain this, it was like déjà vu; we all have had that feeling at one time or another. But it wasn't a déjà vu where it all just fell into place that second. It was more like catching the déjà vu halfway through the experience.

I looked at the sea, then at the track I was walking on, and then I remembered the dream and the great feeling I got of freedom whilst in my bed at home. I said to myself, *I bet the house is around the corner and the park and the cliff edge*. I got to the area where I had a clear view, and there it was, my dream made reality.

There was the house I saw in my clear dream whilst I was about to just fly off the cliff with a hang glider. The park was there, and I walked over to the cliff where I was standing in my dream and faced the blue sky and clear blue sea. Then the most amazing thing happened as I stood there: all of my thoughts of frustration and all the energy that was negative and all of the thousands of thoughts I had built up from my life and experiences at home, all of these powerful, endless thoughts in my mind were released, all of it just rushed out to the sea and sky. I was left standing there with such an amazing feeling of freedom and a clear mind, which I had never experienced before. I was standing on the edge; behind me was like all the collective consciousness, and in front of me was just so clear, no collective consciousness, just clear blue sky and sea.

It was at this moment that I looked from left to right across the ocean as far as the eye can see, and I could clearly see the curve of the world. This let my mind see life from a different perspective, with an open mind, not the intense focusing on negative thoughts. The feeling I got after realising this was, "I'm on top of the world." To this day, it still stands as one of the best experiences I ever had. It was truly amazing. I looked behind me, just like in the dream, and there was the house and park. I did not have a hang glider to take off with, but all the rest was real.

I then had a realisation; my anger towards my father changed to, "Oh my god, Arthur is making me who I am becoming." He was making me so sure and definite about all that was happening in my life. My father was who he was, and his mind and his beliefs did not let him see what I saw. He viewed life in a more materialistic way of looking. He could, however, balance things, as his thinking worked off a sense of balance, but he would not believe any of these experiences unless they were somehow proven to him. He was a huge part in my game, in my mind, and in every experience, as his role in my game was to say that none of these experiences were really real and that I must have been on drugs or crazy to have these experiences, and the solution was to see a shrink. So this was my father's role in my game, and I knew that these experiences were real, and I felt things and knew things but that was not good enough. I needed to prove to him, to explain how it worked, in order to get him to see what was happening, to get him to believe based on how it worked time and time again. So I just realised here, after I released so much from my mind, the truth came from within me; he was not the enemy, although it felt like that sometimes. He was a team player; he, his comments, and my personal intake of how these comments affected me, all of this, drove me to put this game on paper, analysed and proven to the best of my ability. We're a team in my game, and that I can now see.

The perfection of life—failure for me to see this was due to a clogged up mind and a lack of understanding. We really were perfect for each other.

REPROGRAMMED MY MIND

I then reprogrammed myself. I flicked back through each time I was listening to my father, how I felt he was making me believe that there was something wrong with me. I reprogrammed my own mind and understood then that all I experienced was true. I flicked through my mind, and on each event that happened, I was able to relive it mentally for a moment and agree to myself that it was true, it really did happen, there was nothing incorrect about the experiences that life was giving me. After doing this a while, my mind became reprogrammed. I realised that I was still on my path in life, but somehow I needed more ways to explain all that had happened and to get some sort of proof for these events, and that was where my father played his part.

So I got the experience of freedom and a clear mind, and I fixed up all the things that I was unsure about before, denying my own experiences because I couldn't prove them to my father but I could to myself. The programming went on. I went through my mind as if it were a filing cabinet. I flickered back through each time I had a chat with him and each time that I felt he was telling me I was wrong or on drugs or dreamt it up or. I stood there in each event and relived each one for a couple of seconds. And I said, "Arthur, I'm true to me, all of it is true that I said and experienced. You can't deny everything, Arthur."

I basically reprogrammed myself; although there were many events, conversations, and moments, it still didn't take too long. I was free of Arthur in my mind then for the past that happened, and I could see and understand that what I experienced was all true. Arthur was the driving force for me, he was making me who I was becoming. He was also in me; the real Arthur didn't have all the conversations with me, but what he did say in many chats that we had was the core of all conversations that created the endless dialogue between us in my mind.

THE IMPOSSIBLE

But I was still left with this dream—reality experience; my mind could not understand how it was all working. I got a taste of that experience, the same feeling whilst I was on the other side of the world at home, weeks before it happened. Then in Australia, I got the full experience of that taste in real life. That's what was getting me. I agreed to myself that what happened was just not possible given my father's view of life, but I also knew it just happened. So there I was in my most amazing experience, but I just could not understand what happened, for each time my mind penetrated to the core of how it works, I still could not definitely see how it was working, how it was really happening. But that was enough for one afternoon, and I just had to let it filter through my mind until sometime later, when I could make a definite, accurate sense of it. This experience was truly amazing for me.

REALISATIONS

In all of my driving around this time, I was very in touch with my sensitive nature; the more I was connected to my spirit, I could feel everything around me. I could even feel the flow of traffic and the energy involved in it. I could clearly feel when the traffic stopped, that it was static energy, no flow where we needed a flow. As I was driving around and listening to the radio, everything was amazing for me, and I realised that what I was really doing here was getting away from all I was doing at home. I was still me and didn't like going into café Internet shops; if I wanted to write an email, I was unable to think or write whilst I was in there, as all the energy that inspired me was gone. I was away from the televisions and thought I would never have to watch one again for the rest of my life, as it tortured my deep thinking mind. I could feel all that was affecting me to the finest detail. Each time I drove around in traffic, I would drive slower so I would be at the back of the traffic. Then as we all were going through the lights, I would go through the lights when it was yellow so all the cars behind would be stopped at the red light and I had no one around me.

It was the energy in me, the negative body of energy, that got activated when I was in company or had people around; it wanted to be alone. This energy was what I was desperately trying to get away from, and it was the energy that was driving me to the relative opposite, to be awakened, to be spiritually connected with myself.

So my direction in life became where I felt good, and that was at places like Vacluse and places of pure amazing views and beauty; the freedom spots where the ocean met the sky were where I could get my fix and feel good and then I could hack the hustle and bustle of life for a while.

Realisations were coming in all the time. One was, "This is it, I'm halfway to my goal. It's all about staying in Australia no matter what, and I can't ever forget this. It's all about Australia and not going back home no matter how bad things get. It will work out eventually." The other one was, "It's the bridge and it's all about the bridge, not just the walking on the bridge and the experience that occurred halfway across it but the building of a bridge, that's what I'm doing, I'm going to build a bridge. That's what it's about."

I thought, *How will I remember this? What if something happens like it did before, if I was to lose my mind again, get stuck in a haze again? What if I wake up one morning and forget everything?*

These valuable pieces of information became my life's importance; I did not want to ever forget this inspirational vision. So I thought I'd get a tattoo of it. If not across my forehead, so that I saw it every morning when I looked in the mirror, at least on my two arms. To get a tattoo of Australia and to get a bridge tattooed across my other arm. These tattoo images were golden in my vision, and it was a way of capturing a picture that opened up the essence of my spirit and my whole life.

Well, I took a good long drive up the highway. I could feel how perfect the driving was for me. Music and travel and a big open road, passing amazing views all around me, was ideal for my well-being and thinking, understanding, remembering, and creating.

I went on and then saw a signpost for Newcastle and then one for Gosford. When I drove into Gosford, the lights went red, and I looked to my right and saw the front of the shop, which became crystal clear as I was looking at it. It was a tattoo shop. I walked in and said, "Top of the morning to ye."

The lad behind the counter said, "I don't believe it, an Irish leprechaun just walked in; well, what can I do for you, Irish?"

So Mike was his name, and he began to tell me about his grandfather, who was Irish and came over to Australia a long time ago when the first ships arrived. I was having fun with Mike, and he was just one happy-go-lucky sort of character.

To my amazement, there were two lads in the shop wearing rockers gear; they were dressed like punk rockers. Based on previous experiences, more so on passed on beliefs, my mind labeled these people as some sort of violent group and far from respected by society. But how incorrect was that belief system?

These lads were so friendly; Mike was a classic, he just loved cracking the Irish jokes and sayings, and he had all of our accents perfectly acted out. He was funny, the two lads were very funny, and the whole shop was completely welcoming. They were great trusting lads. The lads were in a band and told me to hang out for a good drinking session. Then we started talking about tattoos. I said that I would have to draw up the pictures I wanted, so that was a sorted deal done. I went on a session. The lads bought cans of Jim Beam and told us all in the flat upstairs to help ourselves. The lads were all in a band, and the apartment upstairs was almost like a studio, how deadly was that, I thought. The lads were spot on; they really did know things, and they all spoke in this smart, intellectual conversation. They were really on the ball but also with lots of tattoos and earrings. Really, the statement "Don't judge a book by its cover" fit them perfectly.

I realised that we all tend to have our minds made up, we make judgments about a person and even judge a group of people by one lad's appearance; that attitude is just ridiculous. The lads were gents, and even when they went across the road for Sunday dinner in a classy pub, they were spoken to politely: "Well, gents, what will you be having today?"

It was like living in a game as it always was. But in a town with the same name as Newcastle, England, these lads were all walking around with tattoos and being treated like the best gents in the town, highly respected by everyone and not fearful like Al Capone's gang. These lads were just so different than people at home could picture.

Mike told all his granddad's stories of coming over to Australia and being held captive and beaten by the English. After Mike had a few drinks, he sure did have anger against all English people over all his granddad went through. I could see this was a passion, not from experiencing the reality himself but from reliving mentally all his granddad told him. I could just see it all, all the fights in the world and hatred was to do with the history, the stories passed down through generations.

Then as I walked out to the hallway, I saw a lad named Ross, and he was crying to himself. I said, "Are you all right, mate?"

He looked at me for a few seconds and said, "It's just my daughter's birthday; she would have been one but they all died."

I said, "Very sorry to hear that; sure, have another drink and we'll get the music going."

Ross said, "It was that song that reminded me, we all had it on in the car. What happened was . . ." He was full on eye contact with me when he was telling me. "Three weeks ago my girlfriend and kids all died in a car crash. My girlfriend went drinking that night, and I told her not to but she had the kids, and when they were all driving home, she crashed, killing herself and all the kids. In it were our two sons, and the youngest was our baby girl; she was just three months old. But she was the key to the whole family; she was the key to it all, and I ran down the road and the car was turning over and over, and when I got there, there was blood everywhere."

So what was I thinking straight away? I was thinking, bloody hell, everyone in the house must know this, as he was just crying in the hallway and everyone can see him, but no one paid attention really. I also thought about how it didn't add up: "One year old birthday," "she was three months old," and it happened "three weeks ago." But that was not something to say, only it was something in my personal mental folder of "What the hell is going on?" The other thought I had was, that dream of that family was some sort of goal for me to strive for, and on a mystical level, was I being told about my future? Why was this told to me? Was I living a life of complete struggles and hardship just to get to a goal that may have me take my own life anyway? So I left it be for a second, went out to the kitchen, and what I keyed in on my phone is still on my phone beside me here. I had a folder called "Put into book" (I constantly tap in and out of realisations), and written in that folder was a text message about Ross's story.

Later on that night, I went out to my car to lock it up and take a breather from the apartment, just me and energy again. So as I got into the car, the drink was bringing up my frustration, and I asked myself, "Why live? How could that have been true, and if it was true, why did he tell me and particularly if it wasn't true, how did he know?" So this became a main priority for me but in a very questionable manner.

The next day came and I woke up after a two-hour lie-down on the couch; we went for a meal and I asked the lads about Ross. They said that they didn't really know him but that he told one of them that he was just out of a mental institution. I then told them what he told me, and Mike said, "Sure, it can't be true, as he is only twenty years old. He's just a mad man, I guess."

I thought about it and what I was left with was, he was perhaps a mad man but a mad man that was perhaps extremely sensitive to picking up the thoughts of those around him and a convincing liar. Human nature has many strange things going on that may always be unknown.

I drove home and back that weekend. Got tattoos and had a good session up there.

THE DON

I went back to Kirribilli, and the place was infested with amazing good energy. This feeling was great, but I couldn't work out who was around me. Who was this happy energy? I had to keep thinking things like, had I been here before? Who died that I knew? I realised that I would be happy to meet this happy spirit, but I didn't recognise the feeling, nor did I have any idea who this was. It was someone who knew me, I could feel it, but how could I forget this connection? "Who is this?" I asked out loud.

Just then, a car pulled out in front of me, and the registration plate stared me in the face; the letters were "DON."

I knew someone was around me or with me, and this was just too hard to deny. There was a comforting feeling all around in this area that I was being looked after. This was funny and happy and good for me—there were no negative feelings involved, my mind was open, but who was Don?

I don't know a Don, nor did I know this person, nor did I have any idea what was really going on here. All I could do was laugh and go with the flow. I went to Gosford a few times afterwards, but when I got up close, it began to rain very heavily. The tires on my car were not the best, and the car did a full spin around on the road on my way up. There were no other cars around, it was a bendy road, and lucky for me it was quiet, but the car wouldn't go in the same direction. Other times when I went to go back to Gosford, the feeling just wasn't right and either it rained or the car spun around and I would be back in the direction of coming back to Kirribilli. Kirribilli and I were magnetised for reasons I was unsure of at the time.

There was a school just outside this town, and I passed the school a few times. I also went inside once to use the Internet. I then looked at the name of the school—Donald James—and knew there was some connection deep within me about that school, but I just couldn't recall what it was. After flicking through my programmed mind through stories and events, I recalled when my father told me a story about his uncle going over to Australia and that he was the principal of a school. Donald James was his name.

So I thought I nailed it there when I remembered that story, but how much of a coincidence could that be? I didn't trust my own judgement, as the whole idea just seemed a little far fetched. I decided to go into the school and ask a few questions. I walked in and went over to the girl at the reception desk. I said, "This may sound strange but I have to ask you a question."

She said, "Go on."

I said, "A granduncle of mine went to Australia and worked in a school over here, and I think it could have been this school. His name was Donald."

She paused for a minute and then said, "Oh my goodness, that's a blast from the past. Donald was an amazing man, he did so much for this school, but he passed away many years ago. Did you know he died?"

I said, "Yes, I believe I did."

The receptionist was well into her fifties and knew Donald; she was very surprised that I just came in and asked. I too was very surprised that he worked there, and little pennies were dropping into my life as to what was really going on. Still, I stood there and wondered, how did Danny know to give me the address in Kirribilli? What was really going on? How does it work? The girl said, "Wait there, and I'll get someone to see you."

So then a teacher came over; the girl had informed him of who I was, and he was delighted to meet with me. I went into his office, and he laughed as he talked about Donald. He said, "We called him 'the Don' all the time. The Don taught my year how to play rugby. He was some man, even when he was seventy-three years old, still he was smoking away and playing rugby. The Don would say, 'Come on, you bleepers, and tackle me like men.' We couldn't go too hard on him as he was an older bucko at that stage, but he insisted that we don't take it easy on him and to tackle him like firm rugby players. So when he got in our way, we would just pick him up and put him down out of the way. We were all big lads then, and when he first started teaching us, we were just kids. Do you smoke?"

I said, "I do, cigars at the moment."

So he said, "Come on and we'll go out the front for a cigarette." I looked at the teacher in the eye, as I tended to do whilst talking to people, and he said, "You have the same look in your eye as the Don, you both have these real intense eyes. I'm sorry, it's hard to look at you in the eye, as it's like looking at the Don."

He was getting a little uneasy as I reminded him so much of the Don, only I was younger than the teacher and the Don was his teacher. But he told me so much about the Don anyways. Then we went back inside and the teacher said, "The Don was some carpenter; he could make a table or anything out of any piece of timber. Like, if there were logs or any waste out the back of the school, stuff that we would have thrown out, the Don could turn it into anything."

I said, "Carpentry is my trade too."

The teacher said, "The Don's in a few of these books here; you can have them. I'll give you a copy for yourself or to send home to your family."

I said, "Yes, brilliant, I want to send one home to my father, he told me about the Don when I was a kid."

I got the books and the teacher said, "Call back down again some time, because the principal would love to tell you some stories about the Don. I'll tell you this, when the Don's funeral was on, there were over three thousand people at it. In those days we didn't have email or things like that, the phone was just constantly ringing. The people who came to the funeral ranged from judges of courts to shopkeepers to all the students; everyone was there, and people came from everywhere to be at his funeral."

So I left the school with two books, and even though I felt questionable about going in and asking a question, it turned out to be quite incredible. There were only good words and great words spoken about the Don. He was a legend, and they even gave a trophy in his to the best student of each year. He sure was some man, and mentioning his name in the school put a smile on everyone's face.

LARRY AND COWBOY

So what did happen when I went to Australia? Well, I experienced the opposite of what I was experiencing at home. How did it work? Well, there is the mind, the body, and the soul. The mind went from closed and blocked and trapped to open and free and clear. The body went from pain and blocked energy and frustration, along with drink and cigarettes, to freedom, very little smokes, little drink, and a complete change in emotional energy. The spirit was affected by emotional energy, and it went from entrapment to a great sense of freedom, from emotional sadness and pain to a spiritual experience, which was the great opposite, and the depth of one brings out the intensity of the other.

After one month in Australia, I got a job and started working. There were a crew of us in the job, and all was going well. One lad on the job, named Larry, was a big man and he worked very hard. He didn't tend to stop working hard at all. He would even work through his lunch breaks at times. Nobody wanted to work with him, as they thought it was punishment. But something told me that I should start talking to him and even work with him. I saw a connection between

Larry and myself, and I wasn't too sure what it was but I felt that I should have a chat with him. I could clearly see that he was working so hard because there was a lot on his mind, as I too was just like that, so I had an insight as to what was going on. After I was talking to him, I was asked to work with him, and the lads laughed and said that it was punishment, but I was happy enough. Call it a gut feeling, call it intuition; I reckon "connection" is the best word for it, but I knew before we met that we were going to be mates.

I started working with Larry and asked him why he worked so hard. I said, "If you worked for yourself, you would make a lot of money, but why work so hard when you're on a set wage?"

So I got him thinking, got him off his strong fixed working mode, and we had a chat.

After a day working with Larry, I thought to myself, *I'm going to ask him does he believe in anything; I want to find out his views.*

I was taking a chance, because if he was like the other lads, there would be all sorts of talk about me, and I couldn't have that. But I went with the feeling and said, "Hey, Larry, can I ask you a question?"

Larry said, "Sure, hit me with it."

I said, "Do you believe that anything happens after we die, like, do we go anywhere or is death just the end?"

Larry began to tell me about how all that interested him for a long time. He told me about how he went to different churches and about his seven-year interest in all religions, Christianity, churches, and Jesus Christ.

I said, "What got you interested?"

He said, "I went walking up the hill one day in New Zealand and was experiencing my own hell, and that was all that was happening for me at the time. I then shouted out to God, after I had enough, and said, 'All I have experienced is hell, where is this heaven? I want some of it.'"

Larry was driven to a point in his life where he had enough, and he just shouted that out to the sky. A lot like when I had enough and went out behind the house and shouted out to the sky after one of my interesting negative conversations with my good friend.

Larry said that the Bible says, "If you ask, so shall you receive."

I said, "Well, that seems to be the case, Larry, as I was cracking up and shouted out to the sky, and then things happened for me, and now I'm here."

So there was Larry, walking up the great big hill, and a man came out of nowhere and after he startled Larry, he said, "Why are you not at church? You should go." So Larry took this to be a sign of some sort and decided to check out the church. Larry went to the church, and after hearing about all their teachings, he decided to check out another church to get their version on what was called the truth. So when Larry went back to the first church, they barred him from going in, as he was checking out other churches. So Larry came to the conclusion that all they were really doing was forcing their beliefs on people and not letting them have an open mind about anything.

I said, "Fear and guilt control?"

Larry said, "Exactly."

I said, "What did you do then?"

"Well," he said, "I checked them all out, and I even read the Bible, and it all just doesn't add up. Like Jesus was a real person, and he sure did make a change in the world, and it's 2,000 years later, and no one has matched Jesus or has even come close to understanding what was really going on. In the church, they are teaching the New Testament, and it is completely different from the Old Testament. Mind you, none of it was written around the time of Christ, it was three or four generations after Christ. In the Old Testament, there are many great stories, and it talks about how John was incarnated from someone else and so on about five times. So it explains that there are many lives that we live, well at least John lived anyway. But in the New Testament that the church preaches from, none of these great stories are involved at all. It's all about no sex before marriage and can't do this and can't do that and that God should be feared. Well, after seven years of searching for the truth it, became to full on and I didn't ever really find any great answers, so I don't know why that man on the hill referred me to the church, as what is the big deal about going to different churches? Surely there is just one God, and the church kicked me out because I went to another church one week; what's that all about? There must be a God, and there was a Jesus, so why are they all teaching different things? And none of these organisations are teaching from the closest book that was written at the time. So I had enough and left the churches after seven years, and I don't know, I give up, still no heaven in my life."

Larry was a classic, and I asked him if he ever saw the Monty Python film about the Holy Grail; he said he did and he loved it, just like I did. Then Larry asked me about my views.

I said, "There are heaps of Gods everywhere; they're all from the same energy, but I'm starting to see how all the mythology stories from Greece are actually true, for there is essence in everything. Everything is alive, and it's all one big game, Larry. I am not exactly sure what really happens when we die, but we are still here. I'm not even sure that all the people who have died even know they're dead. There is so much going on that really is all unseen but can be felt, if you know what I mean."

Larry said, "The Bible talks about angels; do you believe in angels?"

I said, "How do you think I got here? As crazy as it may sound, yes I do. I always figured that life is a game to be played out, but I couldn't quite get my head around how it all works. First I came to the conclusion that it's all mapped out, but then I realised that I had free choice, and I therefore understood that an influence must be directing us all the time. Something that is unseen by us but really influences our lives behind the scenes, if you know what I mean. Like something had and has to be working with us all the time in order to make things happen and for us to go certain directions in life, and now I have come to the conclusion that angels are playing a major part to the game and that they are the unseen energy influence that works with us through life so we get the feeling of free choice but we are guided in directions. The funny thing seems to be that it took me a lot of frustration before I finally shouted up at the sky and said, 'What the bleep is this crap all about? I've had enough.' Soon enough, things changed for me, and soon after that, I got a flight for cheap to come to Australia and so many amazing things happened. But it seems to be that I had to shout out for a break in a way before the change came about. A lot like your statement on the hill. While I was going through life, I was thinking that if there was a higher power, how can it let all of what was happening to me and not give me a break? But then I came to the conclusion that if I don't ask for a break, why would this energy interfere? And it was only after I did shout out to the sky that I got a break, and I'm only realising now that all we have to do is ask. Although we think this great spirit knows what we're thinking, we still have to ask for a break or a change or an answer to a question."

Larry said, "You see, you think there are heaps of Gods, and I think there is just one, and this is how simple it happens. We could set up a religion each and get all our followers to blow bleeps out of each other because we can't agree on one thing."

"Well Larry," I said, "I fully understand that. But really, at the end of it all, there is one love, one high power, but I'm sure it's divided into so many different things, for everything has a life force in it, and all of it really makes the essence of life, the source of it all, the creator."

So my gut feeling was correct about having a chat with Larry, and he became a very good friend. The feeling, the intuition, the gut tells the truth when our own mind tells us lies. The feeling holds the truth in all moments. If one was having conflict between one's own thoughts and one's own feeling, go with the feeling, as it won't let you down.

Larry mentioned that the Bible says that one day there will be a universal language; he asked what I thought that would be.

I said, "I don't know, what do you think it will be?"

Larry said, "English perhaps, as that's the way it is going now, or else tongues, which is a language that I don't understand but I can speak it. When I was christened before, at the age of Christ, thirty-three years old, this language was given to me, and I began to speak it. This is what the Old Testament tells us, and it actually happened to me."

I said, "Feeling is the language of the soul. To feel is the truth. If there is to be a universal language, I would have to say, it will be feeling."

We also talked about the whole thing about the Father, the Son, and the Holy Spirit. After we discussed this, we agreed that it is the mind, the body representing the experience, and the Holy Spirit as your true self, manifesting your reality. I then said, "We live in a system created universe. We live in a game called life, where only now we are starting to understand the workings and mechanics of this game. Once that is done, knowledge is power. I think it up—request it—and things happen. We all think up things and we all get copies of our own beliefs and realities. We all live in our own beliefs, and those beliefs get strengthened due to the middle man, the system that gives us what we think up, what we choose to believe. We think it up, to us it looks like it gets created, but really it is always there, it just gets drawn to us. By who? By what? It's a perfected system!"

To my amazement, Larry said that what I said about the game was the same as what was written in the Bible. Larry and I had many talks, and I fully enjoyed each of them. Religion was something that I sidetracked in my life, as this was a subject that people knew a lot about. It was the unknown that interested me. However, I was interested in listening to Larry, who was a lad like me, looking for answers, and he could educate me to all he honestly knew about religion.

Larry came in one day and said, "You know what, I have been thinking about the type of character you are, and I have come to the conclusion that you are a religious man."

I said, "I am not religious at all."

Larry said, "I think you are, Cowboy." (As I wore a cowboy hat, "Cowboy" became my nickname.)

I said, "Religion is not my game, the game is my game. Religion is a belief system. I am not settling for anything less than the truth. At moments, I feel connected with a higher power perhaps or angels or influences or energy, but I'm not into religion."

The word I would have used to describe myself was "spiritual," I guess, but I didn't say that. Religion to me means no sex, deny your own manhood, and feel guilty for so much. These rules are designed to control and manipulate people's lives, rendering them powerless over their own lives because they have given all their power away to religion and basically a whole load of things that create more problems in life and ruin people's lives. Religion makes people feel small and powerless; they have to do whatever the religion tells them or else straight to hell with you. Religion is a tiny step in the world to spirituality; it is for people who can't think for themselves independently. Religious men pick on the vulnerable and weak minded and take their power away. Others are brought into it because they are taught it by their families and don't know any better. Spirituality is getting connected with the force, the energy that is out there, understanding one's own body, and loving all parts and not denying any parts of the body. Spirituality was the word I was looking for; it doesn't restrict anything in my life. I'm Irish, I can have a drink (mind you, I could clearly feel how that was dragging down my amazing natural spiritual high: drink and cigs are acid energy; spirituality is full on positive energy, or better still, it is the awareness that brings both negative and positive into relativity, into existence), I beat controls and restrictions no matter what it takes, and I search for truth no matter what the cost on my own life, for I have a spirit inside of me. My grandmother had a spirit, and my friend had a spirit, and they all seemed to be happy spirits. Spirituality is about getting in touch with who you are and not denying aspects of yourself.

ANGEL—MATERIALISED

This next section becomes the confirmation on my reality—the truth expressed. "The most beautiful thing we can experience is the mystery." Albert Einstein.

One day, I went to a warehouse to get some work boots. There was a magazine on the counter, and it was opened up to an advertisement with the picture of an angel; it was an ad for a shop in Balmain called Mystery's. So as I really had no idea what I was doing in Australia, and I was only really following what I felt was right in many occasions, I decided to continue to follow what was going on, continue to play the game, to experience whatever life gave me the opportunity to and to get my truths, as that's what it was all about for me. I had to see, can I prove in a material way, what I know in a spiritual way?

Two nights later, I went to the Angel reading class shop and met Liz McDonald, an angel manifested in the material world; she communicated and worked with angels in the spirit world. Liz's card read: "Channelled angel readings, Readings on line, phone, or in person. Liz@angelreading.com, www.angelreading.com."

Liz showed me something that was very interesting. She said, "Put your index finger and forefinger on your forehead." The third eye, she called it. "This is at the centre of your forehead; move your index and forefinger in an anti-clockwise direction and ask your God (no matter who that may be) to cleanse your mind, body, and soul. Then move your hands down from head to toe, cleansing your whole body."

So I said, "In the name of the Holy Spirit, please cleanse my mind, body, and soul," as I used my two fingers on my third eye and then ran my hands down over my whole body to the ground, each time taking in a deep breath and letting out all the negative energy. It was amazing. No more heated moments or nervous feeling. A quick cleanse and I was back on track.

Liz wrote me a note that made no sense to her but it was from some angel to me. It made perfect sense to me, and I was well impressed. It read, "I am the one who you saw before on the cliff." This made me feel happy and connected. She also said, "Write down three things that you wish to happen in your life, and when you wish for these things to happen, watch them happen." So I went with what was said and wrote down the following:

1. To have a job where I can work outside all the time and for this to happen within one week.
2. To have a new accommodation for myself back in Darling Harbour, close to where I stayed on my first night in Australia but half the price as I pay for rent now. In exactly one month from now (I said to myself, *This is impossible*).
3. The third one was for myself and siblings to be together in Australia in one year.

Liz informed me that the angel around me wished to give me a gift. I asked, "How would that work then?"

Liz said, "Someone during the week will hand you a gift and it will be from your guidance, your angel. When the person hands it to you, you will know, and you can come back and tell us about it next week."

So I left then and continued on in life as if nothing happened that night.

So what did happen? Some crazy things happened that week.

It started off with a friend named Ash, who emailed me to say that she was thinking about coming over to Australia on a holiday. Then she emailed to say that she could get tickets at a certain time and did I think she should come for a holiday? Unfortunately, I did not read any of these emails. I didn't see them because I was busy; one night, I was going to check my emails but I was very tired and knew there would be a lot of emails there. Anyway, Ash emailed again and said, "Okay, so if I don't hear back from you, I'll go ahead and book them." And then she sent another one saying, "I'll see you on Thursday, pick me up at the airport."

So that Friday night after I was talking to Liz, I came home to Kirribilli, and there was a great thunder and lightning storm in the sky. It was an amazing show going on; the whole sky lit up with this amazing lightning followed by claps of thunder. It was just happening all over me in the sky, so huge that I thought for a second the world was going to blow to pieces. It was really incredible; I never saw anything like it before in my life.

I went to sleep that night early enough. I got up in the morning and went for breakfast. I said to Jane, the lady who owned the place, "Those storms and lightning were really something else last night, it was amazing."

Jane said, "We were hit by lightning and all the computers blew up. The Internet is down for today, and we have to get a crew around to patch up the damage."

Then later on that night, the Internet was back on, and I checked my emails, but all of them were wiped off the computer. I had no emails, and it was good in a way, as there would have been too many to reply to. But I also knew that there were many important ones that I held onto and important ones that I could have been receiving, but the whole lot was wiped off my account. A very strange happening also because my emails were not saved in the computer, they were in an email account that I log into. But nevertheless, somehow, this really happened.

So it got to Tuesday, and I got an email from Ash saying, "Leaving Ireland now and I'll be in Australia Thursday morning at 9 a.m. so you better be at the airport to pick me up."

I read it once, rubbed my eyes, read it again, then I thought that maybe she was emailing someone else or else it was an old email for me or something, but nothing fit in at all. She was coming on Thursday, and I had no idea about what was going on, but I just let whatever happened, happen. I felt that I had no control over my own life at all, things just happened. So I went into work on Wednesday and asked the boss for some time off, as I had a friend to pick up at the airport.

Thursday, I went to the airport and picked Ash up. So there was Ash, and I said, "Hello there, how are you? Don't get me wrong, this is a very nice surprise, but what's going on?"

Ash said, "Sure, I have been emailing you lots of times, did you not get them?"

I said, "I only got the one that said, 'I'll be in Australia Thursday morning,' so here I am."

Ash thought I was messing first and then she explained what she wrote to me.

I was overdoing myself at that time, sending emails to people and presents to everyone at home, postcards, and just so much communication and gifts. I was racing around all over the place, receiving realisations and thoughts, truths, and understandings to my mind. I was on such an amazing high at the time, a natural high, but I was burning myself out. Having Ash come out of the blue like that was a gift in itself in many ways, and it was like a time for fun after a long streak of work.

I said to Ash, "I want to try and get a place to rent for myself over here in Manly, let's just have a look around."

Ash said, "Get the paper and look in it for places."

Ash was organised like that, she knew how to go about things, even simple logical things like looking in the paper for rental accommodations. I was not thinking in that frame of mind. My mind just was not thinking like that. I would just say what I wanted to do, and I would just drive over and see what comes into my life for me. We went over and I saw a few houses beside the beach; I drove up that road, looked, and turned around. With that, a lad behind me said, "Irish drivers, should not be allowed on the road." He was joking but I didn't know how he knew I was Irish. I stopped and he came over.

He said, "Are you looking for accommodation around here?"

I said, "Yes, there are some nice houses here."

He said, "I'm looking for a place myself, my old flatmates are moving out, so we're all looking for a new place. You see those houses up on the hill? They're the best. It's away from the snobby neighbors here who don't let anyone listen to music. It's half the price of these ones and it's over twice the size."

The three of us went for a coffee and a chat, and it was all good.

So I had his details and gave him mine if he saw any places. I didn't know him at all, he seemed cool and I found out a lot more than I knew before. I then said to Ash, "You see, that's how things work for me; I don't know how they happen but that sort of thing happens for me all the time."

Ash said, "Yeah, really something. I notice the way things just happen for you."

And that was the truth. Over all of that time anyway, I felt I didn't have any control over my own life; all I could really do most of the time was sit back and laugh as everything slotted into place, and with other things that happened, it was only a matter of time before I could see how they were the best thing for me. I was requesting and creating! But more than that was happening. Ash was good at finding out information. I was good at dodging information and just feeling the truth everywhere, which was my education.

We learned a story about the opening of the Harbour Bridge. In 1932, there was a ribbon across it which was to be cut by the mayor. An Irishman rode up on his horse, took his sword, and cut the ribbon for the opening of the bridge. The police arrested him and figured that he was mad, so they brought him to a mad house to get him checked out. He was found quite sane and they let him go. He got fined $2 at that time. I'm proud to be an Irishman. What a classic.

Ash and I had good fun on our holiday, and before she left, she handed me a bottle of aftershave as a gift. When she handed it to me, it felt like I was receiving it from two different worlds. One was from Ash but the reality changed for a moment when she handed it to me, and it felt like it was given to me from a spiritual sort of essence, from a mystical level. It was so strange. Ash then left and continued travelling to different countries; she was just passing by and wanted to say hello.

I went back to Liz's class, and each person told their story. I told them what happened and they all listened in amazement. When Ash handed me the bottle of aftershave, it was like looking at my hand, the gift and her hand in a sense of two worlds. I could see it as the gift from guidance as Ash handed it to me, and it became my special aftershave—the gift from an angel. I was amazed at how all of it went. The lightning, the storms, the loss of emails, the arrival of the Ash, the aftershave as the gift, Ash leaving, and going back to the class was all quite an adventure, just like all the other adventures.

Liz asked what each of us wrote down, and I explained about the job situation and how it worked. So, in one week, the job thing happened. I worked in the same job but was taken from inside the building and put outside to work, and I stayed working outside from then on. I started to see what was happening, even from my Arthur point of view, as all of this was really happening, but the Arthur side of me needed us to continue on to see what would happen with the second request that I wrote down.

ACCOMMODATION—SECOND REQUEST

I had to get out of where I was staying in Kirribilli, as it was too expensive for me. I thought about staying where I said I wanted to stay but didn't really think it was possible, as the first night cost me $260. But I kept the faith. I actually kept the faith so strong that I made no real attempt to look for a place, apart from that one day in Manly.

Then as it came to close to one month, John, a friend I met at the lodge, was also looking to get out of Kirribilli, as it was just too quiet for him, but the owners said that they wouldn't pay his deposit back.

John and I were down in Darling Harbour, having a drink at the bar. There was a girl outside and she looked a little sad.

There were two glasses of wine on her table and I said, "Did your boyfriend run off and leave you?"

She turned around and said, "Yes, something like that, we are having a fight."

I said, "How could anyone fight over here? The place is amazing; sometimes I think my plane crashed and I went straight to heaven."

She started talking to us. Then a bottle was thrown from the top balcony and landed in front of me, smashing all over the ground. I looked up and there was this big lad who was not impressed with me talking to his girlfriend. He came down and wanted to fight me. As he came for me, I stood up and was ready for a full on fight. He was three times the size of me, but it was looking as though I had no choice but to give it my best shot. Then bouncers ran over just as he was coming for me. I was lucky and he was taken outside. We were all seated outside the pub but he was told to move on outside the bar. There were three bouncers holding on to him, and they were struggling. He was full of angry negative energy and began shouting at his girlfriend, and then she left with him. He had issues and was dangerous all right; a big giant with issues is a bad combination. But these situations magnetise themselves to me as I still have this energy in me also.

So after that moment of hype, I sat down and John asked me what I was going to do about accommodations. I said, "I have no idea but I'm working on something."

John said, "You're in the pub, crazy D.J., you're drinking pints of beer; when are you going to look for place?"

I said, "If nothing happens today, I'll have to look tomorrow."

Then my phone rang and it was Paul, another friend, and he said, "Hey, D.J., Sarah and I were just looking at an apartment here, it's beside Darling Harbour and it's really classy. We weren't even going to check it out, as it just looked too posh for us, but we went in on the last minute and they are renting out rooms for $550 a week. Five of us can stay here and it will only be $110 a week. Are you up for it? It has a free Jacuzzi and swimming pool and a free gym to use. Come on up and we will check out the apartment if you're interested."

So we got it; John, Paul, Sarah, and I moved into this fine apartment in Darling Harbour, which was just one hundred feet up the road from the hotel where I stayed on my first night. How good was that? That was incredible! Four of us moved in for starters, it was $550 for us all, leaving us each paying $140 each, which was exactly half of the $280 that I was paying at the lodge. Absolutely incredible; I was just so impressed and so amazed. I had great faith in what was happening. Something was really going on that was further than my own comprehension. Do angels really exist?

So next was the third thing I had written down; after things changed and I changed (I'll explain as the book goes on), I cancelled the third request. I was pretty convinced that my siblings were coming over for a holiday, but I crossed it out. I asked out loud for it to be cancelled and did my utmost best to change it, as I was convinced it was all in motion, which it was. I'll explain why I couldn't have it happen in one year—we will see as the story unfolds.

But all of this information, as crazy as it sounds, still worked. There was no setup of any sort, as the Arthur part of me tried to believe. It really all did happen, and I really just sat at the pub and got a call from Paul, and that was really what he said, and we all really moved into the apartment. It was incredible stuff that happened exactly one month from the date, whilst I waited for it to happen, and that it did, and I ended up paying exactly half of what I was paying before.

Life is a game to be played; all that really is required is knowing how it works and what the rules are (if there are any). We'll find out. Let's chase truth and not settle for anything less. Rule out all possibilities of nonsense, of fear about telling the truth, and let's find the truths.

Requests are thoughts spoken aloud or written down. I believe that my life's experiences are not to be selfless acts, but I am to pass on these experiences to those who need to know. Requests are thought up and sent out. The belief behind the thought is what makes it come true. Actually believing that an angel is present and knowing this is true is the faith—the hope behind the thought or request. And feeling the angel is present is the knowing. There really is an angel, a strong energy influence in the world.

PSYCHIC CLASS

Sometime later on, I went to another class at Mystery's in Balmain. It was a free class and it was on the first Friday of each month. I went once and this is what happened: There were about twenty people in the class. Each person paired up with another person. So there was myself and this lad left. Jim was about forty-odd years old and was from Australia. The girl who was running the show explained that everyone is psychic, and she went on to say, "You know when the phone rings in the house and somehow you just know who's ringing or when you're just thinking of someone and then they ring you? Well, it happens to everyone, and we are all really psychic, so this class is about developing that." So what we were doing was swapping an item with our partner, something that was metal or steel or gold, as it held vibrations of the person wearing it.

Jim said, "Okay, you go first; here is my pen. Just hold it in your hand and close your eyes and whatever picture comes into your head, just tell me about what you see. It may not make sense to you, but whatever it is, just tell me."

So I held his silver pen in my hand. I was kind of worried that nothing would happen, but the trick was to clear your mind of all thoughts and then whatever came in, to say it. So I did what Liz said, and that was to pretend there was an imaginary box in my head where I just mentally pushed all my thoughts into and brushed them all away. I did just that and then I got a picture. In my imagination, my mind, I was in a building. There were white florescent lights there and open offices.

I looked at the floor, and it was like an underlay before the carpet was put down; the place looked as if it wasn't finished getting renovated.

I moved to the window and looked outside. There were three lanes of traffic with cars jammed up, honking their horns. I told Jim all of this and also said, "I don't know any streets like this in Sydney. It's a one way with three lanes. I'm up about four or five stories high. Cars are driving in one direction to my left as I look out. There are offices everywhere on this floor, but it all appears to be unfinished. The floor isn't finished anyway. Okay, does that make any sense?"

He said, "Amazing, I'm about to buy an office block in Hong Kong; that explains the three lanes of traffic, as that is all they have over there, and the office isn't finished yet. Amazing.

"Okay," he said. "What have you got for me?"

I said, "Here you go, my ring." I gave him the ring that my father gave me; all my other jewelry came and went, but I had worn this ring since I got it. None of this I told him.

He started and he said, "Someone close to you gave you this ring; hold on, let me see, it was your father. But he gave it to you at a time when there was emotional upset around. He's quite a stressful person, and it symbolized an emotional moment between the both of you." Then he added, "But you give this to your son." He looked at me and said, "Do you have a son?"

"No," I replied.

"Okay, well, you will soon, and this child will bring smiles to everyone's face. I'm smiling now looking at all the happiness, such joy. You give your son this ring, and the circle is completed, from an emotional time of sadness, from father to son, and happiness from you to your son. Look at me smiling, this ring and story is making me so happy, thank you."

I said, "No, thank you."

LIFE WITH MY MATES AND WORK

I was telling John about many of the stories that were happening, and he said to me, "D.J., I think you have a bigger brain than me." I didn't expect him to say that but that was cool; he figured that I could work out something that he couldn't, and I took that as a compliment, as he was a smart lad. With all the conflict in my mind between myself and my father, this comment gave me peace for a moment.

In work, I was getting negative again, too much in the same place with the same routine, and the body of negativity was arising in me. I felt trapped; my mind felt imprisoned, as I didn't have a time to recharge anymore. I didn't live on my own, I was constantly picking up energy from work to home to everywhere, no recharge at all. I needed something new. After working for three months, one day I went to the job site and the manager, Louie, said, "Cowboy, what's going on? You're looking like a terrorist. You're gone from a Cowboy to a terrorist."

And that was it, Louie nailed it there, I was becoming trapped again. I was mentally sinking. I think my mentor in Ireland was right when he said, "You are running from yourself, D.J." I was in Australia, so I extracted everything from my life from all that was happening at home. I really just extracted myself from home. So I was able to observe any little thing that was ruining my life, wrecking my energy and driving me in a direction of self-destruction. I wasn't a mad man at all, I just needed to be away from things that drove me mad, like constant TVs, advertisements, and programmes that prevented me from deep thinking and creating. I also needed to be free of florescent lights, people's negative energy, and unnatural things, which gave off waves of unnatural energy. I needed to be around natural things; on a social level, I needed timber pubs, and on a home level, I needed a timber house, and I needed to work with timber, which was all balancing me out and making me normal.

So I started thinking and came up with a thought that I just need to get out of work and stop everything in my life again. I made a decision in my mind and something happened then. I was called over to the office and the boss said, "I'm going to have to let you go, Cowboy. Sorry about this, it's just there is not enough work to keep us all going, and we did only agree on a few months work."

He was apologetic and also said that he hated letting lads go and all the rest. I said, "No worries, I need to move on anyway. It was great working here."

We shook hands and off I went. Louie said that I could finish out the day, as I would be paid for it, but I could also leave now and spend the rest of the day looking for a new job, as it was short notice. I left and on I went. It was very important for me to analyse exactly what just happened. I thought about maybe someone said that I was looking a bit dodgy and could be up to no good, as that was how I was looking. I was closing myself off from people and was becoming the opposite of what I was when I started. When I started, I was confident, fun, socialising with the lads, telling a few stories, and giving the lads a lift home. I played songs by Guns N' Roses all the time, and everyone loved it. I had an open free mind and an unrestricted place to rest in which left that comfort in my mind. Then I was closed off, dreading each day, didn't want people to see me looking uncomfortable and looking like a terrorist, as Louie described it perfectly. So I thought up in my mind and clearly sent out that I need out of the job, and then I really was out of the job in a perfect way. This was exactly what happened.

When I was driving back home, I was sad in myself, realising that I had to keep on moving all the time and that I was still me and couldn't handle all this trapped energy with negative waves and lots of things. I was sad in myself and worried as to how I was to get through this life. I was losing all my clear understandings the more I was getting lost in my mind, which were my life's workings. Then I saw something to inspire me to continue my path; it made me think, *Don't give up, D.J., don't give up—it is possible to change things.*

I ended up meeting up with many friends from home, and one day we all went out drinking. We all met up in Darling Harbour at the bar, and everyone was asking what part of Ireland John was from.

I said, "Switzerland," and they all said, "Bleep off." I said, "No really, he's from Switzerland. Why do you think he's from Ireland? He's wearing my jacket, which is an Irish jacket, but he doesn't even look Irish."

They all thought I was joking and just didn't believe he was not from Ireland. He learned English while he was in Australia; the whole time we talked, he listened to me and copied all my slang. He just sounded like me. He was like a child copying words from others, and he was really learning from me talking all the time, and my level of English was really not what he needed to be learning. He had the accent and the entire lingo sussed.

We went out to Murphy's then for a few drinks. We were all on great form, and it was all great fun. Then there were two lads on stage, dressed up as women, and they were saying all sorts of things. I got up on my chair and shouted something back. Sarah grabbed me by the shirt and pulled me forward. I went over the table and landed on the floor, with glasses smashing all around me. This was all okay, although it appeared that we were getting drunk, but nobody said anything. It was still early in the day, but it was all fine. If it was at home, we would have been removed from the pub. Later on, one girl that I knew came in, and she was sitting there just watching me for so long, it was making me very uneasy. She didn't mean to be making me uneasy, I guess, but this was how it was making me feel, and I couldn't relax. Then I was deeply thinking that this drinking session life was not really for me, that I needed to be out of it and needed to be doing something different. These were quiet thoughts to me as I felt uncomfortable at times. I was sending out these thoughts fuelled by this intense feeling that I was feeling.

So what did happen? Well, another girl came over; she was Australian. She sat beside John and I and began talking to us. She was a bit of a head banger but I said hello to her and asked her where was she from. After some time, the bouncer came over and took me outside. I had no idea what was going on at this moment and decided to come back in. The bouncer was a big man with scars across his face. He became very forceful with me and threw me out onto the street. I had done nothing wrong and was getting bleeped off with this big bouncer, so I went for him. I gave him a punch, he gave me a punch. I gave him another punch, and he gave me some punches back. I realised that my punches were only causing this man to take one step back, where his punches were sending me from the footpath to the road. I still didn't give up, and each time I ran for him or the door, I was thrown back outside. This went on for about an hour, between releasing negative energy and having a few drinks. Then the girl came out and told the bouncer that another lad was giving her grief. I then realised that it was she who had gotten me thrown out for no reason, and not she was trying to get John thrown out. The bouncer, after a few panting breaths, told the girl, "No, no more, just stay away from him." I later heard that she was onto John and he was just moving away from her and then the girl was trying to feel up Sarah. She was crazy.

The next day, I woke up on the floor in my apartment. I tried to get up but couldn't. I tried three times to get up, but there were just so many aches and pains all over me. I felt like I had been hit by a truck and run over by a few buses. I eventually got up and stood on my legs. I took off my top and was covered in bruises, and my legs were too. I had gotten some beating from the bouncer and was bruised all over. I was in a bad way, but I was laughing about it all. After contemplating this event, none of it made logical sense; what really happened?

Well, we were in Murphy's and it was going all right. An old friend came in, and I felt that I was getting watched and trapped again; I didn't even want her to meet up with all my other friends in the first place. I then thought to myself about getting out of the situation I felt that I was in. I clearly made a mental decision that I needed out of this situation, and when I did this, the mysterious head case girl came over and caused me to get thrown out. None of it made sense, and I tried to get back in. What I thought up or requested in my head, at that moment in time, somehow an answer came to my problem. I was thrown out just as my mind was requesting out of the situation I was in.

People at home and throughout my life have noticed how things just happened to me. What was going on, on each of those occasions, was that I was not feeling comfortable and wanted out of the situation, and something always happened. Between my mind's request and the emotion in my body, events were attracted to me, fulfilling my thoughts. So I woke up that morning and could just about remember the big fight but couldn't understand how it all came about until I understood that the girl was the problem. But everything cuts deeper than that. What was the real problem? The truth: what one is asking, one is receiving.

AMAZING CONFIRMATION ON EXPERIENCES

A friend said to me, "Blame no one but yourself." I felt this statement was a truth in itself, but I couldn't see how it worked in my life. I was thinking negatively again, and I guess I was blaming others for this negativity in me and began thinking in this frustrated way. To make this statement, "Blame no one but yourself," come true for me, it's not like I created my sensitive nature. I was born with it, and to me, I went through some difficulties. I didn't complain at home, I lived it and left, but I was thinking, is it necessary for me to have to live like this? Am I not allowed to be happy and feel good at all?

I walked down to Darling Harbour and stopped outside a shopping centre. I felt a presence around me and said out loud, whilst no one was looking, "I know all I am doing is correct, and I know all I have said is correct, but there is no one on my side. Everyone at home thinks differently, and even though I don't doubt my own experiences and what I think, I still could do with confirmation on all that I experienced and said, just to confirm that I am still chasing and understand the truth, as I am losing my clarity."

I walked off then and there was a book shop that got my attention, and I entered it. One area of the shop got my attention, and I walked down to the back and there was a book called *Conversations with God.*

I picked up the book, I bought it, and off I went. I sat in the apartment and tried to read, but the TV was on, and no matter how hard I tried to think clearly, it was not happening and I felt I needed out. I wanted to read the book that I picked up but felt that I couldn't read whilst in my sitting room, as there would be a lot of curiosity about that and too much interest for my liking. I felt that having friends around was great, but it wasn't in synchronisation as to what I needed to be doing. Wasting time or watching television was not what I needed to do. I sat there at the table and tried to think about what I needed to get me out of the situation I was in.

I thought, *I need a vehicle to drive, as the old one is nearly out of registration. I need a place where I can listen to music and play some CDs so that I can think clearly. I need a place that doesn't have TV, a place where I could sleep some nights without the TV and just have music. I need a hideout spot where I can read this book. I need a job that pays well and that I get moved around to different places quite a bit, as I need the change all the time.*

So after some thinking, I got a clear thought created from all this thinking in my head about what I needed in my life for it to continue, but I had no idea about how to get past that stage. I felt it was very important to get it clear in my own head about what I needed instead of just watching myself sink into a non-existent D.J.

It was my birthday the next day, but I didn't say anything to any of my friends in the house. I reflected back upon all my other birthdays and remembered that they all consisted of police and court and getting locked up. So I didn't say anything this time about my birthday and just sat there thinking about how I would get myself out of this mess. Then my flatmate came back and said, "Hey, D.J., there is an English couple that I was out drinking with last night. They have a Mazda van that they want to sell. They were talking about selling it for $2,400 but no one has looked at it yet. They are so broke, I think they will sell it for a lot less. I asked the lad would he sell it for a $1,000 last night, and he said that he would, so I reckon if you give him $850 for it, he would take it. It looks great from the outside, but I don't know anything more about it. Do you want to have a look?"

I couldn't believe it; what was going on? By the sounds of what my mate was saying, he was giving me the best birthday gift that I could ever get, and he didn't even know it was my birthday.

I said, "Let's go down and have a look then. Can we go now?"

He said, "Yes, come on, we'll check it out."

So we went down and met the lad, and he was in a spot of bother with money and was panicking. I had a look at the van, and it seemed very neat and tidy. We went inside, and it had a big sun roof and had its own built-in CD player and curtains to go around the window. It had two rows of seats in the back, which folded down to a double bed, and the seats could also be turned around to face each other; it was like a little sitting room in the back of the van. The registration was good for several months, and all the papers came with the van. It was still in its previous owner's name from ten years beforehand, and he said that there was no need to put it in my name unless I wanted to. It was some setup.

I honestly explained to the lad that I didn't have the money but that I had a keyboard which I bought two weeks prior; it was worth $850 and I could bring it back. The lad was interested and said, "I'll sell it for a $1,000; if you can get that together, it's yours."

So I went back to the apartment, got the keyboard, brought it back to the shop, got the money, went for a test drive around the area in the van, and I told him that I would take it all right.

He said, "That's great, how much have you got?"

I said, "$900."

"Sold," he replied, and it was a done deal. He explained that he was going home in a week and that his girlfriend was staying on, and he couldn't wait any longer for money. I drove off in the van, and it was brilliant. I had timeout for a second, and I realised that it had a CD player and radio in it with big speakers in the back. It had curtains around the windows. It had seats in the back that turned into a bed; it had built-in heaters; it was registered; and it was cheap to drive. This van had everything that I was thinking up in the house; it was the answer to all my problems, and my buddy had just given me the best birthday present I have ever got. It was just perfect.

I came back to the apartment with the new van, and it was all happy days. I told my mate in the sitting room that it was the best birthday present I ever got, and the others said, "It's your birthday, D.J.? Why didn't you say so?"

So I explained that I didn't like to celebrate my birthday, as I seem to get locked up each year it is on, so I just wanted to stay in the house all day and not really go out.

Sarah thought what I was saying was a load of rubbish, but I explained about different years and said that it was just another day in the year that I would rather forget about.

So the next day came, and I went out and about. I wanted to get my tax back for the three months' work that I did, but I was having problems. I was to be owed $3,000 back from paying tax. I went to the tax office in Sydney. I had my blue bag and all my papers in it. I had a bit of stubble on my face and had a cowboy hat on my head. I learned that none of my tax had gotten paid for the whole time I was working for my boss, and therefore I was unable to claim it back. The bleeper did me over and a lot of money too, I might add.

I walked outside and lit up a cigar. I was trying to think for a second about not having any tax paid by the boss the whole time he gave me pay slips to say that he was paying it.

Then three coppers ran over to me and told me to drop my bag. I started nervously laughing as they were full on, but I was laughing about what I was previously saying about police and my birthday. So they checked my bag, thinking it was a bomb and that I was a terrorist.

I said, "I'm an Irish Catholic boy, a simple man just looking to get my tax back from working."

They said, "We just got a report that you were looking a little suspicious and that we should check out what was in the bag. We got a report that you may be a terrorist."

So after I gave them my name and date of birth, they rang that into the office and I said, "Okay folks, I'll be off now, was just inquiring about tax."

I texted Sarah then and said, "The coppers just nabbed me; they thought I was a terrorist, but I'm a free man now."

Sarah told Paul, "D.J. was not messing, the police came after him the day after his birthday."

So what was really going on?

Well, I tended to worry a bit around my birthday, as I really didn't like to be the centre of attention, and I used to think, *How will I get out of this one*? I would picture in my mind about a black room that was closed off from everyone and a place where I could think and breathe and relax. A prison cell seemed to be the place that matched that, and each time I thought up or requested that I needed to get out of the game, fuelled by all that energy I was feeling, I ended up attracting a situation and getting carted away by police and put in a cell. Mind you, if there was one thing I detested in life it was cells. But a thought in one's head should be carefully thought up as to what was really best for the person at hand. But it got to a stage where I couldn't quite recall the thinking before the event, and all I could do was remember all the previous events, and that led me to the conclusion that for some reason the police always came for me on my birthday and took me away. The truth of the matter was, I would think up a way for me to get out of the situation I was in, just like needing the van, and each time I did get locked up and away from people and out of the game, in a sense. But this time I was just looking dodgy; I was thinking I should be dodging the police because they always seemed to come for me at this time. Thus this look of dodginess was attracting the attention of the police, and they did come over and question me, and of course I convinced myself and even Sarah that the police just come after me on my birthday.

Can you see what is going on? This book is about trying to explain the unexplained. All of those times that I got locked up, I was doing it to myself. In the Canary Islands, I got locked up for forty hours in darkness, as I requested just that. Other times I asked out loud to a system governing the game of life, and it became my reality. Let's continue on and unfold the madness of D.J. The truth, no matter how shocking, no matter how offensive, no matter how frightening, no matter how unbelievable it may appear to be, nevertheless, the truth as this game will go on!

Then I was talking to another friend about having no job, saying that I was in trouble with no money. Then my friend got a text from her friend who had a number for a company that was looking for workers. I rang them up and explained that I had a van, and I got a job working in different areas for an agency that paid well, and the lads running it were so sound. The main man was an Irishman, and he was just happy with getting all Irish workers working for him; he was a gent of a man. All of my jobs involved moving around after about two weeks at each job. Perfection, to say the least!

One day, we were back in the apartment and the news came on; I was focused on it and started to think in a deep sense about it all. There were a few natural disasters in the world, storms and destruction. I was watching it in deep thought. I could see it all, I was flickering back through things in my mind, and when I was in deep thought, I was penetrating to the core, the reason why and not just a maybe but a definite.

Sarah said, "D.J., you look like you're in deep thought there, do you mind if I ask you what you are thinking about?"

I said, "Not at all, Sarah; all of those disasters on the news, the storms, the floods, all of it is caused and created by people's thinking, a collective consciousness, Sarah, it's created by the people."

She said, "Oh, that's very deep, D.J."

So I said, "Sarah, what is your verdict on life? Is there one life, are there many lives, how is it working, what do you think?"

She said, "I think that we have many lives; I think that we have to be a child, a woman, a man, and in each life there is something different for us to experience."

I said, "I am not the only one who thinks like this, that's great." So many of my age group were really thinking like me; we're a new generation, on a higher frequency, more awakened.

I noticed myself sinking in many ways, and I was losing my connection that I had before. It was like I was in two worlds at the same time and drifting into heaven and drifting back into earth. Both places were in the same place; it was just the amazing feeling that I was receiving and my mind connected to my feeling was letting me see in my reality where I was. But then things were catching up on me; I needed a change and was getting tired from running. Spiritual energy change created an enlightening world for me. Negative energy body in me brought to attention, created a negative world for me where all I saw was negativity in people and places and my world.

But when I got out and was driving around, I was happy. I was driving around with my friend Paul; we had the music pumping and that was my fix. These were the times I was most happy; it did me a world of good. So there we were, driving up William Street, the main street in Sydney, and I looked over to my left.

Something just caught my eye, and I saw a lad talking to some people and said, "Look at that, would you, Paul, that's John from home over there, I bet you it is."

So we rolled down the windows and opened the sunroof and shouted out "John," whilst beeping the horn. It sure was John, and he couldn't believe it; he ran over, we were in traffic and had to keep on the move, so the side door opened and John jumped in, and we kept driving.

"John," I said, "how the hell are you, chief?"

John said, "I didn't know who was in the van, I thought it could have been you all right, great to see you lads, it's been crazy."

The last time I saw John, he and I and our other friend Joe were in Ireland, and we decided to meet up in Australia, because I was going straight to Australia and the two lads were going to Australia via Thailand, where they were to have a holiday first. But Joe got murdered over there. John explained that he took Joe's body back, and they had the funeral, and he was at home for a while and felt that there was no point staying at home, so he came over to Australia. There we were, as I told John that I would meet up with him in Australia and we did; sadly, just John, but that's it, you know. I guess these things have to happen in life. So we talked for a while and then decided to meet up in a pub later on that night.

John and I met later and had a chance to talk about Joe. So I said, "Fair play to you for coming back over."

John said, "There was no point staying at home, and Joe, I don't know but he died in a beautiful island off the coast of Thailand."

I said, "John, now I don't want you to think that I'm crazy, but I know Joe was murdered, but I reckon in the deepest sense that he chose that himself, that he wanted to go, and it's just what I reckon, mate. What you think?"

John then said, "D.J., this is amazing; I think the exact same thing, and I have told all the lads this at home, and none of them can understand it. But Joe felt depressed all the time, and even though when we were all out and we had fun, he still felt depressed all the time at home, and he used to ask his mother, 'Why this depression, all the time, why do I have this depression?' So when his throat was slit and he was lying on the ground, I ran over to him and held him in my arms, and he looked me in the eye just as if to say, 'I'm happy to go, this is good.' D.J., he was happy to go, he was in one of the most beautiful places in the world, and he would have realised that the depression was still with him, and he was happy to go. I'm delighted that you're saying this to me; I have told all the lads this, and they just don't get it at all. But you do."

I said, "I have thought about it a lot; I needed to know myself the reason why he was murdered, apart from what happened. I needed to know why it happened, and my only conclusion in this case is that he must have choose it, in the deepest sense, like from his subconscious mind, of course, but that's what must have happened, you know."

John was great, and we two only seemed to be on our frame of mind, but that was okay; at least we understood each other and confirmed each other's thinking. That was all good.

Then I was in the apartment and the weather was getting bad. It was raining and cloudy. I could see the difference in the city and how dull it all looked. I was thinking, is it just the weather that is making everything amazing and also dull and sad? Because when the sun was out everything was given amazing life and colour and all the rest. But when it was dull, it was like Ireland when it rains. It can be very depressing, but I was thinking was all that I experience just the sun giving the place life, or what was going on, as there is such a difference now?

The truth of the matter is, it was everything that was giving everything life. There really is a spiritual essence in everything, and it really is just our own state of mind or level of energy or level of consciousness that stops us and lets us see the truth and slowly separates us or connects us from and with everything. Just realise this: the mind has 50,000 thoughts per day. That is our own energy getting dished out into 50,000 places, thoughts per day. All my thoughts rushed out to the sea in Vacluse, and I was left with a crystal clear mind plus spiritual experience, and it was all really real. But then my mind started to think again, how is this possible, and energy began to be dispersed everywhere again.

There was something that this girl named Lora said to me. It went like this: "I had a dream about you, and you were on the beach."

I said, "Really, a dream? What happened?"

Lora said, "You were on the beach looking out to the sea and behind you was your girlfriend, and there were three kids there. Two lads playing away in the sand and your girlfriend had a baby girl in her arms."

When she said this, it was a little scary for me, as that was my dream, my goal, and I never told anyone about it, but was I sure of that? I said nothing and mentally flickered back through all the conversations I had with Lora, and no, I never told anyone about that. I asked Lora if I told her that, and she said no. But there was the Arthur part of me that said, "She's telling lies, you told her in the pub the other night."

I carefully thought about it, and no, it was my secret, she really did have a dream, my dream, and it was about me. I was receiving confirmation of my own goal. *How is that possible?* I thought. Even though I had my own visions myself, my own dreams, my own tastes of experiences, and all the things that happened for me, I still questioned it as if I was my father. So between this and the Gosford conversation, I realised that it was somehow possible, and I just needed to get my head around it as to how it was possible. I actually found the answers now, for it is all here in the now, the end of the race, but again I'll explain when the book gets to that, so hang in there.

THE BOOK

So anyway, what did God really have to say for himself or herself?

I asked for clarification on all I said and experienced and all I was doing and thinking, and this book became clarification. I got into the back of my van and laid the seats out (I also paid to get all the windows tinted, which I got for a great deal), and I had my music playing away with my big speakers, the sunroof was open, and it was all like my own little sitting room. Brilliant!

The book was called *Conversations with God* by Neale Donald Walsch. This book that I took great pleasure in reading explains so many truths that we know inside us, and only when we read the words on paper do we connect in amazement with these truths. If you have not come across this book already, I hope someday that you get the chance to read it, as you will then be very amazed at all you thought yourself was actually correct. Throughout the whole book, Neale asks God questions, and God, apparently, is replying, writing through Neale.

Whether one really believes this is God writing or not, still this book will have a huge impact on your beliefs and your life. For me, it was exactly what I asked for: confirmation of all that I experienced in that amazing spiritual awakening.

The book talks about relativity and dyads, also about time and how it is perceived from our three energies. It also talks about our emotions and how it is the power that attracts. The collective consciousness affects the world's changes, and people, if their thought is strong enough, can produce amazing results. Also everything derives first from a thought; people's illness comes either from their abuse to their body or from their frame of mind, all starting first with a thought. The author mentions reincarnation, and God explains that Neale had 647 lives so far, and he was everything in them, including a king and peasant. When psychics are mentioned, God explains that everyone is psychic, but only some people use it.

Neale has written a very interesting book, and I recommend reading this book and the others that followed. God seems to be really the creator of a game called life, many interesting truths are told, and it sure does make perfect sense. The invitation is there, delve into it if you like.

At the start of this chapter of my life, I entered an amazing world, an enlightenment that my own little mind could not even think up or come anywhere close to imagining this reality. This reality came from a deeper part of me, a deeper part of existence that was not ruled by the mind.

Most people believe that they are their mind and that's it. Little do they know but when they were children, they knew then that more than mind exists. But when so much of our conversation and civilization consists of mind-orientated goings on, we get lost in our minds, and when we lose our minds, we are as good as dead. But I have good news for you! We are more than just our minds, and this chapter of my life let me see that so clearly. I entered a new world, so enlightening and fully enjoyable.

What really happened? The world stayed the same for most other individuals who were around, but my world changed from an inner awakening of the self/spirit/soul/energy, and it became alive, alive I became. I connected with so much essence that is out there, that the eyes and the mind can't see. The mind, although it is a great tool for us to use, still it exists in illusion to so many truths that the world holds before us. All you have to do is look at our world and see the truth in this, for there are not many loving acts going on in this game of life. One would wonder how a perfect game came into existence—clearly it was not created by our minds, for our minds cannot even understand the true reality of all that exists. Illusions have to be taken away, and at this stage of the game, a good stripping off of illusions, bit by bit, would go down very well.

CHAPTER EIGHT

Independence

This chapter in life seemed to consist of heading in the opposite direction to where that enlightening world derived from. It could have been the awakening of deep energies inside of me or it could have been the relativity of life, or it just could have been my higher or deeper self was out to experience all of it. The more I left my spirit and the more I went back into my mind, the more problems I encountered and the more I became lost. But nevertheless, I had issues, and at some stage they would have to be dealt with. *Can't run forever, D.J., for you cannot hide from what's inside.*

KARMA

I was working with a group of lads, and one day, one lad was telling us that someone stole his sandwich from the fridge in his apartment. We thought this was very funny, as we all lived in different shared accommodations and could relate to this. The next day the same lad came into work to tell us that the person who stole his sandwich had their phone stolen; he said, "What goes around comes around, a circle has to be complete and he got his, ha ha."

I noticed that each person that left Ireland and went to Australia noticed things like that. They all said, "What goes around comes around. A circle has to be complete." Also, each person I met bumped into friends of theirs from home, even next door neighbours and long lost school buddies that they hadn't seen in years. It seemed to be that Australia held this awareness, this energy, these truths, and the mystery of how life really works. It's very hard to see all the mysterious connections when we live in the same area most of our lives, but when we all went to Australia, we all had a new perspective on life. This was not fully understood but I met a lot of people who were like minded in my thinking, without me saying a word.

Karma is behind the saying, "What goes around comes around," in people's actions. If someone does something bad to someone else, it will happen back to them.

So everyone was on this karma, not the "craic," but the karma.

Karma is a subject that explains actions and reactions to people. I began to ask myself, what is karma? Is it really another programme in the game, like "nature," perhaps? But if it was a programme, it would have to be worldwide and it would have to exist in a spiritual essence rather than seen by the eye. But who runs it all? Like, just imagine this: If someone stole something, for example, who would cause this bad reaction to them? Is our creator around all over the place, making the bad happening? No, so who is? Does this source have a heap of angels or spirits or something, different frequencies of energy all over the place, doing all the work? Possibly, perhaps, but then who is justifying the action? The person could have been thinking that they deserved what they stole, or in other cases, one needs to be cruel to be kind. So if angels are doing it all, they have to know our model of the world and how we perceive reality and our own actions for them to balance out the action to a reaction. There is just too much there for that to be simply possible and a perfected natural flowing system in the game. I had to work through the mind and find the one core answer that brings all of this to existence.

HOW KARMA WORKS

Karma is a mind thing. I'll give you a very simple example and you can see yourself.

There were two men living only a few doors away from each other. One man gets up in the morning and he gets in his car. As he drives backwards, he hits something and stops. He gets out and sees that he just ran over the other man's cat. The cat is dead. He panics, doesn't know what to do. He picks up the cat, puts it in a bag, and places the bag in the wheelie bin. He tries to pretend that it never happened, but he knows the neighbours love their cat, and his whole day is spent thinking about how he will get out of this mess and what he is to do. He is panicking big time.

He doesn't tell the neighbours.

Another man lives a few doors up the road. He's a hit man and he kills people for money. He gets a call to do a job and he is to get $10,000 for the job. Off he goes, sets himself up, shoots the man, and then his work is done. He comes home and sits down and has dinner with the wife and kids.

Who gets the worse karma? Is it the cat man or the hit man?

How does it work? It works on the principle of a bow, thoughts in the mind. Karma is created by thoughts. The hit man was just doing his job; he didn't think about any of it. The cat man thought a lot about what had happened and tried to cover it up and pretend it didn't happen. He might get away with it, as long as the neighbours don't check the wheeling bin, but it's eating him up. He is thinking so badly of himself, and no matter how good he acts out that he knows nothing about the cat, he can't manipulate his own mind. He is constantly thinking that he deserves bad things to happen to him for his punishment over what happened. He creates his own bad karma, creates bad things to happen to himself on either two levels: by his thoughts that he should be punished or by his thoughts on creating the feeling of guilt for something—creating that emotional energy and attracting the bad things to himself. And the more thoughts he places on that bow, the bigger the reaction will be.

Then all the bad things that he thought up and created actually happened. He would be thinking so badly of himself thus creating bad things, whether sickness or accidents or whatever, and then he can't take it anymore and confesses to his neighbours. He releases this secret that he was keeping for so long, and when it comes out to the open, he is okay again. No need to think badly again and create bad happenings in his life.

You see how it works? What you think, you create. For you are the creator of your own karma.

PLANTING SEEDS

While I was working, I met a lad named Patrick Fitzpatrick.

Patrick was about forty years old; he ran away from Wexford when he was a kid and made it over to Australia. He worked hard and bought a house and is now doing very well for himself.

One day Patrick told me about, "Do you know how everyone seems to have a Holden car now? Well, I met a girl nearly twenty years ago. When I asked her what she did for a living, she told me that she worked for Holden, planting seeds in the minds of young boys so that when they grew up, they would want a Holden car. Can you believe it? This was her job, and she appeared to do it very well; look at them all driving Holdens. Planting seeds, D.J., in the minds of young kids."

I said, "I know, all seeds have to grow; how come you told me this?"

Patrick said, "I don't know, I just felt that I should tell you."

"Thanks, Patrick, that is a fantastic piece of information. I see it all now."

It's the mind and a seed. There were advertisements on the television twenty years beforehand about Holden cars, and when each kid saw it, their minds were made up that they wanted a Holden car when they grew up. It worked, nearly all of Australia lads have Holden cars, it was their dream to have one; I asked many of them and they said that they always wanted one, that it was always their dream, and when they got the money, they bought a Holden car.

But was the dream really theirs? Or was it planted there from a television advertisement, an effective television advertisement. One could ask, what difference does it make? But this is how the mind works. Plant a seed and it will grow in each person's mind. There is so much in this planting of seeds, so much to be said for it too, but I'll leave it on that note there.

With some of these points between manifesting to seed planting, should we have laws against these things or should we use these truths from a personal level of understanding and compassion?

A QUESTION THE MIND CANNOT ANSWER

After I worked for some time, I had enough money to go up the coast of Australia. I had a lot of fun with many friends that I knew and also met up there. But when that trip was over, I began to think about what my next move in life should be. I really wanted to be at that dream that I had before, where I felt so complete in life, and I was trying to bring that into my reality now. But my timing was way off, and I was hoping that I was younger than I thought I was in my dream. I thought that I was driving to a new way of life, a fulfilment of some sort. But when I was up there, I started thinking away, really needing to cut to the core of my future before I continued on and looked back in regret.

I was thinking, I can work hard, make money, build a company, own this and own that, and for what? There was no end to this. There were no limits, no time when the mind doesn't stop wanting to be in power off. It is just a frame of mind that people get into and have a need for more and more money and control and power. But there is no peak to that, no limits, where one is completely happy with themselves. There is no filling of the emptiness within. No completion, only an illusion of satisfaction for the mind, that will never stop striving to own more and more. I thought, *If I was to get a job and meet a girl and settle down and have kids, would that make me happy?* No; something was lacking, something was incomplete within me. I was not ready to live that dream, but I had no idea what I was missing. Due to this deep thinking and needing to make a choice in life, I began to have a sort of mental breakdown because I couldn't make a decision in my mind. I couldn't go backwards but did not have the answers to go forwards. If I could just come up with the answer to living life, I could focus on that and either physically bring it into my life or attract it, as that was how I lived my life. But I did not feel complete within, nor could I waste twenty years of my life going in a direction that would leave me feeling the same way at the end of the race.

For me it was like, I made it all the way up to the corner of Australia, and I was here, the foundation was all done, but could I live the life? No, I couldn't, something big was missing, and I didn't have any idea what it was. I was not who I wished to be; I was seriously incomplete. When I made the decision that I couldn't stay up there and needed to turn around and go backwards, at that point it was not good. It's like a man would rather die than give up his beliefs. I didn't know what was true any more, and I was thinking that if I go all the way back down to Sydney, which was 4,000 kilometres away from where I was, I would surely start dying and would eventually die. Where I was then was a happy place, full of amazing freedom and beauty, but I was not in synchronisation with this sort of life—there were many experiences left undone, but I could not find the answers in my mind. After torturing my mind, searching for an answer that was not comprehensible to the mind, my thought then at this moment was, I'll drive back down the road fast and turn off the cliff road and go over the cliff and into the sea, where there will be no trace of myself or my van. I wanted to die or just wanted for something to happen while I was driving down. Each time I drove to one town, I turned around and went back to another town. I couldn't make the decision, and there was no fixed thought in my head. I wanted get out of the game.

I finally decided that I should work my way back down to Sydney; I needed to get a job and get set up, as mates were coming over and all the rest. All my friends suggested that I should hang around and see what happened. So I explained that I had issues with myself, and one girl said, "We all have issues, all of us do; we are the issue group. All of us have issues that we need to work through."

She was funny and perhaps she was right, but I said, "My issues cut deeper than all of yours, and I should move on."

So I left and travelled down. I realised that focus was the way forward. To construct a thought in my own head and create that in my reality was the way forward, but I didn't want anything to happen. I didn't want my own thinking to create anything; I just wanted something to happen without my own choice on events, as I had no mental direction anymore.

When I got to Sydney, my friend Roger was looking for accommodations, and we decided to get an apartment. We moved into a shared accommodation, and the thing that took me out of my frame of mind of self-destruction was really looking out for Roger. I needed to get Roger set up, but I had no interest in setting myself up. Living a normal life with TVs (for relaxing; with a mind full of unsolved answers, this was not enjoyable for me) and working and being influenced by many people's energy was not something I looked forward to. So I decided to fight for Roger's survival.

Roger and I had no money at all, but we didn't tell anyone else that. We needed money and were thinking of ways to get it quick. I checked out my emails, and my mother wrote that she should sell the car that I got her, as a gift before I left, as she had two cars, and although it was a great gift, she didn't really need it. So I emailed back and said, "Yes, sell it and could you put some money in my account, as I have none for rent and Roger is less organised than I am."

So she sold the car and put money in my account, and we all got something good from it. The rent was due, and I paid it. I got Roger a job working for the company I was with before I went on my travels. The owner and manager were great and got us work straight away. We worked that week, and when we came home, we cooked dinner for ourselves. Roger was cooking and teaching me how to cook. He played songs by the Wolfe Tones in the kitchen, and the girl called us Irish rebels. All the songs were about Ireland and its history. Many were depressing songs in ways, but this was what Roger wanted to listen to. In the kitchen, the florescent lights made me feel uncomfortable. I had myself in a frame of mind of worry and a sort of depression and all the rest, and it was becoming a sickness in me where I couldn't snap out of it due to a loss of beliefs and a loss of direction. I had to live a real normal life like everyone else, and throughout my 50,000 thoughts per day, 40,000 were, I wish I could just die or go to sleep forever.

We got beer and cigarettes and smoked and drank away in the kitchen. Once I was away from the television, I thought I would be okay. But all my energy was in my mind, and my mind was thinking all sorts of things, and cooking became a difficulty. I had to be shown how to do everything again. So after I fought for survival and had us set up with money and jobs and the rent was all paid for, I decided that I wanted out of life, out of the game, or to just have something happen. I was full up with all the energy body inside of me, the complete emotional negative or suppressed anger body inside of me, and I was getting very depressed.

I was working every day, but I was very sad and didn't know what to do anymore. Whilst I was planning my ending, I reckoned that all I did was balanced out; I was justifying my past and fixed things at home after they were all unfixed for a while. I got away from everyone, and most of the connections were broken between us all. I figured that if I wanted to die, it was my choice, and there was nothing more I could do to help out the others. I really began to get very depressed within myself and had no great urge to live. Roger was drawing pictures, and that was what he did. He had a passion about art and drawing. I sat in front of the TV and fell asleep, and Roger turned around and drew a picture of me. It was a great drawing, but I looked so depressed and had lost a lot of weight. What you think, you become.

PLANNING AN ENDING

I wanted to get my van fixed so at least I could drive off a cliff listening to a good song, and that was my plan. I owed myself a nice send-off. I was sick of feeling the way I did for so long, and I had enough of it all. I couldn't remember any good times, as I was in a spiral in my mind, and all that it held were the like energy thoughts, for they were all attracted to each other. How I was feeling at that particular moment was attracting all the other times I was feeling that way, all the other memories and past experiences. It was a like attracting like energy. I could not recall the natural high I had when I came to Australia or any good times. I was sinking and going deeper.

I went back to Mystery's, and I told Sandra, the owner, that I was really thinking about ending the madness and all the rest. She got someone on the computer to talk to me, and he looked up my astrology chart and said that this was a time of depression for me, but no one knew what was on my mind. We discussed my options for a moment, and both of them told me, "If you do decide to take your own life and end this, you know that you will have to live this life again. This life is your soul's way of evolution; if you cut this life short, you will have to relive this life again to experience that which your deep self wishes to experience, so you would be better to try and relax and just get through it."

Sandra sent me to the healer that was in the shop, and he had a chat with me. He told me to lay down, that he was going to heal my energy. He told me that I was a healer, but I just didn't know how to do it and that he could teach me sometime if I wanted to learn. He did his healing work on me, and I felt a lot better afterwards. He told me to look in the mirror, and I did look five years younger than when I came in. I asked him what it felt like for him, and he said, "It felt like pulling a big black snake out from inside of you."

Sandra told me to go have a chat with her friend who was a psychiatrist, and I did. She was very nice and said to me, "The Gemini mind is known to have a chattering mind." She also said, "Did you ever get your birth chart done, an astrology birth chart? I got mine done, and it really did give me a clear understanding of myself."

She was very nice and told Sandra that I was a very nice lad and that she enjoyed my visit. I felt I needed help from a vet shop to give me the needle to put me down. I couldn't see a future for me in my mind; all I could see was no direction, no future, no goal, and I lost all my faith, my hopes, and dreams in life.

There was a garage at the top of my road, and I called into the mechanic. I told him something was wrong with my van's clutch, and he said that he could fix it for $50. I told him that a shop in Bondi said they would charge me $600; I asked, "Are you sure you can fix it for $50?"

He said, "I don't think it is your clutch, I think it is just a cylinder that has gone."

So I brought the van over. I couldn't use the clutch in the van, so I had to let it roll and then put it in gear and keep going, hoping for green lights all the way, and when there was a red light, I had to slow down way beforehand and move at a slow pace until it went green, because I couldn't actually stop. I got the van over to the mechanic, who was a genuinely honest man, and he said that he would have a look at it for me. I was taking the train to work; trains, energy, people, static energy, no music, depression: it was all bad for me.

My outward world was draining my energy, and it was so negative because that energy was in me also but I didn't see that nor could I see past the negative world that I was looking at. The energy that was kept down in me for so long was brought to attention, as I had lost all hopes and dreams in life and was only thinking negatively, thus bringing the energy to attention.

One day at the train station, as everyone was changing trains, I walked along the edge of the railway. I was looking at a train speeding towards me and looking at the track. I was thinking if I just fell over, it would be as simple as that, I'd be out of my mind imprisonment. I then looked at the driver, who put his hand up and waved and shook his head, saying, "No, don't, don't, don't." He could see this intention in me about jumping to my death and having him run me over in his train. So really, for the driver's sake, I couldn't do that.

As I was walking on our road in Rockdale, I really was at the stage of wanting to give up on life, but then a handicapped person came walking up the road. He had great difficulties in his legs and couldn't walk properly, but he was trying. As I was walking at my normal pace, I was three times faster than him, but he wasn't giving up on life; he was trying, struggling, but trying. But even in realising that, once I had fixed the thought in my head that I wanted to die, I became happy and had a choice to make as opposed to no decision in life.

I got on the train again, and as I sat down, I saw a familiar face in front of me. It was a teacher from my school years prior. She was there with her husband and son. They had come over to see their son from Ireland, who had moved to Australia and we had a chat for a minute before I got off. It was these little things that were getting me through this period by bringing me back to the old reality and reminding me of family at home. I couldn't go on the way I was forever; I tried to survive, whilst I was in the city. I was in a lost haze in my mind, and it occurred to me that living this way of life was so difficult; it was very hard to survive in Australia and make a successful life and a good name for the family at home.

I decided that if I was going to die, that I should get rid of everything I owned first, like all the books that I picked up along the way. I got it all together in one case and was going to get rid of it somewhere. I thought of the wheelie bin outside but then something came on the radio about checking the rubbish bins, as no one has claimed the lotto. So I got all my belongings, all I wrote about energy and all the rest of it, and distributed it all in different bins around the town. It was all great information but I didn't want anyone to have any information about myself after I died.

Before I went to bed that night, I put my shoes beside the heater. They started smoking away, and the room started filling up with smoke. I was in such a worry state of mind about actually going through with taking my own life and all the problems that I had that I wanted the room to go up in flames and burn me to death in it. This is actually true. So let's pause for a second here. My frame of mind was due to a lifetime of struggles and chasing a goal only to find I was not ready for any of it. My frame of mind that consisted of extreme worry actually felt that burning to death would balance it out. Worry is heart of all evil. "Evil" spelled backwards is "live," which is just an interesting point that I have noticed here. The only reason I got out of the bed to take my shoes away from the heater was the others in the house. There was no way I could cause harm to others, but if they were not there, I would have watched myself go up in flames. This was the power of the mind and the power of the state of mind; you see, any issues I had were not balanced out in my life at home, and all of it I took with me, like baggage I was carrying around with me, and there was not one good thing in my world that could have me fight for survival, unless I was helping out others.

Then my friend Lora rang on the phone; she was in Sydney and was having problems with her friend, who was not good to her and all the rest. Her friend left Perth and came back to Sydney, and then Lora left her relations' place in Perth and came back to Sydney a week later, but her friend wouldn't let her stay in her place. The girls weren't getting on too well, and Lora was counting on me to fix up her life. She wanted to stay with me, but I said, "We just moved in and there is no room here."

I was in a bad way and wanted to die on my own, not with Lora making a big deal out of it. Lora had this real full on negative energy; it was created from worry and insecurity and all the rest, but it was an energy that was taking me down too. I couldn't have her around me if I was thinking of any hope for myself. So I met Lora in Darling Harbour; she was saying that her life was a disaster and that Australia was crap and that her friend had no time for her.

I said, "Sure, you may as well go home then. There is bleep all I can do, I'm in a fix."

Lora had money and was staying in different places. She seemed to be making a mess of her life in Australia, so she thought I would fix it up or something like that. I said to her once at the start that if I could help when things got really bad, I would be there to give her a sense of security for herself to do the Australian experience for herself, but she was creating misery all the time in her life and with her friends, and it was all so clear. The girl had money and even relations in Australia, but she was walking around, looking for attention from me. I told her many times that my life was to be lived by me and not her, and she said she understood that but none of it was registering. Lora just spent all her time worrying and creating problems for herself, I reckon, and if she got wind of me wanting to do myself in, she would make me the reason of all her worried problems and thoughts. I would be the cause and excuse of all her problems, and it would be her story for life. I could see it all and had to carefully plan out my own escape.

I made up my mind to have it all over with; I went back to my place. My flatmate was shaving his head with a razor, and I asked him to cut all mine off too. He laughed and said, "Are you serious?"

I said, "Yes, all of it, if you wouldn't mind sir."

I had no hair on my head and lost about two stone in weight, as my frame of mind was burning my energy up, as this thinking was so powerful. I went out drinking with Roger; there were no pubs as such, they were all gambling places and slot machines and pool tables and televisions. I hated the places, as they were just so bad for my frame of mind.

The mechanic fixed up my van for me and told me not to worry about the bill. He was sound and was helping me out, where I felt the whole world was against me and I just couldn't battle anymore. This stranger fixed my van up and told me to come back and pay when I had the money. Like come on, where would you find a mechanic like this? Did you ever hear the likes of it? He gave me the van and told me to pay a small amount of money when I got some. I paid him and then I was free to do my own thing again.

So I went to the chemist and bought some sleeping tablets. I went to a hardware store and bought myself a utility knife; my work was done. I wrote out a text message for Roger that I didn't send but I still have saved here. It read, "There's an envelope in my room for you, buddy. The van is at Goldberg apartments, the keys in Darling Harbour pub."

The note said, "Sorry mate, none of this is to do with you, I just have my own issues. Here is my bank card and here is my pin number. It was going to happen sometime anyway so just continue on and have the fun. There is enough money there for a good session anyway. Cheers mate, take it easy."

I rang my father up and said, "How are you doing?"

He said that he was good and asked how I was.

I said, "I just want to apologize for fighting with you throughout life and that none of it is your fault. I just wish to make peace and let you know that if anything ever happens in the future that it's nothing to do with you." So I made peace with my father and a few others, and I was all ready to go.

That night, just when I was about to go and finish off my plan, my phone rang. It was Chris, an English lad from when we started work with the first job. He said, "How are you getting on? I'm around the corner and I'll be up in a minute for a session."

I said, "Where are you? How come you're ringing me?"

Chris said, "I'm just at home in Nottingham; it's my lunch break in work, so I just thought of you and decided to give you a buzz."

That was the first time I had heard from Chris since I met him in April of that year. These things were putting me off my plan, and although I didn't really want to die, I just felt there was no hope for me in the world and there was nothing else I could do. I put it off that night and left it till the next night. Then my brother rang me the next night from home; he was out drinking and was on top form. He gave the phone to all these people to have a chat with me. He ran into a pub that he had been barred from to put Jake, the barman, on the phone to chat with me. It was funny; Paul was in the background trying to throw him out of the pub, and my brother was shouting out, "It's my brother in Australia, Jake wants to say hello to him."

After Jake said hello, Jonsey left the pub and gave the phone to other friends outside the pub. Then he was in the background shouting out to the whole town, "My bro and me love each other. We love each other and we're not afraid to tell the world."

He was like a mad man in the town, which was his usual drunken self. He was funny and put me onto so many different people that I hadn't talked to for a while. It was good talking to Jonsey and everyone, and it brought me back to who I once was and brought me back to the home frame of mind.

LIFE WOULDN'T LET ME OUT OF THE GAME

Each time Roger and I went to the supermarket, I would drive; one day, I said, "Roger, would you mind getting the shopping today?" Roger said, "D.J., you say that as if we take turns; you have only been in the shop once." I said, "Sure, but I'm the driver, Roger."

Roger did the shopping, and it was because the store's bright lights and unnatural energy was bleeping me up, bringing my negativity to attention and leaving me like a zombie. I was in a dark mind, plus I needed dark places.

Then Roger mentioned that Danny would be coming to visit in two weeks. I said, "Danny is?"

Roger said, "Yes, he's coming over to see you, D.J.; it was planned, wasn't it?"

I forgot all about Danny coming and didn't know what to do. I called him and told him to cancel his holiday, as none of us had money and we were just setting ourselves up. Danny said that he couldn't cancel it and that he was coming over. He said that he didn't mind if we were working, that we would all just go out after work. Danny was sound but I called him again and told him to just cancel it till a later time. But he said, "It's too late to cancel it, D.J., I'll be over in two weeks."

Now I felt that I was really in a fix. I wanted Danny to cancel his holiday so I could do myself in, and now that he was coming over, there was no way I could go through with it. I decided there was no way out and that I better get some help. I made an appointment to see a shrink, and she tried to find out what my problem was, but I wouldn't really give her any information. My mind was closed off, and I was not letting anyone in; I just wanted someone to put me back to the way I was once, to put me back to the messing D.J. that Danny knew me as. But no one could really help. I was in a bad way, and I wished I was dead and was constantly in that frame of mind, planning out how I could pull it off at this stage. I had the sleeping tablets and the knife to finish me off, but there were still connections with people that I couldn't break away from.

When Danny arrived, I was in a frame of mind that I couldn't get out of. I pretended that all was fine but was unable to be my funny self. Danny just laughed at Roger and me as we were driving around in the van. We were both singing the same song, and Danny laughed and said, "Look what Australia is doing to you lads, you both even know the words of this song." He was just delighted to be on a holiday and away from home.

I was coming around at times, but I was just acting it out; that's the trick: fake it till you make it. My mind was thinking about how I would get through life like this, and it was just as well I was away from everyone at home, as I couldn't have them see me like this. So we went out drinking; the beer and cigarettes were making me worse, but I had to be sociable.

We went out a few nights, and Danny loved it all. I had forgotten what I was like when I first came over, but I remembered that it was a good time, and looking at how amazed Danny was jogged my memory.

Danny's eyes lit up when he saw that Murphy's was a twenty-four-hour bar. We went in and had a drink. I couldn't stay in there for long and couldn't get any help or answers, and then a song by Reef came on with these lyrics: "You cannot hide from what's inside." That was it, that was my answer; the problem was inside of me, and there was no way I could hide from it. I left after a little while and said that I would be back in a minute. I walked down to the harbour and asked the game of life, "What is wrong with me? I need help, need to be fixed, can't live like this. It's Danny's holiday and I can't even get on form. I'm dying inside."

Then Lora rang me; I didn't see this as help, but this seemed to be the help I was getting. She was in town, and I said that I would meet up with her. We went out for a drink and she asked me about a text I sent the week before, saying I was going away for a while. I explained that I was just about to do myself in that night, only some geezer from England rang my phone. She couldn't believe it, and her mind went wild. She saw me as the person to look up to for help and guidance, and I was planning to do myself in. So I became the reason for Lora's worried mind after that, but she was concerned for me and cared for me, so that was nice too.

Danny and Roger were getting happily drunk at this time. Roger was happy, as he was thinking very highly about us Irish. This was good; it's an eye-opener, since our country felt suppressed for years by the English, and once we get to the other side of the world, everyone loves us. One day, Roger and I had gone into a shop where an Iranian man was telling us that his people were like the Irish, that we all had a passion and that he loved us. People loved us Irish everywhere we went. People from different countries told us that they didn't like the English much but loved the Irish. So Roger felt about ten feet tall at times. He was a true and truly proud Irishman.

Anyway, Lora and I left the pub and met Danny and Roger at Murphy's. Later, as we were walking up the footpath, Roger saw some girl talking on the phone, and he put his arm around her and began walking with her. He was on great form and was just messing away, where no one took offence to that. He was walking well ahead of Danny and Lora and me. There was a part on the footpath where the building was getting done up and it was all boxed off. It was like a tunnel, where it was very busy as the people were walking past each other. So Roger was on ahead of us, walking along with the girl on the phone. He was lost in the crowd. As I got up closer, a crowd had formed around someone on the ground. I pushed through the crowd and saw Roger, out cold on the ground. I quickly picked him up and held him against the pole. I thought he died at first and shouted out, "Help! Come on, Roger, wake up, man."

Roger then began snoring, as if he was asleep, and I knew he was alive. Danny was there beside me, and someone came over to tell us what happened.

He said, "A group of lads were walking up and one of them turned around and cracked your friend over the head with a bar. I heard the smack from the far side of the road, and the lads ran off that way."

Danny ran after the lads, but could not find anyone running away and he came back, the whole lot became too much for Lora, and I don't know what happened to her. Two girls had stopped to help, and one of them took Roger's wallet out of his pocket. I said, "What the bleep are you at?"

The girl said, "We're nurses and I'm ringing an ambulance for you now, just want to get his ID."

So the girls rang an ambulance, which came after a while. We put Roger into the ambulance, and Danny got in with him. I said, "I'll follow you up to the hospital."

I had my van in town this night and I got to the hospital, and the doctors and nurses wanted confirmation from Roger's family before they would operate on him. Danny rang Roger's house and spoke to his little sister.

I said, "Just operate, will you? You got to fix him up."

Roger got a severe bang to the head, and his brain was swelling up. They had to cut his skull open to let the pressure out. He had gotten beaten for no apparent reason. The girl he was walking with ran off, and the lads had not tried to rob him or anything like that. I couldn't get my head around it. I then started thinking it was something to do with me, and I was blaming myself in ways. But it was nothing to do with me, it was just that frame of mind I was in that I wanted to take blame for everything.

So after they let the pressure out of Roger's head, he went into a coma, and there were all sorts of drips and machines around him. It was not looking good. There was a 50/50 chance that he would not pull through, and if he did get through it, he could have been left handicapped, so we were told.

Danny and I stayed there for many hours and then decided to go. I started to head back to our place, driving up the main road at top speed. I drove up over a hill, and there was a police check-point on the road. They stopped the four cars in front of me, but I just sailed through; when I looked in my mirror, they pulled over the two cars after me.

Danny said, "Oh my god D.J!" and I said, "I know, someone's looking after me."

The next day, we went to the police station to make a statement about what had happened. So we were in there, and the coppers were trying to make out that we had started a fight and that Roger just got a beating for it. They were saying all sorts of things, just like they do in Ireland. I realised the coppers were no different in other countries; they were the same gang everywhere. I explained what had happened, and Danny did the same. He had the phone number of the witness and told the coppers that they should ring him up, as he had seen what happened. One copper then tried to say that maybe the witness was one of the gang members in the attack. I reckon the coppers were watching too much *CSI* programmes and detective movies. We told them what had happened and gave them the number for the witness. I just wanted to get out of the place.

Roger's mother and father came over to see him. We went back to our place, and our flatmates informed us that they were moving up the coast; if we had two other people, we could rent the house out for ourselves, but if we didn't, we needed to leave. I told them about Roger and what had happened and that we didn't even know if he'd make it. No matter how difficult my life was beforehand, this was all becoming too much, but all of these problems were stopping me from continuing my plan and driving me to fight for survival. I asked the owner of the house if we could stay for a week or two so Roger's parents could stay here. But the owner had no pity and did not want to help out. In fact, she told the others that they hadn't paid for a deposit and wouldn't be getting their money back. She was surprisingly unreal but that was it. No one got back their deposits. Many people are scammers, even this one, who looked like a nice old lady.

Danny and I were homeless, and Roger's mother and dad were coming over. What else happened that night? Well, there was a homeless man on the street, and some gang member took a sledge hammer and ran it through the homeless man's head and killed him. The place was gone mad with attacks.

I really did not like hospitals myself nor could I relax in them, and I had the whole world on my shoulders then. My life was to be in Australia, and it was all falling asunder on me, and I couldn't get out of it all. Each day we went to the hospital to see Roger, and he was in a coma. His parents came over, and there was a priest there. Danny and I were skeptical of the priest at first, but it was a blessing that he was there. He said that Roger's parents could stay at his place. It really was a blessing that the priest was there; over all my years of really disliking priests, I understood that even the church, which could hold such low members like child molesters, also had the balance of that; there were a few good saints in there too. There was no real definite in much, only that each group holds the good and bad, and it's all relative. So this priest let Roger's mother and father stay with him.

After a week of this, Danny and I decided to get out of Sydney, as there was nothing we could do. We told the others that we were going up to Byron Bay for a few days, as Danny was on his holiday. We drove off up the coast to Byron Bay. Danny was a gent and a very positive person. He was the balance that we needed to balance out my negative thinking. He thought in terms of positive happenings and events, and he just saw the best in everything and everyone. He was a great laugh. I was sorry that he was stuck with me, my energy in my low times. He was snapping me out of it, wakening me up and giving me things to laugh about. He was a classic; between this holiday and giving me the Kirribilli address, what more could a mate ask for?

I put off my own problems and began worrying about Roger. I previously thought that I just wanted to die, as I just didn't want to live anymore, and then I realised that I would need to look after Roger if he was okay, and this was what I must do till everything was okay again.

One day, I got a call from Roger; he left a message on my voice mail.

He said, "D.J., I'm okay now, I woke up and the doctors reckon I'm okay. I just have damaged my brain, and I'll have to learn how to walk and talk again. Where are you? Come on back down to me."

I was nearly crying as I listened to Roger's message. I told Danny that we all should just go back to Ireland with him, as nothing was working out. I had applied for residency, but it failed, as the papers got delayed somewhere.

We drove back down to Sydney and went to the hospital again. A few days later, we all met up with Sarah and the rest of our crew, and after we went to the hospital together, we went outside and had a chat. I was doing nightshift work at the time and spending most of the day with Roger. Sarah looked at me and said, "You're going to fall asleep in your job tonight; when did you last sleep?"

I said, "I don't know, four days ago. I'll be fine."

I worked all night, the job was indoors with lights all around, and it was a lot like being in the hospital for me. The whole lot of it was filling me up with a heated, intense, negative energy. I had a lifetime struggle getting away from places that bleeped me, just so I could feel normal and have fun, only to end back up in that situation again.

Danny and I were walking across Darling Harbour, and he said, "Let's go to the market and get some pints, and then we'll call up to Roger in the hospital."

Whilst we were walking, I went into my thinking about all the problems; it was a spiral created in my mind, and just one thought could trigger it off. There I was, rushing through a spiral in my mind that my mind was trained to do over all the years. I just collapsed on the ground and laughed at myself as to how my own thoughts had such an effect on my ability to even walk. There was nothing in front of me stopping me from walking; it was just the state of mind that had me like that. What I was thinking in my mind was not really in my reality at that moment and, therefore, not really real, but to me it was. All that spiral of thoughts took me off my feet, and I was on the ground, laughing at Danny and hoping the ground would open up and swallow me whole. A mind can be trained in any way, but for me it was worry, which was a wasted energy really. But yes, of course I had to take it to its peak to fully understand it and, I suppose, to write about it.

After a while, Danny left and went home to Ireland. But before he did, he was in the hospital with Roger, and we saw how well he was getting looked after. Roger was getting the finest of dinners; mind you, he couldn't eat it, so Danny ate it himself, Danny asked the nurses if I could get a bed there, as I was homeless. The nurses said that I had to be injured, and I said that could be arranged. Getting a bed in the hospital and getting looked after by nurses was a pretty good idea, apart from all that energy I would be taking in.

On one of Danny's last nights, Roger wanted to go for a walk around the area; the doctors said it was okay but he couldn't go drinking with us. I said no problem, and Danny said that we would look after him. When we got outside, Roger said he wanted a drink. I brought him off on the wrong direction, so we could just have a walk.

He said, "D.J., I'm your mate, and I have been stuck in that place for two weeks. I hate the food, I hate the place, and I need just one drink. It's a nightmare in there."

I looked at Roger and thought that if I was stuck in there, surely I would go mad and need to be out, so my heart went out for Roger. We went for a drink, and I just stood beside Roger the whole time, so he wouldn't get a bump off someone or so that I was ready if he needed anything. His skull had been put back in place with a few pins and stitches, and it was very delicate. So we had one drink and went back to the hospital. Roger's parents were at the front door of the hospital and told us that the police were out looking for us, going from pub to pub up Oxford Street. We had gone to Kings Cross, which was the opposite direction. So we were in the bad books for a little while.

I really tried to get my head around the reason why Roger had been attacked, but I couldn't link it with anything. I thought about energy attracting and wondered if Roger's anger or hurt inside himself had attracted the attacker, but I couldn't pinpoint the reason. The incident was never going to leave my mind until I nailed it.

KINGS CROSS

Lora was still onto me about sharing an accommodation, and when she rang me to suggest that we get a place together, I said, "Okay."

Lora said, "Really? I just didn't think you would, but that's great. I'll look for a place."

She began looking at places; both of us were homeless as well as mad, insane perhaps, crazed with worried minds. She couldn't find any place, but I went to look at the apartment where Chris had stayed with his girlfriend before. I had been there and they were nice apartments. It was in Kings Cross, which was a five-minute walk to Roger's place. My job was to stay sane, fix Roger up and help him to learn how to walk and all the rest, and set up a life for myself in Australia, plus work every day to have money to pay the bills.

I needed a place that was pretty much away from people. I was unable to live in a shared accommodation, and there was no attempt of me moving into a place with backpackers, where there are six people in a room in a crammed building. I was full of emotional energy, and this would be felt by people in a backpack place, thus causing problems in my life. I needed someplace where I could try and get my lost mind together instead of having it more and more lost in a building full of people. I also needed someplace where I could keep my van off the streets, as the registration was running out on it, and the way I was creating my life at these times, I would have gotten stopped and locked up and lost my van. I was almost afraid of driving, as my mind was manifested with disasters and I was just looking for an excuse that it was time for me to leave the game of life. I could see no future, and the end of the road was coming, for I had no dream to follow.

We took the apartment; it had an underground car park there, plus the registration building was across the road so I could renew the van's registration. I was working in different places and was assigned a job at a private house in Ryde. The morning I was told to go there to work, Roger was sent to a hospital in Ryde. It was an hour's travel away from where we were. Roger was to stay there for a few months to get brain scans done and all the rest. He was basically to be kept in an institution until they decided to let him go. Roger knew this and I did too. The house where I was working was around the corner; I was to do some timber decking and a few things. When I arrived, I went to a different house; two men at the door called out to me and asked if I had a hard session the night before, but I explained that I didn't have a drink at all. They looked at me strangely, as what could have me looking like I was hung over and stressed? The answer was I was completely worried and lost in my own mind.

I found the right house, and the man of the house explained to me that he had a brain tumour and did not have long to live. He was a gent of a character and told me that he just wanted me to fix the house up so his wife could sell it if she wished. They had a daughter between them, and it was very sad. I had a chat with him each day. I didn't say much but listened to all he was going through. I had nothing to say really, only that my friend was in the hospital up the road in the same condition. He was telling me about the things that were happening while the tumor was taking over. He was getting more tired, and his speech was getting bad; he couldn't say words properly. He loved listening to classical music while he napped on the couch. He was telling me that the only real sad part about it was that his daughter would grow up without a father. I wanted to tell him, "If you could have my life, I would give it to you, as I am unable to live my life."

In the evening, I would go see Roger, who was around the corner, and see how he was getting on. I met many patients in there, and nearly all of them had been in attacks or accidents that involved a head injury. Some of the people had been in there for years and never snapped out of it. I looked at one lad and figured that could be me sometime if I keep living this life. Roger wanted to get out of the place, and they were keeping an eye on him when I arrived, as he had escaped from the hospital and they found him up at the shops.

I explained to Roger to just get the tests done and then I'd get him out of there. Roger was sticking it out for the week, and I was down there each day after work. This went on for a while, and each evening I went back to Lora and my new apartment. She and I were just friends, issues had us magnetised together, and when I asked life for help, Lora was what I got. Life had plans for us.

Roger's parents had gone back home, and I told them that I would look after him.

I would get the bus each morning from the city. It was all a nightmare for me, really. Because of the frame of mind that I was in, I was resisting my outer world. I was tearing myself apart, hoping that I was dead. I had no hope, I had no dream, I was just existing here, magnetised to these circumstances. I hated my life and my world and who I was and where I was. The more heated energy I took in from all of these situations, like the buses, the hospital, the jobs, the apartment with Lora and her energy, the more of this I took in, the more it affected my mind and the more negative I became, the more sad and depressed I became. With all this energy, my mind became crazed with thoughts. These thoughts changed my energy in motion to negativity; it was a vicious cycle with no light at the end of any tunnel.

Kings Cross was full of mad people, and I was stuck in one big collective consciousness. I was constantly getting burnt out from the apartment with the energy, to the bus with the confined space, the people and lights. I couldn't stay awake on the bus and needed the bus driver to chuck me out at my stop, as that was the only way I could deal with this. Everything seemed to bring this energy in me to the surface and add to it on a constant basis.

I bought a lotto ticket from the shop and settled with myself that if I didn't win, there was no hope for me. I would go to work, not that I really knew what I was doing as a carpenter any more. I didn't even care to listen to the radio anymore, and that really just showed how bad I was getting. But the man of the house where I was working gave me a radio and insisted that I listen to it. All I was attracting was this sadness in my world, even on the radio. One day, a song was playing on the radio that represented my feelings, story, life, and moment: "Behind Blue Eyes."

I went back to see Roger in the hospital, and the whole place was bleeping me and Roger up. He had lost so much weight and looked so frail and sick whilst in there. We both weren't eating, and both our minds were a little bleeped up at this moment. He asked me to do something, and asked the nurses if they could let him out.

The nurse and I had a chat, and she said, "Has your friend Roger always been like this?" She was concerned about his loss of appetite and how much weight he had lost.

I said, "Yes, he's back to normal; he is always giving out and is a grouch. You got to let him out, this place is destroying him. He will start eating when he is out of here; he'll be brand new in no time."

The nurse said, "So he is always in bad form? We thought he was just like that since the attack. But if he is always like that, maybe he is coming along fine. We'll do a few more tests on him and then let him out."

I walked around and stopped at lottery shops and bought tickets. I figured if someone was looking after me, surely they could just let me win some money, but no such luck ever came. I kept playing each week, and all I was living for was to win the lotto, but it never happened.

You'll never get what you want . . . for the very wanting act pushes it away. I thought I needed it, but I must not have really needed it, must have really needed something else, and that was coming.

KINGS CROSS—THE END OF TIME

What I was doing was, I was leaving one place where I was staying, which was making me very uneasy and filling me up with energy, and walking through Kings Cross, where I wanted to live, as I would be close to Roger. That place was also making me feel uneasy, trapped in the little collective consciousness and the energy of the place. Then I was walking down to get the train, and all the circumstances were making me feel terrible. Trapped energy—my own negative energy was unable to be kept down, and when it was brought to attention, I was losing my mind. When I'm in this situation too long, I cough up blood. Too much energy in me is getting brought to attention. If I wasn't on the train, I was on the bus. It was too much; I had to close my eyes and go to sleep or search for peace of mind to slow down my crazed mind from spinning its endless thoughts, fuelled by the energy in me. Then I walked to work, on a job where I was just completely bleeped up and unable to do simple tasks, but still I somehow managed to pull it off that I was kind of okay. Then I would leave work and go to the hospital. I really disliked hospitals due to how the florescent lights pulled my energy to attention, also giving me more unnatural energy, hence my sensitive nature. Throughout my life, I made choices to bleed away without going to the hospital after an accident, even if I needed stitches, because the static energy and lights really bleeped me up and filled me up with the most unpleasant energy.

One day, I saw Roger and he said to me, "D.J., I know you're guilty for something, I just don't know what it is yet."

So I looked guilty; not surprising, as I constantly had this negative energy addressing me. I wished I were dead or free of all the negative energy attracted to me that was really bleeping me up. There was no way that I could look sane, relaxed, or comfortable, thus making me look guilty to the one person I was helping so much. Then after all that, I was back on the bus and then I was back at the apartment with Lora, who was full of negativity from worry and other issues. I did this for a long time; I was strong but it was all killing me. I was dying, mentally, emotionally, physically, and spirituality. I sure was dying. There was no timeout, there was no balancing the energy, there was just all of this that was just so bad for me and my nature. I was hoping to have a fatal accident at work, and that was my constant thought at this time. I wanted to say to the man of the house, "If I could give you my life, I would give it to you and take your place no problem. I would be delighted for someone to make use of my life and not wish it was over like me."

After a couple of weeks, the man of the house where I was working died, and Roger got released from the institution. The three of us were on this same vibration; none of us could eat and we were all dying. Then the man died, Roger got released, but I stayed in my mental energy issue institution. Around this time, I was walking around Kings Cross, and there was a mental home up the road. I walked past it and thought about signing myself into it. I thought to myself, *If I was in there, I could stay alive, but where would my family think I was gone to? If they came over, it was game over for me.* I then figured that I could work out each of the people in there, help them, and there would be no one left but me. It's my nature to help others, but I can't help myself. I brought myself to the realisation that I was not mental home material. I was a player of the best game in town. There's a thin line between genius and insanity down here on earth, but I was not insane. I just needed to change all I was doing, needed to get out of the energy bubble, and needed some freedom.

This state of mind can wreck your head; my hair and teeth started falling out. I was sick with blood from my ulcer, and all the symptoms were to the point where to die was the only freedom. I was lost in my own mind of worry. Given my model of the world, I was in hell, thinking the worst-case outcome of events in every situation, as hell is in the mind and heaven is in the soul. I spent a lot of my thinking just planning my own suicide, and other times I planned on fixing my life up.

When Roger got out, he didn't want to stay in my place in Kings Cross, as he felt the whole area was so dangerous. So he got a place in a hostel over a pub in Bondi called the Royal, and he was happy there for a while. Sometimes he talked about wanting to go home, but I would tell him, "It's terrible at home, you can't even get a girl there. We will be sound, Roger, as all the bad is over with."

I worked on different jobs and had to take the train to a few of them. I was thinking about how I would get through the day, and all my thoughts were about that. When I woke up in the apartment, I looked at myself while putting on my trousers, and I was like a three-year-old child one particular morning, unable to do much at all. Lora was good in many ways, but she was worried a lot of the time; she said it was because of me and the amount of blood that I was coughing up every few days, which could seem believable, but she was just like that any way all her life really. She couldn't stand getting on buses and would walk two hours to work instead of getting the bus. She got a job around the corner, cleaning up some premises. But the energy off Lora was fuelling me also. I needed my own place, just to recharge my batteries, and I did not have that. There was no recharge for me at all; it was just plenty of discharges for me. I was gone past the stage of help and couldn't do much for myself. I needed to get away from everyone and everything, but I had nowhere else to go to really. I couldn't just pack up and leave Lora there.

I was really worried and rang my brother for a chat. I told Jonsey that I might come home, as I couldn't seem to make it over here. He said, "Don't come home, whatever you do. It is crap at home, nothing is happening. Home's not a good idea, bro."

After I hung up, Lora walked over to me, and she was her worried self. I looked at her and realised that she was just like the way I was carrying on. She was the reflection of me. All the worrying and ringing Jonsey and all the rest, it was my level of energy that was attracting

Lora. We were just the same, and I was making a choice here. I was not going to be like this, I could see myself in Lora, and I chose differently. I was not going to contact people because I was worried; somehow I was going to beat this. I just had to get myself together.

I went walking in Sydney with Lora, and she asked me how was I feeling. I said, "Do you see that building over there? Well, to be honest in this moment, I would love to just get up to the top of it and throw myself off it."

I was starting to see that Lora's energy was connected with mine, and I was taking in all this insecurity energy and energy issues, and this was how I was feeling. If I walked down the street on my own, I felt quite okay, considering. The worried mind was one thing, it was the mind and how I was living in worry. But the feeling was a sort of numbness at these times, and it was enhanced from Lora's energy. The whole time I didn't want to say anything to Lora, but I was thinking to myself that she was trying to help me out and I couldn't hurt her feelings, but she was very insecure, and her vibration energy was burning me out, making me feel the same, and I just wanted to throw myself off a building. I was the same but I was feeling double of this. Once I got away from Lora, I felt I was okay, as good as could be expected anyways. I appreciated Lora's concern for me and wanted her to be happy in Australia and for her to meet up with her friends and all the rest, but she just wouldn't do that at all. It was like she was stuck to me like a magnet. We were a worried ball of insecure energy. It was the attraction that brought us together. I only gave in and got a place together when I was at that level of energy. We needed each other, I think; she was there to help, yes, but also she was intensifying my energy. It was not her fault; it was my sensitive nature, and I was in some mess really. I was dying on all levels; I was a dying man.

It was coming up to Christmas. Each and every morning I woke up with the thought of, *I'm still alive in this life and this mind,* and I would cough up blood each and every morning. My mind was killing me. My mind was connected to the emotion in me and all that I was taking in. My mind and energy could not be separated, and both were killing me; I had internal bleeding on a constant basis. Lora was going mad in the apartment because she was just doing that while I was around. She was doing so because I told her to go out with her own friends over Christmas or even go with my friends but to leave me alone. This was driving her mad, as she wanted the two of us to spend Christmas together. She started throwing things around the apartment. I didn't want any memories of Lora and me at Christmas, as the feeling was not a Christmas feeling at all. I went into the bathroom and filled up the bath. I got into the bath and sat there, thinking. I played a CD, and it was the soundtrack from the film *City of Angels.*

As I was having a bath, I decided to get my options together. I realised that I just couldn't go home, as I would be walking into my own grave as a complete failure to my life's path. Not that anyone would know, but I would know, and I just couldn't do that to myself. I reflected back upon everything in my life. I was searching for a good memory to help get myself out of the frame of mind I was in. My thoughts were just all bad and all negative, worry really. I thought of many things, but all I could think of were things that ended in a disaster, as this was the frame of mind I was in, and this was all I was attracting mentally. I could not for the life of me recall anything that worked in my life, anything that didn't end in a disaster. Thoughts are energy, and I couldn't recall one positive good memory; I just couldn't remember any, at least any that were really important to me. I was carrying all that baggage around with me, as nothing was cleaned up, left behind, it was all energy that was attached to me, that all came with me.

Lora went a bit mad in the apartment, as her mind was racing due to her own problems and insecurities. She was thinking in her own mind that she and I would at least be sister and brother forever and not split up, but I told her that I didn't want to spend Christmas with her. She was very frustrated perhaps, and she broke a thing or two in the apartment, but I didn't care as I didn't have to look at her, but it created a great strong negative energy. I lay there in the bath and was numb, feeling the negative, frustrated, stressed, insecure energy that I was always dodging from Lora, but perhaps this time I helped to flare it up, and I couldn't cope with it at all. It took over my energy, and I could feel it all, it was entering into me—my mind was about to just go into pure lost negativity. I needed to get out and at a rapid pace.

I figured that I would quickly do myself in and reckoned that whatever frame of mind I would leave my body in, I would be like that on the far side. I needed just to find peace of mind before I left. I plugged in the hair dryer and thought there was no way I could continue on. A song came on the CD, U2 was singing, "If God will send his angels." Just there, I found peace of mind for a split moment in that song and dropped the hair dryer into the bath. I was ready to go, as I had absolutely no other choice at that moment. I gave up on all of my struggling life. I just had enough.

But I didn't die, and then I got a fright where I came out of my mind. I became separate from this crazed mind fuelled by negative energy for a moment. I found something and wanted more of that something. I drove myself to the point of self-destruction. I got out of the bath, and all the energy was still there. So I wanted to get the toaster and have another go, but Lora was too full on, and I decided to leave it to another time. Lora then came into the bathroom and asked what was wrong with her hair dryer.

I said, "I plugged it in and dropped it in the bath."

She was freaking out, but I was hoping that she would see what she was doing to me and stop doing it. But no such luck there. I asked for the hair dryer and shook the water out of it; amazingly, it still worked.

I got changed and realised that I needed to get out of the apartment to try to understand that peaceful something that I found. All of my worries were pretty much going away, as there was a shock on my mind. It was a frame of mind that had me there. Then I looked at it as a sickness that I had; I was a sick man. Then after that stunt, I let go of many worries and saw that it was Lora's energy that was bleeping me up. So when Lora shut the bathroom door in one of her tempers, I snuck out the door and left. Lora liked having a big drama scene more so than wanting to have time out or be on her own at all.

I walked down the road and went to the pub; I started to become myself again. Who was I? That was a good question, but I started to be in the present moment a bit more. There was a band playing music in the pub, and I sat down on a chair, feeling at one with my environment, a feeling so distantly familiar. I felt relaxed, peaceful, and more aware of my nice friendly environment. I began to analyse what the bleep had been happening, and I just looked at the whole lot as if it were Lora that had me feeling that way. It was all to do with the energy from her. I had woken up from the imprisoned mind that I had been held captive in.

I walked up to the bar and saw a girl that I thought I knew. She had her back to me as I looked in the mirror in front of us, and it was

Lea from Nth Coast. I walked to the end of the pub, as I wanted to surprise her. She then got up to use the bathroom, and as she walked in my direction, I stepped in her way and said, "Hello there."

She jumped at first, and then she burst out laughing and gave me a hug. Lea and I had a few great sessions, and she was great fun. She had gone out with Danny years ago, and that was how I knew her. She said, "I just arrived here two hours ago and knew you were somewhere over here. I was just saying to my boyfriend to get your number off Danny at home so I could get ahold of you. How the hell are you?"

I said, "Well, isn't that just something? I'm great, Roger's out of hospital, and friends are scattered all over the place. It's great to see you." So I met her boyfriend Glen, and he was a gent. This night it was all changing for me.

We all planned to have a Christmas session together, which I thought would be good. Lea wanted to know who I was living with. I brought Lora out to meet the crew another night, and she was getting on well with them. I told Lora to contact them any time and go out for drinks, as they were all very nice and wanted to get to know her. But Lora really wouldn't let me do my own thing. She said she was concerned for me, but when I explained that I was fine and that I wanted to do my own thing for Christmas, there were problems. There was no right or wrong. Perhaps one could think that I was a bleeper to want to get away from Lora, but given my nature and these circumstances, I had to. I had to stay sane and had to keep the energy body in me down and not fuel my mind with crazed thoughts. I had to be free. This became an impossible task. I tried to get away from Lora, and each time I did, I would drive her energy wild, which in turn became a part of my energy. I was imprisoned in my mind again, living in a world of crazed, spinning thoughts. I realised over that Christmas that I must finish myself off.

BRIDGE CLIMB

When it came to New Year's Eve, I got away from everyone and walked down to the Sydney Harbour Bridge. I was fuelled with negativity again and accepted the fact that I was happy enough doing myself in. So in this heated moment, I reckoned that I should climb the Harbour

Bridge with the flag of Ireland I had with me; I thought if I got to the top when the fireworks were going off, I would be on television for all my friends everywhere to see. At this point I hoped that I would be blown to kingdom come or else that I would fall off; either way, I would wake up dead somewhere and would have gone out with a spark.

That was the plan, so off I went. You may think I was a madman at this stage, but you have to understand that if you were in my mind, it was a great plan, as I just had to die. There were no other options that I could possibly think of. There was to be no way out, and there was no way that I could get out of life, alive. I walked down to the base of the bridge, and it was a good 150 feet up to the roadway and the same again to the top of the bridge. At this stage, I had lost a lot of weight and was nowhere near as strong as I used to be, but I was going for it. I started climbing the bridge. I got up two pipes all the way and just pulled myself up those 150 feet. When I got to the top, I was out of breath. I then took a breather and started going crossways to get to underneath the bridge before I could climb over the barbed wire and start the climb again.

There I was, all on my own, and I was up a great height over the water. I was thinking that if there really was someone looking after me, like the Don perhaps, that he would just appear in front of me and stop this, but that didn't happen. There was a police boat in the water, and they were shining their big spotlight up at me; they were moving it around, and I didn't think that they could see me, but I was in a haze of madness in my mind. I climbed up and was hanging on the side of the fence on the bridge; up I went and over the barbed wire.

There I was on the foot part of the bridge, getting ready for my second and final half of the bridge climb. Then there were security lads way down at the end, and they started running up. They were a long way away, but I looked over the edge and saw the police boat shining the torch at me. I started to wake up to reality, and the reality was that I was on the bridge and a lot of people seemed to know I was. I ran across to the far side of the road, but there were a bunch of fire department lads climbing there. I couldn't believe it and was thinking, how many people are climbing this bridge? But it was only me, and I was looking at all the people. I ran back across the road and hid behind a power box. My heart began racing, and I started to wake up; I became more in the moment instead of in my racing mind. After I took a breather and woke up, I realised that I was in trouble and thought about what my choices were now. As I came to my senses, I realised that I didn't really want to die, and what was more important than not wanting to die was to not get caught by all these people, as I could just kiss my residence good-bye. I stood up and looked to my left, and there was the police boat. I looked to my right, and lads were climbing the bridge and had just gotten over the side to get me. Then I looked behind me, and the security lads were catching up on me. I had only one option, and that was to run to the other end of the bridge. I figured if I went to climb it, the lads would catch up on me anyway, and all of it wouldn't be the perfect leave-in-a-spark TV show. So I ran, and a heap of people were running after me. I couldn't believe the situation I was in, and Lora didn't even know with her mad carrying on how she was fuelling my mind with these crazed thoughts.

I ran and ran, and as I was coming to the other side of the bridge, there were a set of steps leading back down to the area known as the Rocks. There were two security guards there at the entrance to the steps. When they saw me running towards them and a whole load of characters running after me, they too ran towards me. Now this was it. I had put myself in a pickle; what was I to do? I quickly observed my choices and reflected on my intentions. So whilst running I came to the conclusion that all these people running after me were making me feel like I really wanted to live now. If I stopped running and they caught me, I was practically as good as dead anyway, or even worse, as it would be a slow painful death over the years to follow. Lads were running towards me, behind me, and beside me, and there was a wall on my left-hand side. I saw a tree that was a far distance from the bridge, but it was an option. It was my only option, and I had to make a dive for it and pray that I could manage to stay on it. I quickly summed up the possibilities, and one was, I was facing fear itself. Another was, if I miss the jump and fall to my death, at least it would all be over; another was, what if I make this jump? Wouldn't that be something, and who in their right mind would chance it after me?

As I jumped up onto the wall, I was surrounded by all the people who had been chasing me. I didn't even blink or stop for a split second; I jumped from the Harbour Bridge, which is 150 feet high, to the tree. I made it and I hugged that tree with all the love and fear I had. I wrapped my legs and arms around it and was intensely in the present moment. I got such a fright whilst I was in midair; I think my heart missed a few beats, but it was a leap of faith. I slid all the way down this great big tree. I came down it at good speed and landed on my feet and fell over. I then ran towards the Rocks, which were just in front of me; there were over a million people there, and I could get lost in the crowd.

So what happened? Well, I ran into the crowd, and a bloke took the corner from behind the pub, and I bumped straight into him. I looked at him and he looked at me. It was Roger! What are the chances of that?

He said, "D.J., what are you doing? You told me you would be at McGuire's, and you're in the wrong place; what are you running for?"

I pointed up to the bridge and said, "Look." There were a whole load of people up there, looking down at me, and I was correct in my thinking: none of them followed me in my jump. It was far too risky to chance it for any sane-minded person. I gave my Ireland flag to Roger and said, "You hold that, and I'm a free man."

Roger went wild when he saw all the people who had been chasing me. I told him, "I jumped off that bridge. I climbed it to get on the TV for all the crew at home with the Ireland flag, but I didn't quite make it all the way."

As we were standing there, Roger's phone rang and he said, "Sorry D.J., I wonder who this is."

It was the crew at home from Nth Coast, our friends, and they were saying, "So it must be nearly fireworks time over there for you and D.J. How are you getting on?"

Roger said, "You won't believe what just happened . . ."

After a while, Lora turned up on the scene and asked me what I had done. I told her what I did, as I was hoping that she would understand that I couldn't take any more. She asked me why I ran off on her and left her back there, and I explained, "It is the energy that I'm getting off you; it's killing me and driving my mind wild. I have to get a break from you. Why won't you just stay with your friends? Can you not see what you're doing to me?"

Lora hung around for a while and wanted to get pictures of us all together, but I wouldn't stand next to her in any of them, as I didn't want those memories, nor did I want memories of that frame of mind, which I felt was degrading myself in that style. That wasn't me, I was stronger than that. Lora and I had a bit of a disagreement, and then she had a tantrum and went home. I again was filled up with that energy, and I couldn't meet up with the other friends the way I was. I had to lie down in the park and close my eyes for a short while, just to search for peace of mind and relax my own energy. The problem in my life became Lora, but I saw her as a nice person with issues like me. I really didn't want to hurt her feelings. After I found peace of mind, I walked into a pub off the road, away from all the people. I texted my mates to see where they were, and they all met me in the pub. We had a great laugh, and that was how I wanted my New Year's to be: with good mates, nice vibes, and having fun. I didn't mention anything about what happened, and I guess I just moved from one experience to the next.

Later that night, I fell asleep on a park bench, and there was a man nearby who had made these signs himself that read "We love it," "That's why we do it, we love it all," "We love the drama, the excitement, the fear of survival," and "Don't deny it all for we love it all or why else would we all do it?"

He had some very valid points on his signs, but I reckon only people like me who have broken free from mind and are awake in subconscious mind could actually comprehend it. I fell asleep, and when I woke up, one of the man's signs was over my face, protecting me from the sun. The man had put it there and off he went. He was a silent preacher and had a heart of gold. There was hope in my life. It was almost like I found a new energy in me, and this was opening up a world of hope and possibilities.

I went back to the apartment, and when I looked in the mirror, I saw a grey patch of hair over my right ear. A full on grey patch of hair; I couldn't believe it. I heard many times before about people getting a grey streak through their hair from a fright, but it wasn't that I disbelieved this, it was more to do with, how could that really be true? I tell you now, it is true, a grey patch of hair at my age, shocking. Getting old for me was more frightening than taking my own life.

D.J.—LIVING OUT MY CHAPTER

There was another area where I could hang around with some friends, and this I did when I was well again. I previously met another lad named D.J., and he was over in this area. He was from the same area as me in Ireland and had the same name as me. I asked him how he got on for New Year's, and he explained that his mate was having a leak down at the Rocks on New Year's night and someone pushed him into the harbour. He reckoned that that was a bit much and asked me what I had gotten up to. I told him that I had climbed the bridge and that it was probably on the news. He said, "I thought I had a mad night but you take the biscuit; take care, man, I'll talk to you again."

So shortly after this, D.J. went back to Ireland; he hired out a bed and breakfast and got a rope, a box of sleeping pills, and a Stanley knife. He hung himself from a rafter, slit both his wrists, and swallowed the tablets. It was his second or third attempt to do himself in. D.J. and I were very connected. It was crazy for me. I realised that we were connected and that I was D.J., we were both on the same experience, and the story just went two different ways. D.J. went home and killed himself. But I did the leap of faith and a few other things that moved me up a notch in vibration and onto another awareness about life. D.J. died; it was just like he was living out my chapter, my choice, but it was his; a strong connection, I think.

I then had the perspective to see and hear what people would say about that, as if he was me, only I was me, watching and listening to what the others would be saying about me. Skipper, one of my mates, from the Canary Island holiday, who I didn't particularly have much time for anymore, said, "D.J. was a very selfish person to do that."

I got angry over this statement and said, "What would be the amount of torturing pain one could receive before it's not called a selfish act?"

Skipper said, "I just think, no matter what, that it is a selfish act to do."

I said, "You haven't got a clue what someone goes through for so long before they can finally give up and actually do themselves in; you just have not a clue."

I was on the edge a lot, but I was listening to others. Another friend who was there didn't say much, only that poor D.J. must have had a few problems. Some of D.J.'s mates went home for the funeral. They said that he had tried to commit suicide before but someone had rung him as he was going to do it. It was freaky; it was just like a whole load of people talking about me, but I was there to listen to them all.

I didn't say anything about me and just watched to see all that happened, as if it was me. What a connection really, D.J. And D.J.

MOVING FROM THE AREA

I realised that I was living off these people's energy everywhere I was going, and I so desperately needed positive energy or just to be on my own to make my own energy or even let my own energy get hold of me. I needed to be me. The whole place was getting me down, I could see it all so clearly now and feel it all so clearly. My mind was thinking clearly again but on a new level now, and this entire energy intake was becoming so clear. So I told Lora that I was moving out of the apartment, as it was just too expensive and it was pointless living there. I needed out, as I was changing myself. I needed to leave all those memories and madness behind and start again in a fresh place. I left my worries behind me and was becoming a new man. Different friends of mine lived in different places, and each said that I could stay at their place. So I told Roger about this, and Lora and Roger and I went around to look at a few places. I didn't mind where we lived or if we all split up, but I was there for each of them to make their choice first. Roger stayed where he was, and finally Lora picked one of my friends' places that was far away from the city.

HELPING STILL

I found a skilled company that would sponsor me as a carpenter. I organised it all and went for the appointment and met up with a solicitor. I still tried to help Lora out but felt that I couldn't be around her too much. I told her that I was getting sponsored and that she too could get sponsored if we pretended that we were a couple. I could see that she was like the old version of me, and I wanted to help her, but I really couldn't let her bring me back to that old cycle again. I was a nice guy, I had a heart, I cared, but even after attempting suicide (twice) and killing the imprisonment of my crazed, fuelled-with-energy mind, the worry energy was still there from Lora. It was time to say, "Enough is enough."

I had to do a trial for thirty days, and then I'd be in. My friend Chen took a few pictures of Lora and I in the van and outside the house and all the rest, and we filled out the forms and sent them in. My one-year visa was to be finished by the first of March, and this was January heading into February. Things needed to happen at a fast pace. I started working at the airport, and it was all right. I was able to get Lora and myself four-year sponsorships. Lora was to have the best end of it, as she could work anywhere in Australia. I had to work for my company, and they really were not paying much money at all. I was getting $550 a week some weeks. It was extremely hard to survive on, between lunch and petrol and sponsorship. Lora paid for half of the sponsorship, which was her part, so we both helped out in that category.

LORA AND I

The truth of the matter is, we attracted each other, like energy attracts.

It was only when I was at Lora's level of energy that life magnetised us together. We had issues with ourselves, and that's how it works. We were drawn to each other for us both to work through our own issues together. That's what it is about, and that's why people are drawn to us; we are constantly evolving, changing, growing up. But were working through our own difficulties, and whilst doing so, we attracted the like energy of others. Like a group of people with the same interests or problems or goals; it's all like energy attraction. There are just an infinite amount of energy levels, but once we're on the note of energy and that it really is there and really does exist, then we're halfway there to understanding the game.

But with my nature and Lora's energy, I was feeling all she was feeling, and I was so insecure and all the rest; it wasn't really me, as I had my spiritual experience before, and that was my security. But all that I was getting from Lora, I didn't say much. I only did actions, threatening my own life, and then shared what I did with Lora, hoping she would stop what she was doing to me, but she really had no idea what she was doing to me. My philosophy was, *Whatever is meant to be, just go with it, D.J.*

Then, of course, she was more worried from all that I was doing, and it was a snowball effect of worry and bad energy and insecurity. This was something that I wanted to stop, but it got so much greater. I went jogging a few times around the area to try and help myself. Lora wanted to go jogging with me, but I would just leave without saying anything. So from Lora's perspective, I didn't wish to be around her anymore, and from my perspective, I had to get away from her, as it was her energy that was bleeping me up. I needed to be away; I had to fight for survival. I asked her if I got her the four years, would she live her own life herself and leave me to live mine? Eventually she agreed, but I think that instead, she went home.

I should have explained to Lora what was happening. But it was only after she was gone that I clearly understood what was happening. I thanked Lora for being there; that was the truth of the situation. I was torturing myself mentally for a long time, and even though I fought to say alive for my family's sake, and my friends were on my mind, I needed someone to push me over the edge, and that was where the gratitude was, as in that I had found something. I found me in all the madness out there, I found myself. Thank you.

During that chapter in my life, I lost 2.5 stone in weight, I got a patch of grey hair on my head, and I coughed up half a litre of blood nearly every day in the month of December, all because of negative energy. The lyrics of the Reef song explained this chapter so clearly: "You cannot hide from what's inside."

Between losing sight of my future, turning my back on the only goal that got me through life, losing all faith in the game, resurrecting the negative energy in me, searching in my mind for an answer that cannot be found, and threatening to do myself in on a constant basis, I found something. You see, I was searching for something in life, something that gave some fulfillment as opposed to living in the mind, constantly trying to dodge the negative energy in order to have some sort of clear mind. I was searching for a way of being—not a way of survival. I was looking for something that cannot be found by the mind's thinking, as it was incomprehensible for the mind. I refused to waste twenty years chancing a promised fulfillment by the mind that would never arrive, just like tomorrow will always stay tomorrow. After I worked out many things in life and life's illusions, I came to a very tricky illusion that just didn't add up, as I could see that if I continued on, I would get played by my mind, where there was no point of satisfaction. My mind became tortured, as I couldn't work out the answer that was deeper than the mind's understanding. I could not run forever, and my mentor was right when he said, "You are running from yourself, D.J."

My mind started to short circuit, and my thoughts started to freeze after my many attempts trying to kill it. And in doing so, I found something—this game will go on!

CHAPTER NINE

Time for a Change

Once Lora left, I went down to the supermarket every day and got myself dinner. I got potatoes and chicken and steak. I cooked dinner for myself each evening, as I was thin from that last chapter in my life, when I couldn't eat because of all that energy. I got a few night shift jobs with my old company, who were always there to help me out. I would work at my sponsorship job from 7:00 a.m. till 5:00 p.m., and all I could get was $550, but it had to be done. I then would drive home and get dinner, cook it up and eat it, and then start my night shift job from 10:00 p.m. till 5:00 a.m., working as a carpenter again. My rent was $320 a week, so I had to work and work. I still had a huge amount of energy in me, and it came to good use, as I was able to work all day and about four nights for a few weeks. I remember at one stage I worked for thirty-six hours straight; I liked the feeling of being relaxed then, as the energy was finally burnt out—my mind was at ease and it was a nice feeling.

I came to the conclusion then that it didn't matter how much work I did, I would still not have money behind me. Rent and van and petrol and registration, and there were always things that had to be paid. I tried it all for a while, but it wasn't working, and then I decided to change my thinking.

I needed a way out. I was working night and day; I had one Saturday night off, and it goes without saying I had to have a session with my buddy Chen. I needed a way where I didn't have to pay this amount of rent a week (I was paying for both Lora and me, and she was gone). I had fixed my body up; I was stronger now. I deserved a break. I deserved some fun, and it was about time I had a girlfriend. I just needed something to happen.

At my night shift job, there were a few other Irish lads. One of them said something in an accent that I hadn't heard around much. I copied his accent and mentioned a county that he was from.

He said, "Ha ha, what part of Ireland are you from? I know a lad who has an accent like yours, his name is Duke. I'm sure you would hardly know him."

I said, "I don't believe it; Duke is over here, really? He has a brother named Tomas, and they are from Nth Coast, Ireland I lived a mile away."

He said, "That's it, Nth Coast. He's a friend of yours, hey?"

I said, "I haven't seen Duke in about eight years, but yes, he is good friend. Can you get me his number?" So I told Roger about this story.

FRIENDS

I got Duke's mobile number and gave it to Roger. I told him, "Right, for the whole week, let's just text Duke and pretend that we are some girls that he met one drunken night. Abuse him and do lots of messing but don't let him know who it is; don't answer your phone unless you give it to one of the girls at the bar. We'll arrange to met him on Saturday night at the pub, and then we'll let him know who it is, okay?"

Roger said, "Sound, D.J."

He came up with a girl's name for himself and thought of all sorts of things to say. So we both texted Duke some amount of slop, and we were even sending the texts to each other to let each other know the slop we were sending and who's was funnier. This went on for the whole week, and then I texted Duke to say that I'd meet him in the pub on Saturday. Duke was sending texts to both of us and ringing both our phones, and when it came to Saturday, I picked Roger up and we drove to Coogee. At this stage, I think we had taken the messing and abuse too far, because Duke had turned his phone off and wouldn't answer it.

So I rang the lad that I got the number from; he had gone back to Ireland but had left his phone in the apartment. The lad who answered knew the lad who was staying in Duke's place, so I got his number. I rang him and asked him was Duke around. Duke got on the phone and said, "Who's this?"

I said, "It's Paul [a friend that we both knew], I'm in the Coogee Bay Hotel pub; why don't you come for a drink?"

Duke said, "Paul? Really? I thought you went back home with Sarah."

I said, "We were up the coast, and we broke up after a while. Sarah went home but I came back to Sydney."

Duke said, "I'll be right down; you're in the C.B.H., yes? Give me ten minutes."

So Roger and I got a drink and chilled out. I said to Roger, "Let's really wind this lad up and pretend that we haven't seen each other until tonight. Say that we didn't even know each other were over and just bumped into each other."

When Duke arrived, he saw Roger and me.

I started laughing and said, "Duke! What a pleasant surprise, my dear fellow."

Duke said, "D.J.! Oh my God, I haven't seen you in years, man; how are you? This is mad. You guys must be with Paul; are you?"

Roger said, "No, man, Paul went up the coast with Sarah, and then he went home, I think."

Duke said, "No way, Paul was just on the phone and said that Sarah is gone home and he came back down; he wanted to meet me here for a drink."

I said, "Paul hey? That's great, I haven't seen him in years."

Duke said, "How is your head, Roger? I heard all about it at home."

I said, "What happened to your head, Roger?"

Roger looked at Duke, who said, "D.J., were you not over here with him when he got attacked?"

I said, "No, I just met Roger here on the beach; what happened?"

So Roger went on to tell me about his attack, and we were playing it real cool.

Duke said, "Hey, let's go look for Paul; he must be around here somewhere." So we got up and went walking around, looking for Paul.

I was surprised Duke didn't cop it at that stage, but out came another classic from Roger. He said to Duke, "You know about Paul and his cross dressing now, don't you?"

Duke said, "What do you mean?"

Roger said, "Well, Sarah and Paul broke up because he kept wearing Sarah's clothes, and it kind of got out of hand."

Duke said, "What? Like underwear and that?"

Roger said, "No, well maybe, but dresses and all that."

So I said, "Right, lads, let's get back on track here. We're looking for Paul; he may be wearing a dress. Will he have a wig on, Roger?"

We were just laughing so much, and I was waiting for the point where the penny would drop for Duke. Then Duke took out his phone and turned it on and rang the number for one of the girls who were sending him text messages all week; he said, "Who owns this number?"

At that second, my phone rang in my pocket, and Duke said, "You two bleepers; I bet this other number is yours."

I said, "That was me on the phone."

Duke said, "You two have my head melted. So did you really only meet each other today? What's going on? Is Paul really around? You'll have to tell me the truth from the very start."

So we had a good session with many laughs, and Duke showed me his apartment. He explained that I could move in there, as he was leaving soon. The rent didn't have to be paid too much, since the landlord was on the missing list; some people were paying rent in the complex, but others were getting away with it. I decided that was what I was going to do.

POLICE AGAIN

Chen and I had a chat with his landlord and explained that Lora was gone and it was too hard for me to pay rent. The landlord was sound and understood, and I moved out. I left the apartment better than how I found it. I left cutlery and plates and all the gear, where there was nothing there to start with.

The night I was moving out, I started to move my gear at 5.30 p.m. There was a blue light flashing away at the door of Chen's house. It was an alarm light, but it didn't make any sound at all, it just kept flashing. I got all my gear out from the apartment and started loading my van. People on the main road in front of the house were coming home from work, and they must have thought I was robbing the house, as the alarm appeared to be going off and I was loading up my van. I walked back into the flat, which was out the back, and was just getting the last few things. Just then, a man scaled the back fence, two others came from the back garden with battens, and in the same second, they were in my flat, telling me to drop what I had in my hands and to place my hands against the wall. It was a full on raid from the police station, and it was too hard core to take seriously.

I burst out laughing and said, "Come on lads, relax, it's my place, I'm just moving out."

So they brought me around to the front garden, and there was Chen and his friend. The coppers ran into their sitting room and asked who owned the van. Chen jumped up and said, "The lad in the back; it's nothing to do with us."

Chen told me afterwards that he wasn't sure what I would be up to at times, due to my shifty look. So the coppers wanted to see everyone's passport to check us out. They wanted my driver's licence and passport. I stood there for a second and started thinking. I counted all the police whilst Chen and his friend were getting their passports. There were nine police officers. I said, "What's going on? You lot must be the whole police station. We live here, these two lads are my mates, and I'm just moving out from the back."

One of the officers said, "Have you your licence?"

I said, "I moved some of my gear down to my new place, and that's where my licence is; sorry."

"Your passport, please," said the officer.

I said, "You might find this hard to believe, but immigration has it, as I'm getting a sponsorship."

It was becoming funny for all of us, and they asked if I had any ID at all. I looked in my pockets and found my airport ID, which I showed them. I said, "That's better than a passport, that ID there. I work in the airport, and that's my pass card."

So myself, Chen, his friend, and the whole police station had a nervous chuckle about the whole lot, and then one of the officers said, "Well lads, at least you have a good story to tell your friends in the pub. See you all again, and lads, get your landlord to fix that alarm light or there might be more calls about break-ins."

MANIFESTED NEW LIFE

I moved into Duke's apartment; I had my own bedroom out the back. Duke said that he'd be happy on the foldout couch until he left. He went jogging each day, and I decided to join him. He was good like that. He didn't laze around and depress himself watching programmes on television. He listened to music, took time out from everyone, and went jogging and did some exercise. He also drank energy drinks if he could get his hands on them. We went jogging around the pitch and did many stretches, and he explained how to get in shape. I gave it all a good bash, and the next day, I couldn't move. I was only really easing myself into it compared to Duke, but it was still a shock to the body anyways.

We began having outdoor BBQs in Coogee. It was simply organised; one lad, named J.C., went around and got some money off everyone. He then went to the supermarket and bought the food. The cooking device was built into the ground for anyone to use. It was all perfect, and we bought cans of bourbon and food and had these outdoor sessions. J.C. was great fun; he found a toy shop that sold these cap guns, and he bought one. They were only $2 and the caps were $2, and he was set up. When I saw him in action, I had to get one myself.

Whenever there was a disagreement in the house among Roger, Duke, and I, I would say, "Right, lads, there is one bullet in the gun. You have to aim it at your own head and shoot it. If it's a blank, you're okay, pass it to the next person. Whoever shoots themselves in the head loses the argument; this is how we should solve all our problems. There were eight bullets in the gun and now only one, so here you go Duke, let's play Russian roulette."

Out of all the times we did this, Duke lost the most times, Roger lost a few, and the gun just never seemed to go off for me. I would have been happy with a few bullets to the head, as I felt it helped me stop the last of the trained negative thinking mind that was nearly dead. It was very funny, Duke nearly always lost, and he tried all different methods to keep from shooting himself in the head, but he nearly always got the bullet. Then one day we were in the pub, having a few drinks, and another disagreement broke out. I handed the gun to Duke and he threw it on the floor and jumped on top of it, breaking it to pieces.

He hated my gun at that stage and said, "The bleeping thing always shoots me in the head."

The next day, I was back up at the shop and bought one for Roger and I; we relived our childhood years, shooting each other as if we were pilgrims on the streets. The noise woke Duke up, and he said, "What the bleep is going on? I thought I smashed that gun up last night?"

I said, "I don't know, I just woke up and it was under my pillow, all fixed up."

Duke said, "My bell end it was; I broke that gun up real good. The magic gun is dead."

When all the crew who lived upstairs heard Roger and me with the gun, they all wanted one. It happened that there were just heaps of us with cap guns. When I was driving down to town, the sunroof was open and the van's sliding door was open. The Victor Street crew were out having a BBQ, and all of us in the van were doing a drive-by shooting at the lads. We were all reliving our childhood years; Coogee was such a fun place.

LIZ MCDONALD

I heard that Liz McDonald was in town. This time she was in a shop down at the Rocks, doing readings for people. One day, I walked in and there was a lad sitting behind the till.

He said, "Hello."

I said, "I just came to see a friend of mine named Liz McDonald."

He said, "Did you book an appointment? She's quite busy."

I said, "No, I didn't."

He said, "Well, there is someone due here to see her at half two, someone at three, and someone at half three and four."

I said, "What about now?"

He said, "There's a girl to see her now. But she's not here, hang on a second." He rang the girl and then said, "Okay, she said that she will be late. Well, what's your name?"

I said, "D.J."

He said, "Well, it's meant to be, I guess. It's your turn, which will be $35. Go on and head upstairs."

He was amazed. Intuition for me and it worked. I went up to Liz, and she was surprised to see me, as she was expecting the girl. I told her the story, and she laughed and said, "Okay, sit down."

The reading commenced:

Liz said, "Grandfather on spirit side, very strong with you. He's a guide. He helped you a lot in finding this position in work. He wants you to get in touch with a union.

"One year from now, you will be living somewhere else.

"Female coming into your life, there will be a desire for you to live with this woman, but it may not be good for you because you may get stuck in a situation that you won't feel comfortable with and will have nowhere else to go, due to financial reasons.

"Can see you being happy and comfortable here, but you seem to get in your own way of happiness, and sometimes when you drink, you are not always the nicest of guys.

"You're attracted to cheap women. You wear your heart on your sleeve, and at present I see you falling in love with a girl who is involved with someone else. Don't do this to yourself. Don't put yourself on the line for a woman. What you need is someone really available, but I see you afraid of someone available.

"Michael's talking. Michael the Archangel. Apparently you talk to Michael? He is saying he hears you—he loves your sense of humor—sometimes he doesn't know how you come to certain conclusions but he's not here to judge you, he's here just to help.

"The Don is here; he died here. He looks at you as his. He says you're just as stubborn as he was—he is saying it with a smile.

"You're very good at manifesting. Please put into the pot, the relationship you want. You're not ready to have it, but put into the pot what you want. You look at the wrong people, so it reinforces your belief that you can't have what you want. You find yourself feeling very vulnerable and very threatened whenever you care about someone, and negativity comes up in you—jealousy and not trusting—all due to previous relationships.

"Guidance will tell you if something is wrong or someone is cheating on you, so trust that and trust your intuition.

"Your instinct is very spot on, so trust it. You have a huge issue with rejection; welcome to being human, a lot of us do.

"Your relationship problems are to do with your mother. With your mother, you had to please her or do the right thing to get attention from her. Not that she was a perfectionist, but she was someone who was quiet. Her affection had a string attached to it; what she gave you had a string attached to it, and you had to do things the way she wanted you to do it or she had to manipulate you in some way, but not all the time. She withdrew a bit as you got older, which made you internalise that you're not good with women and you're not good, full stop. A sense of judgment, coming from your mother, verbalised negativity. Where you felt judged and you couldn't do the right thing no matter how hard you tried kind of thing. So you put yourself in harm's way whenever you look at a relationship with a woman because it reminds you how you can't please and how you are not good enough. This is all stuff that comes from your mother. Doesn't mean she didn't love you, but I will say she is proud of you. So how do you fix that?

"This is step number two, if you want to do that, and that is healing the inner self. The more you talk to your ego—the more you go on and on in your head—it tells you what you want to hear. Your ego thinks it is in control. You are getting a lot of love and support from the spirit side to help you get over your childhood—you go in and out of depression due to your childhood. Your father stuff is here too, but we're focusing on relationships and that's more your mother."

Liz continued, "There is a lot of doubt in you, and that is because of how you were treated as a child. You were not nurtured as a child. Healing your inner self means getting out of ego and into the self and healing your perception of yourself. Here is a little boy, all he wants to do is love, all he wants to do is be accepted—that's you! And here you have all this crap, your parents fighting, your parents not getting along, okay? You're going like this: what do I do? How will I fix this? You are very much in your feeling, you feel overwhelmed and very insecure. They start fighting and then they start to pick on you and use you as the middle person between them; here you are, not knowing what to do. And when you want to please one, the other one gets angry; you please the other one, and the one gets angry. There is nothing you can do that is right. So you feel helpless and you feel angry and you start getting angry at them, then you start to rebel. You don't listen to anything they say to you—you understand?"

I replied, "Yes, I remember, they were not bad to me as such, but I was used as the middle person, and that was very frustrating."

Liz said, "And you set your own course, and that's part of the reason why you came here, you wanted to get away from that crap, and look, you're much more well adjusted and happier. So in order to come to full terms with this, in order to release all this stuff, to heal your relationship with you, so you can get on with your life. They have got their own problems. As you are going through these processes, it is not about what anyone else said to you, it is about how you feel about yourself because of what they said to you. It has eroded your belief in you—so you don't feel you can be loved and you don't feel you can be happy.

"Because of all the crap you believe that they have told you—it's all crap. How do you fix that? By getting out of your head and into your soul self.

"Restate whatever thought, whatever feeling, whatever emotion that you want discovered and how you feel about you. Then you follow a practitioner's voice inside of yourself, and your own soul will help you see what was going on, why you created it, and why you choose it.

"Part of you is angry at putting yourself through all of this. But the nice thing is, you're through it and the hard part is over. Now it's just healing from that so you can actually have a nurturing, loving relationship.

"And that is all within your ability, and I'll say this: there is a possibility, if you want this, to have your own business in the future here in Australia, okay? And I will say that there could be some friends back home that you might sponsor to come out here, friends of yours that are also in the same crap and sick of it. Mates! And you help them come over here, and they want to be supportive of you as well."

Three things were written down for me by the Don and Michael the Archangel:

1) Trust = mistrust.
2) Healing inner self.
3) "I love you completely and I accept you exactly the way you are."

Number 3 was for me to say to myself, as I was not accepting myself the way I was, as the negative energy was still in me, but accepting that could be a way of moving forward.

THE MANIFESTO CONTINUED

There was a girl who lived next door to us. Duke was telling me that she was a monster and that she was always giving out about the music being on and she hated Irish people and parties and all the rest. Whenever I heard a conversation about the next door neighbour, I figured I never wanted to meet her.

Anyway, one day, I had the music playing in my room, and then there was a knock on the window. I looked up and there was a good-looking girl standing there; she said, "Would you mind turning the music down a little, as I can hear it next door."

I said, "No problem at all, I'll do that now."

So she walked off, but I checked her out and she looked very nice. I was thinking that there was a lot more to this next door neighbor than what I was hearing; she had a New Zealand accent and a soft voice and also looked very cute and attractive. So the next time I saw her, I said, "Are you any good at massages as I just did my back in, in work?"

She said, "I have to work now but I'm off at two o'clock, if you're still awake."

I said, "I might just nod off around that time, but here, look, I'll leave this hurley stick beside the window; just give me a good hard smack with that stick, and I'll be up."

She didn't wake me up that night, but she wrote a little note for me and signed it "Rachel." Our apartment was a little rough looking, to say the least. Duke and Lin (another girl who stayed in the complex) were always giving out about the next door neighbour, but I didn't know what the problem was. Duke started to bang on the wall to upset the girl to show me what she was like. The hurley sticks came out, but she didn't come in, and as Duke and Lin were hitting the wall, Roger joined in.

Just then, the door opened. Duke dove onto the bed and pulled the covers over himself. Lin hid behind a lamp. I just stood there. Rachel came in the front door, and Roger stood there with a hurley stick in his hands, giving the wall one last bang. It sure was a funny sight to see. Rachel was not too impressed and told me to calm down my wacko friend.

I said, "Sorry about Roger, he just got out of a mental institution, and he drank all his medication money."

So Rachel hung around for a little while, looking at Lin behind the lamp and Duke in the bed; she asked me if I would like to go for a walk. I said that a drink would be great sometime, yes. We went for a drink and got on great. It was such a fun night with many laughs, and I could then see that I was to have my relationship with Rachel, as she was an available girl.

So what attracted Rachel and I to each other, apart from we may have fancied each other? What was the real truth? Rachel explained to me that she didn't like Irish people, because all the ones that she met living in my place, twenty of them at once, were drunk all the time and singing Christmas songs and doing Irish jigs and mainly just heaps of messing. But Rachel thought that I was different; she said that she could see a green aura around me.

I said, "I think I know what an aura is, but please explain?"

She said, "I see it on people sometimes, it's your energy around you, who you are, what level you are at perhaps. Some people have a blue one, and they all mean different things."

I said, "What's blue mean and what's green mean?"

Rachel said, "My old boss had a blue one, it was rushing around him like a snake. He was a fantastic boss and made sure everyone was happy in the job. He constantly gave everyone positive feedback, and his whole main priority was that the happier the worker, the better the business would do, and more customers will come in, and it will be a great place to work. He did a great job, and everyone loved working there. He spent the whole day making everyone happy and looking out for the workers as number one.

"The green aura is very good. It means healing energy. It's only because I saw your aura that I was interested in you."

Rachel told me sometime later that she had asked the universe for me.

I said, "Really? I did something like that too."

So what did I do? I thought up that it was time for me to have a girlfriend, someone to have a relationship with. I wanted someone who was a little older than me and was smart and could even teach me a thing or two. Someone who looked great and fit (goes without saying really, but it's most important to get it right in your head first). I then said it out as if I was talking to someone, perhaps the Don or my higher power. But I was talking to myself, getting it clear about who and what I was looking for.

Rachel also did the same sort of thing, only asking the universe and signing off with, "under the grace of God, in a perfect way." Which was something that I needed to learn. Signing off this way would have saved me many difficulties before.

I quickly reflected on my last request to life itself and could see clearly that all I asked for had worked out perfectly. I was in a nice relationship. I had many friends and we were all having so much fun. My job was good—I did not make a huge amount of money but I made more than I did before. Also, my rent was free; I did not have any rent to pay. Things had changed, just the way I asked, just the way I felt that life should give to me, and here I was living this change.

Also, due to all that killing of my mind—it short-circuited itself and I was connecting with a deeper part of myself yet again. Not just a spiritual experience like before but really finding myself. I was tapping in and out of inspiration. I still had questions that needed to be answered, and this was what was in my mind always.

THE ILLUSION OF TIME

Rachel asked if I would like to go for a walk (for our second date). I decided to take her up on the offer, and we went on a walk. She asked me if I a spiritual person behind the messing side of myself. I said, "Perhaps I am, I'm more of a truth chaser—I don't settle for anything less than the truth." We began talking about different things, and I told Rachel about my Vacluse experience. I was finally letting it out and talking about what had happened.

I said, "I had a dream about a place in Vacluse. I was in Ireland at the time, and it all seemed so real. I was on the cliff edge and was about to take off on a hang glider I appeared to have in my arms. I decided to look behind me to see where I was in the dream, and I had a good, clear vision of all that was behind me. The more important thing about it was that I was leaving a collective consciousness behind me and flying out to the sea and sky in front of me, which was so clear and had no collective consciousness.

"But the real thing that happened," I said, "was the feeling. I felt the experience when I was in Ireland, and I classed it as freedom awaits me in Australia, and then when I got to the place, it was all real, everything was there, and it was amazing. It was like catching a déjà vu even before it happened. I knew everything was there, and I ran around the corner, and there it all was. I walked to the cliff edge and was in the same place where I was in the dream. The only difference was that I did not have a hang glider in my arms. But as I stood there, all of my thoughts from many things that happened at home all rushed out to the sea. I received a clear mind and so many realisations. But still, not only that, I had this amazing feeling inside of me, as I had the full experience of the feeling of freedom. In the dream I had a taste of that amazing feeling, the amazing experience. So Rachel, I'm left with how could this be possible? Different sides of the world and yet I could feel the same experience. Yes, people can see things before they happen, and there are many psychics around to tell people things. But this is so much different, it's all to do with the feeling of the experience, and something has to be ruled out of the equation for it to be possible, you know."

That's when I got it. I continued, "Time has to be ruled out of the equation for it even to exist in the first place. Oh my goodness, Rachel, time is not real, it has to be an illusion. It's all working off the feeling inside us and how we're filling up the emptiness inside to completeness. That's how it works; all there is, is now, Rachel. Time has to be an illusion, as it's the only way it can work. I experienced the experience myself, and it is only now, as I'm telling you, that I'm also getting answers. Take time out of the equation; it's the only way all these insights can work, and all of it is perfect. Time is not real, it's an illusion."

Rachel and I shared the afternoon walking along the coast and beach, and it was amazing. They were the places where I could think the clearest. It was all to do with the collective consciousness that I was stuck in all the time at home. I'm still on energy (vibration energy) and thoughts (collective consciousness) as the true workings of a game. I had this worked out at fourteen years old, and it was here when I was nine years older that I experienced the madness and insanity of it all.

I left this theory filter around in my mind, heart, and soul for some time (or for some moments) until a later date.

PRACTICING MANIFESTATION

So there I was, in Coogee. Rachel suggested that I stop saying that I was broke and pretend that I had lots of money; she explained that's how it comes your way. I thought this was a very interesting factor as my theory was, think it up, call it forth, believe it, and manifest it.

I decided to check this out, take on the task at hand, and see what happens. I walked around town, telling everyone that I was the richest man in Coogee. Everybody! I stopped people on the street and people in the beer garden. I said, "I'm the richest backpacker that the Coogee town has ever known." "Really?" was the reply, and I said, "No kidding." I was quite convincing, and when I just about convinced myself that I was, things started to happen.

A friend moved out of town and left his van behind for us, as he owed us some money. He asked me and another friend to sell it. He owed two grand and wanted to sell it for four. Then they all left, and the van became mine; now I had two vans. My friends left from our block of apartments, and they each said that I could have their apartment; they felt there was no better person to give the keys of their free apartments to. I had three apartments, two vans, and a New Zealand girlfriend.

Then Tom, another friend, said that there was an apartment next to his place, and no one had lived in it for six months. He opened it up, and it was like a storage room. He said, "D.J., I have a place for you to move into; it's yours, mate, if you want it." I had four apartments for free, two vans, a New Zealand girlfriend, and I lived in the nicest town in Australia. I became the richest backpacker that the town ever had.

LIFE SURFACING MY NEGATIVE ENERGY

I needed to finally rid the negativity within—you cannot hide from what's inside. Life could be a raging stream until this was over, but many things must happen to get this process started.

Rachel and I decided to go to a mind, body, and soul exposition in Darling Harbour. I was very happy that she was into what I was into. She and I loved understanding one's self and anything to do with the direction of awareness and spirituality. We went and it was great. It was in a huge hall, set out wonderfully, and there were stalls and sections where people sold different things. It was all very interesting. There was also a big room with over fifty psychics in it doing readings, and I decided to go in and have a chat with one of them. I bought a ticket, then my name came up, and the reading commenced.

Basically, this reading went from my relationship with Rachel to family and some very bad news. The girl told me first that the relationship that I was having would not last, that we would go our separate ways after the relationship reached its peak. Surprisingly enough, this did make sense to me. Deep down within, I felt that this was true, and all I asked the girl was, would Rachel be okay with the ending, and the girl said that she would, as we would want different things and would drift apart. She told me that I would leave my job and that I would get my break in life by working with this new guy, who was going to offer me a job. The other thing that she told me was that my father would die in one year or less. I was shocked and couldn't believe it. I refused to believe this, but she insisted on it and explained that this was what spirit was telling her. It did not make any sense to me, and then she changed the subject and told me to check out the aura photo stall and get a picture done for myself. She also told me that I had to be ready for a lot of changes coming my way and to accept them as part of my process as a learning phase.

I went off looking for the aura stall and got a picture taken of me from this hi-tech camera. I had read up on this before; in the 1960s, it was proven that people have auras, and a camera was invented to take pictures of them. The aura is our energy; the colour of it explains it all: what type of spirit we are, the level we're at, and what state it is in at the present moment.

My aura picture showed me standing in the middle of a bright green oval energy field. The outer part was green, but where my body was positioned was all red with only a green patch, where my heart was to be positioned. The green area was my energy; it meant healing energy. The red, however, was all the energy that I seemed to intake over the years. The red was causing the internal bleeding, but it was also strength, a force, a power within to drive me to do what I did.

So what was going on with this girl telling me all she told me?

Well, I figured then that the Don was with me a lot, and I figured that I should listen to what I was being told. It did make perfect sense about Rachel. I figured that this girl was not telling lies, but maybe some of her information was not clearly heard. For my father to die on me would be one of the greatest disasters I would have to face. Arthur and I were creating this story. The aura was a good idea, and the picture explained a lot.

As life went on, Rachel's father died in New Zealand. I am not sure whether the girl got it mixed up as to what spirit was telling her, or perhaps spirit was telling her that my father would die to get the emotional energy in me to surface and perhaps get rid it.

RELEASING ANGER—LIFE'S REFLECTIONS

I was driving up the Carrington Road on my own and saw this man on the side of the road, walking up and down. He was only about twenty-seven years old. He seemed to be very angry and shouting out at something; nobody really, the sky, himself. He appeared to be going mad. This energy in his body appeared to be leaving him; he was shouting and walking up and down the road, and it was some sight to see. This was all I saw, and then I drove on. What was happening there was a great big energy that was in him, negative and angry, was leaving him, and it was clear for me to see. Plus it was for me to see. My spirit was attracting this event to me to see. Then I drove on.

Later on, Rachel and I decided to go to a few classes that I was very interested in checking out. One was a meditation class; I met the lad who was running it at the mind, body, and soul exposition. Rachel and I went to one class. It was all about breathing techniques and a few exercises. I was interested in the workings of this class more so than anything else. I began talking to the lad afterwards. We were talking about breathing techniques. He explained that newborn babies breathed from their centre, deep in their stomach or belly. As people get older, they don't breathe that low, but it's very important to breathe like that. Adults breathe from their chest. When older people breathe, they breathe in but only fill up their chest area, maybe their stomachs at times, but not deep down breathing. We don't take in, focus on the depth of our intake, thus our body doesn't get all the oxygen that it needs. We have to breathe faster for our bodies to do so. When people get very old, they tend to breathe in, just giving their necks air. When they breathe in, all the air is brought to their necks and not the rest of the body, slowly suffocating themselves. It's a smart move for anyone to breathe deeply. It gives us more energy, our body gets a better supply oxygen much more quickly, and we don't suffocate ourselves. Once I understood the information, there was no great need for me to continue the class, or so I felt.

There was another class that I tried to understand, but it was something that I would need to experience myself to fully understand it. The class was on astral travel, and its opening page read, "The Astral Plane, Lucid Dreams, OBEs, Dream Symbols, Concentration, Awareness, Visualisation. Free intensive interactive workshops designed to take you on an unforgettable journey."

There is so much I could write about this, but basically it was about out-of-body experiences (OBEs), and apparently anyone can do it. One hears of stories of it happening to people when they have a car crash or some other near-death experience. Anyone can do this in a relaxed state of mind whilst also staying conscious. One needs to relax their body and go into a complete relaxed state of mind, where they connect with their soul self and then detach their spirit from their bodies. They will be conscious in their spirit, and the spirit is connected to the body at all times by an endless cord. The spirit can then go places by the power of their thought; if they think of a place, they will then be there. Gravity and other laws have no effect on the spirit once it is out of its body.

I went to a few classes, as this was what I wished to do. I was fascinated in the theory end of it. The girl who was teaching it was very well spoken and confident.

I went to a few practical classes, but one day, we all sat in someone's sitting room and went into a meditation, and I fell asleep. My snoring disrupted the rest of the class. I was embarrassed when some people said afterwards that I stopped them from doing it. The organiser was very nice and told me not to feel bad; she just suggested that I get some rest at home before I came; she also said that I must have a very stressful life.

I couldn't do it with a class at all, and I had to drop out. But I got the information on astral travel. It can happen, it does happen, it's very possible, and it's not a scam; the course was free.

JOB

I met up with a person named Jackass; we had a chat about construction work, and then he offered me a job. He asked if I was interested in being paid cash. And trusting me said, "That would suit me great, as I'm applying for residence, and my visa is a little unstable at the moment." He seemed a little dodgy at first, in fact nearly all the time, but I thought that added to his character. I went to a fortune-teller after the mind, body, and soul festival to get more information on my father, where I was told he would be just fine for a long time. The girl also told me that I would work for someone who was older than me and that he would help me and teach me the business and be very good to work for. She said this man would be the break I needed in life.

I started working for Jackass, and I was doing a lot of great work too. I agreed to get paid by the hour, and that sounded good to me. I felt that I was finally getting my break in life and I could make a few dollars instead of struggling all the time for the work I did. However, I soon noticed that Jackass often fought with his workers, and even though they had been mates for years, they quit, but I still believed that he was all right. I put in a great effort to do the best work for him. I worked for him all that week and told him that I needed to be paid as I went along, as my last job didn't pay me too well and I was broke.

Jackass said, "That's okay, mate; how much is okay? Would $100 be fine?"

I said, "Yes, that's perfect until I get my wages."

Over the next few weeks, I kept asking Jackass about my money, and he said that I had to send in my forms of how many hours I did and where I was working and all the rest, as there were many people to pay. I did exactly that, and his response was that he didn't get the papers; well, he said that he got the first week but not the second week, which I knew was impossible as they were both together in one envelope. This sort of nonsense went on for a while with Jackass, and along the way someone else had offered me a job that paid more money, but I decided to stay loyal to my bleeper of a boss, as I just couldn't imagine that I wouldn't get paid for the job. I was running around doing work everywhere for Jackass, fixing up jobs that others were making a mess of. I did three weeks' work for him, and he said that he was just waiting for a cheque to come in and that he would pay me soon.

It was the Friday on the third week, and I needed payment big time, as I had nothing to eat and could not afford petrol to get to work. I went down to see Jackass, but he was on the missing list. The owner of the house where I was working asked if I would come back on Saturday, as he was in a rush to get the job finished. I came up on Saturday for the owner. I was so worked up at this stage from spending the whole evening looking for Jackass and ringing different people. There was a new lad on the job, an Italian, and I told him that I had not yet gotten paid and that I had worked for Jackass for three weeks.

After I shot a few nails out of the nail gun, I told the Italian lad, "I am going to crack up if I don't get paid. I told Jackass that I'll be out on the streets because I cannot pay my rent and that I am starving of hunger, and he still has not paid me. There is nothing left to my life if he doesn't pay me, and I'm going to take that son-of-a-bleep down with me. I feel it all coming, and it's going to get nasty. You might not even have a boss to work for after this."

The Italian lad went on to talk about how hot headed the Irish can be.

I was so mad all that weekend, and Jackass was still missing. All that happened throughout my life and all the times I kept cool, calm, and collected, carrying on regardless, this event took it all too far, and all of that pain and anger and negative experiences and energy was coming to the surface in me. I was becoming a very dangerous, angry person, and there was not any room in my head to consider any other situations after thinking about what I was going to do. There was to be no life or residence after I felt what I was to do. Nothing meant anything any more, and that was it; I was cracking up.

I saw Rachel and she said that karma would get me if I did anything to him. I said, "Bleep karma, nothing is going to stop me. I have to get that money or else I'm taking that bleeper down."

That whole weekend, I was going mad and was turning into one really sad and angry person. All the people who knew me from having fun saw a different side to me. All the sadness and depression and frustration were coming out in me, and they all commented on just how sad I looked. They said that they had never seen such a sad and angry face before.

Monday came and I said, "That's it, I'm going to bleep up this bleeper big time."

Rachel said, "I thought you were a spiritual person and all of that nice side that I saw in you for so long; what is happening to you?"

I said, "Rachel, I am really a mad bleeper, I have been hiding my true nature for so long, and over all that happens in the next few days, you will realise that you're better off not knowing me."

I drove my van to the job, but no one was there. I rang so many different lads, but none knew where Jackass was. I rang Jackass's phone so many times, but either he had it turned off or he just wouldn't answer me. Rachel wanted to come with me, and we ended up driving around looking for him. Finally, I saw his father's van on the road; his father, I felt, was as crooked as Jackass. I pulled into the lane behind him, as there were three lanes on this road. There was one car between me and the old timer. I followed him to see where he was going. When he pulled over to the second lane, I did too. Then when the light went green, he took a right turn and moved quickly up the road. I did too. I was catching up to him, and he knew straight away that it was me. He was on the move, and then my phone rang; it was Jackass.

I answered it. Jackass asked how I was and what I was doing. I said that I was fine.

Jackass said, "I just received a call from the owner of that job you were on, and well, he is a very tricky man to deal with."

I said, "Where is my money, Jackass?"

He said, "Well, the man you were working for has not paid me yet, and he is now holding off on it."

I said, "All I want is the money that we shook hands on and that I worked very hard for."

Jackass said, "Well, I will pay you when I get the money for that job, but Mick says that it is all done wrong, that all the squares that were put down were done wrong."

I said, "None of it is wrong, now where is my money?"

He said, "If it is all wrong like what Mick is telling me, it will all have to be taken up, and that will cost a lot of money, and I cannot pay you for that work." He was talking tripe in its lowest level of form.

I said, "Forget about that job then, where is my money for the stairs job and all the evenings I was taking out timber and all the other jobs that I did? Even if you paid me that money, I wouldn't be so bleeped off, I could live and feed myself and pay rent."

He said, "Well, that job you did for Mick is all wrong, and it will cost a fortune to fix it. I think you owe me money."

I got off the phone and felt that I was going to take great pleasure living out my nineteen-year-old foreseen event, but instead of on me, on Jackass. By this time, his father, the snake, had gotten away; they were playing their little games with me. All of my dreams, my life, my residency in Australia, all of it, whether it was to be true or not, didn't come into how I was feeling at this time. I went quiet, as it all just went too far, no more Mr Nice Guy for me. I drove to a gun shop, to get myself a licence and a gun (or just a gun). All of my anger over so many years of not saying anything was coming to the surface. Nothing mattered in my world anymore, apart from Jackass and my money. The gun shop was closed, what a shame, I thought, and the reality, what a lucky bleeper.

I then thought that if I killed this bleeper, I would release my pain, but maybe there were other ways that I was to learn. I drove back up to the job I was working on (where the squares were supposedly put down wrong). The front door was closed. I walked around the back, scaled the wall, jumped into the back balcony, and strolled onto the job. The Italian lad was talking on the phone; I said nothing, only looked around at the lads finishing off the job.

The Italian lad spoke into the phone, saying, "Sorry Jackass, could you hold on a second?" Then he said to me, "Are you looking for Jackass?"

I said, "Yes, mate," and he handed me the phone.

I said, "Hello, Jackass; the job seems to be going very well here, without any form of hiccups at all."

He shouted, "What are you doing on that job? I'll get my lawyer to remove you from that job if you don't get off it now."

I said, "Are you sure you have it right, Jackass, about the job, as it all seems to be going perfectly well here."

He said, "I'm calling the police on you now for trespassing on private property."

I said, "No need for all that carrying on, Jackass; just making a point, and that is, there has been nothing wrong with any of my work in any job, but you won't pay."

I gave the phone back to the Italian lad and said, "Thanks, mate; perfect," and I left. This event was bringing all my energy, all my deep down negativity that was in me for such along time, to the surface. I reckoned at that point there that I knew how a person feels when they are just about to blow themselves up, and that was how I felt. I felt happy to blow myself up as long as I took Jackass with me. That was the mental vision I had to match my feeling. I don't think many people in their lives even come close to the frustration that I was going through at this time. Nothing meant anything any more, and it all became me and Jackass at this point.

Roger had gotten a lot of money from a claim, and he went for a trip up the coast. I was always concerned about Roger and was always there to look after him. But when it came to the crunch, when I needed some looking after, Roger was gone up the coast, drinking all his dough, and there was none for me. I didn't ask Roger for money, nor did I feel that I should have been paid for looking after him. I had looked after him unconditionally, but Roger saw that I was cracking up over not getting paid and that I had no money to do anything. He knew that I had given my savings to my other so-called friend who deliberately done me over beforehand, and still he just went off and did his own thing. So I was reaching the peck of anger at this stage, due to not getting paid and friends of mine that I looked after and how they repaid back that friendship.

I went down to Jackass's office, and they told me he was away on holiday. I met up with Chen and was filling him in on the whole lot; he asked me what I was going to do.

I said, "I suppose it is about time that I learnt how to get money off an employer the legal way. I'll open up a court case against him, that's what I'll do, and I'll represent myself in court."

I was thinking this was what I needed to learn in life; everything happened for a reason, and my constantly thinking mind was constantly searching for the reason. Australia was a beautiful place, it was my home, but some people were not what I imagined to be in such a nice country. Not all people, just some people, that were brought into my life and I theirs at these times of my life, for reasons beyond my understanding at these moments. All that was happening in my life was to get this energy body in me to surface, and it sure was working.

I met this really nice woman named Jade, who owned many apartments complexes. I briefly told her what was happening and said that I had no accommodation. She rented me an apartment and said I could pay her whenever I got back on my feet. It was a great spot, was a big place, and had a great view all around. It was three stories high, and many of the residents were Irish. I couldn't help but notice that "Knightsbridge 1919" was written across the front of the building. I always try to delve into the spirit side of life to see a connection, as if some spirit was helping me out. I realised that my grandmother was born in the year 1919, and I felt that could be a connection. After I moved in there, I did some work for my good friends in the agency, just to pay rent and buy a little food. My whole life at this time was about Jackass and me not letting it go, as it just set me back so far. Jackass was based only a few streets away from my apartment, and then he moved to a new place; where was this new place? It was on the same road as my new apartment. The building I was living in was one block away. I could see his premises from my window; it all seemed like it was meant to be that I was not going to forget about my money. Life placed this Jackass in the view of my front window!

I was set up between the fortune-teller and all these insane happenings in my life, all to connect with the anger body; adjustments needed to be made. But there was no way for me to see that I was getting played—by a higher power, the Don, life, divine intervention, or my deeper self.

I decided that maybe I should learn how to get my money back the correct way. Maybe that would be a good lesson to learn. I opened up a court case against Jackass. I was to represent myself, and after getting information on him from the Internet, I could open the case.

It was all organised and filed away. I had the letter at home to give to Jackass; I was going to do it in person. I went out with Rachel that night for a walk down to Kings Cross. The night before, I found it hard to sleep; it was hard to pinpoint what had me like this.

I couldn't sleep or eat since I thought about opening up the court case against Jackass. As I was walking back with Rachel from Kings Cross, I said, "Something is really wrong."

Rachel said, "What is it?"

I said, "I don't know but I'm not well inside, something is very wrong."

Rachel said, "No, you're going to say it's us moving in together," and she was getting worked up, as we discussed moving in together before

I said, "No, you're not helping; let me sit down, I need to think. It could be anything, someone could be sick at home or someone in trouble. I don't know what it is."

That night when I got back to my apartment, I rang Jay, the manager of my old job, who had given me a good reference. Jay told me not to give Jackass the court case letter, explaining that if I did, I would have to leave the country since my visa was not stable. I left the letter on the floor and never sent it out. The next day, I began to feel better.

KNIGHTSBRIDGE 1919

The new place Jade gave me had no televisions or distractions or any negative energy; it was a place where I could breathe, even think and be me, a place where I could call home and a place where I could listen to music, especially the lyrics, and get the mental stimulation from the music I was often deprived of in many places. It was a place where I could get out my papers that I kept from lots of pervious experiences and perhaps even stop all the highs and lows I was going through, a place where I could finally put an end to the madness and sort out my life, a place where it felt like a home sweet home and didn't feel like a battle zone or a war zone. I wanted a real place of rest where I could create sense and logic to the madness in my life. All I really wanted was a table, a chair, and my CD player, tape deck, and radio, where I could take out papers and tape recordings and get it altogether.

The room was painted blue, a light blue that gave off a cold feeling, and I needed to change that to feel comfortable. Everything gives off a feeling: places, people, colours, pretty much everything. Rachel and I went for a drive all around the Vacluse area, as we heard that on certain days, everyone in Vacluse left out items and stuff that they no longer had a need for. We were hoping to come across some paint for our new apartment.

So Rachel said, "Hey, let's ask the universe for some."

I said, "Who, life or the game?"

Rachel said, "Either, why not?"

I said, "Well, it's important to get it right about what we need first; what color paint do you want?"

Rachel said, "I don't know, what do you think?"

I said, "Cream would be very comfortable for the walls and white for the ceiling, and maybe some designer red paint or some other color for the skirting. I think I want to paint the unit silver and red; yes, that be great."

Rachel said, "Okay, now I have to ask it out loud and say 'Under the grace of God in a perfect way' at the end of it."

I said, "Okay, let's see if life's essence is working today; go for it, girl."

Rachel said, "We are looking for paint for our new apartment. If we could get colors like cream and white and even some red or blue for the skirting all for free today under the grace of God in a perfect way."

So I drove around the area, but I found out that we had the days mixed up as to when people left things out. In fact, I had the day right but it was once a month instead of once a week, so there was nothing out. I then drove up the cliff road where I had my amazing experience, and there was a skip on the other road to my left. I slowed down as I passed it and reversed back. I said, "Right, Rachel, this is our only hope now, and the question is, is the universe working today?"

We went over to the skip, and I got out and had a look.

It was amazing; I said, "Have a look at this."

She got out and came over; the whole skip was full of cans of paint, buckets of the stuff with no writing on it. I opened one up and it was a greenish color, so that wasn't good. I opened up another and it was pure white; I put it into the back of the van. I opened up another tin; some buckets were half full, some empty, and some full. I came across another white one and said, "What if I mix the white with some of the green, sure that would be a cream, hey?"

Rachel said, "Yes, let's make our own colours."

I put the green and the white into the back of the van. Then I opened up another, and it was red.

I said, "What were they painting in their house with red paint? They're as tasteful as us."

There were also some timber blinds there made from cedar timber; they were very fancy looking, and I'm sure they were very expensive, as cedar was expensive in Australia. I put all of it in the van and off we went. All I had to buy was some silver paint from the hardware store across the road for the unit.

We began painting, and we painted ourselves a very nice, very comfortable sitting room, which changed the whole feeling of the place, and it really was very nice. We fixed it all up and had it looking great.

BIRTH CHART

I went over to Mystery's, the shop owned by Sandra. A lad named Mick was there. Sandra introduced me to him and explained that he printed out birth charts; was I interested in one? I was and got one printed out. When I went over to collect my birth chart, Mick said, "This is really something; you really have to stay away from negative people. Are you okay?"

I said, "Yeah, yeah, I worked that out by now."

Mick said, "No, really, like there are not many places you can go; this is really something, so sensitive."

I said, "Sure, give it to me and I'll look at it later, mate; thanks."

I read it first. It was all very interesting but I did not fully understood it. Then I read it again and got a marker and highlighted certain parts. There it was, in black-and-white print: negative energy and how I pick up on it, and when it's inside of me, it attracts the negative circumstances in my life. It even mentioned having accidents with my hand at work due to negative energy. It was making a lot of sense to me. I could see how I was controlled, played by my own astrology chart. But once I started to understand it, I stopped getting played by it any more. I started to rise above it once I understood it. It's like when a person tells his friend that he is doing something, where the friend doesn't realise that he is doing it until it is pointed out to him. Then he stops doing it. He become conscious of it and doesn't continue it any more. That's how the astrology worked for me, because I was understanding it, I was choosing to not let myself get influenced in that way anymore. I understood it and got a new perspective on it. I rose above its influences. Once it was understood, I ceased to be played by the birth chart. Amazing!

I could see that I was picking up on the negativity around and how my life was full of torturing states of mind and events and feelings.

I could see that I was picking up on energy everywhere. I had my own truths, but this chart was making things very clear for me. I could see that I was getting stuck in a collective consciousness everywhere I went, and energy was ruling my life. I could see that no matter how strong I was to be, there was no choice but to finally give up on life at one stage. One part read, "May just give up just before success in life." That was it for me; it was planned out. I was meant to give up on life, as it was part of the process for me, the influence of my own astrology chart. The perfection of it all was all there on paper. I could see that I was living the life of the chart from day one.

Here is some stuff from my chart:

Mercury in Cancer; these people are extremely susceptible to consciously or subconsciously absorbing the thoughts of those around them. Whatever their ideas may be or however they may have been generated, Mercury in Cancer individuals need to find some means of personally expressing themselves. Methods and motivation for learning, communicating, and transportation are subject to their prevailing mood at any given time.

Moon in the third house; this moon indicates emotional identification with their primary education, siblings, and what is going on in their immediate environment. They tend to be deeply affected by positive or negative circumstances and relationships in these areas.

Their negative potential includes those who are accident prone, have limited memory, and lack mechanical or communicative skills. The moon suggests the desire to write or teach.

Moon square Venus; sometimes they are discouraged from reaching their personal goals because of financial and family burdens that slow them down. However, the energy of frustration in this respect is often turned into constructive channels that lead to their ultimate success.

Mars in conjunction with Saturn; in youth they are apt to have confrontations with authority, even though consciously or subconsciously they want order and structure in their lives. They are apt to hold in anger and frustration until it surfaces in unwise actions that cause accidents or other regrettable situations.

Saturn in the third house; the biggest lessons in life involve thinking, learning, communication, and the development or use of basic skills. Circumstances may prevent or greatly restrict their early education. Negative factors suggest that they can suffer from depression. Relationships with neighbors and schoolmates can be stable and long lasting. They can be the soul of authority, reliability, and strength to their family and neighbours.

Pluto in the fourth house indicates those who may experience trauma in childhood, most likely as the result of the death of someone in the family or because of physical or mental abuse by a family member. Whatever may have actually happened or how they may have felt about it, childhood experiences ultimately leave them with a sense that they have no control over things.

Moon in conjunction with Saturn indicates those who may be too severe and inflexible toward everything and everyone, including themselves, tending to look at things negatively, picturing the worst-case scenarios.

They tend to be deeply affected by negative circumstances, which can cause depression.

I don't know if anyone has any idea what all that is like. But I couldn't generate unless I was on my own. I had a body of energy in me that seemed to be attracting all waves of negative energy in my surroundings. I had no choice but to eventually give in and decide to give up on life, to kill my mind's cycles, the programmes of depression from negativity, the negative waves that seemed to be attracted to me, the energy body of Lora that was the reflection of me. Constantly picturing the worse case scenarios in my mind, I was a goner.

I began to think about who created this chart; who wrote it? Who chose it? We live in a game called life, with laws and rules. It is a perfected system, but how does it work? What if I did it to myself from an existence before I became me in this game? We always exist as we now know. Could I have picked my own date of birth and created all of this life for myself, where I was to be influenced by this astrology? At these moments here, I was really beginning to wake up, to try and understand it all, to understand myself and who was the controller of my life. Who was my controller? When I studied the chart again, I felt that certain events should have happened at different times, but then I realised, the truth is, it's all perfect for all of us. The only thing that makes it less than perfect is our lack of knowledge, our lack of understanding of the whole process.

So who created it? Either we did it to ourselves, or the life was already mapped out and we picked the one that we wished to play. We'll get back to this.

I BEGAN WRITING THINGS DOWN

I decided that I was going to write a letter to my father, as that was what it was all about for me, to let him see all I found out. All of my life was all about him and me, whether he was with me or not. He was always there, and it was about time that I could finally write a letter and let out all of the things that were in me, all of the experiences that I wanted to share with him and the view that I analysed from both our perspectives. I still managed to be alive, and it was time to write him this letter. I had no money, I had no visa to stay in Australia, I had no proper job, and even though all of that was my life, this letter was more important than everything. I put together a letter that included our charts and numerology, and I also wrote about the illusion of time, karma, and the conclusions to many happenings.

At the end I wrote, "You know, all of this is just a taste. Just a sniff of what is so. It is just a glimpse of real reality. It's just a taste of life. It's just a taste of who we may or could become. There is no time and there is only now. Present moment is a moment in which you Pre-sent for yourself. Your whole reality was thought up in your mind, and challenges brought forth are created by your soul, i.e., you.

"Present happy thoughts and they will become your reality.

"The more you know about you, the less there is to know, full stop."

I was finally letting clogged-up energy, experience and information out of me after so long. After I wrote this letter to my father, I released some of the energy and information in me, and then things started to happen. I was breaking through all the influences and restrictions on me, searching for the reason for all of this pain and discomfort and negativity I had to experience and go through. I was searching for the controllers of it all and was rising above numbers, astrology, understanding science, and chasing truth. This writing was what it was all about for me, to show my father all I found out and to try and prove the existence of the mystic side of life, until I realised the bigger picture.

CHAPTER TEN

This Book

The next day was August 7, 2004, and I was in the apartment with Rachel. I was talking about Jackass and how there was just no way I could let it go, not all that money, but I couldn't think of anything else to do. He set me up from the start and bleeped me over.

I was really getting worked up. Then I just realised something overwhelming to me, and I said, "It's all about the book, Rachel, that's what it's all about, the book, the book, this driving force in me is to write a book."

At this same moment, there was a smash in the bathroom. I walked in, and the bottle of aftershave that Ash had given me (that Liz had said would be a gift from my guidance), which was on the top press, came off and smashed all over the floor. I said, "Rachel, that's it, no more getting looked after by an angel. I did it, I'm here now, it's the book, this is what it's all about, the whole lot. I now see it all."

All the negativity, the frustration, the experience of just feeling like I was happy to end it all—I turned all that energy into a love and determination to write this book to pass on these experiences that life has given me, to those who need to know.

On Saturday, August 7, I started this book. I began to write all about different things that happened. Once I wrote it down, another memory seeped up through my veins and produced a thought in my head, where I wrote it down also. I was not too sure what I was to write a book about, only all I experienced. Things started happening after this day.

All the information that I needed in order to add substantial evidence to my theories came to me either by someone showing it to me or on hearing it on the radio. All the theories and truths in me started to come alive in me and attract the backup in my environment.

A couple of nights later, something amazing happened, something that changed everything for individuals like me, something that I experienced myself. I now know we can all experience this.

OUT-OF-BODY EXPERIENCE

On August 9 at 3.30 a.m., I astral travelled. It was an absolutely incredible experience. I went to bed with Rachel. Everything was good, relaxed, and chilled, which did not happen too often in my life. I lay in bed and said to myself, "I am going to let myself astral travel tonight."

I was in a relaxed state. I lay there and let my body fall asleep. I let my mind completely relax, no thoughts racing around (since the Kings Cross time really). But I relaxed my mind and let it fall asleep while I stayed conscious.

At 3.30, I had my arm around Rachel, and she was asleep. Then I started sliding off the side of the bed. I grabbed Rachel with the arm that she was lying on, but my arm was still there. I was falling, sliding out of my arm and body. I then started to shout out her name, but as I did, all that came out of my voice box was "Ra . . . !"

I had no voice any more as I slid out of my voice box. I slid all the way out the side of the bed. I was waiting to fall on the floor, even though my body was still in the bed, but it was me that was this energy, and if nothing was underneath me, I would of course fall. I slid out and just hovered on the side of the bed, just over the floor. I stood up but had no weight. There was no gravity pull on me. I moved onto the bed and did a complete spin, head over feet and again, and I said, "Look at me, Rachel, look at me."

But she didn't see me; sure, she was asleep. I was weightless, my voice was in my mind, in my thinking; I was not really talking, I had no voice box. There was my body and Rachel in the bed, and there I was on the bed. It was very freaky. I didn't look at the mirror in the room, as I was told that if a soul or spirit saw itself in a mirror, it would get some fright compared to how we normally see ourselves. But I'll tell you this, it was incredible. Then I was thinking so many things and was very shocked and just in awe about the experience.

As I was experiencing this, I was thinking that I could just go off and experience this to the full, but then I thought, what if I couldn't get back? I realised that this was amazing and this was really real, and it was all I needed to know that this really existed. I went back over to my body and lay down on top of it, and then I felt myself back in my body and jumped up. I was then in me, I was in myself again. Of course Rachel woke up then, wondering what was going on.

I said, "I did it, oh my god, I did it; could you not see me hovering over the bed?"

Rachel said, "No, I was asleep; did you astral travel?"

I said, "Yes, oh my god, what an experience." I got up and went to the fridge and got a drink. I was racing at a pace up and down the sitting room, just thinking and imagining, if everyone can do this, the feeling of everyone being aware of being able to do this, changes everything.

It can be done; I had done it, but none of it really meant anything to me unless I experienced it, and I did just that. I experienced leaving my body on a very conscious level. I was no different from anyone else, as we can all really leave our bodies. We really were not just our minds. We really were the energy that feeds our minds. I knew all of this, but the knowing and the experiencing were very different. Now I really knew that which I knew. We are that energy, that soul, that spirit. That soul is really a part of the force, the great energy, the all that is. So therefore, we really are part of the source itself, the energy, the vibration intelligent energy is really us. We, all of us as people, had the power to do anything; we are everything and all of us are the vibration energy source that existed. This energy, cut in half and half again and again and again, is us. Religion and governments and all the people in power would have us believe that we were powerless, when in fact we are everything, all of it; all of us are. Nothing else matters, only the matter in us, the energy and our thoughts; all else was really illusion, the game we are playing. Astral travel; give it a go, what can you lose? It's a fantastic experience and really can happen.

I was told that it happens each time we go to sleep, but we are not conscious of it. Then we have dreams and go back into our thinking minds again when we wake up, and all that is in our mind is all that we then know. There is so much going on. I haven't taken it further than this. I had to come backwards to get this down on paper, and maybe in the future, I'll be able to do it again.

I guess this was what happened to me that time I was in the U.K. when I watched the two lads break into my car and steal my camera and my lighter gun. I left my body; we all do when we sleep, but somehow, just perhaps once, I remembered. I brought it with me when I woke up but could not comprehend it, and now I see. Somehow when my body was asleep, I awoke in my subconscious mind and watched them breaking into my car, as I was there to hear the lad say, "Look at this crazy Irishman," as he found the gun. I watched them and heard them, and my body was asleep in bed. Then I woke up in my body and somehow carried this experience, this knowing, with me from my subconscious mind to my conscious level, and I was just amazed and could not understand what had just happened. Now I see, I see it all now. We really are all the same with the same sort of matter in us all deriving from the essence that makes life real. If this has ever happened to you before, you may just now understand what was happening. This is truly amazing; I feel so privileged to have this experience and share this with you.

We are all amazing!

BEATING RESTRICTIONS

At this stage, I rose above and understood my astrology. I read and understood all my numerology, which I will get back to. I stopped all the cycles in my mind and freed myself. I connected with the true essence in me, which is me. I knew and understood that time was an illusion. I then left my own body in an amazing experience. But when I was in work, I still had this anxious energy body inside of me. I broke free of everything else, searching to find the truth of this energy, searching to be free of it, as it was attracting all the bad in my life. It was a constant race for me to break and beat every restriction there was and see through each illusion, to find the torturing control of all—this energy within me.

One day, I couldn't break through anything more; I then surrendered. I had been struggling, running, fighting, beating each and every restriction there was, and then I did it, I beat them all, the energy attractions, the highs and lows that governed my mind, breaking through the restriction of time and mind, entering the subconscious, I left my body, freed from another restriction, and I surrendered, leaving any other restrictions fall to the side lines. I became free. There was nothing else I could beat or understand its illusion. I had the energy, the life in me to beat it all, bring it on. But that's it, I did it, I stood there in my sitting room towards the window and said out loud, "I surrender."

Then I felt this great overwhelming feeling. I shed a tear, as it was the first time I stopped and had to reflect back and accept things.

"I surrender," I repeated.

1st stage = Denial
2nd stage = Anger
3rd stage = Acceptance
4th stage = Forgiveness
5th stage = Beat all restrictions
6th stage = Realised all illusions
7th stage = Stopped time
8th stage = Found myself
And the 9th stage = Surrendered

Surrendering to the game of life is a very important part—it's accepting that all that can be beaten is beaten, and then I won.

The next day at work, I was realising things; I was mentally getting there, there was not much else in my mind, I was searching for the truth, and there were no other restrictions or influences stopping me. I went searching for the core of this energy in me, and there it was, as it all became clear for me. It all came from my family, all of that emotional anger and negative energy came from my childhood years, from day one till about when I was sixteen years old. The strong force of energy in me called anger piled up with my sensitive nature, picking up emotions and negativity. There was not much conflict in my house or much shouting or arguments, but there was the energy there. Usually it was passed on from generation to generation, and that could have happened in this case, but there were also other reasons. These reasons don't really need to be explained, for they are not part of the story as such. The main reason for this energy intake was for me to take it in and race this game through all restrictions and illusions in order for me to rid this energy, and in doing so, I found all the other illusions along the way. This was the perfection of my game. This energy that I received was the drive that put me through everything intensely. First I saw it as the pain and crap that I had to go through. Then sometime later, I realised that it was strength to beat every restriction there was, to beat every control that was on me, and the strength to search for what I felt was the controller of all of my life, as so much was happening in my life and I couldn't understand it. And there it was: it was me. I was my own controller, and the energy in me, which was the inward reflection of my outward world, was passed down.

AN ENLIGHTENING MOMENT

This was the moment that I realised the energy, the pain body in me, was actually an illusion, it was not really me, it was passed down. I realised where it came from, the core of it all. I was walking up a staircase on my job and entered an amazing moment. I was to fix a window that was halfway up the stairs. I placed a ladder on the landing and climbed up to the top; the window was very big; it was like a church window, full of fancy glass. I was wearing red shades at the time, as I felt they let me see things much more clearly. I was literally looking at my world through rose-coloured glasses, and this was how I liked it to be.

The sun came and shone onto me through the red glass. I was in a moment there. I became intensely in the present moment. It was incredible; everything around me was so intensely colorful, and all of my energy was in this present moment. I looked at myself as I was sitting on top of a ladder. I looked in front of me, and there was the sun shining through this colored church window glass. There became no past in time; there were no past tense thoughts and no future tense thoughts. All thought and awareness entered the moment. I entered into this enlightening moment, and it was just so incredible that it was very difficult to get words to match. Everything became intensely alive in the now.

Coldplay's song "The Scientist" came on the radio at that moment; the lyrics include "Nobody said it was easy . . . no one ever said it would be this hard . . . I was just guessing at numbers and figures, pulling the puzzles apart . . . running in circles, chasing tails, coming back as we are."

The words in this song fit perfectly with how I would explain how I got to where I was. The next song that came on was "It's All Good," by Damien Dempsey, with these lyrics: "I am an angry man, yeah—I vent it when I can, yeah . . . the negativity, yeah, Pushed onto young Paddy, yeah, is a shame, who's to blame? . . . It's passed down." This song was from Damien's album called *Seize the Day*.

My whole environment was telling me what I knew and needed to know. It was confirmation on that which I just worked out. My surroundings were in synchronisation with my very being. My body had a shift of energy, which was attracting these truths to me. I was in synchronisation with life itself. We all are, all the time, only I was awake to see and there was no time in my world. I was intensely in the present moment. I had seized the day.

I made it to a goal in the game, the balance point in my life, and it all became amazingly so clear and so real. I could see my position in the game of life, as if I was in one of the tarot cards, as if it was all a card itself in the game. As I sat there on the ladder, my phone rang; it was Rachel. I said, "Well, isn't this just something? I've done it; I am intensely in this moment here, time has stopped, the sun is shining in through the church glass, and I'm directly in the centre of it all. I'm in a moment here; this is truly incredible." Rachel said, "This is great, things are happening to me too, I'm more awake then ever before".

From that moment there, I was compelled to write down everything: what was going on around me and the reason for all my experiences in the past. As I was on a higher vibration than before, I saw the mechanics, behind the scenes, of the experiences that happened in my life. I laughed as I realised that all the energy in me had made me who I was, had driven me to this level of existence; the deeper the pain, the freer you can become. It's all relative until it's balanced out—I was at the balance point.

Thoughts came about different experiences in the past, and many songs on the radio triggered off different memories. I wrote them down, and then another memory and thought came, and I wrote that down and I could let that thought go. Then another thought came, and I wrote that down, as I was realising the real story to it. I filled a notepad with these stories, which were these experiences. Then I carried around a tape recorder and recorded everything in the one moment, how everything became absolutely perfect in the now. I needed to prove this existence, this experience, and pass it on. Any question I thought of entered into my reality right there; someone in the background could answer it for me, but they may have been talking to a friend or a song would come on the radio, giving me the answer to my mind's question. It happened all in the now—in this one moment. Everything that entered my mind was in synchronicity with my surroundings. This was all truly amazing; words cannot even describe. I can't even analyse this experience as there is nothing to analyse, it is a stage of being, not something the mind can even comprehend, as one needs to be in this state of being, their true energy that supplies energy to the mind. It's a deeper understanding that can only really be understood when experienced.

LOOKING AT LIFE INTENSELY IN THE NOW

I could see in this awareness that it was my thoughts that were making me sick, and my thoughts were fuelled by the energy in me. The energy around me was the reflection of what was in me. The energy outside of me was magnified to my energy, having me thinking unhealthy thoughts, thus having me getting sick. It was a state of mind fuelled by negativity and, for me now, a state of soul being alive, and I was in the eternity—the now—but I could see that this negativity was in me, attached to me, and I saw now how it all worked. When all thoughts stopped, as time and mind were in synchronisation, what was imagined as heaven was here, just where we were. I had complete awareness of everything in front of me, around me, not walking around unconscious, as I used to do, but very much conscious and intensely in the present moment. This was truly amazing.

MICHAEL AA

I got out my phone card and rang my mate Tommy at home. Tommy wasn't there, but Marian answered. Marian and I began talking, and she was telling me about a few things that she really wanted to do. Then she spoke to me about Archangel Michael, and I said, "Oh, that's what's going on; Michael AA is up to it again. He has us talking." Marian then said that she needed answers to things and was longing for them to come. She had asked Michael AA to help, and with that, the phone rang, with me on it. I had not spoken to Marian in years, and we were now having the conversation of a lifetime. I asked Rachel to tell Marian what she always says on the end of her "requests" and "thoughts." Rachel explained to Sarah that she should always say at the end, "by the grace of God in a perfect way." *It's a system we live in, a universal system.*

That night, I stayed out all night long and didn't have any sleep until the next day. I decided to have a lay-down beside the harbour, and Rachel came down while I was half asleep beside the water at Darling Harbour.

Rachel wanted to get a drink of coffee whilst I was laying there asleep, but she didn't want to leave me there. When I woke up, she had a coffee cup in her hand; she said, "This nice guy came along and said, 'Hi.' I said, 'Are you having a nice day?' He was friendly and harmless—he went and got me a coffee while I looked after you. He came back with a coffee, and we had an interesting conversation. His name was Michael, and I saw that he drew angels. We talked about that. He said, 'I am Archangel Michael.' Woo, I thought, you who were sleeping would love to hear about this. He told me lots of stuff about his girlfriend trouble and his time in jail for beating up the son of a cop, who was beating a girl and her two daughters. He told me about his oppression by police, his adventures, and lots of stuff. He was funny. We talked for another hour and eventually you woke up. You met Michael and said that we would come and meet him at the coffee cart next week—he was cool."

I was not sure who this person really was, but between this and a few other incidents that happened in my life, I was led to believe that Michael AA seemed to be in my life in many ways. Michael AA was a spirit who we believed was high up in the angel world, not really in the physical world as such, but I guess he had no limits. I believed he was letting me know that he really existed, as I was in a clearer reality now than before, and I was getting constant confirmation on this spirit world. Maybe he was letting me know that I was getting closer and closer to his vibration than I thought—thus him manifesting himself in my reality to show this connection. Either way, it was all amazing.

LATER ON I MET LARRY FOR A CHAT

I saw Larry in the pub and told him about my "Enlightening Moment," which was what I called this intense manifestation in the moment. I explained how I entered the now after many attempts to do myself in and finally stopped my mind from believing it was real. I said, "Larry, time is an illusion."

I was planting a seed in my mate Larry's head for him to work out.

I apologized to him that it might be a difficult one for him to understand, but nevertheless, it was true.

I told Larry, "I was in my apartment and wrote down the word 'NOW' on a piece of paper, and I held it to the mirror and looked at myself and the paper. Larry, the mirror reflected it back, and I WON. I won the game, I won it, I am a winner. It's all a game; you should get with the programme, Larry."

Larry said, "There was only one man who started time in the first place, one man."

I said, "J.C. himself?"

Larry said, "Correct."

I said, "So much madness in the world existed because of this illusion. Everything would end, if we could just stop time for everyone; there would be no fighting, no wars, none of the bad negative things that the mind insists on creating in the first place. The mind is separate from everyone else. The soul is connected with everything else. The mind is destructive, and the soul is loving energy. To enter the temple is to leave the mind and enter one's own true self, the soul. There is no justifying or judging in the spirit; like in the mind, each and every action one does is justified by the mind. Heaven is here; it's just whether you can live in your conscious, your subconscious, or your superconscious. Those are the three ways of being, and that's where all the truth lays. Not outward observation but inward observation."

Larry left that pub looking very tired; I didn't like doing that to him, but I had to tell my mate the truth. He came back with something good.

He said, "The mind cannot conceive that there is no time."

I said, "I know. Thank you for that, Larry."

THE ENERGY IN ME IS CONFRONTING ME

After a while, Rachel and I were not getting on. I felt that she was attacking me with negativity, and she seemed to feel that I was not giving her any time. The truth was, all my energy that was coming to the surface in me was attracting Rachel's energy, her issues, also having her deal with them. There was even more to this; it was almost like she was attracted to something I needed to develop within myself. We were magnetised on a few levels.

I went for a drink in the local bar and had a laugh with some mates.

Sammy was there; he was from Ethiopia. He was a small lad, about forty-five or fifty years old. He was young at heart, and each time I saw him, he was dancing around to the music. This time, however, he was a little sad.

I said, "What is wrong, Sammy, you can tell me?"

He said, "I have a few problems; the thing is, I can't tell anyone about them."

I said, "Tell me; sure, I have seen it all."

Sammy said, "My mother is dead; she died some time ago, but I saw her standing at the end of my bed a few times when I woke up. I don't know what to do."

I said, "Well, I too have had friends who have died and they are around, so all the people who die are still around. All she wants to do is to let you know that she still exists and is happy. This is a good thing, Sammy. She doesn't want to scare you; she just wants to let you know that she is good and that she is there for you. She wants you to be happy, and I'm sure she is too."

He said, "Really? I was not sure what to do or whether I was going mad, but you have made me feel so much happier inside. Thank you."

Two Muslim lads came into the pub. One lad put his money down to have a game of pool, and the other lad stood at the wall. I walked over to the lad at the wall, where my drink was, and I said, "I'm just in here having a quiet drink, I hope you lads aren't going to blow me up to kingdom come, are you?"

The Muslim lad said, "No, not at all, I'm not into all of that, but be quiet, as my friend is. I don't know what to do; can I talk to you for a second?"

I said, "Sure, what's going on?"

He said, "My friend is getting caught up in all that Muslim fighting, and I don't know what to do. My country is going mad, they're all wanting to fight and be terrorists."

I said, "Well, do you know what's going to happen next in the game?"

He said, "No, what?"

I said, "Well, now is the time for a holy war, and that's what some of the Muslims are trying to create. But the thing is, there is going to be a spiritual revolution. So if you get them all to calm down and relax and stop the killings and just wait for it to happen, then you will be an inspiration in your country. Do you see that picture up there on the wall?" I pointed to a painting of some inspirational man.

He said, "Yes."

I said, "If you stop your country from fighting and let them all know about this spiritual revolution, then you will be in a painting like that one, hung up on a wall in your country."

He said, "How are you so sure that there will be a spiritual revolution?"

I said, "Because I can feel it so strongly that it overrules me."

After that, he left the pub, left his friend there, and off he went on his mission.

The next morning, I got up and went over to get my van. I was walking around the corner and coughed up blood. All the energy in me was surfaced around my chest. My mind was connected with this energy, and all my thoughts were about how I saw this world as so negative. I was walking on the footpath beside the road; I went over towards the ditch and got sick pure blood. Approximately a liter of blood, nothing else, only blood. I was thinking that if this bleeding ulcer in me burst and I died, all of this would have been for nothing.

I needed to get everything down on paper. But this energy would not leave me if I had unresolved negative thoughts in my mind. I needed to address any negativity in my life, in my friendships, as it all had to be harmonised.

I was addressing situations with people that I felt had this same energy in them, or rather we connected with this energy once upon a time; things were not resolved in my life, and I needed to resolve them. My father was one of these people, and we had some negativity let out from both of us over conversations. I wrote him the following email:

> Subject: Re: apology with some reservations.
>
> I apologize with some reservations. I am touched by some of your affirmations of love. Unconditional, and I understand the clime you have lived under to place hard work seven days a week ahead of all things. I realise you may have read my long letter down the track. My "venom," if that is how you have read my email, is to be articulated by my sheer disappointment in you not reading the words of my heart and soul on paper. An explanation of events that have taken place between us in my life that have caused me to be disparaged, at moments in great despair. The fact that I took valuable time to write to you and the postage of money that I can hardly spare is something that adds to my anger . . . my anger even perhaps an over reaction to time and events is still me, and I wanted your love and respect to be there to read and reply to me at that moment. I know there are things that I don't know about you as a fellow human and father—your struggles etc. on all life's fronts. Hopefully there will be a point in the future where we can sit and discuss things on an even platform—to learn and to grow as individuals on this planet.

He replied back:

> Thank you for your email. I fully understand your feelings at my first reply. I should not have replied until I

> had read all of your correspondence in detail. There is a lot to digest and I feel privileged that you choose me to confide in. I, however, should have waited. However, your outburst is what I could not accept. I have been moved by the amount of pain and anguish you have been going through, and my heart is saddened by your feeling of not being cared about. You want a happy and good relationship with me? Well, there is nothing more important to me in the world. I will read through your mail again at the weekend and email you then. I don't have the chance before that. The time taken this time may be well spent.
>
> Love you. Your dad, Arthur

So I was addressing all the situations I had to go through. By either conversations with my father or others or by addressing it all to myself, writing it down, releasing it from myself. Then the most amazing thing happened:

I was in the pub, and Roger arrived back from the coast. There were two New Zealand lads there. One came over to see Roger, and he began to talk with us. He looked at my chain, which was a New Zealand bone chain.

He said, "Do you know, for some reason I have studied bones for years, and it is very unusual to see this type of bone. It's from the old old days, it's from the old animal, the wild boars that were around in the old times."

I said, "It's got soul, yes?"

He said, "Most definitely, that's it, soul."

Another New Zealand lad was there, and I said, "You two are from the islands, and us two are from Ireland; we're all islanders!"

The place was going, as the buzz was there. I walked over to the bar, and it was inside of me: the whole energy body, the huge great weight that was inside of me, was coming out. For the first time since I was born, I was feeling a change in my stomach. The whole time it was weak, negative energy lodged in there, and all the attractions that it brought to my life were leaving me. Rachel was there, but she didn't understand this fantastic experience. I was telling her that I had never in my life felt like this. I said, "It's leaving me, and it was there so long that I don't even know any different. This is amazing."

Rachel wanted to leave the pub. We went back home, and she was getting very worked up and having these angry tantrums. I said, "Will you stop? This is the most amazing thing for me. Live it with me, don't make it terrible; it's great."

So what was happening? Well, this great big emotional body, this energy that was lodged in me for so long, bottled down and kept inside me, destroying my insides, was leaving me. It was moving from my stomach to my chest; it was so great, so big, and so strong. Energy does attract like energy, and it is only now from this observation point of view that I can see what was happening. It was attracting all of Rachel's bottled-down problems from when she was a kid and with her family. She became really angry (which was not like her), and she was going on about her family and crying and sobbing and coming in and out of different rooms and wouldn't leave me alone. It was too great of an experience for me to go through it like that. I packed a bag and said, "You have the whole lot, keep the apartment; I'm moving out. This is too good for me to miss out on."

I moved out for a week and analysed this great experience. The whole energy body inside of me had left. It moved from my lower stomach, upwards. When it was all in my chest, my chest was so compact, and I could feel it all so clear. It was like pushing a big heavy ball through a garden hose. This almost solid weight was leaving me. This went on for a few days, and then it all left me. The energy that was in my mother (that was passed on or passed down) and my father's energy (that was passed on, or passed down) left me, plus all energies that I picked up along the way. I became the freest, happiest man alive. I tried to pinpoint how it happened or what caused it to happen so I could help everyone. But it was just when I shouted out, "We're all islanders," that it started leaving.

The real reason, however, for this happening was that my mind was constantly spinning its endless thoughts throughout life, and at this stage, I manifested myself in the present moment, in the now. All distracting thoughts stopped, all conscious mind thoughts stopped, and full awareness entered in. This was the key to being free. Full awareness intensely in the *now* frees us of this energy, as the energy is only kept down by our minds constantly spinning thoughts around.

See it this way: the energy cannot leave us, as it needs an escape route or a hole in order to leave. We have 50,000 or 60,000 thoughts a day; it is like the solid material that stops this energy from escaping. Just like a solid piece of material is not really solid—it is just so many atoms racing around that gives us the appearance that it is solid. Science actually proves that there is actually more space in solid material than there are solid bits in there. Our minds act like the solid cap that stops this energy from leaving, and we spend all our time trying to bottle it down or keep it deep within so that it doesn't surface in us. We really need to get rid of it, but we don't know how. It takes the shift in consciousness, from mind to within one's self, the subconscious awareness. Then this energy naturally leaves us because our mind does not stop or block it.

The mind is a tool for us to use. Disease is created by set-in-motion thinking, which is connected to the energy in us; it all completes a circle. Either our mind's thoughts create this energy in motion or the energy in us, that is passed down onto us, makes our minds the same, completes a circle, "chasing in tails." Live in your soul self and see that this energy is not you, it is attached to you, and you're cured.

It left me, and I was able to relax, chill out, and feel comfortable within myself. The huge energy body left my body after twenty-four years of it. What a strong force this energy was, and I saw that all those problems with Jackass brought it all to the surface.

But I was not going to thank him. Maybe I should but I am not; I felt that life could have done this to me in another way. That way, I felt, was unnecessary. Also, I was not truly enlightened, so I could not thank this man.

When I was ten years old, that energy was a part of me. There were many years before where I had great pains in my stomach. There was a time as a child where I ended up in hospital. I remember being in the hospital, as it felt good, I was happy in there then. I was not at home, due to different levels of energy intake. It was always the energy feeling for me; it felt relaxed. There were times where I just stayed away from my house and tried to rid this energy by doing dangerous stunts, but when I was ten years old, I realised that this energy that I was dodging for so long was lodged in me. It was a part of me, it was inside of me, and I had no choice in life, as I had to take it in. I remember asking, "Why are people being so bad to me? I'm the one who helps change things, who does good." This was it, energy bodies passed down from family with my nature and this energy; it all became a part of me.

A Guns N' Roses song will always remind me of this: "It's been fourteen years of silence, it's been fourteen years of pain, it's been fourteen years that are gone forever and I'll not ever have again . . . I am past the point of concern, it's time to play."

INTENSELY IN THE NOW—CAN SEE IT ALL

I went to the post office across the road from where I was living, and there were four people serving. It didn't bother me any more to be in this place, the bright lights were not drawing the negative energy in me to attention; as the energy in me was released, everything was just so clear in the now. The people serving were, well, it was just so clear, funny clear. There was a man who was dressed like a librarian with white hair and glasses. There was a woman who was dressed in black with a veil over her face; there were two others also just dressed in a religious way: a Jew with a hat and a Muslim. It was so clear to me. All history is past, held in the mind. Their religions were belief systems passed on through generations, and this was what they believed themselves to be. Basically, all in the now, they were four people dressed up in different ways, and none of them saw that they were in the eternal moment, all the same stuff, all from the same energy source. They were all completely separated from each other, and the separation was their history, religion, place of background, country of birth; it became all so clear. Their beliefs in their minds had them all believing that they were so different, but there we all were, in the post office, in the one moment. Actors they were, but they believed that they were real, that all these beliefs in their minds were real. They were just people with an infinite spirit within them in the one moment, all the same, they just believed different things. Everything became so clear to me as I was awake and knew the same essence that gave them life was the same essence that I had woken up to, that was me. I saw their minds operating, I saw their body language, their separation, and holding dear to them their beliefs that were passed on or passed down. It became so clear to me, and it was hard to keep a straight face. Everyone walking around living in their thoughts, their minds, no one was really awake in the moment; no one was, only me.

It really was just incredible, even now, and hard to find words to explain this. A game, like a play, actors all in one room, but it's called real life, and the actors actually believed all that they had been taught, their beliefs, all of what they thought they were was real. The mind was like a computer with a series of programmes running, constantly thinking of many things at once. Many beliefs were running away in their minds, which gave them the makeup of who they were. But they didn't see the truth; if they could see the truth we would have all been laughing away to each other. The truth was, I was my spirit now; I saw and knew that their spirit and my spirit were from the same spirit; we were all the same essence manifested in this game called life, and they did not know that nor were connected to that—they were in their minds and their beliefs, what they thought was so real to them. So only I was laughing to myself as never in my life had I ever seen life in this inspirational clear state. Maybe when I was a kid I was close to the now, but of course I had to work things out, to get the programmes running in my mind, all the seeds I was taking in, planted in my mind to be worked out, the collective consciousness and all the thoughts everywhere.

Our lives are to complete a circle and come back to what we were like as newborns; we didn't know about time then, nor did we care. It's all one big circle, and it is our aim to try and get back there. The same principle as human nature is to love, to hate, and then to love again. Relativity is the definite in all things; everything is governed by it. We go from a perfect child to thinking in our minds, and the only way we will find happiness truly is to find ourselves again inside ourselves; that's where the happiness is. Have you ever seen how much happiness and fun a child gets from the simplest things in life? Inward observation not outward observation is the way forward. We all at a young age start thinking, trying to work out why, building up our own philosophies and directing ourselves in outward observation for most people all the time. The more one thinks and searches in outward observation all the time, the further they become from the truth. It's all reflection of what's inside. What a game; can you see how it works? Inward observation is truth, firstly realising how the body is acting, body language, and then our feeling, then the deeper aspect; one can find out who we really are, what a game, and most don't even know it's a game. And that's why we're all in trouble; the world is falling apart because people, all in their minds, create havoc, thinking one day I will be happy: "If I just blow this country up here and wipe out all these religious people here, I'll be happy then," or on a personal level, "If I just work all the time and make money, then I can buy myself a place in paradise and be happy forever." Tomorrow never comes, it's always today.

It's all illusion, the mind is never happy; there is no happiness in it, only a frame of mind one could call happiness compared to the other torturing frames of mind there are. The mind is constant; if I have this, I'll be happy. When I own that, I'll be happy. Our own minds run us into the ground and actually kill us, the disease, the sadness, the searching for happiness but not ever finding it.

Our minds, our thoughts create our illness, our pain, our discomfort, our sadness, our bodies to age—some rapidly and others not so rapidly, depends, of course, on what one is thinking. The younger looking person will of course have had more fun in life. Happy times and fun times is the way forward, makes us look happy and younger. The constant thinking, working things out, is good for the mind but may make our hair go grey in a short time. The conflict in the mind from how one feels and how one thinks is not having it altogether and of course creates the sadness, and it's really only a matter of time before we get sick and die.

When I looked in the mirror and saw a grey patch of hair on my head, that was it; I had to rapidly sort out my life, rapidly stop time, stop my mind, and stop growing old. For I was only a young man and just couldn't be having grey hair at my age. I haven't had all the fun yet, I'm doing it all backwards, the old serious part of life while I'm young and then the young part after that. Now I'm at the balance line in my life. If my calculations are correct, I therefore should have a life where it may be balanced out from all I went through, hopefully for me, as this is my theory.

The mind, the body, and the spirit connected creates happiness.

If you could look at it this way, everything is all over the place, and everyone is too. The whole idea is to bring everything together, ourselves together first, and it's then when we realise that we are all in this together.

Scientists have just found out that the stuff that is in trees and plants is the same stuff that we are made from. The core of all the stuff, the stuff behind the DNA and the atoms that are our most broken down form, is the same stuff that everything and everyone in the world comes from. Now, at this evolutionary state in our world, it can be proved that we are all made from the same thing. The only thing that is not funny about these religious belief systems is that the people actually believe it to be real, real enough to kill so many others. The belief of, if my mind is wrong, then I too am wrong, and that is the mind and how it works. Two minds on different frames, different beliefs, will have no other real choice but to kill each other at one stage, unless they can agree to disagree, but this is what were talking about here. This is how it works: see the truth, see the illusion, or we're all staying in this mind torturing infested hell and dying too, I might add.

EMAIL FROM LORA

Lora sent me an emailed with all sorts of things. She was talking about having to leave jobs and get new ones every three months; she couldn't get on the bus, and she was asking me questions about why her mind was the way it was. I could see that she was still herself, the old me, a lot like I was at Kings Cross. So I sent her back an email, hoping to help her. This is what I wrote:

> Yes, we are all there to tell you to move on and make a life of yourself, to follow a dream. It was so hard for me but I'm here now. I made it, and the main thing that made it so difficult for me was the worried mind, as it destroyed me. Once a worried thought came in, it joined with all the others that were put off, it all acted as a spiral of destruction. But now I rose above it, I'm free now. I met a person who did birth charts. I gave him my date of birth and time I was born. I got twenty pages on who I am, amazing stuff. At first it was like reading another language, but I read it again and again. Then I underlined different parts, in different colours. For example, how I got so affected by people's feelings, I'm extremely sensitive, it reads. All the highs and

lows that I read, once I understood them, I rose above those influences, and I didn't get played by the game anymore. Life's a game, hey; denial is the only thing that makes that not true. If you were to get with the programme, find life's rules and then become a player, once all that information is understood, you rise above it all. All the hurt you have received, you write it down on paper; when it's written down, you can read it from an observational point of view. It leaves you with a clear mind. If your room is messy, clean it up, it leaves you with a clear mind. You are a Gemini person, music is just as important as fresh air. You need to travel, need to communicate, as these things give you the buzz. That's why I really needed to get my papers as carpentry worker, as it's my green card to travel the world from job to job. My last job was one of the longest I was on for ages. Five weeks, it was great fun with six Irish lads and one Australian. But now it's over, I'm broke, the van's in the garage. I don't care though, I've no residence but hey, I'm happy. I'm happy but how did I do it?

Well, between dreams of places and then ending up at those places, I figured out something quite amazing. I realised that time could not possibly be real, as it must be built into the system somehow. For how could it be real if I could have a vision at seventeen about being thirty and the feeling was great and I was on the beach? There is no time, the mind uses it as a tool for survival, the mind needs future and past tense to exist, worry is in the mind. Worry attracts worry, and down you go into a depression, negative attracts negative, and away you go, but hey positive also attracts positive so hence the saying, positive thinking will get you far. If you rule out time you end up in a place called nowhere. Time stops, you realise there is only now, time was made up by man, it's not real. When you're in the now, you start to see what is real and what is not real, you also see so clear; as mind judgement illusion disappears, you start to see every answer to every thought you have in your head is right there in front of you. Only you could not see it before because your mind lives in past and future tense all the time, it does not rest. And if you believe you are your mind like 95 percent of people do, then you do not rest. Nothing harms you in the present moment, it is the worry and negative thinking in the head, constantly thinking the worse case scenario, that harms your body and your world. You were convinced you would die if you went home; look at yourself now, not a bother. You will always be here in the now, even when the body you use called Lora dies, you will still be here now. But what do you want then? You want to play the game again. When you're in, you want out; when you're out, you want in. The solution to this relative madness is to die before you die. Need to get out of your mind—particularly if it is as negative as you say it is. You need to control your thoughts, and the way to do it is by not focusing on it, don't give it energy; once you don't give it energy, the thoughts go away. Nowhere then becomes now here. The beauty of this game, the trick is to let go of negative things and to rise above your own game. Once you rise above all influences, then you'll love life, love yourself, love everybody, for you find out they're all a piece of you as were all pieces of the same thing.

All there is, is now; you may be thinking, what if this happens when I'm forty and this and this. Forget it. Get in the now, get a cap gun and shoot yourself in the head until your thoughts freeze; in between those thoughts is peace. Once you get a taste of it, practice slowing down your thoughts, focus on your inner feeling, and then you will learn to get better and better. If you catch up on me, you will realise that what you have here in front of you is more important than winning the lotto itself. You become free. I wish you the best on your journey through the programme. Always remember, there is no right or wrong, only what works and what does not work. Stick with what works and keep an open mind for the love of God. Blockages on one's mind are the causes of all destruction.

Lora replied back, saying:

> "Yeah, cheers, I'm still broke and it doesn't get rid of the hurt or make me want to not jump under a bus."

I replied back, saying:

> You don't get it. It does completely get rid of the hurt, and it does completely take away the fact of wanting to get hit by a bus. Hey, there is a man who did what I did but even better and in a complete different way, and better still he wrote about it in a book in such fine detail. More so than I could ever do; he's a legend in my eyes, I only read half the book as I'm so busy but it's only 102 pages long I think. I read the fifty pages in one night, it would only take two or three nights, so could you get the book for yourself? The book is called *The Power of Now*. Do you even know who you are? A friend that I met on a few occasions named D.J. went home and got himself a rope and sleeping tablets and a Stanley knife. He hung himself, slit his wrists, and took all the tablets. I can help people now who wish to help themselves, and I am not wasting my energy on anything else.

Lora wrote back about being so worried and her mind was making her old before her time and that I was taking pity on her and a few other negative things.

I replied:

> Subject: Power of Now: NOW-WON. Such a powerful word. Get with it. That book *The Power of Now* clearly shows you how to stop your worried mind. I have a mind that doesn't stop analysing until it analyses what interests me, but negative energy and worry distorts that thinking. The worried mind is created by yourself, it's terrible but only you are in control of it. You have trained your mind to worry. One worried thought triggers off the spiral of worried thoughts in your mind. It's up to you to put the effort into just reading this book; when you take the haze

> of worry out of your mind and break it down, you realise what you are doing. You can start to train your mind to think positive or funny thoughts. You can practice this quite simply by observing your own mind, your own thoughts, and think positively. What you think, you create; what you experience, you become. What you send out, you receive. If you think worry, you're sending out worried thoughts, and what comes back to you, only worried moments. You are creating your very own reality all by yourself and no one else. This book called *The Power of Now* will take you from being five steps behind everyone to five steps ahead of everyone. Plus the peace of mind, the comfort of the body, and no more tortured soul. It is the book of books, well worth it to keep reading it until you do understand it; each word is so helpful. I don't take pity on you, I am doing my best to help you. I don't think anyone else would email you if you drove them to sit in a bath and throw a hair dryer into it. I feel that I am more than helpful to you, and I also feel that you must like being the way you are, as you don't seem to want to snap out of it. Of course you will not always be the way you are now; it just feels like it now. Once you're out of your worried mind, you may even laugh at the simplicity of it all. Once you clear your mind of all the negative wasted energy and fill it up with positive thoughts, that's where the magic lies. If you get out of your mind and find yourself—that's where the real essence of life is. There are no limits one can go, positive thoughts create positive reality. Go for it.

So Lora wrote back:

> "I got your book. Walked to town for it, looks kind of difficult to read."

I have a question: how do you forgive someone who's not sorry, who hasn't apologized? You can't, you just can't, so it eats you up inside day after day.

Then I replied:

> If you write down the word NOW, place it in front of a mirror. You will see how far I made it up the game. Are you going to catch me or what? I'm sailing away. You won't catch me in Oz, as I'm leaving in one week. The only way to catch me is to use your mind, body, and soul. Have the three connected, stirred up with some understanding, and you're nearly there. It's the pain body inside you that eats you up. It's created from even one bad experience, any bad experiences. Then your thoughts on the issue, if they're negative, and they will be, that's what eats you up inside, so you must find the positive reasons in the bad experience. Everything happens for a reason. Even when you're driving my energy wild enough for me to put the plugged in hair dryer into the bath, or climb the bridge, I could be like you and let that experience destroy me inside, but I don't, I see the good in it. I didn't talk about going to kill myself, I just tried it; it was such a build-up of so much, and then my mind hit its depression again and my life was full of highs and lows. After I did it and after you left and then I moved to Coogee, my mind didn't worry like it used to. I could see if I started worrying, I would end up sick again, so I learnt from that experience, I didn't let it eat me up inside. I started to live inside, and that's when all the good things started happening. It was more difficult than this, but if you get the gist of what I am saying, that's the important thing. I forgave everyone to myself because it too was eating me up, I forgave them because they didn't know that they were all killing me, they didn't know what they were doing, like you, you didn't know how great of an effect you were having on me. But nothing forgotten, forgiven but not forgotten; that way, I'll try not to put myself through it again, these experiences will stay in my memory, and they won't affect my health.

ENERGY ATTRACTION AS ALWAYS

I met a girl named Rose in Coogee. Rose longed for answers about spiritual essence and beating restrictions and all the illusions, and somehow I came her way bursting with information. I began talking, and Rose was very interested in the present moment, the 50,000 thoughts in the mind, how to see through the illusion of time, and many interesting things. Then some other friends of hers came around, and they were like me, we were like one awakened, intense ball of energy. They knew this stuff; they were not influenced by time, they lived in the now, they knew about energy. They told me about a book called *The Maya*, meaning illusion, and that it had all of life's illusions in it, but it is kept in a place where we cannot get to it. One lad told me that it was his life's mission to steal *The Maya* from the authority people who had it.

I was on a wavelength, a pulse, a vibration of energy that was on a different level of consciousness, an expanded level. I was attracting people on this same level—I would never attract these people into my life if I was not on this level of consciousness myself. Energy attraction is a constant truth in this book, as no matter what level or vibration I am on, I am attracting the like energy out there. Not just the people but the material too.

There was a book that was attracted to me and I to it, The Power of Now. Between energy attraction and requesting it, it came my way. I realised that there was so much I could write about the essence of now and the reality of it, the eternal moment of life. I had tape recordings and things written down trying so hard to explain all of this, but I knew I needed to write about all the other experiences that happened, and there was no way that I could write all the previous experiences and this new reality, as this now could have a book all written for itself.

I could not dismiss this experience, as it was the destination, whilst my experiences were the journey. One could not go without the other.

I stopped walking and stood still, requesting to life, "Could I receive some paperwork on this reality, as there is way too much for me to write down and explain in perfect detail? I have so much to write already, I need some documentation on this reality."

Later on that day, I had the feeling I needed to go to Balmain to see Sandra. I just went over to say hello and see how she was; she said, "Hey, have you read this book before? It's called *The Power of Now.*"

The Power of Now came my way when I entered the now intensely.

This was exactly how it happened for me, and to me, this was perfect.

HOSPITAL

In the job I worked at, I made some money, but all the money that I made seemed to be gone that weekend, due to bills and rent. My car broke down, and I had to pay $1,000 to get it fixed. I also had to pay for my van to get fixed up. The mechanic did it for cheap, but the parts were expensive, particularly the Honda. The night I left my own apartment because I couldn't handle Rachel's negativity, I drove to Roger's place. Then the gears went in my van. I figured Rachel was making spiritual requests that I would have to come back or that something would happen so I would have to stop. Rachel was spirituality evolved. This was what I understood to be the reason for this event at this moment, and she later confirmed that to me. I was still analysing how it worked, and I noticed it worked better with the emotion behind it; the greater the energy, the quicker and faster the answer or happening was served. I had just gotten my van fixed and had to take it back to the garage again for a new gearbox. I had to pay $3,000 on the car and van. I came to the conclusion that it didn't matter whether I worked or not, as money went as quickly as it came. When I was working, I just went through all my cycles in life, my self-education for the book. Nothing else was of importance, really. All these experiences that were happening were for me to write down and prevent the bad ones from happening to others.

One day at work, I was thinking about how I shouldn't have to work; I should be given the time to write and all the rest. I worked that day, and then in the evening I was struggling to fit some timber, and I only had myself to work with it. I tried to clamp all the timber sheeting closed whilst fixing it. I wrapped my arm around it and clamped it off my chest, pulled it tight, and cracked my chest bone.

I then realised that anytime I thought that I needed time off work, I usually had an accident, either cut my hand badly or cut my leg with a skill saw or now I broke my chest bone. Thoughts and requests create reality.

The next morning, when I woke up, my breathing was very bad; I couldn't get a deep breath. So I said to Rachel, "I can't go to work, I'm too bad." I rang the boss and told him, "Remember yesterday I cracked my chest bone by trying to clamp that timber together?"

He said, "Yes."

I said, "Well, I'm gone very bad now and need to get it looked at."

"Go for it," he said. "Ring me when you are out of the doctors."

Rachel wanted to go with me since she didn't have to be in work until nine o'clock. We drove to Kings Cross Hospital. I didn't have my passport, and Rachel reminded me of this, so I went back to the apartment to get it. The pain in my chest increased as I went up the stairs. I couldn't find it and was getting frustrated. I couldn't breathe properly, and Rachel came up.

I said, "Look, let's just go."

We went to the hospital's emergency department. There was a lady behind the counter and one patient outside.

As I looked to my right, I saw a soldier in uniform outside the other department. His face was cut to bits, he looked at me and I at him, and to me he looked like he was out of a movie, as he didn't look real. We went in, I gave the reception girl my details, and we sat down. Someone sat down behind us and said, "I'd know that accent from anywhere, my mother was from Ireland. It was a big move for her to a land of snakes and spiders but fair play to her, she adapted very well."

I felt at ease with this person and at ease in the hospital. There was only really the three of us. He reminded me of someone out of the circus with his grey moustache and wavy hair. We talked about why we were in the hospital with compassion and helpful ways on both our parts. Approximately one hour later, I was getting impatient. I asked the receptionist if I could go out for a cigarette, and she replied, "You're next; if you do, you'll be at the start of the list again."

I looked around and only saw the three of us there, and then I said, "Right so, I'll sit down."

After a minute, I got called in.

I had a chat with the doctor, and then he put his ear plugs in and held the end piece against my chest to check my breathing. Just then, I heard horrific screaming going on. It was very intense and reminded me of the screaming in my house when we were broken into when I was a teenager. I said to the doc, "Can you hear that screaming going on?"

He took out the ear plugs and said, "What?"

I replied, "The screaming, can you not hear it?"

He listened and said, "I'll go check. I'll be back in a second, just wait there."

I said, "Go on, will you? Check it out."

As I sat there on my own, I got a flash in my mind of this crazed lunatic, filled with hateful negativity, running after someone. It was like a clip out of a film that I saw, and in my mind he was running after someone. I got up and walked towards the door to look into the corridor. I got shivers all over me with this mental clip I saw. The feeling was absolutely horrific. Rachel then came running in; her hair was all tossed and there was blood on her face. Her lip was cut, and there was blood on her teeth. I couldn't believe what was happening; had the screams been from her? I had only left her for five minutes and wondered what had happened to her.

"Oh my God," she said, "some crazed bitch just attacked me."

The look on Rachel's face was of pure shook and horror. While a nurse was looking after Rachel, I ran out to the waiting room. There was an old Chinese lady there. I went out the front to check out what was happening outside.

I went over to our friend and said, "What the hell is happening? Why were you not helping Rachel? I heard screams going on for ages."

He said, "It all happened so quickly; the Mission Beat people brought her in, and she just went mad."

I said, "Where are they?"

I couldn't find them and went back to Rachel. I felt for her pain so much; this had been a vicious attack on her. I could feel it, heard the screams, saw the clip, and experienced it in a way where shivers were all over my body. I felt so sorry for Rachel to have experienced it. We hugged each other, and she cried on my shoulder.

The police then came. I told them about the crazed attacker, saying, "This girl should be brought to a veterinary and be put down. Come on, Rachel, let's get out of here."

We started walking out, and one of the nurses said, "Where are you going? We need to check you out."

I replied, "Just outside for fresh air." We left and walked up the road.

The nurse ran out and handed Rachel a form for victims of a crime. I asked what happened in detail, and she told me.

"A woman came in," she said; "it was so strange. She had two men on either side. We made eye contact as the door opened. I thought she and they were coming over to me to get some help off me or something like that. She walked straight over to me and as she got close, her eyes had a rage in them, and she attacked me, pulling my hair; she had the strength of ten men. There was no stopping her. She threw me on the ground and went crazy on me. It was like the two men stood either side of me, and I couldn't even run. It was all so bleeping weird. The crazy one was screaming like she was possessed or something, so vicious."

I brought Rachel to Randwick Hospital to get fixed there. Afterwards, I drove back to the hospital and left Rachel in the car. I asked our friend, who had been sitting directly behind us, what happened. He said, "She came in and walked towards us. As she got close, her eyes became so evil. The only time I have ever seen that look was in an animal once going off, a very vicious look."

I asked the doctor what happened with the crazy girl.

He said, "She is acutely psychotic."

I said, "What did she say?"

He told me that she had said she saw the devil. "The rest was delusional," he explained, "and very hard to make sense off."

I walked back out to the waiting room. The old Chinese lady was there and she stood up. She looked at me and I looked at her. She looked straight at me, her eyes just lit up, and I kept walking but looking straight at her. Then I got it, a shiver straight through my body; all my hairs stood up whilst we intensely looked at each other. She knew me or knew what happened; it was so weird, and all the different feelings were having me so edgy. She was just looking at me in amazement and knew I was intensely in the present. The whole lot was like some sort of play, like a drama starting off with the soldier and then all that happened. The feeling was of hairs standing up and shivers throughout the lot. She must have broken through mind consciousness and was also manifested in the now.

It was like she recognised me. It takes one to know one, and we were both in the shift of consciousness and fully in the now.

I tried to make sense of what was going on; that was why I went back in and asked everyone. Logically thinking, none of this made any sense. But on my findings on the workings on life, things kind of started to make sense. One of them was, Rachel was asking the universe for money, needed money, wanted money, "Send me money now," and she wasn't even doing the "under the grace of God in a perfect way." She was just demanding to the universe. The experience came her way. This event happened in front of many witnesses in a hospital, and when we were leaving, the nurse insisted that we take the victim claim form. Money had been manifested in Rachel's reality. Of course she would not get it straight away but down the road; she would get a payout over this attack.

Now, in this moment that happened for Rachel, there would be many reasons on many levels all in the one moment. Opposites in energy attract, meaning that the crazy girl was full of hatred and negativity and saw Rachel as the opposite and attacked. Also, on Rachel's self-development, having me around intensely in the present moment was bringing her into it also, but there was some residue of energy in her that needed to be released, and this attack shocked the mind, froze the thoughts, and released this energy, thus leaving her to come into the present moment, as my energy was bringing her in that direction.

If I was to be part of this event, life would have had me there, but I was not to be in this event; this was just for Rachel to experience. It was like we were on different frequencies with different vibrations of energy, and I was not to be in it. I was on a different vibration awaiting Rachel to move up a notch from the residue of negativity to full awareness. It was when I got called out of the room that this all happened. And soon enough, I connected with the Chinese lady, us two were in the now—intensely. It was as though that event was not much to do with us but that we were bringing someone else into the now, and that was where our part was played, and that was the closest that we could get to the event.

This gets deep, but this awareness was seen when one entered the subconscious mind, when one was in the now. Life became so amazingly awake but even scary, as I knew the more I knew, the less I knew as a world of unlimited possibilities opened up, and also I felt almost vulnerable as I was so open in a world of unconscious people torturing each other, acting from their delusional beliefs. We were on the other side of the bridge, and even though others were in the room, the Chinese woman and I could not explain what was happening to other people, but we knew it ourselves. We were in a place called "nowhere," according to our minds, but we knew that we were "now here."

SEEING THE FUTURE

Rachel and I were talking about going to New Zealand, as her father was sick and I had to go somewhere. I said, "We can heal your father, I see it."

Rachel said, "Heal him? What can we do? We aren't healers."

I said, "We must become that, as I can see it; we'll do healing work on your father, you'll see."

I guess that I was connecting to my emotional energy, and insight was coming to me. Then I had another vision; I could see it so clearly. There was a man who took all my papers for my book, all the pictures and the conversations that I had, and he stood out over a lake. There was another lad watching, and he didn't really play much part in it, only the two lads were together; they knew each other. I came out and saw this and this was it. There were no actions what I did; all that was happening was this man was holding all my stuff out over a lake, ready to throw it in.

I was thinking that this event would be in New Zealand and said to Rachel, "What is the point in me even writing this book, if there is someone going to wreck it all on me? What's the point?"

Rachel didn't know what I was talking about, as she had her own mind clogged up with problems. I was thinking that the two lads could be people Rachel knew, and there really was no one in the world I felt I could trust.

I also saw some form of a celebration, a happy time with lots of happy people. Three events I saw clearly, but in what order? Why? Who knows?

So what did happen in New Zealand? Well, Rachel and I took a Reiki course, and both of us became healers. Rachel worked on her father, healed his energy, but it was time for him to go, and he left peacefully. But his spirit was there at the funeral, Rachel and I knew that and explained it to Rachel's sister who needed to know. It was sad but bearable for her sister then.

About the man and my book: I moved into an apartment in New Zealand, where I was living with two other lads. Rachel and I weren't getting on, and I needed time out, and Rachel needed more attention. It wasn't working, and Rachel moved out. One lad who was there was stealing things on me, and one night he broke the lock on my door. The other lad was a good bloke and didn't seem to know that his flatmate was a thief; he was known to the town as a thief. So I could see how it was all to work out. The thief and I were having some form of conflict. I put a padlock on my door after that, and a few days later, I went down the road only to come back and find that he had broken into my room; he had looked through all my stuff and opened my cases. I couldn't believe it—it was so clear that my room was broken into, but he sat there on the couch with a grin on his face and claimed not to see anything.

When the other flatmate came back to the apartment, he saw the conflict between us and said, "I might just ask both of you to leave if this continues," as he had his own problems in life to deal with. I could see it all so clearly; none of this was to do with Rachel—I had rented this place. But there was a lake outside, and there was me and the book and these two lads in the vision, the same boys.

The thief just had the urge to create conflict with me, and the other bloke didn't know what was going on—just as I had seen in the vision. It was all so clear; I didn't have to relive this, I didn't even have to live it once. I told the lad, "Okay, I'll move out." He was surprised, but I said, "Thanks for having me and see you around." I packed all my stuff and left. I got my own place.

But it's like going to those fortune-tellers or mystics; we are told things but we don't have to let it happen; all of it we can change. We do have the choice to do that. The celebration, yes, there was a bit of a celebration at Christmas time, where I got to meet many interesting people from New Zealand and some long-lost friends from home. We had a lot of fun.

SNOW BLIZZARD IN SYDNEY

I told Rachel about my theories on how the weather can be controlled and how it works. I was explaining that the weather can be changed by a collective consciousness, or perhaps it was always influenced by us, that the weather was in movement with the energy that we as people put out there. It was influenced by the minds of the world, a complete collective consciousness. I knew this was so because at the core of all existence, thoughts still do exist, but I just don't know exactly how it works scientifically. But then something amazing happened.

Firstly, I had left my apartment and walked to the post office. That post office just amazed me. I, my energy, became fully aware in the present moment; it's funny, actors, characters, all in the now. Then I went to a shop to print out some stuff. The shop was straight across the road from me. Then I felt it. I looked up at the sky. The sun was shining but I could feel a change. It was a clear day but I could feel the energy involved; I could feel the change in the day. I went back to my apartment and stood in the kitchen. I could feel it coming, I could feel that a big snow storm was about to arrive. I had a CD with Christmas music and put it on the CD player. I got out my camera and took a picture of the clear sky so I would have "before" and "after" pictures. I knew what was about to happen and took a collection of pictures to show just that. But only the feeling, opening up to one's own sixth sense, one's intuition, lets one know what is coming.

I then texted Rachel and said, "Happy Christmas."

She texted back, "It's only September, what are you talking about?"

I texted again and said, "Wait for the snow." I started snapping pictures from the bedroom, which had a clear on view of what was to come but still only showed clear blue skies at this moment.

Then it happened: snow fell in Sydney, Australia. Not just little snowflakes but big heavy balls of snow came down from the sky. Rachel rang to ask what was going on, and I said, "It's snowing; it's just started, can you not see it yet?"

Rachel said, "It's not snowing, it doesn't snow here . . ." Then she yelled, "Oh my God! Look at this, it's coming over; people are running under bus stops; the snow is huge! Oh my God!"

I whipped out the camera and took more pictures; snow balls were coming in through my window. It was amazing. I was not sure what was happening, but I was completely in synchronisation with this storm. Before it even happened, I could feel it in my body, in my stomach, all over me, and the bigger the feeling became in me, the more clearly I knew a storm was coming, and a snow storm at that. It's like my mind was connected to my feeling and this feeling my mind was understanding. It controlled me, the feeling I could not deny, this snow storm controlled my whole energy, I became at one with the freak snow storm. The noisy mind did not distract me from the world's emotion. I was now fully connected with my environment.

The mind with all its analysing on weather maps and forecasts could not see this coming, but connecting with the energy that feeds it, the mind knows it all. Stopping the noise that the mind makes lets each and every one of us see what is going to happen in our surroundings. There are huge benefits in connecting with our deeper essence of our selves.

Over this period the weather was going crazy all over the world, and each and every change in the sky's atmosphere changed how I was feeling. Sometimes when Rachel and I would go for a walk and it was sunny, the energy in my surroundings would change, and I would feel all of this and say, "It's going to rain heavy soon," whilst we were walking around without a cloud in sight. Within ten minutes, the heavens would open up and it would pour rain. This happened over and over again for this whole year, intensely from rain to snowing in New Zealand and all sorts of blizzards and storms. I could not deny it; it overruled my whole mood and feeling and energy. I felt happy that I was getting closer to the world's emotion but also sad that I experienced so many storms.

ROGER AND D.J.

Roger was leaving Australia to go home, so we met up for a beer in the Royal Pub in Bondi. He mentioned time again. It had driven him so mad. He must have been thinking about it since I planted that seed in his mind the week prior.

I had nailed the fact that time was an illusion. I not only let it filter through my head for so long, I completely connected with a deeper self and entered a new level of consciousness. I was completely living and experiencing that there was only now. I said, "Roger, I've done it. Time is an illusion."

He was shooting pool, and he said, "How can time be an illusion, D.J.?"

I said, "It is, Roger; it's not real."

He walked around the table and took another shot. I watched as his mind was racing through thoughts, trying to work it out. He walked around the table a few times and was getting so worked up in his own head. This went on for about ten minutes. I realised to myself at that moment, that it was all going to be a war against the mind and the spirit, and that was what was on the list in the game of life. The mind was fed by the spirit, but it believed it was real and would not give up on itself no matter what, because for the mind to understand there was no time was not possible. As the mind lived off future and past tense all the time, time was what made the mind become real. Roger was like a walking encyclopedia; he did know everything about facts and Irish history and so many things. So there it was; two friends, one in the now and the other in his mind for so long, intensely.

Roger came over and said very angrily, "Are you trying to deny that you were born on such a date and that you're not twenty-four years old now?"

I said, "No, I am twenty-four, Roger. There are many more illusions involved that unravel themselves one by one once this concept is realised, but the biggest illusion of all is time itself is an illusion. I live in the eternal moment of now."

You see this, this was the problem: the whole thinking from day one in the mind and the mind believing it was real; for example, a person would rather die than give up their beliefs. So we were talking about the most difficult thing for Roger to accept here.

He stormed around the table; he was getting very hot headed and came back to me and started barking. His emotion then became my energy, and I said, "Come here, you Roger." And I spoke in his ear and said, "I have done it, I wish to show you the truth; you're just like some others. You will watch me die over and over again rather than understand the truth. You better listen to me."

My bark back at Roger was a taste of his own medicine; this frustrated energy came from him, not me, and he asked me to calm down and relax. I was perfectly calm and relaxed after I said that to Roger, strongly and clearly.

Roger was a little startled and said, "Let's just forget about all this and go to another pub."

I said, "It is fine, Roger. I'm just making a point."

We went to a different pub, and even though it was crowded, nothing affected me any more. I was not lost in the consciousness of it all any more. I had risen above this mind influence; I could see all the people dressed up in their different ways, and it was just like a play, just like a game. Everything was very clear; there was no haze in my mind. There was nothing. I was in the now, not in my mind and not influenced by a collective consciousness. We got a drink and sat down. Roger, who completely lived in his mind, was telling me about something. I didn't bring it up, nor did I mention anything about it.

But Roger, for some reason, was compelled to tell me, "There was a man who tried to work out the triangle and that there was no way that he could measure the length of one side without knowing two of the angles and one length. He locked himself in a room, where he tried every single way to see if it could be worked out, but it couldn't. It was infinite. No matter what way he tried, it would still lead to that he needed a certain amount of information to work it out."

Infinity and time; calculations leaving an infinite answer each moment it was done. Roger was nearly onto it!

But then, Roger was getting worked up again as he was racing through thoughts in his mind. The mind has about 50,000 thoughts a day; half were in the future tense and the other half can be in the past tense. From the second we wake up in the morning and leave our dream state of being and enter our mind, we are constantly thinking about what we have to do, what we did the night before, and so on, constantly thinking. I wanted to share this with my good friend Roger, but he couldn't understand. Why? Because he was still intensely in his mind; he was his mind. If I was getting him to deny his own thoughts and mind, he would fight for his survival, and it could be a battle to the death between us, as he believed he was his mind, and his mind believed it was real. It wouldn't give up.

This was why people meditate: to slow their thoughts down; after many years of doing so, they could perhaps make it to live in between the thoughts. It was in between the thoughts where the now was. The thoughts racing around in the mind were the time; they created the reality of time. But it was all illusion. I did it by going the other way. I brought my mind to a racing point where it was killing me, making me sick, coughing up blood, and racing through about 80,000 thoughts a day. Then I cracked it, burnt it out, and finished it off with my trusty cap gun.

So Roger was getting worked up again, and I could feel all the energy off him, thus giving me his frustration. It was not my energy; it was coming from Roger—his racing thoughts were changing the emotion in him, from Roger energy to frustrated (can't work this out but somehow know it is real) energy, and I was feeling it all too. I put my two arms up, clenched my fists, and banged them down on the table, and I got up and went to the bar. I had to snap him out of it, as he was getting lost in his thoughts. This unexpected bang brought him a lot closer to the present moment than the racing of thoughts. The more he was racing through his mind, the further away he was getting. The answer cannot be found in the mind, the thinking; it cannot be worked out in the 50,000 thoughts, even if one races that to 80,000 thoughts, as they are going the wrong direction. The thoughts that we have, and the more we do think, the faster time goes for us. If we slow them down or are bored, for example, the slower time will go for us. Can you see? It's our thoughts in our mind that has time speeding up. But the fact of the matter is our racing mind speeds time up; the boredom, which is the slowing down of thought, slows time down. It's an illusion that the mind loves, as it needs time to even exist.

I sent a text message about this to my brother Jonsey. I explained that time was an illusion but did not explain so much about the now. I started off with the illusion of time, and he said, "I'm onto it, D.J. Sure, we don't have time in our dreams; it is only when we wake up that time seems real."

I couldn't believe it; what a response. I was happy to understand that my bro was all over this.

Roger and I were chatting again, and I said, "I am going to find out why you really had that attack in the city. I will get the answer and will inform you of it when I do find out the real reason for that attack."

He said, "Ah, it doesn't matter, D.J., I'm grand now, and we got through it all. I have to say that it must have been hard for all of you when I was in a coma.

I said, "It sure was, you had the easy part, being asleep."

Roger said, "Yes, I know."

I said, "Roger, what about that time when you went up the coast and Jackass hadn't paid me that money? All the time I looked after you, for the whole time you were over here, you got your money and went up the coast. I'm there for everyone but nobody's there for me. I looked after you for ten months, Roger."

He said, "No, D.J., you looked after me for twelve months."

He knew how to handle me at this stage. That one liner gave me a feeling of appreciation, and I left it be.

With all this talk about time and spirit and astral travel, I went to bed that night and had a dream about Roger and me. In the dream, Roger and I were standing there, looking at each other. Then it happened where we swapped over, and I was in Roger's body, looking at me, and Roger was in me, looking at his own body. We became each other. We were in the Royal Pub. It was all crazy. Then Roger went off with my body and went to the hairdresser's, where he got a complete botch-up job done on my hair, and he came back and laughed so much. Then he was hanging out of different girls and acting the mess in my body, and I couldn't stop him. It was a mad dream.

A SAMPLE OF NUMEROLOGY

One day, I was on the job doing some work and met this lad. I said to him, "Have you studied science?"

He said, "Yes."

I said, "Well, you then know about negative energy attracts negative, positive to positive, and to break it down, like attracts like." He understood. So I said, "People who are 3s attract that level of vibration, other 3 people. Like my mate Larry, he's an 8, and he thinks that everyone will vote for John Howard, as we all need money and he's the best man for the job. I had no idea, nor did I think like that at all. Larry would be attracting all other 8s or like minded people, and given his model of the world, all the people would think like that. He would think that everyone everywhere was thinking like him, but not the case at all. We attract each other; you may be a 7 like me or maybe an 11, both having the same essence in them."

We added him up and he was a 7. Since I said I'd write my book on August 7, everything was coming forth to me. It was an energy attraction. We attracted people on the same vibration as ourselves. Some people would be in our lives, in a group, and we wouldn't want to talk to them. We didn't logically understand it, but within we knew there was no connection and thus no connection happened. But all people that we did talk to were all on our vibration of energy. Or are there to get a part of us to develop, that is—raise a vibration in a part of ourselves like opposites attracting. I'm attracting the like energy of the 7s and the opposites, as the 3s, and Larry was attracting 8s and its opposite, the 2s, which is spiritual or emotional. Larry knew all about that in his life. Life's a game, and I was an awakened player.

SEPTEMBER 11

So what really went on with September 11 (9/11)? Well, 9 is the end of a cycle. Numbers only go from 1 to 9; 1 stands for the beginning and 9 emphasizes the end. The end is usually war in our world; 11, on the other hand, means spiritual, and I guess it is out of the mind's nine cycles, a number away from the primary; it means spiritual. People who have birthdays that add up to 11 usually have some passion to present to the world in some form, whether it be art (like Roger) or singing (like Madonna). 11 means spiritual expression; 9/11 means war/spiritual. That's it! It was not just one attack against Americans by Bin Laden to balance out their actions against the Muslims. It of course could appear that way, but the truth of the matter was, it was a spiritual war. It was the start of an "awakening" to a "spiritual change." It really was a shocker, but it also was a comfort to know what was really going on in the really real world. Nostradamus wrote that during our time, there would be a Holy War. "Holy" is a word to describe spirituality. Who's trying to create the new Islamic change? A certain group of Muslims are. Will they stop? No. What's required? Understanding; we as people couldn't let ourselves live by their Muslim laws, but their laws were coming from old rules and laws towards spirituality. We need to create a new type of spirituality, a new understanding, an open mind understanding, not a closed mind, not a life of fear, but a life of understanding and fulfilment.

9/11 means spiritual war. The number 9 goes into the number 11, so who's going to win? Number 11 will win, for it holds all the other numbers. 11, spirituality, will win, so what's required? My advice would be to delve into one's self and feel and know the truth within, for it is in each and every one of us, as it is impossible to have life without this essence within, and make it an enjoyable change and not a disastrous change like the experience of 9/11. What's required? Knowledge and understanding! Right; I'll do my best to play my part, and all I can pass on is all that life has given me to experience, to give my part in understanding.

I'm not sure if people will understand what I am writing here, as I am finding it difficult to put experiences down as clearly as they were.

But even if a few people understand all I'm writing due to all I experienced, if they connected with it, this could help them out a lot, help them to get back in tune with themselves, follow their own truth, and give them confidence by explaining who they really are.

TONIGHT

I thought of the word "now," an amazing word that directs us to this whole existence. Three letters we're talking about here. Swap them around, what do we have? "Own" and "won."

I went to the Palace Bar in Coogee. Everyone and everything was so clear. People were so clear in this existence, in this presence, with no noise in my mind at all. It is always now, always, and I'm after breaking through all illusions. I have fully entered this now-ness. As I walked around the top floor to see if any of my friends were there, I saw Casey talking to some bloke. I stood there in front of her looking at her.

When she saw me, she became so intense and said, "Oh, my God, D.J., you're standing there like the body of Christ." We connected (intensely in now).

I don't know how she came out with that, but she said it intensely, as if she was in the now, completely awake; maybe she was sensitive like me and felt what I felt. It was the now, the awareness presence I entered, and she could see me like that, where others could not. She must have awareness in her, and others were not connected to their spirit energy or subconscious minds. It takes one to know one. Girls are more aware and have their own presence in themselves. Most lads are in their minds.

Casey and I had a chat. She asked how I was, saying, "My friends said you looked sick and lost a lot of weight. But you look good now."

I said, "Well, a few things happened, causing me to deal with some issues, and I confronted them and released them, and now I'm me."

Then, as we were in the now, there was a girl at the bar; we saw each other and she came over. She took a cig out of her cigarette box. I had a lighter in my hand and lit it. She looked at me, eye to eye. She had a steel cross on her chain, and it reflected the light and shone in my eye; clearly another connection in the now. This vibration I was on, this consciousness, was attracting the essence around me, and it was a very intense awakening. I told Casey three things that I felt she should know, two tricks to life and the truth:

1) The trick is to die before you die.
2) If you don't go within—you go without.
3) And the truth: The intelligence of vibration energy is inside us.

She said, "That's all so true, I'm working on that, Thank you".

SPIRITS—GUIDES—COMMUNICATION

Rachel saw someone in our apartment. She said that she thought it was a ghost, as the person disappeared. She then gave me a description of what she saw. She described the appearance so clearly, and I couldn't help but wonder if it was my grandmother, as the description fit perfectly, right down to the wavy grey hair. Rachel had some gifts herself, and one was to be able to see these spirits when they were around. I'm not sure how it works, but she seemed to have sensitivity in the eyes; somehow she saw spirits. She also had another gift: she can hear what they are saying. I would imagine that they had no voice box, as they were out of their bodies. I experienced this myself, but somehow Rachel can hear them talk when they whisper in her ear, which was how she explained it to me. She said, "I hear what they are saying when they lean over my shoulder and talk in my ear." She has done this before but never told me about this until I explained that I felt spirits around but could not see or hear them. The feeling is so clear and so profound that I know who is there.

We attracted each other on many levels. It was not only a tester relationship for both of us but a deep, meaningful relationship with issues and spiritual energy attracted; between the two of us, we could see, feel, and hear the spirits that were connected to us. And this I felt was amazing, as together we could achieve something that would prove I feel and know spirit is around. It would confirm my story—it would make the truths of spiritual essence manifested in the material world.

THE DON—MATERIALISED

Spirits were around us in the apartment, and I felt it so clearly. I was not taking too much notice about this, as I was so busy writing this book. But knowing they were around was adding to my amazement and happiness. I felt them, I knew who they were and what was happening, and I was just observing. The door to Rachel's cabinet had gotten locked some time prior to this, and no one could open it for three weeks. One day, it opened all by itself, and all her CDs and other things were in there.

Just then, she saw someone walk past in the kitchen. I was looking at her from across the room, and she was just staring into what appeared to be space. There was a glass bowl on a tripod on the cabinet in the sitting room. Rachel was in the sitting room looking into the kitchen; she said that someone was there. I felt the Don around and smiled, as I knew that he was winding up Rachel. The glass bowl just jumped out of this tripod and fell on the cabinet. Rachel was standing right in front of it, and it happened right in front of her very eyes.

She jumped back; looking scared, she said, "Did you just see that? It just jumped off the tripod!"

I said, "It's okay, it is the Don; he's messing. I am just amazed that he can move things."

Rachel said, "This is happening for a while now. I vaguely see an older man and an old woman in here at different times. My keys went missing the other day; they were gone from where I left them, and then later on, they just turned up on the cabinet. I am positive that they were not there. Why are they doing this to me?"

I said, "I know who it is. I can feel Don around now. He's in the sitting room; I don't know why he is getting your attention, but it sure is funny."

I knew through experience that spirits were around; angels can make things happen for us if we ask them. But I was trying to analyse how they could physically move things, hide keys, and so forth. Well, they were spiritual vibrations, like all of us and everything. Don was a spiritual vibration without a body, while I still had a body. So they could do anything, according to my theory. Everything had spiritual essence in it to give it structure and life. Material objects had essence in and around them in order to keep the molecules together. Everything must. So the Don could move things and hide anything he wanted to. I would just love to see a bunch of keys floating around the room, though—that would be really something to see.

I sat down to write and could feel the Don messing around. I kept saying, "Don, I have a whole folder here for you. I have got your pictures and information on you. You're going to have to help me here; there is still not much in the Don folder. Come on, Don, talk to me, will you?"

Keys went missing on Rachel, and drawer were locked. I didn't know Don could move things; they all could. It reminded me of that film *Ghost*, where Patrick Swayze was murdered and was trying to move things for his wife. That was the only way I could imagine it must be. I had no definite thoughts on the exact way it was for people who had passed away. So I talked to Don and asked him to talk to me. He probably was talking to me all right, but I couldn't hear him. He knew Rachel could hear, and so he played some games with her, for her to see. Then Don spoke to Rachel on October 9, 2004, and she wrote down all he said:

The Don said:

And then we were all brothers.
Life was simple and happy.
I had let go of restrictions of a previous time.
Nothing mattered but teaching.
My heart was open to a world of learning and liberation.
I felt free and worthwhile because I was helping others.
I also felt that this was part of an important thing in the world.
I did not care that I did not have children
What I gave my students was better than
I could give my own children.
My heart became open in a way
That I had always wanted it to be
I felt safe and never alone again
This family guided by a higher purpose to assist others was the best—
The rewards was seeing the progress in my students. A divine life.
Life is perfect, was perfect.
I lived to be an inspiration and strong guiding force to others.
My feeling in my heart was the only reward I wished for and received.

Rachel then said, "Okay, tell me about D.J."

The Don replied:

D.J. wants to be a teacher, Will be a teacher
Is more sensitive and passionate than me
His sphere much broader
His mind is too
He could teach me about the world if we sat down for a chat
I love to listen to him when he is inspired

He is a visionary and has a dream.
He must continue and will create a beautiful set of new teachings.
Eyes and minds won't see at first but will after, it will be amazing.
He is my big brother—I look up to him
This cannot be explained but it is so.
We are connected from a time before when we were friends but I always looked up to him for guidance and leadership.
The universe supports him to follow truth.
Mr D.J., I love you for what you do is all divine and full of love—you are my champion too.

So I began to ask questions to the Don, and he would then tell Rachel, who in turn would write it down and show me.

D.J.: "Hey, Don, I would love to sit down and have a chat with you—you are my hope and inspiration. Don, can you tell me about Roger's attack? Was it his energy body inside, his hurt that can come out as anger, attracting the attacker's same type of energy? Can you give me your thoughts on this, can you tell Rachel?"

Don: *"Some people do have emotional problems that can cause a reaction in their lives—I have observed this in some people, although there is no right; in truth, emotional problems (that is the pain body) tend to create pain outside as the outside can reflect the inside if not addressed. Your friend Roger is a very sensitive but blocked person. He felt so different; that made him act out his inner pain in an aggressive way at times. He needed proof that he was a victim. So he became one. Now he has learnt from this experience; he hopefully will not repeat it."*

D.J.: "Roger thought it up many times and sent out these thoughts that he was a victim in life and thus manifested that in his reality. He needed proof that he was a victim and thus became one. This is also our connection when we were living together, as I too believed that I was a victim. This is so amazing and so clear now.

"What about Rachel's attack? It happened at St Vincent's Hospital. A girl came in with two Mission Beat lads, and Rachel and the girl connected with eye contact. The man behind her said, 'She just went off,' adding that he only ever saw that look in an animal going off. We know about the money and not asking under the grace of God, and we have our own theories on it, but can you give your thoughts on this please? Thanks."

Don: *"The girl was and is very evil; she is a victim herself but she has many bad energies attached to her. She wanted to attack someone, as she feels much pain and needs an outlet, so she saw Rachel so trusting and open and saw vulnerability and attacked because she sees her as weak—which she is not but appeared to the girl to be. She is filled with rage at her life so she must lash out. She will only attack an open person like Rachel as she hates that. Rachel does not know what to make about it, she is confused and still working it out, but she saw hate and danger—is still in shock."*

D.J.: "Will Arthur understand the whole story between me and him from the numerology pages I sent him, which show that he became influenced by emotions the year I was born for a nine-year cycle. Will he see I am a victim and not really a bad lad?"

Don: *"The problem with Arthur is he doesn't like to get in touch with his feelings, and you are asking him to look at them and take responsibility for them. He has a very rational mind, which will ultimately brush off spiritual ideas as being something akin to witchcraft, but he won't admit it to you. He is not really deep enough to see how your theories work, and if he does realise, he will feel responsible for causing pain to you, so he would be quite likely to avoid it. He does love you but finds it very difficult to understand you. You are very different; try to understand that he has a long way to go and be compassionate; he is a victim of his own thoughts and fears and can't get on top of them, so he avoids them. You must try to understand this about him—he does not intend to hurt you but you are actually speaking a language he doesn't understand—understand."*

D.J.: "Clearly Don, thanks. Hey Don, do you know my grandmother? Is she one of my guides?"

Don: *"Intimately is not a word I would use about your grandmother. We are all connected but not to the same degree I am with you, for instance. My job is to guide you and watch over you when you travel from point A to point B—she is not doing the same thing, she watches over you. It is a bit different but though we both help you, I do not have a close relationship with her."*

D.J.: "Ah, so that's why my car would spin around on the road and magnetise me to Kirribilli. I was well impressed by that trick. What is the story with all the radios breaking around me since the hospital attack?"

Don: "*The energy has changed around you, and it's affecting stuff. Once your energy is perfectly harmonious, everything will be harmonious.*"

I was looking at a picture of the Don and his group of friends; I asked, "How come the old timer at the opposite corner of the crowd is so sad looking?"

Don: *"He wouldn't say but I reckon he did not like getting old, and he lost touch with his inner child because he was just too serious about life. We humoured him; he may have needed a woman to cheer him up, but he never got one, so yes, he's a grumpy one all right."*

Rachel: "How can D.J. communicate with the Don?"

Don: "*He needs to wake up; if he asks for guidance, I will show him things—not in ways that he is thinking. I am in everything, nature, life, his surroundings—he just has to see. Happy I am, I want him to be too—he needs to relax, take time out, and slow down and breathe in.*"

That was pretty much the closing off of that conversation; it really took place exactly as written.

Anyways, I don't think that I ever saw what I needed to see. I didn't ever relax as such, as my whole life was coming back into my mind, experience by experience, as I wrote it all down just as it was. But I could see that the Don, like many other spirits who have died and left their bodies, could exist in this world but was not governed by our universal laws, like relativity, energy attraction, gravity, time itself. They were above this and were very happy. They seemed to be able to get into nature, that is, make birds fly directly in front of us or to get a bird in the sky to stand beside us. They had the power to put their essence into our material world. They could control and manipulate what was in our surroundings. Life after death seemed to be a happy place with many talents to be learned. It just seemed to be our existence in our minds that made us feel less happy. We lived in a world where there were many problems and unsatisfying ways of living. I believe that if we could just make our world more and more like their world, without leaving our bodies for good, soon enough we could have what one calls heaven on earth. I hope and pray and send out my thoughts that some day, that day will manifest in our reality in this lifetime.

CHAPTER ELEVEN

The Science of Numbers

> "Know thyself; then thou shall know the Universe and God."
>
> (Pythagoras, 598-504 B.C.)

I got all the information in this chapter from Dr David Phillips and another numbers legend named Mark Gruner.

The way that I attracted this information was, I started to see that everything worked off a vibration energy, and even as complex as people are, I figured that there must be a way to analyse people's vibrations, not just the negative and positive energy but a deeper understanding of people, the levels of vibration that they were on. Once I had an open mind on this subject, I attracted it into my life. I was just so happy when it came my way, as all of it is already done, it all exists, just like everything exists in life already. It is just a matter of tapping into what it is you would like to know more of or that which you would like to experience.

You do not need to read this whole chapter; I just wrote it all in so that readers can see their own numbers and the influences that they have in life. I will guide you through this by putting down examples.

Introduction: The study of numerology had its beginnings in the research of the Greek philosopher Pythagoras, who discovered important recurring personality traits amongst individuals who shared similar "ruling numbers." Ruling numbers were directly related to the individual's birth date, and this led Pythagoras to the conclusion that certain numerical formulae lay at the bottom of everyone's personality and behaviour.

Pythagoras discovered a pattern of life forces that affect us all. This knowledge can be used to better our self-awareness and to achieve a more harmonious balance within our lives on both a personal and environment level.

This tradition introduced many hitherto unrecognised aspects of human expression and personality, and when the same practice is employed today, humans discover so many secrets of their inner selves so that life no longer remains a mystery. Such revelations are the purpose of this chapter and this book.

RULING NUMBERS

Our vibrations are broken down to each individual's numbers, and the numbers are explained as follows. The ruling numbers are your pathway in life.

Of fundamental importance is the number that reveals the basic guidance of our life, the number of our pathway. This we call our ruling number or destiny number. It is that important number which is found by obtaining the total of each individual number in our birth date; in all instances but three (11, 22, 33), it can be resolved into a single number. The method is illustrated by the following examples.

Birth date: May 18, 1973 (5/18/1973)

5 + 1 + 8 + 1 + 9 + 7 + 3 = 34

3 + 4 = 7 ***Ruling number 7***

Birth date: November 6, 1948 (11/6/1948)

11 + 6 + 1 + 9 + 4 + 8 =

2 + 6 + 1 + 9 + 4 + 8 = 30

3 + 0 = 3 ***Ruling number 3***

This is very simple to do. The 0 doesn't need to be added in, as it doesn't change the outcome. The whole theory of my own philosophy is that everything is working off a vibration energy. With my nature, I could feel vibrations from others, hence "bad vibes" and "good vibes" and all the energy attractions throughout my life.

So what is to be shown here are these vibrations in people broken down to fine detail. There are twelve vibrations and twelve astrology signs. There are twelve animals in Chinese astrology. There are twelve chapters in this book. Twelve is the name of the game. The twelve vibrations are summarized as follows:

NUMBER 1 PERSON

Positive attributes: Independent, active, original, ambitious, courageous.

Negative attributes: Stubborn, lazy, selfish, dictatorial.

Purpose: Ruling 1 people have incarnated with two prime purposes: to learn to readily adjust to life's many vicissitudes and to help others to adjust. As life becomes more complex, human adaptation becomes more vital. Yet to 1s, the adjustment presents no problem. This quality greatly facilitates their helping others, both in mediating between people and in assisting them to harmonise with external circumstances.

Distinctive traits: Their innate power of adaptability to people and circumstances makes 1s popular in almost every walk of life. They possess a natural ability for making people happy, although, because they prefer not to delve too deeply into other people's problems, they do not always realise why others lapse into disharmony. In fact, they do not delve deeply into their own lives, contenting themselves more with the pleasures of the moment while their air of self-assurance can easily mislead others into thinking they have total command of themselves. This self-assurance is usually based on their physical and social aptitudes (such as in sports and at parties), noticeably diminishing where emotional involvement is concerned. In a light-hearted manner, they are artistic in expression, with a sensitive touch, which makes them good instrumentalists and capable judges of quality in clothing and materials.

Recommended development: The most important aim for a 1 is training to strengthen their individuality. They must not allow themselves to get lost in conformity or mediocrity but rather expand their powers of awareness by a conscious application of disciplines; these are indispensable exercises in self-enlightenment. To a 1, they are doubly beneficial. Based on silence and meditation, these exercises cover such essentials as memory training, moderation, fortitude, compassion, harmony, and order.

Overall: These people are confident, debonair, and bright, with a general happy disposition; they possess an extremely sensitive touch and are very capable in buying and selling.

NUMBER 2 PERSON

Positive attributes: Co-operative, peaceful, gentle, reserved, analytical.

Negative attributes: Introverted, moody, sentimental, overly sensitive, pessimistic.

Purpose: These people have a special ability to work with and under the guidance of dynamic leadership. They are not leaders in themselves, nor have they the desire to lead, but they possess a unique ability of seeking out and associating with the type of person or organisation with which their own diligent capabilities may be most appreciated. Their special role is to complement by providing loyal support.

Distinctive traits: They are intuitive, sensitive, reliable, diligent, and compassionate, possessing the important ability of peace-maker, sometimes to the extent of reforming (and in this emerging new age, this is a very valuable virtue). They are less motivated by ego than most people, possessing the selfless and noble ability of merging their ego with that of their associate when desirable.

Recommended development: These people should employ their intuitiveness to develop self-confidence and to choose as friends and associates those who appreciate their distinctive traits. This is important for their personal development. As they mature, 2s naturally discover the importance of emotional control—how to use it as an aid to their sensitive expression. It will be a considerable benefit to them to develop their mental faculties, especially powers of deduction and memory. Such development will firmly anchor their self-confidence.

Overall: These people are supportive, intuitive, exceptionally reliable, peacemaking, compassionate, egoless, and expressive through their hands.

NUMBER 3 PERSON

Positive attributes: Artistic, self-expressive, effervescent, optimistic, happy, imaginative.

Negative attributes**:** Extravagant, vain, nomadic.

Purpose: As these people emphasise the mental aspects of life, it is clear that their purpose relates to their thinking capabilities. For them, the understanding of life and development of personality are related to their thought processes as opposed to intuitiveness or practical involvement. Their service to the community is similarly most beneficially expressed through thinking, planning, analysing, and so on.

Distinctive traits: Their active brain, lively sense of humour, and general mental alertness contribute to make 3s highly successful in their working life and among their social contacts. They are often the life of the party or the brightest person in the office, but this success does not always operate in their homes. While they are socially bright and breezy, with constant companionship they often become critical. This can be very wearing on close associates, especially spouses. They enjoy helping people so long as they have rapport on a mental level and the other people are prepared to be co-operative.

Recommended development: These people must learn to develop sensitivity to the feelings of others. In recognising that life's experiences are a constant school of learning, their success rate is greatly improved when they learn to live in harmony. This makes for a more positive outlook on life. 3s must learn not to blame others but to use their natural power of resilience to bounce back with renewed vigour, looking upon the experience as a helpful opportunity. It will be of great benefit to them to broaden their base of expression by cultivating their intuitiveness and by being more practical in day-to-day affairs, especially around the home; for example, by actually cutting the lawn rather than theorising about how it should be done.

Overall: These people are assessing, mentally alert, planning, analytic, and often have a sense of humour; they also often have marriage problems.

NUMBER 4 PERSON

Positive attributes: Trustworthy, practical, dignified, tenacious.

Negative attributes: Dogmatic (to excess), narrow-minded, repressive.

Purpose: While we are incarnated on the earth plane, human experience is usually related to the material. This is especially so with 4s, whose development in early life is to recognise how well they express at this level. But as these people mature, they find their purpose elevates to more of an organisational one, thereby allowing for greater scope in gaining awareness and wisdom.

Distinctive traits: These are people with a natural flair for using their hands and often their feet. Their love of practicality keeps 4s on the go. They can rarely sit still and watch others do the organising, invariably coming forward to offer worthwhile assistance. They are among the most systematic, reliable, and trustworthy of people. This is especially evident in detailed work, where their accuracy and practical ability are second to none.

Recommended development: Three important avenues of development should be undertaken by 4s: relaxation, mental application, and expanding intuitiveness. Relaxation is important as a means of detachment from material concerns and from physical involvement. It also provides an excellent basis for mental and spiritual development. Such relaxation is best achieved through meditation techniques, which direct thought into channels of concentration and then relaxation. The most suitable forms of mental application are in memory training and the employment of academic principles related to manual skills (engineering, for example). Seeking the principles behind outward manifestations will assist with expanded intuitiveness. This can also be achieved through practical involvement (doing it yourself) in music and art, as well as through the study of the science of numbers.

Overall: These people are practical, organising, orthodox in outlook, often materialistic, interested in sports, and very capable with their hands.

NUMBER 5 PERSON

Positive attributes: Versatile, adventurous, sensuous, progressive, happy.

Negative attributes: Self-indulgent, aggressive, irresponsible, inconsistent.

Purpose: The mastery of sensitive expression (whether through verse, prose, painting, sculpture, etc.) is one of the real refinements of all human life. However, it can only be achieved when adequate freedom prevails. It is just this type of expression which 5s seek to develop as a means of acquiring the command and understanding of their emotions. But few of them are aware of this, feeling only the drive for freedom, ignorant of its real reason, which is to learn to constructively direct their lives by means of it.

Distinctive traits: They are intuitive people, with a strong artistic flair, gaining immeasurable pleasure from being free to express themselves.

With such freedom they are lively and dynamic, but if confined they tend to become sullen and apathetic. Yet they are usually very good natured people with a strong determination to enjoy life and to help others do so as well.

***Recommended development*:** Very often our search for freedom is a hankering for those pristine days of carefree innocence, the recollections of which are occasionally stimulated to bring to our consciousness a glimpse of many incarnations passed. But we cannot live in history, except to use its lessons for our further development. Thus, when current circumstances appear to restrict us, we should be aware of the lessons we are intended to derive from them. Then we can move on, graduating away from such confinement. There is a need for 5s to develop more attention to detail, for in this manner they gain a wider perspective of life through greater practicality. They should accept suitable opportunities for travel to develop their powers of observation as a means of understanding more about life.

Overall: Their nature is independent, intuitive, artistic, adventurous, moody—oscillating between joviality when free to be emotionally expressive and sullenness when feeling suppressed.

NUMBER 6 PERSON

***Positive attributes*:** Responsible, conscientious, humane, loving, unselfish, tolerant.

***Negative attributes*:** Nervous, cautious, jealous, narrow-minded, pessimistic, interfering.

***Purpose*:** Here we find people who excel as creative artists, as dramatists, or, on a more private level, as exemplary homemakers and comforters to mankind. This implies a very important responsibility in human affairs, one that demands a deep, loving dedication. All people with this ruling number possess such capacity, but often they become so physically identified with their responsibilities that anxiety and emotional worries entrap them. 6s must learn to master those situations into which their great capacities for love and creativity draw them rather than let the situations control them. To this end, they must learn the art of loving detachment so that they may express their beautiful creativity without being imposed upon.

Distinctive traits: Their exceptional creativity finds every opportunity to express itself at work, at pleasure, and in the home. To 6s, the home is the most important place, as it occupies a considerable amount of their creativity and is second in importance only to their loved ones within it. Being great humanitarians, these people resent injustices of any kind and are exceptionally loving, unselfish, and tolerant.

Recommended development: Let those with this ruling number learn that love is a state of being, of freedom—not of possession. Possession is foreign to love, often destroying love, as it produces restrictions and anxiety. Love is a state of joyousness and is above emotional limitations, yet it can call upon emotional expression to indicate its presence (but no more than indicate). Love should not be confused with or limited by, the emotions any more than the celebration of Christmas should be limited to the giving of gifts. 6s must learn to develop a wise firmness. This will not hamper their creative development but rather permit it, for it will ensure they are not imposed upon by unthinking or selfish people.

Overall: These people are creative, loving, just, unselfish, tolerant, and home loving but inclined towards deep worry and extreme anxiety.

NUMBER 7 PERSON

Positive attributes: Analytical, reserved, dignified, peaceful, trustworthy, affectionate.

Negative attributes: Sarcastic, pessimistic, lackadaisical, inconsiderate, quarrelsome, secretive.

Purpose: It would appear that the manner by which individual human development takes place in life ensures that each soul incarnates as a

7 when it is necessary to undertake a major step forward. The unique aspect of this ruling number is its almost limitless capacity for learning through personal involvement. Enlightenment gained in such a way invariably qualifies 7s to be able to share their experiences, making them excellent teachers.

Distinctive traits: These people are found among the most active in all walks of life. Although not always conscious of it, their driving force is a need for personal experience. It is a fundamental law of human life that personal experiences become the most memorable, consequently the most valuable when they are the result of personal sacrifices. This is the path of the 7. Many of them appear to have rather sad lives, suffering losses in love, money, or health when their actions are in conflict with their higher guidance. But they possess a tremendous natural fortitude as well as an inherent confidence and deep philosophical understanding, recognising that everything occurs for a purpose.

Recommended development: It would be of great benefit to 7s if they embraced as much discipline in their lives as they seek to teach others. By this means, they will evolve a more reliable intuition and a well-balanced philosophical outlook. They are naturally slow learners due to their need to experience so much for themselves. Parents should take special note of this characteristic and permit their children with this ruling number to learn at their own speed. The family must realise that children with this ruling number learn rapidly until age seven, at which time they seem to need to stabilise. Their academic learning rate decreases markedly between the ages of seven and fourteen, a very important period of spiritual growth in their lives, when they turn inward for the first time.

Overall: These people need to learn by personal experience; they dislike discipline and are assertive, philosophical, teachers, and helpful, leading a life in which many sacrifices must be experienced.

NUMBER 8 PERSON

Positive attributes: Powerful, successful, independent, confident, active, forceful, creative.

Negative attributes: Dictatorial, thoughtless, interfering, materialistic, intolerant.

Purpose: One of the most important aspects of love is our ability to express it. One of the most important components of successful human relationships is a fluent ability to express appreciation (itself, a vital embodiment of love). It is in these two avenues of expression that 8s find greatest difficulty, consequently an essential feature of their purpose in life is to transcend these limitations. Growth in this direction comes with the realisation that rather than inhibiting their independence, such improved relationships strengthen the confidence others have in them. This, in turn, creates greater personal security and improved happiness in their lives.

Distinctive traits: A strong air of independence and dependability, together with a self-confident manner, are distinctive in the attitudes of 8s. Both qualities work in harmony to equip them for positions of seniority and responsibility, where many are found in industry and commerce. But their independence transmutes to an undemonstrative attitude of coolness, bordering on indifference, in the home. This is related to their difficulties of self-expression, an inhibition which maturity often helps to overcome. Their love for helpless creatures—for animals, infants, the dependent, and the very sick—is constantly expressed.

Recommended development: Every effort should be made to overcome the undemonstrativeness they unvaryingly exhibit towards their loved ones. Until this is achieved, they will not find real happiness in the home. They must learn to eschew aloofness and to express overtly the appreciation and love they possess for their spouse rather than hide these feelings and expect the spouse to know they exist. A successful marriage cannot be achieved when one partner takes the other for granted.

Overall: These people are independent, dependable, self-confident, undemonstrative, commercially oriented, and deeply concerned for the sick and the helpless.

NUMBER 9 PERSON

Positive attributes: Compassionate, generous, humanitarian, sympathetic, philosophical, trustworthy, idealistic, sensitive, benevolent, artistic.

Negative attributes: Impatient, dictatorial, insincere, inconsiderate, overly emotional, indiscreet, impulsive.

Purpose: This is a powerful ruling number in the affairs of man. Those who possess it are intended among the guardians of our cultural heritage. They are far more suited to art than to science, to humanitarian pursuits rather than to commercial ones. Most of our potential philosophers, reformers, and cultural leaders are to be found with this ruling number, although not always are their idealistic concepts the most workable—it is an important aspect of their purpose in life to translate the idealistic into the practical.

Distinctive traits: Responsibility is their forte; they are exceptionally honest and intensely idealistic. Honesty is so natural to them that they assume everyone to be so inclined. This often leads to great disappointments in people. They would rather give money to needy people than save it for themselves. They have very definite thoughts about life and its ideals, about humanity, and how people should be motivated. Even though these ideas are not always the most practical, 9s will always strive to implement them, for in these areas they are ambitious people.

Recommended development: The strong idealism of 9s does not make for good judges of character. Yet once this limitation is realised, it can be remedied by their studying a reliable guide to understanding people, such as the science of numbers. Such a study will help them to investigate all aspects of a person before drawing conclusions. This in turn will help develop intuition. Patience and persistence are two other important traits these people often lack but which can be cultivated from the numerological study of their own and other people's personalities.

Overall: These people are responsible, extremely honest, idealistic, ambitious, humanitarian, and very poor at saving money, with a serious attitude to life.

NUMBER 11 PERSON

Positive attributes: Intuitive, idealistic, visionary, cultured.

Negative attributes: Sarcastic, thoughtless, introverted, materialistic.

Purpose: These people are among the few who are potentially best equipped to guide mankind into the emerging new age. It is a very responsible incarnation they have chosen. Unfortunately, many find that as they recognise life's physical attractions, they are diverted from their higher purpose. As we move into the new age, we are becoming aware of those profound metaphysical forces that express themselves through the faculties of clairvoyance, intuition, ESP, and spiritual healing. A high proportion of 11s will be found forging ahead in the developments in this field.

Distinctive traits: There are extreme differences between the lifestyles of 11s who live positively and utilise their exceptional spiritual powers and those whose life appears difficult and colourless. An uncompromisingly high level of morality, profoundly reliable intuitiveness, and inspired driving force are clearly in evidence. They are extremely dependable, honest, and just, with a deep love for family and friends, together with a sincere compassion for all life.

Recommended development: Spiritual faculties do not mix well with commerce for 11s. Consequently, their best avenues for development lie in those professions that can facilitate growth in spiritual awareness as well as provide adequate monetary rewards. Their natural generosity and spontaneous habits of assisting people in need—admirable virtues, indeed—create a more than average demand on the financial resources of 11s, so they should learn to recognise priorities and be guided by their intuition rather than any desires for recognition. They are often tempted to reject assistance for themselves when in need but must learn to be more receptive and recognise the benefits that can accrue to the giver and receiver of such practical co-operation.

Overall: These people love refinement, beauty, and all things with have a deep cultural substance; they are highly sensitive, intensely honest, and compassionate, often preferring to avoid the life of hard business.

NUMBER 22 PERSON

***Positive attributes*:** Powerful, successful, artistic, emotionally controlled.

***Negative attributes*:** Materialistic, dictatorial, insensitive, overbearing, obsessive.

Purpose: As human life continues to evolve through stages of progressive enlightenment, there will always be people with outstanding leadership whose purpose is to guide such evolution. This they achieve in much the same way as some outstanding directors guide the unfolding of a movie or a play—they might take a minor role in it themselves but never the starring role, preferring to guide from behind the scenes where the decisions are made and the entire overall design is formulated. In whatever walk of life they find themselves, if 22/4s are living positively, they are invariably at the core of the organisation. With the approach of the new age, the role of these people is particularly crucial, for their personal enlightenment is a beacon whose light will illumine the path and guide countless others, many of whom will not realise from whence came the guidance and encouragement. It is generally not characteristic of 22/4s to be found in the limelight of human affairs; in fact they work far better in partial anonymity so long as they gain sufficient recognition by way of respect and co-operation to facilitate their work.

Distinctive traits: One of the most noticeable traits of 22/4s is emotional control, which is fundamental to their purpose. So it is for this reason that they adopt it rather than from any desire to be exclusive or difficult to understand. Actually they are very sensitive people with deeply loving natures, although only their closer friends come to realise this. 22/4s rarely fail to accept a challenge, especially if it involves human welfare. They will be found in some of the most difficult and seemingly dangerous environments but are usually cool and careful in the execution of whatever work they are directing. Their capacity for responsibility is limitless, and because of this, others come to depend on them, too much perhaps, producing both an unfair burden on the 22/4 and encouraging a little laziness on the part of the other person.

Overall: This is the master number whose bearers have the most extreme levels of personal responsibility. They are highly intuitive, with a very tight rein on their emotions and an intense concern for human welfare.

For this unusual number, I'll give an example: Margaret Thatcher, born October 13, 1925.

October = 10 = 1. 1 + 1 + 3 = 5. 5 + 17 (1925) = 22.

Recommended development: For all 22/4s, it is important to ensure that life provides a balance of work and pleasure. To be sure, they have such a considerable aptitude for work that they often dismiss pleasures as a waste of time. Their development along artistic and cultural lines through hobbies, such as singing, dancing, painting, writing, or similar pursuits, will greatly help them to express their feelings more capably and loosen them up emotionally. They must always endeavour to have good academic training and are never too old to get it. (Lack of opportunity in childhood is never a valid excuse.)

NUMBER 33 PERSON

Positive attributes: Humane, emotional, highly sensitive, dependable, trusting, loving, compassionate.

Negative attributes: Nervous, introverted, overly emotional, highly strung, overly physical.

Purpose: A 33 would possess extreme combinations of the positive and negative character traits of a 6. So one can refer also to the number 6 in regards to this number character. The total emphasis of this master number lies in their extremely loving nature. They strive for justice and will protect the underdog regardless of personal consequence. They are tolerant and dependable individuals; harmony is extremely important to their well-being. They are also highly sensitive and emotional people who wear their heart on their sleeve. 33s are at their best when dealing with children, old folks, and the infirm, for here their compassionate nature is able to fully understand the problems and worries of these individuals.

An average 33 would possess far more positive than negative characteristics, but again somewhat more humanised and less angelic. Harmony is essential to these people, harmony of home, work, associates, and companions. Similar to 6s, they place their desires secondary to the creation of a happy home environment. They usually enjoy a large circle of friends who all have similar characteristics to their own. They abhor violence in any shape or form and would go to any lengths to avoid a confrontation that could result in physical exchanges. 33s possess a natural affinity with animals and will often "walk where angels fear to tread" within these areas. They are life's natural worriers, who invariably spend a great deal of time worrying over the smaller, unimportant, day-to-day problems that frequently occur. However, when major mishaps and traumas arise, they can be relied upon to keep calm and carry on in the face of adversity.

Overall: This person is an emotional power house with much capacity for good and a sensitive and compassionate nature. They love harmony and abhor violence of any kind towards any creature.

DATE OF BIRTH

The following section explains the influence of each date, ranging from the first to the thirty-first, of any month.

1st

Strong will power is evident, coupled with independence and exceptional analytical ability. A practical, idealistic person who is capable of devotion to causes and people. Encouragement is important, and although a sensitive, independent spirit is enjoyed, they must learn to express the great latent energy and power within them.

2nd

These people are emotional, sensitive, and intuitive. Other people appreciate their understanding, which cries out for affection and love. They must beware of becoming depressed and moody, as this turns their emotional awareness inwards, causing anxiety and mental turmoil. These people can find it hard to bounce back to reality when depression sets in. Rhythm, music, group activity, dancing, poetry, and other fields that nourish their talents are advisable.

3rd

This is an artistic day number full of vitality. Restlessness is evident with this day number. They portray an easygoing, sometimes couldn't-care-less attitude. The natural ability to express themselves makes them great actors. They have a great imagination, which combines with their other talents.

4th

The love of home and family life is paramount within their lives. They have an affinity for such hobbies as sculpture, music, and painting and could well profit on numerous variations of these pursuits.They must beware of being intolerant or dominant over others. Love expression is somewhat limited. Basically, they should always try to maintain surroundings of a happy nature, attempting to undertake pleasurable pursuits in hobbies and leisure times.

5th

These people are versatile in all areas of life. They have an infectious, sparkling manner. But they need to balance this and localise their energies. They prefer to associate with lively individuals who possess the same extroverted nature and love of variety and freedom as their own. Consequently, this attribute makes them precarious marriage partners.

6th

These are humanitarian people who seek to find the good points in others. They are life's natural givers, dispensing spiritual love to one and all. But they often receive little in return. This capacity to love obviously produces a firm basis for marriage and friendships. They get on very well with children but have a great tendency to worry. Harmony is essentially their key note. Consequently, music should provide the best outlet for their natural ability.

7th

These people should always investigate new people and seek to avoid deception in business matters. Their set ways do not with make them easy people to live with. They should learn to relax more and make a special effort to commune with nature and meditate every day. These people frequently desire to be alone with themselves for at least some of the day. They need to do this to harmonise negative influences of others associating with them. This is a testing day number that often burdens the holder with obstacles throughout life. It's essential that they gain knowledge, thus allowing them to impart their wisdom to others in need.

8th

People born on this day number make ideal businessmen and women, as they are able to conceive a grand plan and plan accordingly. They should avoid forming partnerships, as not many can conceive the ideals of an 8 person. They are scrupulously honest and trustworthy. Though they are idealistic, they also have the potential to rise to the very top in most fields of endeavour.

9th

Many people will benefit from the humane efforts of those born with this day number. Sadly, the desire and ability to help others is often not reciprocated, with the result that they are frequently used and abused by one and all. They should always take extreme care in their choice of career or vocation, as their open-mindedness leaves them vulnerable to deceit.

These people often experience "one way" marriages that invariably finds them giving all and taking very little in return. This is a beautiful day number that realises fully the need to help others—it is sad that these qualities are often abused by unscrupulous individuals.

10th

This is a fortunate vibration, showing a good mind, determination, and the will to succeed. They are creative people with the ability to promote any idea as long as they believe in it. They can handle multiple tasks at one time. They must not let home affairs overburden them, as this could reduce their ability to keep hold of their many business reins.

11th

This is a "Master Day Number" that often shows a tendency towards erratic personal behaviour, being up one minute and down the next. These people are highly strung and inclined to be nervous, but this tendency is often balanced by their strong intuitive gifts. They should make a conscious effort to keep in good health, thus building a barrier against the effects of nervous energy.

12th

This number shows a great love of life, coupled with the desire for action. Possessing great magnetism and imagination, they have the ability to change other people's opinions to suit their own line of thought.

Their mission in life is usually fully known and realised, and as such their gift of imagination steers them adequately on the right course to success.

However, their life seems to follow a series of highs and lows, mostly caused through their desire for immediate action. They are inclined to be distracted by temptations (not necessarily romantic) that should not be succumbed to, as their line of direction and ambition could be sadly affected.

13th

Far from being unlucky, this birth day number produces excellent managerial potential with the ability to motivate and stimulate others to work beyond their normal capacity. Anything to do with the earth, such as mining, geology, building, or construction, is definitely suitable for a person born on this day. Their stubbornness often hides a good logical mind, but they must learn to listen rather than to dominate conversation. A harmonious home environment is essential for their well-being, as they are unable to work under emotional stress, often taking work problems home and vice versa.

14th

These people possess a prophetic nature that combines harmoniously with an ability to reason things out on a down-to-earth, matter-of-fact level. They have a flair for business on a grand scale, which can be utilised to its fullest when self-employed. Artistic hobbies are advised, even if only to subdue their natural gambling instinct which, if not controlled, could produce disastrous results. Due to their doubtful choice of friends, this number attracts many hangers on who find it relatively easy to take advantage of their trusting nature. This is a very powerful number, which if misused could be destructive to themselves and others close to them.

15th

This is an excellent, harmonious vibration. Their understanding nature, together with their ability for dedicated self-sacrifice, makes them loyal and worthy subjects for any deserving cause. Music often exerts a profound influence upon these people. They are generally fond of life and realise that maintaining a correct balance of health is necessary to their existence. Their generous, charitable nature guarantees close, everlasting friendships.

16th

These people must control a basic tendency to become irritable with others. This, when combined with an aloof nature (this day number's weak point), could cause disruptions amongst those closest to them. People born on this day number cannot be told what to do. They intensely dislike interference from others and will, if provoked, erect a mental barrier that will completely ignore the suggestions of the person in question. If they learn to open their minds and hearts to the world, then people would be attracted to them of their free will.

17th

This is an excellent day number for banking interests and general financial affairs. Great success is promised in these pursuits if they can become less set in their ways and learn to unwind. They should try to use their lofty minds and proud spirit to help manage the affairs of others. They are incidentally doubters of occult subjects and should learn to keep an open mind even when proof is seemingly lacking.

18th

People born on this day number often become associated with vast community efforts, where their natural gift for administration can be enjoyed. Usually the first attempt in any particular field is not successful. They must learn to continue their efforts and "try, try again." Luckily their judgement and reasoning are sound. However, they should be aware that opinions should at least be listened to even if not acted upon. Problems associated with marriages and friendships often occur; however, this can be overcome if they dedicate themselves to making these close associations work. Effort is needed, and effort must be given.

19th

These people can rise to great heights and then fall swiftly to great depths, if they allow emotion to overrule their gifts of logic and perseverance. Their versatile nature can enhance their success in many pursuits including medicine, law, art, and music. They frequently possess an inherent carefree nature, although this is not necessarily displayed openly. Despite their nonconformist attitude, they respect responsibility. Therefore, a career in politics or local government could provide an effective vehicle for their original minds. They are continually striving for a better way of life and would detest being kept down or inhibited in a mundane nine-to-five vocation. Those close to them should be aware of this character trait, preparing themselves for difficulties that could occur as a direct result.

20th

Working with others in a small business or in a friendly, sociable atmosphere would attract those born on this day number. These people usually prefer to express themselves in the written rather than spoken work, although they are by no means inarticulate. Their numerological profile indicates a well-educated person who is sympathetic and affectionate towards others. They are not really the manual labour type, although they like to be close to nature and enjoy the open air life. Hard physical work does not appeal to them. Unfortunately, mental pursuits are usually associated with city life, so it is important that frequent revitalising trips to the country are made by people born on this day number, if only to provide a much needed mental break.

21st

These people possess a natural aptitude for dancing as well as a gift for the arts. Their fine voice could be used equally as well in public speaking or singing. They have a good mind, and educational pursuits would be advantageous to them, especially where instruction of others is required, such as teaching or vocational guidance. The tendency to worry excessively, usually over minor problems, often makes them flighty, nervous, moody people. They must learn to express their desires and problems rather than keeping them bottled up inside, thus magnifying them out of all proportion.

22nd

This is a "Master Day Number" that can bring about extremes of nature. Consequently, balance must be aimed for at all times. They experience frequent ups and downs that are usually caused by nervous and physical overaction. Blessed with a strong intuitive ability, they often experience never ending battles between acting out their ideals and trying not to overstep the limitations imposed by society and those within it. They can and frequently do succeed in any field that fulfils their highest ideals. Innovators, artists, and musicians all feature strongly amongst this day number.

23rd

These people possess a sympathetic, understanding personality and must progress through life utilising their gifts for the service of mankind. They are intuitive people able to understand the needs of others, leaving them ideally suited in the fields of medicine, nursing, and psychiatry. They are independent, self-reliant people who are able to work and live unaided by others. This strength of character attracts others less dominant to them. Consequently, they often provide motivational influence to other people's eventual success.

24th

This is an action day number, and as such, these people abound in energy. This is a tremendous attribute if used correctly and if suitable creative outlets can be found, but if abused, an ineffectual, restless person could result. Living with a person of this day number can be both exciting and frustrating, as their life can change direction from day to day. Although they are domestic creatures and seek the joys of a happy home environment with children around them, they find it hard to knuckle down to a life of giving and placing themselves second to their offspring. If this problem offers a threat to their career, then deep down, previously suppressed negative traits will come to the surface.

25th

This day number shows heightened intuitiveness to the extent that people born upon this day often possess both an interest and a gift within the occult field. Unfortunately, although this wonderful attribute can offer help to the community, their own affairs often suffer as a result. In matters of love, these people should endeavour to overcome a tendency to wear their hearts upon their sleeves. Self-expression can often take an art form, being naturally gifted in painting, pottery, and sculpture. This day number is also a testing day number, and the people born on it can often experience greater setbacks and difficulties than the average. Experience produces wisdom, and life can only be learnt by living it.

26th

These people must learn to forget what has happened in the past and realise that the present and future are of greater value. Similar to people born on other day numbers, these people must learn to capitalise on success. Their tendency to spread their interests too far can often negate their ability to reap the rewards of life, thus producing frequent highs and lows in their financial affairs. Love of home and children is very important, but they must allow their offspring individuality and freedom of choice rather then insisting upon dominant parental control.

27th

The numerological profile of these individuals indicates a forceful, determined personality that can tend to be erratic by nature. They do not take easily to direction by superiors and should in most situations seek leadership themselves. They have a rather passionate nature, which at times can be overdone. This is most strongly indicated with the home. Wanderlust tendencies often dominate their lives, and consequently their choice of vocation or business often involves travel. This is a powerful day number than can experience extreme conditions. However, knowledge of this fact, together with correct choice of vocation, can often temper these powerful forces.

28th

Love and affection dominate the life of those born on this day number. A sense of freedom is essential, as limitations and restraints placed upon them can cause very real anxieties and suffering. They should cling to their ideals regardless of what is happening around them.

29th

This is another extreme day number, and as a result frequent highs and lows will be experienced throughout life. Vision and inspiration can work to the benefit of the holder, yet it can often create severe problems in the present. These people must learn that the future relates directly to the efforts of what they are actually doing now. A good home is essential to this number, as it provides a solid stabilising base to their normal precarious existence.

30th

These people must beware of a basic bombastic streak and realise that they are not always right. Their imagination and intuition must be fortified with a greater sense of wisdom, which should be gained from the pursuit of knowledge. They make excellent teachers and social workers. They are loyal and reliable though not above dallying in casual flirtations. However, one area of danger for this day number lies within occult fields. Their constitutions and mental programming does not equip them with the necessary strength to maintain equilibrium in these dangerous areas.

31st

People born on this day number also experience extremes within their lives and, as with other similar examples, must learn to capitalise upon their basic talents and strong character traits. These people possess excellent managerial and business capabilities, provided they also recognise and utilise the talents of those around them. Financial difficulties often occur with this day number, but if a forceful attitude is taken, then these problems can often be totally overcome (or at least lessened). The fear of loneliness, especially in later years, frequently haunts people born on this day, and as such they tend to worry unnecessarily about the future. If they open their hearts and live for today, tomorrow's dream will become a reality.

THE PYRAMIDS—YEARS OF MATURITY

Ancient Egyptian priests knew it. Greeks of the Golden Age following the Pythagorean methods were taught it. The early Christian fathers recognised it. But the modern world is only slowly discovering it—that maximum potential of physical, mental, and spiritual fulfillment can only occur when a person matures to the point, as Pythagoras so succinctly expressed it, of "acquiring empire over the self." This is the goal of life's middle or mature phase, that vital period of growth now symbolised by a group of four pyramids.

Provided neither karmic nor environmental influences decree otherwise, human life expectancy encompasses three phases of unfolding: adolescence, maturity, and fulfillment. The initial period, adolescence, prevails from birth through the many changes in bodily development until physical maturity is reached. At a predetermined age, it gives way to the development of mental maturity. This continues for a period of approximately twenty-seven years, by which time people reach a level of fulfillment in proportion to the success thus far achieved. The degree of maturity attained prepares them for spiritual development for the third phase of life, such as the threefold progression of natural earthly life.

Before we look at the ages at which people of different ruling numbers attain the pyramid peaks, we should investigate the numerological foundations for the construction of our pyramids. These foundations consist of three separate numbers, each derived from the date of birth. They are the numbers of the month, the day, and the year (in that order), each reduced to its single digit.

Construction of a Pyramid

Example: May 5, 1982

Step 1. Reduce birth date to single digits, ensuring that the month number is written before that of the day.

May 5th 1982
5-5-2

Step 2. Build the first pyramid on the first two numbers:

1

5 5

The peak number for this pyramid obtained by adding together the two numbers at the base of the pyramid (if necessary, this should be resolved to a single digit). For example, 5 + 5 = 10 is reduced to 1.

Step 3. Build the second pyramid on the second and third base numbers

1 7

5 5 2

The peak number for the second pyramid is obtained by adding 5 and 2, the numbers at the base. These total 7. Thus, the peak number for the second pyramid is 7.

Step 4. Build the third pyramid on the two existing pyramids.

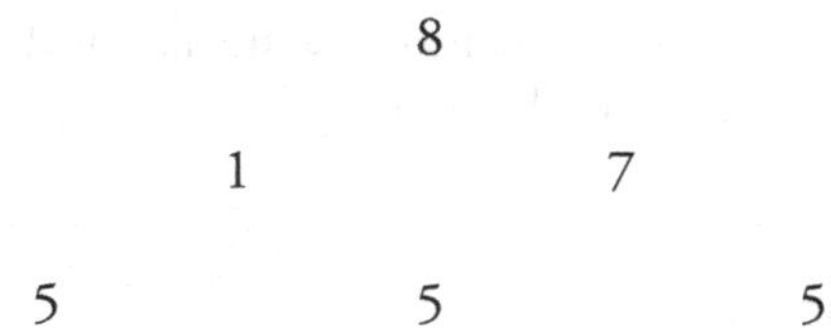

The peak number for the third pyramid is the total of the first and second peak numbers. This is also resolved to a single digit (except if the total is 10 or 11, in which case it remains as these full numbers).

Step 5. The final pyramid is built around the other three, because its base numbers are the first and third (5 and 2 in this example).

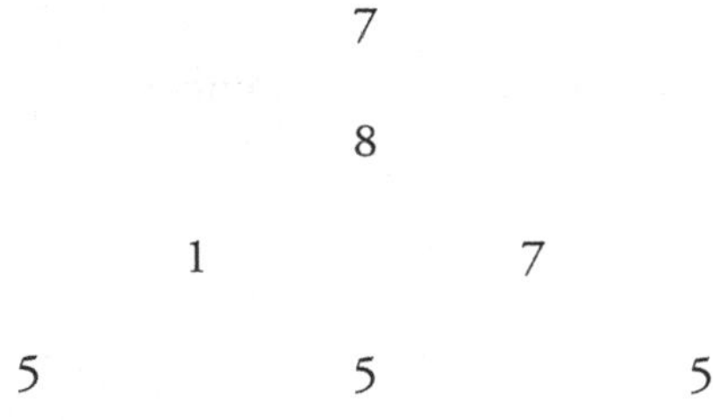

The peak number for this fourth pyramid is the total of its two base numbers, 5 and 2 equalling 7. Usually this would be resolved to a single digit, but if it were to total 10 or 11, it would not be reduced. It is important to note that these numbers are only used if they appear on the third and fourth peaks, for their stronger spiritual influence achieves special importance only as the third phase of life is approached.

To be certain of the year of commencement on the pyramids and the ages at which people of each ruling number arrive at their peaks, the following chart is of material assistance:

Ruling Number 3-36 = age of first peak, as it works in nine-year cycles, 4 by 9 = 36

Tom = 3-36 = 33. After 33 it continues on in nine-year cycles . . . .

Ruling Number of person	**Age at first peak**	**Age at second peak**	**Age at third peak**	**Age at fourth peak**
2	34	43	52	61
3	33	42	51	61
4	32	41	50	59
5	31	40	49	58
6	30	39	48	57
7	29	38	47	56
8	28	37	46	55
9	27	36	45	54

10 (1)	26	35	44	53
11	25	34	43	52
22/4	32	41	50	59
33/6	30	39	48	57

PEAK NUMBERS

Due to the contrasting conditions necessary for each of us to achieve a well-balanced maturity, we need additional help to that normally available from the ruling number. We get our supplementary support from those four peak numbers on our pyramids. The object of the peak number is to provide a valuable source of additional thrust at specific periods during the maturing years. These numbers exert a special influence that commences towards the end of the year prior to the peak year (personal year 8) and rises to its acme of strength during the peak year (personal year 9). This influence can be sustained for up to four years, significantly diminishing towards the close of the personal year 3 following the peak year.

Peak number 1: Will only be found on either (occasionally on both) the first or second pyramids. On the third or fourth pyramids, it becomes a 10. The 1 is an intensely practical number, indicating that a period of individual effort is about to prevail, a period of definite personal expression. For most it will mean separation from previous involvements in which some degree of disharmony was inhibiting personal development, such as in marriage, business associations, or social intercourse. You may be assured that no marriage, business relationship, or friendship will be severed unless it has already served its purpose. Some people will choose to avoid such separations with all possible effort, preferring to maintain the status quo. Notwithstanding, they will doubtless recognise a change in the nature of the relationship, because they begin to exert more of their own individuality and become more expressive. The more spiritually advanced they are (in other words, the older the soul), the more they will exert their individuality this year and henceforth. The direction of their activities is usually consistent with their ruling number; the manner in which they express will depend on their personality strengths indicated by their birth chart.

Peak number 2: Introduces a period when stronger spiritual values emerge. Lifestyle and habits will subtly embrace either a more intuitive or a more emotional manner. Whether the spiritual emphasis manifests as an improved state of awareness (its positive, most constructive form) or as a state of heightened emotions (its reactive and defeating form) will depend on the level of maturity thus far achieved. Obviously, intuitive ability cannot be expected to develop if the individual is held captive by emotion. This is usually a period of hard work and slow progress in material affairs, but we cannot have it both ways. Remember, there is a right time for everything, and one of the most important applications of this science of numbers is to learn what our needs are and the right way as well as the right time to deal with them. To enforce material progress when under the influence of the peak number 2 would be to invite frustrations, conflicts, and emotional enervation.

Peak number 3: Is always a period when the emphasis should be directed towards the intellectual. It is an important period of learning, of reviewing, and of analysing. Many people find the urge for travel particularly accentuated under the guidance of this vibration. At this period in their lives, travel for such people assumes a very important role as a means of learning and expanding their insight into life. If they do not allow their mental faculties scope for positive expansion, they run the risk of becoming destructively critical, exacting, and not surprisingly, quite unpopular.

Peak number 4: Brings with it increased material power. This might be expressed in any number of ways depending upon the general level of maturity, ruling number, and birth chart characteristics. For those people who are prepared for hard work, much can be achieved under this vibration. For those who need to acquire additional knowledge in dealing with the faculties of sense to round off their maturity and who are prepared to involve themselves in physical work, vital development will reward their efforts. But those who become overly ambitious, mercenary, or covetous will find this period one of loss rather than gain. Even though they might work harder, they will make no discernible progress while their motives are so egocentric. This can lead to a serious strain on their nerves and general state of health, which can only be corrected after they reassess their motives.

Peak number 5: Usually introduces significant changes to people's emotional state. These are created through the emergence of spiritual growth and understanding, which leads to greater personal freedom. It is a period through which the psychic powers undergo considerable strengthening, thereby facilitating an improved level of emotional control. In turn this reduces reactiveness to people and to situations. As a consequence, a greater measure of personal liberty develops that prepares the way for increased spiritual awareness. Those who in earlier years were anxious about their financial security now have the means for dispelling such worries with a more balanced view of their real needs and environmental influences.

Peak number 6: Brings with it a very strong power for creative development. It is a period when the highest spiritual and mental faculties can combine to reveal one's vital role in the limitless plan of creation. Such sublime awareness will rarely become apparent to any but the more mature, more highly evolved people. For the majority, those who identify with physical possessiveness, this becomes a period of intense home involvement (or if unmarried, a hankering for settling down in their own home). Tendencies to worry about the home or to rush into marriage should be recognised as merely the procreative counterparts of what would otherwise be a powerful creative drive. Wisdom and patience should be exercised to avoid the need for the hurtful lessons that are attracted when emotions dominate people's affairs.

Peak number 7: Can bring many surprising changes into people's lives. It is the period when we are called upon to share all we have learned thus far. By so doing we experience tremendous progress in our own unfolding, for there is no better system of learning than that of teaching. This is an intensely empirical period in life, for it requires us to undergo much testing. If successful we qualify for the higher teachings that await us during this year. If we have not yet matured to a point of acceptable growth, we must spend more time in preparatory development. Most people during this period of vibration influence are called upon to undertake some form of teaching but not necessarily in conventional scholastic fields. More often their teaching is associated with postacademic fields of human evolvement such as yoga, natural therapies, spiritual awareness, and artistic development.

Peak number 8: Denotes independence as the prevailing force during this very powerful period. Whether independence develops through artistic or commercial involvements will, of course, depend on the ruling number: if it is an even number, financial success is indicated; if an odd number, success through artistic (or for some academic) expression is more likely. Great care must be taken that the power of this vibration is used constructively and that opposing individuals or limiting situations are not allowed to inhibit its transmission. The result of such influences will be clearly discernible in an uncharacteristic aloofness—the effort of the soul struggling to achieve independent expression.

Peak number 9: Introduces a period of pronounced humanitarian activity. This vibration brings with it special opportunities to serve mankind. It is also a period when intense mental involvement is necessary for the greatest success to be achieved—analysing and assessing the needs of others, planning for major changes in vocation, and re-evaluating long-standing relationships and environmental surroundings. Many people attempt to make demands on your time and energy during this period. Some are in genuine need and provide important opportunities to serve. Some will be artificially contrived to attract your sympathy. These latter cases should be treated as individuals needing awakening. Our discriminatory and analysing abilities will certainly be tested and strengthened by such experiences. While some people under this vibration will need to remain at home and be of service, others will be moved to travel to undergo important lessons in development. Everyone, during the first year of influence following the attainment of this peak, will find important changes occurring in their lives. If not involving travel, they will almost without exception move houses, change jobs, or form new circles of acquaintances. Any one of a number of these alterations in lifestyle can occur, depending on the nature of the responsibilities necessary to the prevailing stage in growth maturity.

Peak number 10: Can only occur on the third or fourth pyramid peaks as maturity approaches its zenith. It brings a special strength, a unique power for relating to the needs of others during important periods of adjustment in their lives. This ability is the happy consequence of people's own living experiences and the training instilled by them. With the emphasis on mind power, as indicated by the 9 in every birth date from the last century, a considerable amount of mental adjustment is needed to remould outlooks and lifestyles as the new age approaches. Those older souls who have a peak number 10 during this period assume critically important roles in guiding and encouraging those in need. This is an exciting responsibility that confers upon the giver as many benefits as upon the receiver.

Peak number 11: Is the second of the two peak numbers that can only occur on either the third or fourth peaks. As with the peak number 10, a high level of maturity is necessary to handle its power. Peak number 11 indicates that a considerable amount of spiritual accountability is demanded. Yet the demand will never exceed the individual's capacity. It is a period of high intuitiveness, when the most inspired actions become possible. However, there are certain spiritual requirements necessary for the optimum potential of this period to be realised. These involve compassion, temperance, integrity, and the practice of philanthropy, the sharing of love in its highest spiritual sense. In very practical terms it implies thoughtfulness for and harmony with all life, especially human life. Temperance is the expression of balance and moderation in all undertakings, while meditation is an exercise in enlightenment through a relaxed mind and body, restoring complete harmony to the mind, the body, and the heart. While these disciplines are in practise, the virtue of impeccable integrity must prevail throughout actions and thoughts, thereby ensuring that no negative forces can impede spiritual unfolding, the supreme purpose of this period. The qualities of maturity developed during this period in life bring with them the mental and material independence necessary for the expansion of wisdom during the third and final period of earthly human life we call fulfillment.

THE YEARS OF FULFILMENT

This third phase of life should complete the transition from our younger worldliness to the wisdom and peace that accompany realisation. No longer should our thoughts and actions be held captive under the yokes of ambitiousness and anxiety of those earlier years as a novice. Graduation has occurred. Private and public expression are now those of an initiate: relaxed, confident, and noble.

The sixty or so years thus far accumulated in the body should have matured us to a realisation that only by the twin virtues of truth and wisdom can we now attain the fulfillment intended of our third phase of life. Our loyalties now become distinctly twofold. Outwardly, we must do everything possible to share the benefits of our own worldly experiences, with the general aim of assisting the renewal of our nation's cultural heritage. Inwardly, preparation must be made for the inevitable journeys beyond the earthly plane.

With growing richness in years, senior citizens offer to the younger generations a fountain of wisdom unknown to those less mature. Of this virtue Asian cultures are astutely conscious, evidenced by so many older people in government that we find in the East. The West has yet to learn that youthful vitality must be balanced by mature wisdom for lasting success in life.

PERSONAL YEARS

When you would like to see what year you are in, in any given year, all you do is add your month number together with your day number.

Example: October 14 10 + 14 = 6

Add this number to whatever year you are in now. Let's say it is 2004, for example. That would be 6 for your month and day plus 6 for the year, equalling 12. 1 + 2 = 3. You will be in a 3 personal year. There are only nine years in a cycle, 1 to 9, and then the cycle starts again. There is an exception in this: if it adds up to a 4, it will be a four cycle, but if it adds up to 22, then you are in a master year. If it adds up to anything other than 22, for example, if it adds up to 31 or 40, it will be brought down to a 4.

September 8, 2004, for example, would work out as
8 + 8 + 2 + 4 = 22

This also applies for 11 and 33 personal years.

1 Personal Year: Physical strength is now at its highest peak, making it a perfect time to instigate new schemes, concepts, and adventures. Life will now take on a new challenge, and being physically able to cope with it makes it an enjoyable time. Goals should be clearly set and worked towards, as this is a commencing cycle, and the future should hold greater significance than the past. Problems and disappointments experienced in the previous years will now disappear, leaving the way open to a wonderful, new way of life. That is a powerful personal year that should *always* be used to its fullest advantage.

2 Personal Year: This year is a year for accumulation and consolidation. It affords a much needed breathing space between the hectic 1 and 3 personal years. The previous year's ambitions and challenges should now be looked at and analysed for their practical success and value, for now is the time to streamline, change, and perfect schemes for the future. New ideas and innovations will come as a direct result of mixing with other people, for this is indeed a year of togetherness.

As opposed to the 1 year, when individual pursuits left little time for other people, this is a year of group achievement, when sharing experiences with others is essential. Patience should be exercised this year, as startling, heart-stopping opportunities and decisions will not arise, but behind-the-scenes action is gaining momentum. Take a breather, mix and mingle, and enjoy the company of others, for now is the time to recharge the batteries for the next hectic year ahead.

3 Personal Year: This year is a year to look forward to, as it includes happy and bright vibrations. Life should now be lived to the full. Socialise, accept new invitations, and take full advantage of a lessening of responsibilities. This is a wonderful, happy year for outward expression and activities, but it can be a disastrous year on the business scene. The happy, frivolous atmosphere that now exists could well infiltrate into business areas, causing rash decisions and impractical, unfinished schemes.

However, life is so full on the social scene that little time is left for exhausting business efforts. But unfortunately, it diminishes the bank balance dramatically. However, the next year will quickly rectify this problem.

4 Personal Year: The previous year's frivolity will now be well and truly forgotten as the facts of life are clearly spelt out. This is a year of hard work and effort when one must knuckle down to the task at hand. It is a frustrating year when considerable effort rarely produces dramatic results. "One step forward and two steps back" seems to be the motto of this year. Past failures and successes must now be carefully examined, as this is an organisational period designed to bring a person down to earth. Responsibilities will increase, thus magnifying the effort and hard work needed to maintain a reasonable level of existence. Health and diet should be carefully scrutinised during this year, as physical resistance is low. Tidying up of affairs is now in order as one must make ready for a very hectic year ahead.

5 Personal Year: This is a year to look forward to and enjoy, as the previous twelve months of hard physical effort can now be looked back upon. Anything can be tackled now, provided the governing overtones of restlessness can be somewhat subdued. Travel, holidays, change, and variety will all be enjoyed during this hectic fun-loving year. Daily routine, which was previously tackled with mundane necessity, will now be recharging with physical electricity. "Throwing out the old and welcoming the new" should be the motto for this year, as it heralds a new positive approach to life. One must beware of clandestine relationships that could endanger existing security. A tendency to throw all to the wind will prevail. Balance is an essential factor to maintain during this period, otherwise the dominant theme of the next year could be disastrous.

6 Personal Year: Romance, love, and home are of paramount importance during this twelve-month period. The gay, abandoned, carefree existence of the preceding year is now brought down to earth by the realisation and greater awareness of security and responsibility. This is a year in which the patter of tiny feet (or rather, the ear piercing cry of a newborn baby) could reverberate through the house. Nature reigns supreme in conditioning and preparing for parenthood, and numerology works hand in hand with nature when a person is in a 6 personal year. Nothing of a startling nature occurs outside the home, as occupations and professions tend to take on a new dimension, becoming secondary to home affairs. The burning drive and ambition that was pursued so tenaciously in the previous year is now replaced with a realisation that the end result is purely a material entity as opposed to love of family and home, which has no bearing whatsoever upon financial esteem. The new company that this year brings must be enjoyed to the full, as again nature steps in to test strength of character within the next twelve months.

7 Personal Year: This is somewhat a lonely year when one seeks to look from within for the answers to life rather than sharing problems with others. Spiritual learning and fulfillment is heightened during this period, when the joys of the previous twelve months are now being weighed against the realities of life. Priorities are now questioned and new conclusions reached, often vastly different from previous standards. This is a waiting year when one must be prepared to consolidate and mark time, exercising extreme patience. Future ventures should now be carefully examined, analysed, and streamlined to fulfil ambitions in life. This personal year can rightly be termed as the "lull before the storm," and good use can be made of this somewhat quiet period to strengthen and fortify the constitution, ready for the powerful year ahead.

8 Personal Year: This is an extremely powerful year when innermost dreams and ambitions can be fulfilled. Thoughts and concepts that have been previously conceived can be put into action. The physical body is now at a peak, primed by nature to tackle any task. Now is the time for action, and there should be no need to procrastinate or think unduly about any new venture. Provided the seeds of fulfilment have been carefully planted in the preceding seven years, rewards will eventuate at a pace far greater than originally expected. Consequently, it is of prime importance to be prepared for speedy results, learning to utilise the rewards accordingly. Personal ambition, which is the driving force during this year, is again questioned by nature within the next twelve-month cycle.

9 Personal Year: This is a stocktaking year, when previous values, ideals, and influences should be carefully scrutinised. As opposed to the previous year, this is a period when giving to others holds far greater significance than making for one's self. Home environment, relationships, and associations are important now, as the awareness and appreciation of the finer "free" benefits in life grow. The desire to commune with nature away from the hustle and bustle of big city life is also experienced. This is a consolidation year when debts, schemes, and plans must be finished and cleared from the mind to make ready for a new nine-year life cycle.

11 Personal Year: The vibrations of this personal year are primarily concerned with spiritual ideals rather than material gains or possessions. It is a time when the light at the end of the tunnel begins to glow brighter, bringing new meanings and depth to life. Provided the correct perspective is taken, wonderful, far reaching rewards can be expected. Other people will be motivated and enlightened in the presence of a person in this personal year, as the sign post of life is clearly pointing in their direction. Being an extreme personal year, some emotional difficulties can be expected. This usually applies as a direct result of the desire to question present ideals, circumstances, and situations.

22 Personal Year (my year when I wrote this book): This is a year to remember, as restrictions will now be lifted and the way will be open to plan and instigate far reaching, all inspiring aims and ambitions. There will be absolutely no limit to what can be achieved during these twelve months, as the seeds that have been planted in previous years will now begin to break through the earth and stretch up to the sun. This is the master year, and to misuse it would be a great loss. Physical and mental activity is now at a peak, and the body is suitably conditioned to accommodate the work and effort involved in instigating grandiose schemes. To realise the full benefit from this wonderful year, efforts towards the community or others would hold far greater significance than personal material gains. It is essential that schemes instituted during this year be fully carried through, as the current power and effectiveness will only last for a twelve-month period.

33 Personal Year: This is a year when home conditions will completely dominate life's activities. The general interpretation of a 6 personal year does apply here but with emphasis upon extreme conditions existing. Affairs of the heart will be heightened during this period of life, and caution must be taken against going overboard with any romantic associations. There is a tendency to forget responsibilities in favour of a new, more exciting relationship. Physical awareness and desires now manifest themselves, often creating frustration through lack of fulfilment. Responsibilities previously experienced now act as a mental prison, suppressing personal individuality. Wide open spaces and love of the natural life will now be sought after, and if possible, frequent trips to the country should be taken, as this would provide a natural release valve for the frustrations and mental complexities now being experienced.

INTERESTING POINTS TO KNOW

If you were to look at your personal years now, from this year now and going backwards, you may be very surprised what you find. For example, if you are in an 8 personal year now because your birth date is March 7, 2005 = 3 + 7 + 7 = 17. 1 + 7 = 8, you will feel independent. Last year, you may have felt lonely or looked inward for answers. The year before, you may have been in love or found love or even started a family. The year before, you may have travelled a lot. Before that, from birthday to birthday, you were in the 4 year, working hard, making some form of structure. The year before, socialising could have been the best fun you had in many years. The year before could have been either spiritual or emotional, and before that you may have started new things in your life, whether a new school or a new career, as you were in your 1 year.

Don't you just love it? Now you can see your future—what happens in our lives may be different, but this underlying energy change and influence will remain the same. If you believe someone may be your soul mate, check out their personal years; if you two are in the same cycles, you will be in synchronisation throughout your lives. Interesting points to know!

So the questions still stands, do we really have free choice? Of course we do, hey? But numbers work alongside our nature, the world's nature. Is nature really astrology and numbers? Really, it makes no odds which subject one enters, for they are all connected, leaving the same answers just in different methods. Numbers, I find, are the most broken down simple calculations. No need for complications in life when it can be just so simple. Leave the ego mind out of the equation, and what's the problem? Simple math is what we're talking here. Numbers, from 0 to 9 (and the complicated part: 11, 22, 33), and that's not difficult to understand. Simplicity is the way forward.

What's going on? Well, our energy inside us, our feelings, change at certain stages in our lives, which can easily be predicted by the science of numbers. Our energy inspires our own thoughts. We may feel under a 6 influence, for example, for twenty-nine years. We may love our family so dearly and wouldn't be without them, but then we may change to the 8 influence and then feel different and want to be independent: "I'm doing it all on my own." Finally, we may get the urge to be completely independent. We may feel it's our choice to be like that and perhaps many matters may have happened for us to justify that decision. But if we check out our own numbers, we could see that it was to be played that way, as 8 is to be the influence at that moment in evolution.

So again, what's going on? Well, we're pretty much left with three possibilities. Numbers rule us—influence us greatly—or our energy changes, and it's all just coincidence that the numbers add up. Numbers influence us so strongly, but do they rule us completely? It's a worldwide influence. It's an individual influence. Who is doing this to us? We must do it to ourselves—somehow, our higher selves, our deeper selves, our superconscious essence must pick our lives, for how else could it all work? There is a lot to be said for numbers; they are the proof of how it works.

Explanation of the number 2: Numbers can work a little differently for different individuals. For example, the number 2 can be emotional or spiritual, depending on the experience of spirit, the level thus far achieved, the age of the soul. For some people, 2 is very emotional; when I came to Australia, 2 was so full of spirituality and deep experience; it sure was spiritual. The number 2 may not be brilliant for everyone, but if you get the gist of its meaning, you can make it fantastic. Awareness is the key.

WHO IS TO BLAME? ANSWER LIES WITHIN

When I inform a person that their numerological profile indicates a writing ability, their answer is invariably, "I've often thought about writing, but how do I start?"

Before we begin to unravel some of life's mysteries, we must make a solemn pact between ourselves, a pact of honesty, because nothing of benefit can be deemed from these pages if you do not adhere to personal honesty! Bearing this in mind, how would you now interpret this answer?

It is obvious the person has at least thought about the possibilities of writing, yet they have never explored the avenues open to them to actually put the pen to paper. How do you start? Simply by buying a pen and writing pad, choosing a subject, and then writing. The answer is so simple and free from complexities that we cannot reasonably assume that the solution has been overlooked. This leaves us with one alternative: that the person has considered it but has not taken the thought further because they said to themselves, "I can't write."

This same unenthusiastic approach also says, "I can't sing, I can't dance, I'm a failure." It is a sad fact that the majority of people have such a low estimation of themselves that failure is accepted and success never even considered. A habit is formed by repetition of a particular activity. If you light up a cigarette each time you talk on the telephone, it soon becomes a habit. If you always have your morning tea at 10.30, clean your shoes every second day, or even scratch your nose each time you have a problem, it very quickly becomes a subconscious reflex action. The dictionary defines habit as a tendency to repeat an action in the same way: mental conditioning acquired by practice.

Unfortunately, the same logical conditioning applies to the person who continually says, "I can't," as very soon their mental computer programmes the fact that they cannot fulfil the task in question. We all know that a computer can only act upon the information that is fed into it. Likewise, a computer can only relate true to that programming as it does not possess reason. Who can we blame for this "failure syndrome"? The answer must be ourselves.

LAWS OF LIFE

The First Law of Life: Whatever your innermost mind can conceive, your physical body can achieve. Thought must precede action, for without thought, there can be no action. This simply means that you can be what you conceive yourself to be. If you programme yourself to conceive negatively, then you will be a negative person. But if you reprogramme your computer to think positively and enthusiastically, then you will become a positive, enthusiastic individual.

You no longer need to envy the successful and confident people you meet, because you already know one of the all-important secrets to their way of life. They are what they conceived themselves to be. Think about this concept, savour its implications, and realise its strength. We have discussed the "I can't" syndrome, realising that it stems from our own negative programming. This we must blame upon the conscious mind. Thankfully, however, each of us has a deeper level of mental activity, which we will refer to here as our "innermost mind." This deeper mental level is incapable of creating or activating thought processes that are detrimental to our mental or physical well-being, as the greatest single force that lies within each and every one of us is self-preservation.

It is fortunate that our innermost mind will always consider what is totally best for us as a person, yet it is unfortunate that our conscious mind counteracts this singular individuality by creating confusion, loss of confidence, and loss of direction. We can, therefore, rightly assume that deep down each one of us is a positive individual, yet through circumstances, situations, and conditions, we have developed a negative conscious side to our own personality, which could rightfully be termed as our own worst enemy. It is also frequently responsible for creating frustrations and resentments that can manifest themselves into psychosomatic illnesses and problems.

We all know the result that can be caused by two people constantly disagreeing, yet this is happening within us each and every day of our lives, often with the above result. We can now define our mental activity to be ruled by the following two factors:

1) The innermost mind is always positive, as it reasons on a totally individual basis.
2) The conscious self-programmed negative mind frequently overrules the natural positive forces within us by creating confusion and loss of direction.

From these two assumptions we can make the following all-important conclusion: As we programme our conscious mind, we ourselves are to blame for the restrictions and limitations that it places upon us.

Therefore, the first law of life can be achieved, provided the mental conscious level is prepared and willing to accept the challenge.

The Second and Third Laws of Life: Life's bountiful rewards are available to each and every one of us. Before you exercise your conscious computer to say that the above law is impossible, we will qualify this statement by including the third law of life, which is, "Your desire to achieve a goal in life must be so powerful that it overrules all other ambitions."

To illustrate this point, let's try a small exercise. Dust away the cobwebs of the past and go back to a moment in your life when you really wanted something. Can you remember how you desperately needed this particular thing in your life and how you were prepared to give up anything to get it? Even if you have a bad memory, this should be a relatively easy task, as successful accomplishments are always pleasant and therefore easier to remember. Do you also remember how you amazed your friends, relatives, and associates when you actually did achieve your goal? Yet it did not surprise you; why was this?

Your goal was reached because you had ruled out all possible doubt from your mind that it would not happen. From the point of thought conception, you had achieved it, and it had indeed happened within your mind already. You had overruled your conscious computer and reprogrammed it to concede to your desires and ultimate confidence. You had used your mind in the manner for which it was designed—that of confident analysis and motivation.

The Fourth Law of Life: Be yourself. You are an individual unlike any other person upon this earth. You have a right to individuality, a right to say what you think, and a right to act upon what you believe is correct.

Most people reading this book are involved in some occupation, profession, or trade. Before you became proficient in your chosen field of endeavour, you had to learn the many factors that went to making up the job at question. Success that you enjoyed came in direct proportion to the knowledge that you had gained on your subject. It stands to reason that the best mechanics are those who have diligently studied their trade. Likewise, the most sought after advertising experts have taken the time and trouble to learn their profession. Yet how many of us learn about ourselves?

Our bodies and minds are the only factors that will be with us throughout our lives, from the second we are born to the second we depart from this earth. Doesn't it seem totally and utterly incomprehensible that we fail to take the time or effort to get to know ourselves? We are indeed like a ship without a rudder, wandering aimlessly through life, without a thought or care for direction or guidance. Before we can apply ourselves, we must be aware of ourselves, aware of all the finer points that go to make each and every one of us complete individuals. For without this knowledge, we cannot provide direction, and this factor is all important to our happy and successful existence.

The Fifth Law of Life: Nothing of benefit can be derived from confusion.

Organisation has won battles, launched rockets, and planned massive empires and successful tea parties. To conceive a thought and to nullify all chance of failure is essential, but we cannot overlook the all-important factor of organisation. We have all at sometime in our lives experienced the utter frustration of making decisions whilst in a confused state of mind. Yet the majority of us expect logical results from a disorganised existence.

This may seem the hardest law to abide by, yet in fact, it is the easiest.

The Sixth Law of Life: The scales of life state that for effort given rewards must eventuate. Most of us can remember back to our school days, when we learned the rules of chemistry, which stated, "Matter can neither be created nor destroyed." Effort is energy; therefore, this same rule applies to life.

It is a simple fact that if you continue to put effort into a venture or occupation, eventually that effort will produce results. It may take weeks, months, or even years, but rest assured, sooner or later the sixth law of life will take control and success will eventuate. We can best illustrate this law by using an example. Consider life to be a set of scales. At one end we have a one ton weight, which we will call our "reward" or "eventual gain." On the other end of the scale we have a one kilogram weight, which we will label "effort needed." At commencement, we place the kilo weight on the scales, and as one would expect, nothing happens. We continue to do this for a number of months, but still our effort does not produce results. Most of us at this time would tend to give up, because we seem to be getting nowhere. But if we were to continue increasing our effort by the same proportion each day for years, the scales would then begin to tip in our favor, and the rewards we seek to gain would become ours.

Unfortunately, this law cannot be defined any further, as effort required does not rule in direct proportion to the rewards sought. Often the impossible can be achieved in a very short space of time, and sometimes the probable appears to take much longer. However, at present all we have to know and believe in is that this law of life does work.

The Seventh Law of Life: Encourage and help others as they in turn will encourage and help you. This law of life works on the same principle as the sixth law, that of equal reaction. Encouragement and help is a physical action that requires effort; therefore, it cannot be destroyed. By helping others, we are still loading the scales of life in favour of ourselves so that our rewards can be realised sooner. Try wherever possible to help others. Criticise by all means but endeavour to make your criticism constructive and not destructive, for remember the saying, "What you sow so shall you reap."

We need people, for few things, if any, can be achieved without the help of others. Some people reading this law would say, "Impossible; how can one go through life helping others all the time? Charity begins at home." Or, "In business one can never do this." If you are also having same thoughts, think back through your life and try to remember one worthwhile thing that you did totally on your own without the help, encouragement, or consideration of others. Remember, we are not applying these rules directly to money or material gains; we are relating them to peace of mind, inner happiness, and fulfillment.

This law of life implies that any action created in turn creates an equal and opposite reaction. Self-abuse of the mind is far more detrimental than most other physical abuse to the body. If a person lives a lifestyle out of harmony or character with their true individuality, then their whole lifestyle will suffer as a direct consequence. If we advise someone to stop eating the wrong foods, to take more exercise, or to stop smoking cigarettes, we are, in fact, treating the result rather than the cause.

Why do people smoke heavily, drink alcohol, take drugs, eat food to excess, or indulge in any other single vice? Simply because they need this crutch to help them face the realities of being locked into a lifestyle out of character with their very being. If you can lead a harmonious existence that offers personal fulfillment and satisfaction, these crutches would fall by the wayside, as the body would no longer need them.

CHAPTER TWELVE

The Bridge Created from D.J. to Arthur

This all started when I resided at the Knightsbridge 1919 building.

The 3		The 7
Arthur's	—	D.J.'s
Rational mind	—	Mind and out of mind
Emotional energy	—	Spiritual awakening
Unaware of spirit	—	Full awareness of spirit
Needs proof of any existence	—	Might just have the proof.
To sum it up	—	19 3 7 are the true numbers of this book.

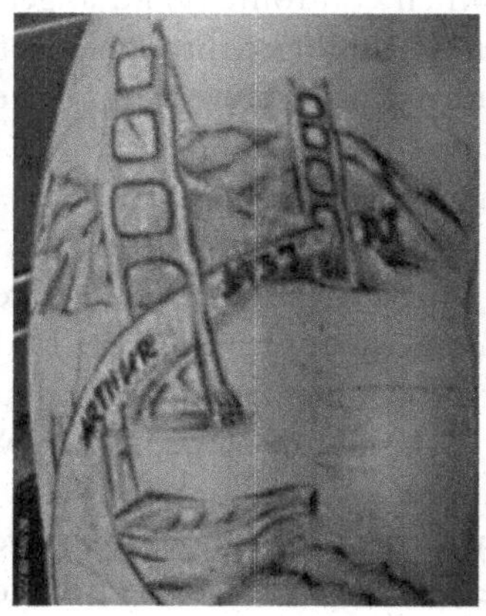

In this chapter of my life, I woke up to a realization; to my absolute astonishment and amazement, I had jumped from one polarity to the other. All those times I was going through the experiences looking up to the sky, looking up at the writer of this story, saying—look at me—look at what I am experiencing here. Now, it was me looking back at myself, as I was the writer, looking back at all the experiences and putting them on paper. I realised something that amazed me: it was me who was now becoming the writer. I did not die and yet I accomplished all that I foresaw on the bridge in Sydney. The story was over, and my spirit had just jumped from living the life to being the writer. And logically thinking, this was the only way it could be; sure, who else could write the story?

COMFORT ZONE

From day one of existence till about four years old, we make up how we perceive the world to be. We copy our parents, we know how they are thinking, and we programme our minds in that sense. If one of our parents is depressed in their thinking during these years of our lives, we will copy that frame of mind, and when we grow up, our tape recorded minds will delve in and out of this core frame of mind. We might not know why until later; for many people it's about the age of twenty-four years old when they confront this frame of mind. The person knows where it came from when confronted, and anger arises first and then acceptance; while some people get through it, others wish they were dead for so long that eventually they bring that experience into their reality. In another case, one parent may come down with a flu or cold, and the child may copy this, as all sickness comes first from the mind's thoughts. When this child grows up, and every now and then he may come down with a flu or cold. These are all examples of the tape recorded mind; some examples are never understood, while other extreme examples are brought to attention on drastic levels.

I met up with a Reiki master named Dave. We talked about how an experience can happen for a person when they're young and that it can be subconsciously carried throughout their lives. He said, "Wait till I tell you this. There was a girl who came over to New Zealand with some friends. She was about forty years old. She wanted to go bungee jumping; she was not afraid to do it. The box went up with them all in it, and as she was standing on the edge with the rope around her leg, she just froze. She just wouldn't move; they had to take her back down. She couldn't understand this herself, and she went to try and do it again. But the same thing happened. She froze and was unable to move or jump or anything.

"She took a Reiki healing course," he continued, "and there is a more advanced part of the course that allows you to send Reiki to your past and future. The girl wanted to find out what was stopping her from doing the jump. She rang her mother and asked her if anything happened when she was young; perhaps she had ropes or something around her legs. Her mother said no. A few weeks later, her mother said, 'There was one thing, when you were born, the umbilical cord was wrapped around your leg.' That was it. This girl could have never remembered that moment herself. But after finding out that information, I showed her how to send Reiki to that event, the moment. She practiced Reiki on it. Then she got up on the bungee jump and jumped with no problem at all; she became free of a restriction that she was unaware of."

So what is going on in our lives? Well, from the moment we are born, our minds are recording all that's happening. The mind is a sponge, soaking up the entire new world around it. Any experiences that take place, there is a series of thoughts placed on that experience, and this becomes our truth. The tape recorded mind plays this over and over again, and a programmed mind is born due to this experience. This happens with all experiences, and it is very hard to change what has happened, even if you remember it. The mind plays over and over again, like a tape recording. The umbilical cord on day one of life can still affect the person throughout life, until the issue is addressed. Day one does make a difference. Day one can create the effect of one's whole life. Not to mention the first four years of experiences, feelings, and programming. If you remember, you can reprogramme your own mind, just like I have done before. But if you don't remember, you can search to find out why you can't do a certain thing and heal that event by Reiki or other means.

ENERGY

Energy is in everything; it is everywhere. Our thought, which is the influence of all, is energy. Our emotions and our experiences are energy. Where we all derive from is a form of energy, a vibration intelligence of energy. Our spirit is energy. Life in all its forms is energy expressed.

We have seen how energy attracts in our world, and we know there are different vibrations of energy out there and in us. Numbers, as seen in the last chapter, can label these levels in us and can do so in worldwide influences. Energy, vibrations, and thoughts are all energy, and that is what the game of life is about.

As I continued writing this book, people and places that had this high emotional energy were magnetised to me. I was working with a crew of people. The boss was the nicest boss that I ever encountered. He was a true gent in the world, like my own father; he was like a father figure. But he had a lot of energy in him; he was an emotional man. He didn't like crowded places, nor was he at complete ease in company. Anyways, the whole time I was working away, we would have lunch in the canteen. This canteen was full of those florescent lights, and it was driving my energy wild. I was hot and bothered. This man had so much of this same energy, but he was the type of person that seemed relaxed in his own company. This energy I was getting off him was very strong fuel, and it was the same energy that I was getting off my father.

I realised that he was not the problem in my life—life was. It kept bringing these people to me, fuelling me with this energy, and in turn this was fuelling my mind. I was able to write down so much about my experience each day when I finished work. I really disliked this feeling; if there was no outlet, I would start to cough up blood, and none of it felt good. But the outlet was this book, and this is what life was bringing to me, to fuel me, to write this whole book in this master 22 year. Some of this energy was in me, and I was still attracting it in my world. But I also saw that some mystical form of life was putting me in these situations so that I finished what I started. It could very well be my own spirit doing this to me, as my spirit was getting my mind to express itself in writing this book.

I realised that my father was a great man, and at times he drove me wild because of this energy, but life was bringing these people to me and creating this for the higher good. We all went out for drinks at Christmas time, and there was too much energy intake for me. I tried to drink and keep it all down, but I was still taking in so much. Eventually I left the pub and walked up the road; I started getting sick and coughing up all of this energy, just choking on the ground really. I now understand why I had to intake this energy and what it was really all about. The solution was, the sooner I wrote this book, the better and healthier and happier my life would be. Life was perfect. This energy fuelled me to write all of these experiences down.

Rachel and I talked about energy for a while, and then she wrote this down:

"It's like your body is a filter, and if it receives good energy—alkaline energy—it feels good. The more you block the energy in your body with, for example, static (acid) energy, it will build up and not be released. The thing is, you must be aware that your body is this filter; how your body feels will affect your mind. So when you realise what things are made of—acid and alkaline energy—then you can watch what you do so that you do not get a build-up of this acid/static energy in you."

"Here are some examples:

Acid	***Alkaline***
Static	Nature
TV/video games	Anything to do with nature
Florescent lights	Natural fibres—clothing
Synthetic	Minerals in home
Alcohol	Calming lights
Drugs	Fresh foods
Even colours	Fruit and vegetables
Rock music	Classical music
Lack of exercise	Exercise
No sleep	Walking
Aggro music	Calming music
Too much noise/ people	Relaxing/yoga, tai chi/martial arts

The thing is, the earth's energy is massive; if we open or close up our filters (bodies) to it, we will experience either happiness or the opposite.

Once the static/acid energy is trapped in the body, it needs a release; more alkaline/natural activity will fix this.

Here is how it works: static/acid energy is not from nature, so when it builds up in the body, it becomes trapped because it doesn't allow the body to breathe the way that natural/alkaline energy does.

So as it's trapped, you will feel a number of things:

Acid/Static Energy

Angry
Depressed
Nervous
Low confidence
Stressed
Too sensitive
Can't think clearly (low energy, no adrenaline)

We are from nature, and our body is like a filter/sponge. We should aim to receive more energy from the universe with the least effort. The more you unblock the energy fields in your body, you then allow energy to flow in a natural, powerful way through your body.

Energy flow creates health, happiness, calmness, and flow in all of our lives; it will allow you then to receive valuable energy at all times from the energy of the earth or universe. It will stop you from feeling those negative feelings in the acid/static state. Because your filters are open then, you're able to receive energy from outside and create a flow inside you. Therefore, you have positive and calm thoughts and will be a creative happy person with good natural energy flow.

Alkaline/Natural Energy

Calm
Happy
Energetic
Always relaxed
Powerful energy
Peaceful

Individuals in this state don't need too much sleep to get energy. They are creative and intelligent; nothing bothers them. They are good communicators and understand life. So now you may be able to understand why people all act differently. We are essentially the same in that our bodies are from nature and are a filter; it just depends on what you are doing with your body. Do you have a connection to that flow of energy in the universe? Look at all the people around you—notice how the calm, happy people look after themselves and protect their energy. You will notice that calm, happy people indulge in alkaline adventures. Therefore, they have a flow of energy in their lives. If you do get an imbalance of negative or static energy, it will become trapped in your body and create a lot of negative feelings: anger, anxiety, confusion, stress, and worry. That is because all energy rises and goes up to your head, creating thoughts that are not positive. Eventually you will become sick from trapped energy and get physical or mental illness, like depression. You may even attempt suicide because you can't feel good at all.

But it's about recognising what you are doing to yourself, and then addressing the situation by doing more alkaline activities, removing acid/static energy from your life. Some people detoxify their body. Others gradually cut down on acid/static energy activities. It's up to you how you do it. But if you have more alkaline energy in you, you will be naturally happy no matter what, a positive person without blocks in energy flow. Once you establish energy flow in your life, always be aware that moderation is the key, but as far as alkaline activity goes, the rule is less is more.

Once you create a good flow in your life, things that would previously upset you will not anymore, because you now are connected to universal energy, which supports your flow. Also do not forget this: When you become grounded, it's like your root chakra is also connected to the universal energy, so the more alkaline energy you create, you will be more connected through this chakra".

Rachel also said, "D.J., you do have a big energy field but by connecting through grounding, you will have energy that protects you a lot more, which means that the universe will support you more and make not only energy available to you but also intuition and guidance."

COLLECTIVE CONSCIOUSNESS

According to my birth chart, I am "consciously and unconsciously absorbing the thoughts of those around" me. I was amazed that it was written there in my chart in black and white. I knew it, I just couldn't explain it as perfectly as the chart did. Throughout my life, I have been living with a hazy mind when I was in crowded places. I experienced racing thoughts in my mind until I was out of the collective consciousness or got drunk, where my mind became numb and stopped working. This absorbing happened frequently, and when I could capture a clear frame of mind, I didn't want to let that go, like the time I stayed awake for so long. When I stayed awake for that period, it was like I found myself and broke free from the mind absorbing all the thoughts around me. I constantly took time out from one party to the next and listened to music on a constant basis, but by staying awake, I slowed that influence down. I constantly tried to analyse why

I could think so clearly on my own but not in company, and the chart explained that to me. The time I was on holidays with many friends, being lost in a haze was frustrating, as I could just about cope with it in life on day-to-day routines, but I was pissed off that it was even happening on holidays. I tried to construct a thought of my own that I needed out of the game, as my mind was becoming the madness around me, and life brought me that experience. I got locked up in a hole of a cell for forty hours. I could think, though, and my mind was at ease as I was taken out of the collective consciousness.

When I was younger, and as this was always happening, I asked life to show me why it was happening; when I was in school, it came to me. I could see people's thoughts rising up, and by the time they hit the ceiling, there was a collective consciousness of thoughts. It was revealed to me, but I still didn't understand how that was affecting me. I had sensitivity to this, and this was all part of my sensitivity. I believe that this happens to all of us—we all get stuck in a collective consciousness, but more so for me. That is, it was more noticeable for me, but still it happened to us all; we all get stuck in that bubble of consciousness. Everywhere I went, I left a consciousness behind me and ventured onto a new place where I could think clearly and be myself, but soon enough the same problem arose.

Once when I was young, I went to a big open green park full of space and trees, and I was amazed at how clearly I could think; I told my friend that some day I was going to live in this park. He thought I was crazy as I explained the clearness of my mind there, but I wasn't logically thinking how I would survive there. Other times, after I got away from the consciousness and was soon to enter a new one on my travels, I saw an island off the coast and thought, *Is this where I am meant to be, on an island on my own, so that I can just generate?* My options in life were to continue on, adapt a skill in mind control, and try and find an answer that was incomprehensible at this stage or live on an island.

I achieved independence at a young age, as I knew it would be a main ingredient for my future decisions. I got a job and made my own income at sixteen years old. Working and making money were the least of my problems, though. I valued the moments where I could construct a thought by myself and needed to find places where I could do that, so that I could bring forth the next experience. Searching and searching for this peace of mind let me clear all my thoughts and manifest my own reality. The only way for me to ever escape this was to kill off the mind and all it was absorbing and find myself, as that was my only answer, but it was unknown to me until afterwards.

DRUGS

People take drugs to experience a deeper meaning of life—that, they know exists and are trying to reach it. I now believe after many experiences that a level of spirituality is what they need, a level of awareness. But people in my generation in particular wonder what spirituality has to do with religion. They may say, "I'll stick with the drugs—look at what religion has done to the people and organisations in the world." It didn't ever bring anyone into the now—only taught more illusions.

The following information is from Susan Blackmore:

> Drugs provide some of the best evidence we have that our mind, thoughts, beliefs, and perceptions are created by chemistry. Take a drug, particularly a hallucinogen, and any of these can change. This means these drugs can be scary and need to be taken with great care and respect. But it also means they have the potential to reveal some of the deepest secrets about our minds and consciousness. A century ago, psychologist William James experimented with the anesthetic nitrous oxide. Our normal rational consciousness, he said, is just one special type of consciousness, while all around it, "parted from it by the filmiest of screens," are other entirely different forms of consciousness, always available if the requisite stimulus is applied. Others meticulously described the effects of inhaling ether chloroform and cannabis and the strange distortions of time, perception, and sense of humor they induced. More curiously, they also described change in belief and even in philosophy. When Humphry Davy took nitrous oxide in 1799 he ended up exclaiming that "nothing exists but thoughts." This raises the peculiar question of whether what James called "our normal rational

> consciousness" is necessarily the best state for understanding the world. After all, if one's view on the world can change so dramatically with the air of a simple molecule, how can we be sure that our normal brain chemistry is the one most suited to doing science and philosophy?

A lot of people in my age group were taking drugs and trying to get out of their minds. They were onto it, all right; out of your mind is the way forward. But with drugs, it's not the real deal, and you then experience the relative opposite; some people die when taking them.

My product: crossing this bridge is 37 times stronger than cocaine,
37 times more hallucinogenic than acid, and
37 times more explosive than Ecstasy.
It's like getting a personal visit from God!

SPIRITS—JAKE

Jake's song was "Viva Forever" by the Spice Girls: "I'll be waiting everlasting like the sun, live forever." Forever young is Jake existing in eternity. If I knew what I had to go through when I was Jake's age, I would have taken that Spice Girl's ticket to heaven myself. But I got through it, and now I just might be getting somewhere. People are energy—energy can neither be created nor destroyed, it can only change form. Having sensitivity like I do, one finds out these truths quicker than others, as one feels what is going on. Like all people who die, Jake's spirit moved on. They can still be around if they wish to be, and they can choose their next part to play, whether it is hanging around or taking the role of a guide or moving on, getting ready for their next life. Spirits are what we know as the life force in us; when our body dies, the spirit still exists in one form or another. I understand that they do not have the laws of life that we have. They are uninfluenced by gravity, by relativity, by the mind, but they have thoughts, and this seems to be their means of travel or transport. To me, I feel that they have woken up; when their body dies, they know themselves, they are after coming home to themselves, they have woken up from a dream. What we see as real reality, they see as they are inside a dream, inside a dream, moving on through evolution, until the experience arise where they are in their Christ consciousness, together with the source of life itself.

DEPRESSION

Hold onto a thought long enough and watch it manifest in your reality or come to you to tackle as you requested. The same applies if you hold onto a worry thought; it will manifest itself in your mind and your reality. Same as a depression thought; hold onto it long enough and it will manifest itself in your reality and you will be feeding it, by thinking or focusing on it, but you may not know how to stop it. A lot of people take their own lives over this state of mind, as not only is it darkness in itself but it leaves the mind separated from everything.

The reason for this could be a whole list of things, a huge file in your computer mind programmed as a child with its core thought of depression, working itself in a spiral in your mind as you jump from thought to thought. When we go around in this spiral, this merry-go-round from thought to thought, these created thoughts, events that aren't actually hurting us in the present moment, but nevertheless, they are very important thoughts, we feel, so it continues. The more times we go though all these events in our mind as they whip around for the next view, each event seems to get to a level deeper, a pictured scenario on an event or a future projected moment. The event looks worse as we realise that we're just not able to cope with it, thus creating a reality of not being able to cope at all. Because these thoughts are energy itself, the core, energy and thoughts, is really just one, but that's fine; no need to confuse anything (or should I say, "no-thing"). Because these thoughts are energy, they attract like energy thoughts. We have a series of thoughts all day long training our mind, having a programme running in our mind all day, then sleep and the sleep feels good, out of mind, then wake up, bleep, back in mind. Need to think, remember what I was thinking yesterday or what was going on. You then pick up from when you left off, replaying the created programme and playing it on. This goes on and on.

Old thoughts are attracted, like energy memories and feelings, and how this has all happened before all comes into your reality, your mind, your feelings, your world. Once you keep searching inside these memories, going deeper and deeper, you can then see where this all started from, the core thought of it all. This process continues, and you are separating yourself from events, people, and places, and it's a one way direction into a great deep depression, fuelled by the emotion within. What happens? You take drugs like Prozac or choose to be out of this world. Drugs distort this reality, enhance colour in your vision, how you see the world as brighter and more colourful. But it is the cause, the first cause, the core, the reason for this depression; is it getting looked at, dealt with, or covered up, suppressed, pressed down?

The core of a depression, the very core I'm talking here, is a lot like the very high awareness, perspective from space, from no-thing. In both states of mind, both perspectives on the world and all around is amazingly the same. Only one is completely isolated and the latter is at one with all. But the only real core difference that makes this mirror image, reflection state of mind, so terrible, is the feeling the thoughts create within. Within each cell in everyone's body is a knowing, a feeling, an understanding of both separateness and oneness. The perspective of the world, the mind, the feeling in a complete depression state of mind, is creating or even having all the energy placed on the separateness part of the cell, thus having the whole body feel like that. To change the energy over to the oneness side, you first need to change your thinking, as your thinking is creating your their feeling and vice versa. How do you change your thinking? The thought in your mind is getting fuelled by your energy. If it's a depression, you can be strong but you may not last long. Your own thoughts will drive yourself to the end, making it game over for you. How do you stop this?

You place your consciousness outside yourself. You picture yourself outside yourself, even approximately one foot away from your head. Once you are aware that you can actually step out of this frame of mind, then you can become the "watcher" of your own thoughts. They will of course continue to race around, like a chicken without its head, but the beauty is you can just watch them die out as you, the watcher, were feeding those thoughts in the first place. For when you become the watcher, you don't feed those thoughts any more, and they have no choice but to merely die out themselves. Then you see that this little method, this little simple awareness, could have just saved your existence as you knew it. This is who you are, you are the watcher, as in who watches your dreams?

RELATIVITY

Relativity not only governs the hot-cold, up-down sort of outward world, it also governs our minds, our lives, and our worlds. Teenagers often feel that they know everything and that they have a fixed point of view on life; they don't see why other people who are older than them are lost, with nothing sure about in life. And the fact of the matter is, as we get older we end up experiencing both sides of the scale, and the only definite that can be brought out of that is balance; moderation is the key.

People in life often feel a certain way and then act out the opposite to portray the opposite of who they are. If they feel worthless in life at a young age, they will strive to be the opposite and soon enough may own a company and be the boss. Relativity governs our lives. Many successful people out there will have experienced both sides of the polarity, from a deep depression of mind to great success. It is all relative. This cycle of birth and death is the greatest relative in our game.

In life we hear, "When it rains it pours," or "It is either a feast or a famine." These things happen because of our mind's thoughts and, in bigger events, a collective of thoughts everywhere. When we are jobless and look for a job and cannot find one, then just as we stop looking, one comes to us (and many more). Or when someone is looking for a girl to be with, he searches each and every night for her with no success, but the moment he stops looking, they are magnetised to him. If he gets married, all the women love him, as he gives off this vibe that he is happy in love, and this attracts other ladies who are just used to men begging for their love or giving them attention. Once your mind knows you have it, you attract more and more of it. Once your mind knows you don't have it, that too becomes your world. It's all relative.

To escape the relative mind and to see past life's illusions, one needs to escape the mind and access the present, stopping time and having a breakthrough, a shift of consciousness within—then one can see that relativity is an illusion, it's all one in truth. Both things come from the one source; that is, the two polarities are an energy split up to a relative of terms.

VISUALISATION

Normal thinking away in the mind does not create our reality. We can think away in a collective bubble of consciousness and spend all our thoughts analysing many things, and that in itself will not bring forth our reality. Producing a thought of our own and placing our energy on that thought will eventually bring that event to us. The story about the car crash that I was in explains this. Thinking and then producing a thought about an event attracts certain events to us; the outcome will be what we needed in our lives. The better way to do all of this is to get it all right in our heads first, and then to visualise that in our minds. After I visualised the car crash in my mind, I could see it as clearly as if it were reality. Then, soon enough, that exact event came to me. I even tried to get away from the speeding driver behind me by changing lanes, and still that event came to me. Visualisation is the key to manifestation.

The whole time that I was stuck in my mind, absorbing all thoughts around me and living with a massive energy field in me with no great outlet, this was not a comfortable state of being. I would then try to visualise my life in Australia. I mentally saw open places, blue skies, a vast land without many people, peace, clearness, freedom, and soul searching. People talk about creating a happy place in their minds so that they don't get bogged down by the world around them. These visualisations were my happy thoughts, a place in my mind that I could access and start to feel better. Whatever we have going on in our mind affects our whole feeling, changes our whole energy field.

Scientists once rigged up a whole load of professional runners with technology that could access their thoughts and all their body muscles and heart rate. They took readings as they were running and then as they sat still but were thinking about running in their minds. The readings were the same. What was going on in their minds triggered off the muscles in their body and speeded up their heart rate, and even though they were not physically running, their mind's thoughts created that effect on their bodies. I have noticed that myself, and I am sure you have too. What goes on in our mind affects our bodies and our energy.

After I visualised my life about Australia, I eventually magnetised myself to that situation, those events in my mind. But the beauty of this next experience was far greater than what my mind could possibly imagine.

SPIRITUAL EXPERIENCE

I arrived in Australia and between all of this visualisation and my birth chart saying I would have a spiritual experience when travelling, and my numerology showing that I was in my 2 year, I had one of the best experiences of my life. Words could not describe the way I was feeling; a new language would have to be born just to explain the awesome bliss of this experience. A spiritual experience is when your awareness connects to your own spirit inside of you and fully connects to this awakening. Your energy in your mind's thoughts become your energy in your spirit.

When I was halfway across the bridge, the sky burst into infinity as I connected to the infinite energy within me. My outward world became the reflection of my inner world. You must become before you can see. When this happened to me, I received so much inspiration as I became connected to the mechanics of the game of life itself. I accessed a programme in the game about thoughts that was so inspiring that I was just in awe about it all. I could see how our thoughts are creating our reality. I could then see that these thoughts were coming from our spirit, to our mind, then to the event that was brought forth and experienced. I could see that as we dish out our energy in 50,000 thoughts in one day, if we could use all of that energy, all of it, on just one complete whole thought, we could manipulate energy itself. I could see the workings of this manipulation and couldn't help but think of the story of Moses parting the Red Sea. One would have to fully connect with their whole being and produce a thought from that source of being with all their energy, also knowing that they were the same energy that was in the sea or rock or any material object and manipulate this. If you asked me if I believed this myself, my answer would have to be, I am not sure, as although this was what I could feel and knew in this adeptness of this spiritual experience; it just seems highly unlikely now as I am back in my mind writing this book. Maybe someday, someone can prove this to be true or untrue; either way, this experience that I had, I was so privileged to have experienced it, and I really hope that you do too. It is a serious eye opener.

ANGELS

"There are two worlds: the world that we can measure with line and rule and the world that we feel with our hearts and imagination." Albert Einstein.

Liz said, "Between the feeling side of life, the spiritual awakening side of life, and the materialistic side of life, I have come to believe that angels really exist. They are the light energy out there that can influence our lives. They are there to help and to guide us on our journey throughout life, only if we ask them to intervene, otherwise they will not affect our evolutionary stage. If you ask it will be given to you as we have all heard before, and this is true. I have come across some people who deal with this kind of work."

THE MIND

The mind is a sponge that soaks up all around it, when you are in your prime years. What you take in may serve you for some (but not all) of your life. At some stage, you may need to reprogramme your mind. This happens by accessing events that have taken place in your life that are stored in your mind and changing the thoughts that you had about those events. You need to be open to the possibility that all you once believed to be true may not actually be 100 percent accurate. Realising this may leave you vulnerable, and you don't want that, but accessing one event at a time and reconstructing your thoughts about that, expanding thoughts on that, opening up your mind to other possibilities, and letting other information in instead of being blocked in any way, will help you greatly.

Rachel once said, "The mind is like a huge house with heaps of rooms. Everything you say yes to, you open a door, and every time you say no, you close a door. So you can choose to live in a big house or a small house. People who live in a house with hardly any doors open have limited experience—limited knowledge and not much fun at all (i.e., that is completely narrow-mindedness). And people who live in a house with lots of doors open, which lead onto other doors and so on so forth, will have an incredible life with lots of learning, lots of awareness, and experiences that go hand in hand and will have an incredibly interesting and positive and fantastic life."

The mind consists of thoughts racing around. It's like a disease, as we don't know how to stop it. Thoughts come in from all angles, and we tend to move from one thing to another. For me, it was madness; not only had I all my own thoughts racing around in my mind, but I was soaking up everyone else's, brought to extremes, and I had to put an end to it all, and here I am now, writing this book.

The mind has about 50,000 thoughts per day. We, our energy, leave our minds when we go to sleep. Some strange things happen, dreams and that, that can't be understood by the mind, but they happen. Then we enter our minds in the morning when we wake up. For the first second, it feels good and relaxed and chilled. Then we think, *What happened the night before?* and *What have I to do now?* Future and past thinking, time is racing, got to get things done, and away we go. There is no time in our dreams.

The mind can be raced up to 80,000 thoughts in any one given day, and there are days where we can chill and slow it down to 20,000 thoughts. And that's it: get out of your mind and enter your own temple, for you hold the truth in you, and that's where your heaven is. It's here in the now. Also, the mind is not the brain—the brain cannot produce a thought, and that is a scientific fact. The mind is the essence that feeds the brain.

KARMA

I had a conversation with a girl about karma; the Buddhist religion explains that one could kill a man if he was bad, as that action could save many lives. There were many things involved in this script in the Buddha religion, and I said to the girl, "It's a script that has been written. If you believe it and then act it out, your experience may just be exactly what has been written on the script. And why is this? Because you believe it to be true; it's your own thoughts and beliefs that are creating your experience. Then when your own experiences match the script, you will think that the script is the truth, the whole truth, and nothing but the truth. And that's pretty much why religions are so effective. The universe, the system that we live in, gives us multiple copies of our beliefs and thoughts, so whatever we choose to believe, that is all we will see in our world."

I then told her the story of the cat man and the hit man, and she said that was very interesting indeed.

Karma actually means, "Effect and result of actions, all actions being the result of thought, past or present."

Karma on a deeper level: People are born with a level of energy that is given to them; they get it at childhood. This is their punishment during life; this energy attracts all the bad events, by energy attraction. It is the energy body that is given to them that gives them the lifetime of punishment and bad experiences. This energy body can be removed from the person if it is put there for reasons that are not from karma, not from the spirit's intentions. The person can be freed of this curse, if the curse is put on them. But most of the time, this energy is there by the choice of the soul to see life from this perspective, whether because of karma or for the individual to experience what it is like to have this energy. But it's the soul's choice to choose this as it wishes to evolve as a spirit. It is what is in the soul's best interest. Most people who have this energy attached to them know what it's all about; they know on a very deep level what is happening, but if you had this problem and didn't know what was going on, all you needed to do was consult a good mystic or fortune-teller. Or you could enter the now and release this energy to stop the cycle.

FORTUNE-TELLERS AND CHOICES

The thing is, for starters, welcome to the game. It may appear complex, but it's not really. People make things confusing, and they don't have to be. So let's keep things simple. Fortune-tellers can tell us about our future. There are some fakers out there, but there are many good ones too. I have my own abilities to see my future, and I have explained how that happens and what happens. I see things, like fortune-tellers can. I see choices in front of me, what cards are on the table for me. Choices in a game, choices of events, but ruled by the same subject, the same sort of experience. It's the experience that I need to experience that's on the cards. Imagine a list of outcomes in your life, laid down on the table, in a pyramid setting. The goal is the higher power, the force, the temple, yourself, finding yourself after experiencing so much. The goal is completion within after collecting so many experiences along the way. So each of us has our lives mapped out in a way. We needed to experience and evolve; that's the name of the game. We keep evolving until we find out who we really are, and we together are the creators of it all.

But the point I need to make is fortune-tellers can tell us things about our own life based on what direction we are going. They can be very accurate, but we have the choice to change it.

Whilst in Australia, I saw in my mind a lad taking my book and throwing it in the river in New Zealand. I was sad that someone would do something like that. I saw the event but had no idea who the person was, what their connection was with me, or how I could avoid it. So I was thinking, what is the point in writing a book if that's the outcome? So even though I saw the event, I realised that once I was in that moment, I could change it. I had the choice to do that. Fortune-tellers can tell you things but you can change them; you don't have to play it out, it can be changed. The number of choices may perhaps be limited, but there is still a choice. There is always a choice. We live in a game with many choices but not really unlimited choices. Our choices can be limited, but nevertheless a choice is always there to make.

Beat every restriction and influence there is, surrender to the game itself, and then you have every choice in the world, for the world becomes your oyster, and that's what it's about anyway.

REFLECTIONS

I got a reading done when I was at Kings Cross, and the girl said to me, "This new job, this new thing will bring the money in. This is all part of your journey, to feel good inside, security. Whatever you don't work on, someone will betray you or do you wrong to get that part of you to grow. Everything is a reflection of what's inside. All that comes into your life is a reflection."

Let's look at this carefully. It's not because I was very untrustworthy that I was attracting untrustworthy people. That's not correct. I was very trusting, and I always tried to get trust off others. In this case, it was not like energy attracting like energy—but rather opposites attracting. There was a part of me, something in me, a part of me that needed to grow, and it was creating the reflection in my life. (Trust equaling mistrust.)

Kids who are bullies don't choose other bullies as their victims. They are attracted to opposites. Some people would be attracted to me and try to get me worked up. When I wouldn't react, they would keep at me until I did react, and then they would back off. There was negàtive energy in me attracting negative events, but there were also parts of me that needed to grow, attracting that in my outer world.

One day, Lora walked over to me when I was talking on the phone, telling someone that I might come home. I was worried, and she walked over to me, and it was like looking in the mirror. She was the reflection of me at that moment. But I changed, and we then separated. No energy attraction any more. I went through many different emotional states. Each change in me, I had some friends that were on that energy connection that matched a part of me. There will be many parts to them too. They too will have relationships, maybe relationship problems, maybe this, that, and the other. But we all connected on one level of energy. I connected with each of these people, these groups of people, and we made each other grow, that part of us that needed to grow. We worked through an evolution part of ourselves. We became one ball of energy, like energy, and we all related to whatever the subject was at hand.

When we see people shouting out to the sky, that's the deepest, greatest reflection. They are shouting to themselves in the sky, to their own reflection, their own soul or spirit inside, creating the dramas in their lives.

Now—Won, Live—Evil, Dog—God, Devil—Lived; these are just some of the reflections of words that I have come across.

All of all is a reflection of all within. We are made up of three energies: conscious, subconscious, and superconscious. Conscious mind creates the past and future in our world, in our minds. Subconscious mind lets us be at one with the present moment, fully. Superconscious mind is what appears to be the great essence that makes life exist. It is the source. To have yourself heading in a direction to be manifested and conscious in these three energies of yourself; wouldn't that be some sort of goal to aim for? It could be the hope that people need in their lives. But in this case, it's not just hope, it's understanding that it's all there whenever anyone fully chooses to go for it.

Time is in the mind, Now is when you enter your subconscious, Source is our superconscious.

If you view everyone who comes into your life for a reason, the part of you that is ready to grow, you will see this reflection. With relationships, it's no wonder that opposites attract, as we often love someone who represents an undeveloped part of ourselves. So instead of judging other people as good, bad, or indifferent, see them as reflecting a part of you and ask yourself what it is that you are ready to develop within yourself. Also keep in mind that those who seem to cause you the most anguish often remind you of what you feel is lacking in yourself. If you did not react at all, it would mean that you were totally indifferent. The fact that you do react means there is something inside you that gets hooked when you encounter a certain behaviour. It is your learning situation that is the reason for this. The game would be no good and have no entertainment if everyone was the same, so see that their uniqueness and our uniqueness is what makes up this great game. No one can tell you how to become more connected or less involved as you control your thoughts. But by knowing how it's all working, you develop a new sense of personal harmony that removes most conflict from your life. You see that there are so many differences in the game, in the players, but in truth we are all one, just on different energy vibrations.

What I realised was, once I changed my mind about a thing or about life and switched it around from depressed thoughts to choosing to love life, then so much happy and loving moments were attracted to me. The outward world becomes a reflection of the inward world.

KINGS CROSS EXPLAINED

At Kings Cross, the end of mind came and a new world began.

Throughout this time, I lost faith in all that I previously experienced. Between all the awareness that I received and the inspiration that once was incomprehensible to my mind, I lost faith in this deeper awakening. Piece by piece, inspiration by lack of inspiration, each experience faded away, and each good feeling was lost the more I left the deeper awareness and entered the imprisonment of the mind once again. The more I became completely intact with my mind's thoughts, the more I turned my back on what I once knew to be real, the spiritual awakening.

It started off the moment that I kept moving to that happy, fulfilled future experience, and the closer I got, the more I realised that I was not ready or fulfilled in any way, as so much was missing. That part there was a turning point in my mind—I realised that I would have to go backwards, that there was something missing along the way, but how far back would I have to go? My mind was constantly thinking, and the answer could not be found in or by the mind's limited consciousness. Between searching for this answer and living back in a busy city in a collective consciousness, it was not long before I became imprisoned in my mind once again. The only decision that my mind (or I) could make on my next step in life was to call it a day, get out of the game. But life seemed to stop me from taking my own life, and when I asked for help and guidance, the answer became magnetised to me: "You cannot hide from what's inside," and my outer world became a reflection of my inner world.

I eventually became burnt out and was dying inside, and I could see that my mind was killing me, coughing up blood each morning and losing so much weight because of this thinking and thinking; I could not find the answer to go forwards, and each morning that I woke up and entered my mind, I realised that there was no answer, there was no future. No matter where I looked, no matter what memories from the past I accessed, I could not find the answers to go forwards. All doors were closing, as my mind was closing them—my thoughts were killing me. I could see and feel the first thought in my head each morning grinding though my head as the reality kicked in that I was still lost in this dead end world that I lived in. Those thoughts grinding through my head became trained to do so and greatly deteriorated my body. I lost a lot of weight over that period. I became weak like my friend in hospital, refusing to eat the food, like the owner of the house where I worked; we were all dying, all on the same vibration, until the crossroads came and each went our own way. I realised that I was dying, that the time had come—it was the end of the race and I had to die; there was no other solution, and my mind must die. I walked around Kings Cross and knew I was losing my mind completely and thought about signing myself into a mental house.

Then I did it: I short-circuited my mind and found something, just a taste, but something that put new meaning into life, and I liked it. Something that allowed me to go forwards, something that didn't need a constant supply of torturing thoughts. Something that you may believe that you can only have when you die, but you can be alive and still have it. The trick is to die before you die. I escaped from my mind, and my new world begun.

THOUGHTS

To create a thought of your own creates your own reality. The present moment is the moment where you pre-send your thoughts out and receive that as your reality. Most people don't have their own thoughts; they just receive others and pass on other people's information and call other people's theories theirs. Thoughts come into the mind and they leave. If you entertain it, give it energy, it will be manifested in your mind. The question of all time is where does the thought come from? The answer is the inspiration is coming from your higher or deeper self, your higher power and the essence of life. Your mind receives the inspiration and creates a thought. Create your own thoughts and create a great life for yourself.

Now, a fright happened at first but then mind kicked in, worry thoughts and so on. And it created feelings of discomfort. One can just stay living in this state of mind until understanding the scam, the truth, the phenomenon, the now.

Attraction with information. When you open up your mind to something, you let the information come to you. When you know something, realise something, it can come to you. Attraction. What's happening is, when you wake up to something, you also see the truth around you. Everything is here in the now, it is just that one may be closed off to the truth and therefore block it from one's mind. It's all here in the now; the question is, are you open to it? Is your mind open or closed? When you open your mind, you open a door in your mind; you let in and also see the connection to the information.

It's all there; if one can take the baggage off one's self or the barriers around one's self, then one is open to it all. All is revealed in the now. It's amazing.

Thoughts. Spirals. Thinking creates reality. Think badly of yourself, and you of course get colds and flu and all sorts of sickness. When you think badly of yourself, it creates that.

Worry, depression; how do you get out of this? You place your energy, your consciousness, beside yourself, focus at a point outside yourself, and become the watcher of your own thoughts. Become the watcher or the witness of your own mind. Be free of your own cycles. Watch your own thoughts and therefore stop feeding them energy, and you can watch them stop. The thoughts have no energy to produce anything or to be kept entertained, and they stop coming, and you watch them die out. This is how one gets out of this frame of mind that kills many people.

What you think about expands. If you hold onto a thought, whether depression or worry or insecurity or whatever it may be, the more you hold onto it, the more you feed it energy, the more it will expand in your world, and you will convince yourself that you have serious issues. The truth is, it is just a thought, expanded.

You simply cannot kill a thought. We simply change form. Always exist. We are intelligent beings, full of thoughts.

The brain cannot produce a thought of its own—it is a scientific fact. The brain is the mind manifested as material. Only the mind is the essence of the brain. This means if you can produce a thought, you have a mind and real essence in you. We only use 10 percent of our brains; science has proved this. No one really knows why that is, but we know we have the potential to use more of that brain. I personally believe that the more essence we acknowledge as us, the more aware that we become of ourselves, the more activity our brain will be doing when we choose to use it.

Some people doubt that your thoughts create your reality. That is because many are just thinking and assessing their memories of the past and living in their mind, projecting their future. None of this is creating your reality. It is not just your mind (as in your head) that manifests. It is the truth, your mind, but this is not explained fully—a missing link.

For creation, you need to clear the mind of future and past thinking, to search for a moment and to produce a thought about what you need in life. It is like producing a thought on a deeper level, but really it is just avoiding the constant thinking that we all do and placing all that wasted energy into a new idea, a new concept, a new thought on something that we wish to draw into our lives. If you do this from the heart or from the spirit, there will be no problem, and if you do it from the mind, you need to put almost all of your energy into it to make it clear. It's the emotion behind the thought that fuels creation. Also, do not focus on what you don't want. Yes and no, relatives of the same focus point; focus on what you do want. When you see how it is done, you will tell people—your thoughts create reality.

But when you think away and you go into your mind, you attract like minded thoughts and like minded energy, the same level of that which you are on until you change your mind. If you focus on depressed thoughts about an event or whatever, you attract the like minded energy in you. This is all within you. The thoughts of a new idea are projecting your life outside of you, and what you are thinking changes the way you feel. So if you are feeling bad—change the way you are thinking.

TIME

Man must always have been very aware of time—of the passing of night and day and the changes in the seasons. The sun and the moon were worshipped in ancient civilizations, and their movements were closely watched. In this way, the first measurements of time were made. A day was simply the time it takes between one sunrise and the next, a month the time it takes for the moon to go through its phases, and a year the time it takes for the sun to return to exactly the same position in the sky. But if we imagine that we are on a rock that is travelling through space, orbiting the sun, and the moon is orbiting us, can you see that time is an illusion?

Our time is divided into past, present, and future, and we too are made up of our subconscious, our conscious, and our superconscious minds. Our past, including past lives and any past, is all held in our subconscious minds. Our present is our conscious minds, and our future and knowledge of all existence is held in our superconscious minds. Our mind itself, where we spend 95 percent of our time, holds in it an imagined future, and it can access the past. When we become conscious, we enter the now, the present moment, causing a shift of consciousness within. But the eternal moments of now, all of existence, are held in our deepest minds, our subconscious and superconscious. By living in our minds, we are living in an illusion, and we do not see these truths.

The timeless in you is aware of life's timelessness and knows that yesterday is but today's memory and tomorrow is today's dream.

Time is an illusion—the moment you grasp this, the happiness and awe that you see and feel will be the greatest treasure you can receive. You will not want to leave the present that you entered, but you will feel compelled to bring everyone else to the same amazing reality, and when you do so, they will constantly analyse it with their minds and eventually bring you back into a less intense state of being, as you have to constantly think to try and explain to them. But the good news is, the more people that move into this awareness, the more everyone else will.

THE NOW

In the now, I brought a tape recorder with me everywhere to try and explain and prove this existence. I recorded many conversations, and some of them were very interesting. As I became completely connected with the source of life, I had so much inspiration all there, just ready to be accessed—I felt I knew everything and had an answer to any problem. Rachel tested that and asked me many questions, and I became full of answers, which were all readily accessed within, as these truths are in us all. When you slow your thoughts down, you let in information from your spirit to your mind, and you realise many things in that moment that you enter. For me at these moments, I am connected with that wisdom, and it's all there to be accessed. This book is not about the recorded conversations, it is about directing you to that eternal magnificence of the now, where you will access all the wisdom that you would like to know in your own world, and the "now-ness" will give you just that. There was one conversation that may help you see this reality from both a man's and a woman's point of view.

Rachel and I were having a chat; here is the tape recording of that interesting conversation whilst in the now:

D.J. (just talking away): "Here I am, looking at all around me. Everything is so clear, intensely clear. The space in between the objects is there, it's noticeable. All objects have essence within and around them to give them this structure, to radiate them. I am completely aware of me, my body. I am not 'out there,' in thoughts, but I am 'in here,' without thoughts, distractions, programmes running in my mind. I crossed the bridge, from conscious mind to subconscious mind. I'm intensely present. There is the nothing and the things. The nothing is the no-thing, the space between, that's what has all the essence of life, the energy manifested here as air. Everything is just so alive, vibrating, radiating. It's like a 'higher awareness,' which it is, but that itself is an illusion. It's actually more of a deeper awareness within one's own energy, within one's own aura. It's like number one awareness is 'outward observation,' number two, 'inward observation,' then this awareness where both number one and two derive from, the present moment, placing energy in deeper conscious mind and using one's own mind as the tool that it really is. The mind is a tool, and you operate it by placing your energy/awareness in it. Move into yourself, your home, your temple, your deep self, time stops and all colors are enhanced, more intense as thoughts and programmes are not taking over all that is normally perceived. All energy is in now. Not 'out there,' family, problems, life, business, etc., have-to-dos. It is freedom, all illusions stop, you rise above all illusions and enter now, the truth, the spiritual essence, that which you are. You find you, yourself. Your awareness is not really 'higher,' or 'lower,' but more so, deeper, clearer, more energy and less thoughts to dish it out on.

"All thought, energy, awareness in the present, which is amazing. Why would you wish to live in a torturing existence, when you can live in an existence of awareness and knowledge and bliss? Whole outward observation changes, becomes amazing, once the change is made within."

"Do you know how and why you are evolving?"

Rachel: "I know why, but tell me then, how?"

D.J.: "This is the best thing ever, right; you're sending the present moments on one level of your awareness to another level of your awareness (yourself) to get over the thought process and issues which is usually a bad experience that you had before, so you have two choices.

"You either tap into this awareness that you are and see what you do and stop it or change the experiences that you had before by tackling that moment, which is pre-sent to you from yourself no matter what it is.

"When you bring this moment to yourself, change it, do something different that you wouldn't normally do, don't think, do it, then thoughts created around that and you make the change in the mind, you have evolved through a new experience—do you understand this? Your deeper self is bringing forth experiences to your mind's reality for you to overcome and evolve until your deeper self and you are one. Your own game is crossing your own bridge within."

Rachel: "What I'd like to know is, what do you think about this?"

D.J.: "This is fantastic!"

Rachel: "Listen to me, as I'm going to teach you something. The only thing that will make anybody happy is if they live in the present moment; it doesn't matter who they're with or what they're doing. That's the whole point of this. For you living in the present moment, for you things are clicking left, right, and centre. But for me, it's like the difference between the future and past. My problem is that I live in the future but I'm cutting out desire like you said and that's it. It's like living in the supermarket and all there is, is crackers . . . or chocolates, or just any one thing. But that's the difference in it. You either have the end of the rainbow or in the present, all of the rainbow and all the colours to go with it."

D.J.: "That's a beautiful description.

"Take time out and create reality now. In between your thoughts, it's here, the feeling. Most people cannot not think of anything; their mind is working all the time. Stop time—stop mind—peace—heaven.

"When I was young, I was so full of negative energy, and how I was searching for the now was racing bikes or cars, and I would drive them so hard, but it was releasing what I had in me, my racing thoughts, it was my fix. The speeding around was taking up so much of my thoughts, and I was finding the present moment and that was it, that's what I was always searching for, that inspiration from the essence within. Now I'm here, no racing, no nothing, I'm here now."

Rachel: "That's why people do the extreme sports, that's what they're doing, or like racing drivers, it brings them into the moment."

D.J.: "Yes, it's only when it is brought to the extreme that time stops, the now is found, even just for a moment, but that's what we're all searching for, to break free of the illusion."

ENERGY ATTRACTION IN THE NOW

Later, there was a conversation going on between two lads. One was named Clive and the other was the owner of a hostel called Tom. Clive was talking about the ego and the mind. Tom said, "Yeah, you need a balance between the ego and mind," and he began to talk about experiences where he left his body. He was explaining he was flying around, looking down on people below. Also, once when he was driving his bike, he felt the wind was so strong that he or his soul was getting blown out of his body. Clive looked at him in amazement.

I cut in and said, "Yeah, I just left my body on August 9 just gone, it was an amazing experience." I explained that I had been trying to do it for so long and finally I did it whilst lying in bed. I explained the story, and then Tom said, "You see, you were not believing what I was saying, but this man comes over to explain his story."

I said, "Yes, lads, the mysterious chain of connection, hey." I said to Clive, "You see, all you said was about the ego and look what you started."

Clive said to the owner, "I'll see you next year, yeah?"

"No," he replied, "I'm building a new place, a new bed and breakfast called B n B, as Be in Being yourself to Be."

"Very good," I said.

He said, "And there will be a wooden sauna deck with beautiful Chinese gardens and lots more." He was getting so excited. He left then and I had a quick chat with Clive.

I said, "You asked about the ego; well, the ego is made up of what you want to be as others view you. How you act according to and to impress others. You need to live in your heart and your soul." I was explaining to Clive how I did it and how I felt I got to where I am.

Clive said, "Well, it worked for you and that's great, you know. I can't follow anyone else's belief step by step and call it my own—I have to find my way."

That you do, Clive, that you do . . .

Let me explain in my words to help you understand my definition of this now. You know when you enter a moment, an all inspiring moment; it could even be a goal at a football match for some people, it could be a beautiful naked woman for other people, but the majority of these moments consist of outstanding beauty, scenery, mountains, lakes, and a rising or setting sun all in the one moment; everything stops, time stops, everything in the mind ceases to exist in that moment; that is, all thoughts stop for a moment. It is only a brief moment, but nevertheless a short experienced lived.

Well, that's it—entering the now consists of that inspiring moment, that awareness to be your constant reality and to be our constant reality everywhere. When looking at reality in this constant moment, nothing in the game is really real, it is only the essence within and around that gives the people and the material objects life. It is an awakening of the energy or spirit inside of you, thoughts stop and in your whole reality, time stops, as time is the illusion of your thoughts racing. Then you feel and see that you are apart of all of this amazing reality and, in a sense, wake up; you find yourself coming home to yourself.

Illusions fade away, and the really real world is clear to see. You then know that you are in a reality that is created, and behind the scenes is where you come from. You see that the essence of life is your security, and you are apart of all that is. You have entered your deeper self and you are awake.

In the now, I have done it, this is the end of the race. I have done it, and I have my proof, the experience, which is my absolute truth. I am out of the racing mind and have entered the now, the present. Then, as this racing mind of thoughts is out of the way, the negative energy within me is free to leave as I fully connect with it, see through it, as it is an illusion as opposed to really being me. The racing mind is like a lid on the top of a can—the energy is not free to go, as it can't leave with these racing thoughts in one's mind. All solid material consists of racing molecules, giving the illusion that the item is solid, and with the racing thoughts, the mind is like a solid object, a solid lid on the top of a can, your body—keeping your energy that was passed down to you, kept within you.

By connecting with yourself, there is no need to be afraid to connect with the energy issues that lay within as with full presence, and all thoughts stop, the energy leaves the person as it is not held captive. All my experiences stay with me, as I have become what I have experienced. I then surrendered to the game itself after a full on intense race, all to prove that game exists and how it exists, the rules and the workings of life itself. And "Now" I have "Won"—the best reflection realised.

In the now, one realises so many illusions, one after the other, and the realer reality becomes real—an awakening up. The illusions are, the mind used as a tool goes back to each experience and sees how life is perfect. In the now, you see that it is you in your body and that your body grows old; it ages. Evolution itself goes on, your body gets born and dies, but you are you existing in this universe, and this is where you belong—endless and eternal. Do you get it? You see the body grows old. We still feel the same inside. Only we look in the mirror and we are older, day by day, and before we see it, we're old. The illusion is the body grows old; the time in the mind creates that, the worry, the thoughts, the anger, the sadness, and so on. The soul stays you and only evolves through experiences. The only change that there really is, is the emotional change. Energy in motion, for we cannot "not be." We are always here, being something, someone, some spirit, evolving, experiencing, understanding, finding ourselves, and even emotion is a choice that we make, we can choose to feel different, it's done by changing our thinking.

When you are in the now, you get a strange feeling that you were away for a while, and now, just after waking up, in a strange sense, you feel that you are now awake and were asleep for a long spell. In the now, you can see that the world is going around the sun, creating the day and the night and, after a while, the four seasons. You can see that time is an illusion, that we are on a rock travelling through space without any time. You become more aware of the space in between the objects in your surroundings, as this mysterious essence that is there is also the peace that you have tapped into, within you.

You attract information that is on this vibration. For example, as you see there is essence in all, you may hear that scientists have just found out that objects and bodies are made up of virtually nothing, so vast under a microscope are the atoms from each other, and the atoms themselves are made up of virtually space, nothing. You then know it is the essence that is in the atoms, the bodies, the objects, life, which is you that is manifested into this material existence.

THE POWER OF NOW

I did my best to explain where I made it, when I became intensely in the now, the present moment. It became amazing, all of it. Everything became perfect in unison by the shift in consciousness. Everything became perfection, everything is perfection, it's just all our thoughts and our hazy minds that distort the truth, complicate the simplicity of life and truth. It's all there in the present moment. All that you think of is there in front of you, around you, but you do not see because our heads have so much rushing around in them. All we are thinking, we are creating, and it's all just there. All the answers are there. Heaven is there, it's here; all that stops us from "wakening up" to it is our influences, our restrictions, what we've being taught.

Once we understand our own astrology and how we are kept down by it, "played" by it, we rise above that restriction and receive a new perspective on life, a clearer mind. Then we get out of our mind, and time and illusions fade away.

I realised that I had so much to write in my book already and the question came to my mind, "How can I write all of this stuff? The now could have a book all on its own; there is so much to say, so much to record, so much to prove its existence. I need a way where all of this section can be done for me, so I can do all the rest." My question (what I thought up clearly in my mind) was, "Could I please receive a book to explain all of this?"

Then I went to Sandra in Balmain and just wanted to tell her how I made it, that I felt fantastic, and that I had no more death wishes. I wanted to thank her for all her honest, caring help.

Sandra said, "Hey, D.J., did you see this book before? It's called *The Power of Now*."

"Thank you," I replied.

The Power of Now—A Guide to Spiritual Enlightenment, by Eckhart Tolle, is less than 200 pages long; it's perfect—it's the now. It is where I fully entered before I came back to write this book. I can still enter the now, just not as intensely as before, as so much is back in mind again. But it's a fantastic place to be. I wish this present experience on everyone who reads this book. It's beyond "getting with the programme," it's the realest part of life that there is, it's so real, not a programme for the mind to get with, it's a place for you, yourself in your present to be happy and content within.

INSPIRATION

Can you recall any times in your life where you entered a moment, where you were inspired by that moment? There have been times for me when I realised that the more thinking I was doing, the further away I was getting away from that which I wanted to know. So when I slowed my thoughts down, I let in the very information that I needed. It came from deep within me, and it seemed to me that it was always there, only that my mind, spinning its endless thoughts, stopped this wisdom from entering my mind. Getting this information from deep within may happen once a month, maybe once a year; it all depends on how many times that time stops and we enter a moment. When one is in the now, the mind does not spin its endless thoughts, and time stops and mind stops and you are aware of you; also you are connected with this wisdom within. You do not have to wait for a month or a year; this connection is always with you in the now, and this inspiration is always accessible and can be received on a constant basis. This is really where you want to be, always having this connection.

SIXTH SENSE

When I wrote this book, it was the year 2005. In numerology terms, this is a 7 worldwide year. That means people all over the world will connect or try to connect with some form of religion or spirituality or just question everything about the unknown and the mystical side of life.

After the recent tsunami, I couldn't help but notice that there were no animals killed, leading me to believe that they could feel it coming, that the animals were in touch with their intuition, that they knew something was about to happen, and they got out of harm's way. It was so sad that so many people were killed due to this tsunami; I can't help but wonder that if the people were in touch with their intuition instead of prisoners of their minds, would there have been so many deaths? I believe that if I had been there, I would have felt the trouble myself, as my sensitivity is profoundly turned on, and I would have gotten myself out of harm's way, also trying to tell others too, but they probably would not have believed me.

On a spiritual level, I can't help but notice how this event happened under the influence of 2005, the 7 year. It was almost like life was telling us something, telling us that we must move into our deeper selves to survive in this world. There is not much more destruction the world can take from our minds and our collective consciousness. Signals are going off around the world, collective consciousness is setting them off, and we must try to get in touch with our spirit. Disasters like this bring many people together. The earth is energy; collective consciousness creates all. If you start getting into your soul self, you alone are creating a huge change. I believe this occurrence was created by collective consciousness. But the reason for it happening, I believe, was to get people to move into the next stage of the game, which is all about feeling. It's the new level that the world needs to re-create itself to.

BELIEFS

The beliefs of a person affect everything. Whatever you believe about life and spirituality, the universe (or the perfected universal system) will support your beliefs. That is, whatever you choose to believe, you will only really see that in your reality.

I will give an example that we can all understand. Someone gets insurance on their home. They get their insurance and feel that they are protected. Their thoughts and beliefs are about the house is protected. The belief is so strong because they have thoughts based on the action of paying for the insurance. The mentality is sent out there, and what is received? Protection on their house. Then fifty years pass without an insurance claim. Then new neighbours move in, and they tell them not to bother with insurance; they even cancel their own insurance, as they see it as a waste of money. They cannot manage to keep the belief and absolute knowing that their house is protected, as their own mind knows that it is not. Their minds become open to possibilities instead of protection. If they keep thinking about bad circumstances and disasters that could happen to the house, these fearful thoughts that build up this fearful energy inside of them, the greater the energy within and the clearer they focus on the thoughts sent out, they will draw to them a disaster that will happen to the house. They will say, "Fifty years I had insurance and never used it, and the day I cancelled it, my house got blown away in a freak storm."

How it works is the belief. The universe (which I call a system created universe) gives us copies of our own thoughts and beliefs in what we perceive as reality. That is, we send out thoughts and strong beliefs, and we think that we are asking a higher power, which in a sense we are (compared to our minds), and we receive that in our reality. And thus, whatever we choose to believe, the system created universe supports us in our beliefs. So therefore, we can choose our beliefs, and our reality will be that, and once we change our beliefs, one by one, day by day, our reality will also change for us.

This is why there are huge problems when it comes to religion and different beliefs; the first cause of all is not doing it to us, we are, and our thoughts and beliefs are reflected upon us. Your own mind knows your truth, your actions, your programmes in your mind, the tape recordings of previous experiences; your own mind knows this, so you cannot manipulate a perfected system. Do you see how it works?

I believed and knew and felt that an angel was looking over me, and I did many risky things until the day the aftershave came off the shelf in the bathroom and smashed over the floor. My belief changed to, this is it, I've done it, I'm on my own now, and my behaviours changed drastically. But whatever it is that you choose to believe with your heart and soul, it is sure to play a huge part in your life, but not just yours, also how you affect others. All the beliefs that we have in the world today are on a thin line between insanity and game over. I personally believe that all of the happenings in today's world are to drive the world to spirituality, to drive the people to a realistic view on life and essence.

I have and had a strong belief about living in Australia, and it affects every single behavior, action, thought, and decision that I have made.

The belief is the core of it all, and we all need them.

My beliefs were that I would go up the coast of Australia and live happily, but that didn't happen, and I guess a man would rather die than give up his beliefs. That did happen, and after the dying of my mind, I found a profound peace. Now my beliefs are just my experiences, as I am my experiences.

Some countries believe that a life weighs less than a feather; others believe that it is the most precious gift, and it's the beliefs that are the underlying reason for their behaviour. These are a person's beliefs, so some people don't really believe that they are doing wrong.

Beliefs are the core of all problems in the world today; none of us have the same beliefs, and everything that we do, say, and feel derives from these beliefs that we have. We need beliefs, goals, and dreams, just like we need food, water, and sleep. This is the core, and this is the problem.

This universal system will give us multiple copies of our beliefs and thoughts, as it is the great reflection in the sky, a perfected game. What we choose to believe will be manifested in our reality. It is all we will see. We won't see the real truth through our mind, as our beliefs stop us from seeing obvious truths in our reality. We have to make a shift in consciousness.

If we all followed our own inspirational truths, I'm pretty sure we would be fine, as following that truth within us is the same truth in all of us. The problem can occur when different people in history explain that truth in different terms, where the people follow only one person's words as gospel and not actually connect with the direction that the words are pointing at, the real experience of the now.

The truth is within you. There is not a single person (or any living matter, which consists of everything, everywhere) that does not hold this divine right within. It is not possible to exist without having this in-depth part of your self that really knows the score, which really knows what is what, once it is activated and woken up. The core holds this truth, and all our minds derive from that core; we are separated from our mind's point of view, but from our life's essence, we are all connected.

SPIRITS AM-FM

I was working away at my job with the radio on. There was an advertisement that clearly got my attention, and as I looked around, no one else seemed to hear it, but I heard every word. A woman named Jeanette was doing channelling from people who had died to people who were in the audience. I decided buy a ticket, and soon enough I was there. She was great. She got the spirits who died to pass on funny things to loved ones, which was truly amazing, and she had written a book about it all.

She explained how it all works: people who have died are here but just on a different frequency. For example, waves of energy: "You do not know that there are radio waves here in the room until you plug in the radio. This is the same with people who have bodies or people who have passed away and left their bodies behind. We're on FM frequency, and they are on AM frequency." She also explained that not all people who are taken into mental hospitals are insane; some just don't understand their connection or how to use it correctly.

At the end, she got us all to stand up and lean forwards for "yes" and sideways for "no," and ask the question, "Is there any energy or entities with me tonight?" Most of us moved forwards and backwards, without us doing it, including me—it was quite amazing! I had a sensitive nature and felt this. I felt it all. The Don was with me that night, and my body moved forwards and backwards.

Spirits with bodies are on FM frequency, and spirits without their bodies are on AM frequency. One needs to tune into the other frequency, the other vibration of energy, in order to access this amazing truth.

THOUGHTS ARE THE CORE

> "You are not a human being having a spiritual experience. You are a spiritual being having a human experience."
>
> Pierre Teilhard de Chardin.

A thought is energy, and when you choose to change your life or your attitudes about your entire life, these are really your thoughts on these matters. Your entire past up until this moment is really nothing more than thought. Your entire future from this moment onwards is nothing but thought. The idea of success is really the thought of success. You relate to everything and everyone in this world through the mechanism of thought. It is not what is in the world that determines the quality of your life, it is how you choose to process your world in your thoughts. People and things do not upset us, rather we upset ourselves by believing that they can upset us. That which we think about all day, we start to become, and people are about as happy as they make up their minds to be. If you change your thoughts, you change your world. Whatever you think and believe you are, that you will be.

MIRACLES

To create miracles, you have to be very clear about what it is you need. By being forthright and acting as if you have already obtained the object or condition that you desire, you create such a powerful energy that the universal law gives you what you want or need. But if you talk about the miracle coming, you release the energy from yourself and lose the power that manifests it. You need to keep it clear in your mind (or a whole group needs to keep the same frame of mind) and manifest this in your reality, draw it to you. Also what you wish for others, you bring on yourself. If you truly wish for others to have success in life, success will soon be brought to your life.

I explained to Rachel that the universe (or even spiritual priests) see God is in fact a system that gives you copies of your thoughts. Rachel said, "The universe gives it to me."

I said, "Yes, it appears that way, but the fact of the matter is, you are doing it to yourself, Rachel; you are really the source that is creating it, and that's how amazing you really are. This is the truth. It's a system with your thoughts and your creation!"

MANIFESTING

Manifesting one's own reality is not creating effects out of nothing but merely drawing them to you. Events you wish to experience come forth when you are ready to experience them. Items that are already there get drawn to us, not created by the ego mind but from a deeper source of ourselves, from a deeper consciousness, with great energy for the intent of being sent from the spirit or heart or one's self.

Manifestation: everything is there and is drawn to us after request or inspiration. But real manipulation, I believe, consists of seeing the illusion of solid material and fully connecting with the essence that holds it all together, with one's own essence, and being at one with it, for we are all the same essence. Then manipulation can occur. This is my belief, and nowhere is it experienced, but that's the real direction of manifestation.

Whether you think you can or whether you think you can't, you're right!

Manifestation occurs starting from your heart or spirit or subconscious mind when you get inspiration, then it moves onto your mind where you create it, then the event is brought to you, where you experience it.

CHAKRAS

Wind and unwind, clockwise and anti-clockwise, open or closed.

The Seven Chakras

1st chakra is where we connect to the earth and draw upon this stable and grounding support. Located at our perineum between our tailbone and genitals, the colour is red. This chakra is important for physical strength and stability.

2nd chakra is our sexuality and sensuousness. It's where we feel our power and ability to connect to others from this personal power. Located below the navel, it is orange in colour. This vital energy feeds our immune system with personal power.

3rd chakra is where we assimilate and discern all information, including nourishment and the impact of others upon us. Located in the solar plexus, its colour is yellow. It governs the ability to discern and filter toxic environments, food, and people. This chakra gives us good judgement and discernment, a sense of who we are.

4th chakra is where we give and receive love. Located between the breasts or the centre of our chest, it is green in colour. This is where we connect with others and share this beautiful energy without losing ourselves. This is the chakra of love.

5th chakra holds both our ability to speak our truth and ask for our needs, therefore allowing others in and experiencing other and self clearly. Located at the throat, it is blue in colour. This is the chakra for communication and clear perception.

6th chakra is the ability to understand the vastness of all things and how they work, whether past, present, or future. Often referred to as the third eye, it is located in the forehead and is indigo in colour. It is the chakra for vision, knowledge, and wisdom when applied with the heart.

7th chakra is where we connect directly with life's source, aligning with our higher self. Located at the top of our head, it is violet in colour. This is the chakra for spiritual wisdom.

CONSCIOUSNESS

Here are the seven layers of consciousness in the aura:

The seventh layer, Physical Consciousness, supports our physical reality. It is felt close to the body, and tapping into it feels like you're wearing a wetsuit, as it is dense and strong, and it defines our physical body.

The sixth layer, Emotional Consciousness, is our many emotions that should be constantly moving, since stagnation implies denial or suffering of these feelings. There are no "bad" feelings, since all emotions communicate our experience and truth in the moment.

The fifth layer, Mental Consciousness, is clarity of thought and where negative thought forms are located. Our ability to think clearly and understand ourselves and others.

The fourth layer, Relationship Consciousness, is where we experience our relationships. This is where we hold our past life issues that are unresolved from incidents involving others. Our relationship cords are found here as well. This is where we are connected to all beings.

The third layer, Manifestation Consciousness, holds the grid for our manifested truth, including our physical form. Out of the void comes sound and therefore form. This is the consciousness that holds and supports all form. Often symbols and mantras are used to experience this sacred facet of consciousness.

The second layer, Spiritual Consciousness, is pure light moving outward to energize our entire aura field. One can comb these light rays to fluff the field to invigorate after disease or ongoing depletion. Bliss and expansion are experienced here.

The first layer, Divine Consciousness, is pure wisdom manifested in our entire being, holding and defining our lessons for this incarnation. This belief system, which we define our reality through, is woven in this divine fabric, which then manifests on other levels of consciousness, bringing these beliefs into fruition. All healing must shift this consciousness to live differently.

I have experienced all of these levels of consciousness. I have been on levels 7, 6, 5, and 4 throughout my life, and I have even lived on level 3 as far as I can remember. I manifested myself into level 2 when I came to Australia, and in the now, I entered level 1 consciousness with the wisdom of everything, for a period. I set out to experience everything, and I sure did just that!

PERIPHERAL VISION

The peripheral vision state of awareness opens up expanded awareness and allows us to totally see, hear, and feel what is going on around us. It is impossible to hold onto a negative emotion when we are in the learning state. Our unconscious mind is active, and we are at a peak learning advantage. This is great for children, for reading, for martial arts, for developing psychic awareness, and for being in the now in all the moments.

To achieve peripheral vision, focus on a spot on the wall, really focus on the spot on the wall, high above your line of sight; keep concentrating on the spot and then expand your awareness out to the periphery. Notice what is to the left and to the right of you whilst you focus on the spot in front of you. Keep focusing and then gently let your gaze drift out to the periphery and see how far you can observe. Once you have established peripheral vision, drop your gaze down and carry on with your activity as normal. Notice how much more aware of everything you are and how in tune with your intuition and the surrounding energies you become.

If you are feeling down and emotional, then invoke peripheral vision; it helps you get out of the undesired negative state by leading you more towards abstraction and the bigger picture.

HOW TO ENTER THE NOW

I would never recommend anyone to get into the now the way that I have done it; as they say on television, "Do not try this at home."

The way that I did it was probably one of the most torturing experiences anyone could put themselves through, but you can do it that way if you are driving yourself to insanity like I did.

A more suitable way to enter the now would be to close yourself off from the world and distractions and withdraw within yourself.

You see, we spend most if not all of our lives being extroverted, observing life outside ourselves through our senses.

Three senses are chiefly responsible for drawing our attention; taste (through the tongue), sight (through the eyes), and hearing (through the ears). With our tongue, we repeat our thoughts and ideas to each other and communicate with the world. And in this manner, the impressions of the world enter our mind and intellect. With our eyes, we see the objects of the world, and their forms get imprinted on our minds. With our ears, we listen to the voices of the world and become one with them.

Our eyes are responsible for 85 percent of the impressions imprinted on our mind, our ears for 10 percent, and the remaining 5 percent is formed by the other senses of our bodies put together. If our attention ceases to go out and we thus stop the entry of impressions from the outside, we can, with an inward gaze, realise the truth. We need to be silent, and the eyes should then be used to contemplate that which is within and the ears should listen to the inner peace within.

Whenever we wish to withdraw our consciousness inwards, we must avoid the thoughts of the world that invade us. These are the impressions that have continually entered through our senses. This could be the affairs of our house, our job, our friends, and our family that have projected themselves on our mind's screen and obstruct our concentration. The first step for spiritual uplift therefore is to eliminate them.

You need to create an imaginary box inside the corner of your mind. Once that is done, you need to place everything that is imprinted in your mind into this box and close the lid. The other option is to get an imaginary broom and just brush all the imprints and thoughts off the top of your mind out to the side and be done with them. Both ways, on their own or together, will get you there. It is only now that you can become introverted or turned inward. This may not entirely work perfectly the first time that you do it, but practice makes perfect. You first begin to forget the world and all that you have to do, and the mind then loses much of its fickleness, and a certain amount of concentration is achieved.

Any left-over rambling tendencies are ended in the mind by listening to the sound within, which resounds in all human beings. Then you have achieved complete concentration. This sound current is the heritage of all. We do not hear it because our attention is extroverted. This sound that holds a divine melody resounds at the headquarters of the soul in the body and can be heard at the eye focus by going within. The sound current has the force of a magnet, which attracts the soul and makes it still. Then the soul passes through the sound current to the place from which it emanates. This place is the origin of the whole world. When we listen attentively to the heavenly sound, we begin to be enraptured by its bliss and automatically turn our back upon the world.

The display of name and fame and learning and intellect in the world is responsible for the scattering of our soul's energy and stops us from achieving this concentration within. It is easy to become educated and intellectually advanced, but it is difficult to subdue the mind, collect the soul vibration, and ascend to higher regions.

We cannot see the source of all with the eyes of our intellect; it is only the eye of the spirit that can perceive this. So long as our mind's energy is spread out, it is impossible to get ahold of your spirit. If therefore we control the mind and the senses, we can capture this bliss within. If this does not work for you but you still have an interest, you will attract the information into your life for you to continue on in this, if you feel that it is for your best interest. One way is by reading *The Power of Now*.

A GAME

When you have that second perspective on everything, then you can slip into it. Then you could think; send your mind out there on another observational point of view. You become the watcher in space, and you will always be here now. Then you realise it's a game and whether you're wearing the body of you or not, you'll be here. Then it's like waking up after a dream that was so real—as to waking up to realisation from a mere game. Then it doesn't even seem so intense; you have security, peace, love, joy, and happiness in the background. Clear thought lets you realise it's a game to be played.

Rise above the mind, the time, the astrology, have understanding and an open mind, and you'll become that you are. One trick to life is to die before you die (a stripping of illusions) and then a surrendering to all that is. Our five senses let us see how life is. Our sixth sense lets us feel the energy and vibrations of how the game really is. Tapping into our divine consciousness, our complete awareness, our higher selves, lets us see that all of all is part of the game, and all is illusion. This entire material world exists here on a vibration of energy, on a frequency of waves, which becomes our material reality when we play through these five senses on most levels of consciousness. Everything is and can be labeled and understood via measuring the frequency of it. All of all exists on levels of energy, vibrating at an infinite number of different speeds.

We all exist here on a vibration, on a frequency; this is our place in life. When we mature, when we evolve, when we see through illusions, we move to a higher frequency as our energy changes and we attract that world to us. When we abuse our body through drinking, smoking, or negative thinking, we move down a notch, because our energy is getting dispersed in many different places; the speed of our vibration decreases, and we attract all that which we are on. Nothing is what it seems. All of all is existing on different vibrations of energy. That level, that speed, that pulse can be manipulated, and our worlds can change—knowledge is power! Up a level—down a level, the choice is yours in your game called life.

This is what is happening in our world at the present moment. Consciousness is going higher, speeding up, and awareness is expanding as people are changing. The entire world is changing its level of vibration, higher, higher, faster, and faster, and this is why the weather is changing. The world is ready to change and grow and develop itself into a new consciousness, if you accept the invitation. You have just got to go with the flow! The way forwards is forward, not backwards.

Behind the vibration of energy and frequencies is the first cause, all that is, which has created itself into this energy. The "is-ness" became this energy, separating itself into an infinite level of vibes, which all derive from this consciousness. Can you see how reality is not really reality but merely entertainment for us to live and die, construct and destruct, feel and think and love and hate under natural laws? Our so-called reality is designed for us to wake up to ourselves through evolution. It's a big game of hide-and-seek, as we are only aware of 10 percent of who we are, and we are seeking to find the rest of ourselves, from the tip of the iceberg—to total existence.

THIS IS THE END OF THE BRIDGE

I did mention proving something that has never been proven before; this is for very good friend of mine in Australia named Smithers. Let's just look at that for a moment; this proves that life is a game and a game it is:

Comfort zone. This is proven by demonstration. Have a look at your own life and see how it matches up.

Groups of people in the same cause. Energy attraction. Science will prove that like energy attracts like energy. We as people are made up of energy. This is proven.

People of opposite natures come into our lives. This is proven by the law of science: opposite energy attracts, people are energy.

Past lives and infinite existence. The law of science proves this by showing that energy can neither be created nor destroyed but merely changes form, from one form to the next.

Acid and alkaline. This exists and is proven by its existence. We know it exists in food and fruit and stagnant energy and nature, and as it does so in this, it also exists in colours and music on some less intense degree but can be felt by people with a sensitive nature.

Vibration energy. This is really real and can be proven by science, by lie detectors, by any form of technology that can scan any form of energy, which is everything.

Collective consciousness. This really exists, as thoughts are energy, energy can neither be created nor destroyed, and therefore the existence of this is proven.

Drugs. What has been written about drugs in this chapter was taken from a scientific outlook on scientists who have experimented with drugs.

Spirits. Spirits are a form of energy; the sensitivity of a person lets them know this is true, but also the law of science states that energy can neither be created nor destroyed but merely changes form.

Depression. This is a state of mind that we know is true, but it works off the principle that like energy attracts like energy; a spiral is created, and you can get stuck in a depression. Because you are your life force within your body that feeds your mind, you can place your consciousness away from your mind and stop feeding those thoughts. The proof is how it works.

Relativity. This theory proposed by Einstein not only exists in the material world, it also governs our minds.

Visualisation. This is the key to manifestation, and its proof is in its workings. As it will work for each individual over and over again, this is the proof.

Spiritual experience. This cannot be proven to the mind, it can only be recognised by the spirit within; only you yourself will know if it is true. No one can make you believe; it is a matter of personal connection, which we all have in us.

Angels. This can be proven by the people who work in this field. Angels love to prove their existence to you; that is their very existence. They love it; try it out.

Karma. What we know of karma is basically that what goes around, comes around, and this is proven by the workings of life; all of everything in life works off a circle, from one polarity to the next and back to itself again. A circle needs to be complete.

Fortune-tellers and choices. We have choice in life, as my stories showed. Fortune-tellers really exist; some are very accurate. In order to prove this, you must see it in your own life, as in this instance we need to prove it to ourselves, just as I have done in this book for me.

Reflections. The realisation of this comes from a deeper looking at life, as I have explained it in the book. You may start to see it in your own life, and if so, we will then have proven it all to ourselves.

Kings Cross explained. Energy and thoughts can kill a person; this I have proven to myself, and all I can say is, it's true. You will know yourself as we are all made of energy and all have thoughts, and you too would have experienced this on some degree or another.

Thoughts. These are energy; science can prove that the brain cannot produce a thought on its own. This is proven. Therefore, as we know thoughts exist, they must come from some mystic side of life, as they do not come from the material side of life, so the essence of life is then proven. The thoughts come from the spirit, the subconscious mind, or some deeper aspect of that. Thoughts always exist, they are energy, and they are infinite. This is proven by the law of science.

Time. How does a person prove that time does not exist? Time and mind are inseparable. The proof of the illusion of time is proven by the workings of the mind; if you stop your thoughts, you see the illusion of time. When you dream, there is no time in your dreams, as you are out of that constant thinking mind. I have proven this to me, and I have shown you the way. If it were to work for you and for others, over and over again and again, then this illusion of time is proven to be an illusion.

The now. This state of being exists, as I have demonstrated in this book. It is very difficult to prove this existence, as once you put a label on it for the mind, you have missed the true essence of its existence. You, your spirit, will know that this is true when you have read this entire book and Eckhart Tolle's book, but if you don't connect with it, perhaps you are too identified in your mind. And if that is the case, the only way you can disprove this is by stopping your thoughts and telling me that this reality does not exist. And when you do stop your thoughts, we will both be laughing, as we then will have proven to ourselves the existence of this bridge and this presence.

You see, I cannot prove it as such, but whether you are to believe this existence or disbelieve it, whether you accept the limited proof or try to prove this wrong, either way, you will become the magnificence that you really are. I love it!

Inspiration. This comes from the deep self or from your higher power; either way, it is all one, just a reflection of itself. We have all been inspired at some point in our lives, but can you prove this to the mind? The way of proving this to the mind is by its label, "inspiration," which each person knows exists. You may have heard this statement from various religious texts: "Even before you have asked, I have answered." Now, how do you get your head around that one? When you ask life for something, you are inspired to do so. The inspiration comes from the drop of the ocean that you are, the same essence that is in the whole ocean. All inspiration comes from this ocean, and as you are a drop of this energy, you too get inspired, but your inspiration is not your secret; it is known by the whole ocean of energy, and that consciousness of energy has answered you even before you have asked.

Religions know many things, but some just don't explain it in a way where the person finds themselves at the end of the day; most religions just put more mind illusions in people, but they have the truth also. The good and bad exist in all of life, in every cell of life, as one makes the other exist in this relative world.

August 11, 2004. This really happened for me. An inspiring moment turned into a reality without time. To see and know and understand this truth, it causes one to have a shift in consciousness. The mind will not understand this, nor can it be proven to the mind, as it will only happen when the mind is switched off. Its existence and essence is what feeds the mind. It's almost like explaining to the body that if it did not have a life force in it, it would not survive.

Once people find their God-given right to have this experience, they could set up their own religion; their friends could even set up a religion around them. But it is not the person who found this presence that can give it to you or sell it to you; it is in you. All the person can do is guide you in the right direction. It is for you to get in touch with your soul self and not to pay an organisation to give it to you, it is you.

Sixth sense. This is a sense we all have, and it is not a sense of mystical illusion but one of our realer senses that we all have. Through experience, you will have proven the existence of this sense to yourself. Any farmer will see this in his animals, and pet owners see it in their pets. The proof is acknowledging this.

Beliefs. We all have beliefs, and we know we have them, so that says it all there.

Spirits. Jeanette, along with many others, can prove the existence of spirits, as can science. Once you are open to this possibility, you will attract this confirmation in your life. Spirits are on one frequency, and we are on another, as we have our bodies. We are human beings, we are beings in human bodies.

Thoughts are the core. The core of all existence derived first from a thought; for something to come from nothing, it must first come from a thought. This is proven by science, and if it is not yet proven by science, I'll have to get a job as a scientist and prove it myself. Because it's true!

Miracles. Throughout history, people have experienced miracles, and in many ways the mind cannot understand this, as miracles are thought to come from God. The energy of the source is life expressed, but we live in a system created universe and our thoughts reflect off that system, thus giving us that thought in our realty. The workings of this work, over and over again. The faith in this system that gives us multiple copies of our thoughts is what's required. But the knowing that this universal system exists is what makes this work over and over again. We are in a game, our spirit gets inspired, a thought is produced, this goes up as energy, working with this system, and the experience or the event or whatever it may be, on the same frequency as that thought or request, is then brought to us.

Manifesting. This consists of producing a thought and sending it out there, asking a higher power for something and receiving it in your reality. How it works is how it is proven.

Chakras. These exist, and we all have them. They have always existed in our bodies and have been known to mankind for thousands of years.

Consciousness. This is not an illusion; it is the only matter in existence that is not an illusion. Where does a thought come from?

Astral travel. The proof is how it works. There are many stories of people who have had "out-of-body" experiences, and they have proven beyond reasonable doubt that they have had these experiences. I think that we should start listening to each other if we ever wish to move on from the unconscious existence that we live in.

Peripheral vision. This is a way for you to avoid negative thinking, as negative thinking consists of intense focus from the mind. Peripheral vision gets you to expand your awareness, and in doing so, it is impossible to have a negative thought. How it works is how it is proven. Just try it.

How to enter the now. The proof of this is how it works; if it works for you and for many others, well then, it has been proven to us.

Proof that life is a game and a game it is. Life's a game to be played. Every control can be overridden, and every illusion can be seen through.

Energy and thoughts are the core, the first cause. This consciousness decided to play a game of hide-and-seek. To hide itself and seek to find.

And what happens when it is found? Laugh, love, so happy, and wish to play the game again. How does a game come into existence?

The solar system is a system that is perfect and gives you what you ask for. A soul that gets inspired to produce a thought in the father, the mind, to ask for anything in the first place. There are two choices in the solar system: that is the soul or the system. Mind systems are not working any more; the next step is to go the soul direction. Energy can neither be created nor destroyed, only change form.

The core of the workings, the setting up, the creation of a game:

One (1) becomes two (2) = Relativity and dyads.
One man or woman becomes three awareness, the three (3).
One becomes two in our outward world, outward observation.
One becomes three, in our inward observation, three energies.

Thus creating illusions like ego mind, time, future, and past. We perceive the world from our triune, our three energies between tapping into either. We look at the world and all experiences have opposites, the dyads, the twos. The energies within are the mind, the body, the soul.

The conscious, the subconscious, and the superconscious.

The Father, the Son, and the Holy Ghost! Holy because it is see-through: Whole-y. One became two. One also became three.

A game exists; I rest my case.

A CLOSING PARAGRAPH

Soon enough, Rachel and I broke up and went our separate ways in life. The funny part about it was, when we were breaking up, this song was playing in the background: "It's all in the game of love."

I thanked Rachel for all the help that she gave me, and she also said the same. I thanked her for sharing the experiences with me and helping me to grow as an individual, and she said that the experiences were great, there was always something to do, life was entertaining. We saw that our relationship had reached its peak and that there was nothing more to become of it. We wanted different things and were at different evolutionary stages in life. I don't know too much about relationships, but what I have come to find out is that they are a tradeoff, both people get something out of it. It causes both people to evolve and learn and experience. There are the good and bad times, but I reckon that it is better to have loved and lost than to never have loved at all.

I also wish to make a written apology to everyone I ever met. Some people, I have come into their life and left their life, and the reason for this was just the way I had to live my life, moving from one experience to the next. Others who I have known all my life, I apologize to them for lack of communication and lack of explanation of events.

Many sacrifices have been made on my behalf in order to do all this. All of this had to be done, this became the whole meaning of my being. I need and needed to justify my existence. I did have to push people away and needed to extract myself from people too, close people, family and friends. I did lose value of many things as if I stopped, all would have been gone to waste. I did this to myself; I did so many things that made sure that I stayed on my path to finish what I started. At moments when I became fully inspired, I would do things that would be for my benefit, really to the benefit of this journey. One has to be cruel to be kind, and I was a one man show, closing misguided events on myself to keep myself on track. I even lost value of love as searching for this proof went too far. There were times where I just needed to have a clear mind, and many conversations that people would normally have with their family were not done by me. Free mind for me meant closing down on almost everything and everyone, and many important values were lost.

Each energy change that occurred in me after I came to Australia consisted of about six-month periods before I was fully analysing a whole new change and awareness. Even the manifestation of the now lasted six months, perhaps even less as I began to use the mind as the tool it is. I began to relive my experiences to write the book. But experience begins within, and one can tap in and out of previous experiences.

Also when in the now, one realises that when helping others, you heal a part of yourself that felt abandoned or ignored when a similar thing happened to you. And I guess that is what is meant by the saying, "What you fail to do for others, you fail to do for yourself."

I also just want to say, I love my family very much. I understand them all and love them all. I hope each and every one of them are very happy within themselves and their lives around them. I have always loved my family. Sometimes my mind was gone crazed from being fuelled up with negativity, and I needed to get away, but once I got far enough away, I would find my energy and quickly realise that I loved all the members of my family. They're all legends in my eyes, and none of this would have existed only for them. It's because of my family that this book comes into play. Love is all there is.

There is one main character in my life that has made all of this possible—my father had a huge influence on me because of all the experiences that I had. I would try and share them or at least explain them to him. He disbelieved all that I was saying and brushed it all off. When I spoke about a fortune-teller, his reply was, "People take advantage of other people when they are vulnerable, to take their money and get them to believe things that are not true."

When I spoke about depression and how my thoughts were killing me, he said, "The body is made up of white cells and red cells, the whites are taking over the reds and that is what is happening."

When I said, "We are beings in human bodies, hence the word human beings," he said, "Nonsense, the difference between human beings and Heinz beans is one knows all and the other knows nothing."

I needed to prove all of these happenings to him so that we could move on from there. This went on for a lifetime, as the only way I could even come close to proving anything was to go out there and experience it all myself and see and analyse how it all worked. So for me, I went out there, to work it all out, just so that I could have a close friendship with my father, who was a huge influence in my life.

So as perfect as he is, he believes the opposite of all that is written in this book. Between the two of us, we together make 1. We are the opposites in life—in numbers and in our beliefs. He is a 3 and I am a 7. Together we make 10. It is only because of him that this book came into existence. I did not start off thinking that I was to write a book about all of this; I only thought I would find the answers and give them to him. Between the two of us on different ends of the relative scale, making this game of life explained from one side of the polarity to the other side brings the reader from his perspective all the way to my perspective. Building together a bridge from the material side of life, to the spiritual side of life. Thank you, Arthur, for you are the driving force for all of this; look what we have created. Between energy and "brushing off spirituality as something akin to witchcraft," he is perfect in every way.

Can you see now how life is perfect for me and for us all? Do you see the perfection in this? Because of how my father was born with his rational mind and all that he saw and believed in life was all to fit into this rational mind, his mind does not see anything else; this is basically him. And I was born connected with my inner self, and all that came into my life was mysteries to the mind, based on this vibration that I am aware of as me. There is nothing that I can do for my father to see what I see; there is no point in my game where I can share all with him and get him to say, "Ah, I see now, I understand." There was no limit in this or point where that would ever happen, no matter what I did or explained to him. The perfection of this is, I would have to find all the answers, all the mechanics of how it is working, and then I would have to surrender at some point in the game. There was no other way this game could be played, as at some stage of the game I would have to surrender and then enter the eternal moment of now. Life through evolution is perfect for me and, as I see it, for us all. See the people that come into our lives as teachers, as that they are.

I also want to thank all the characters that have come into this book; they have all played their part perfectly, and each and every one of them are unique legends all in their own style.

One thing that I didn't make clear is the negative and positive. They are what run the game. Vibration energy—broken in half to a relativity of energies. It's there, so we do have choice in life. It does not have to be both for everyone. It's only there to experience once, to let our minds understand what's what. Just like hot and its relative opposite, cold. Once it's experienced, one understands it and therefore then has a choice—a choice to make. We have all experienced the negativity, so we sure as hell know what it means, but do we fully understand the positive energy? Or the neutral energy that brings these two energies into play in this relative world. Have we taken it past the low level? Even the next level—wouldn't that be something? Even to move into the *now*. That takes positivity to another level beyond conscious mind understanding, and that's only the first big step in positive awareness reality, as it is infinite; there are no limits. So this is just a taste so far!

We have choice. We could all wake up and give this higher energy out there the best experience this source ever had. We could all raise our vibrations and awareness, and we could all be the greatest, hugest change in collective consciousness. Who is this higher power, this source of energy where all derives from? It is you/us, your energy, our energy.

You are energy—energy can neither be created nor destroyed, only change form. This is you. Once this understanding becomes a part of your life, a lot of things change within you, thus creating the change outside you. Congratulations! You're a legend!

Between all of these stories and what I have tried to understand after the experience and carefully piece together, we can see that the family we get born into is perfect for us, is planned out by the source of life, the drama, the emotion, the love, the bonding, and the experiences. Once you fully understand your life, even if it is for a brief moment, the part that you are playing in the game of life, all of it is perfect, as once these rules of this game apply in my life, they also apply for you!

Life Is a Game. Once you are out of constant mind thinking, you will be open to the universal wisdom that is always there, just waiting for you to tune into it. Until that moment becomes your existence, if you were to ask for confirmation on all that you realise yourself, you will get it, as life will give this to you. The aim of this book is to open your mind. The aim of the game is to justify your existence.

Also, don't hesitate to drop me an email on djsgame@gmail.com if you would like any more information to help you on your journey.

I do not intend for this book to be about me as an individual expressing himself; I am just trying to bridge the gap between material and spiritual, between the mind and the subconscious mind. It is just that the only way a person can write about spirituality is through personal experience.

I am not intending for this book to be the answer to our problems of this time, but merely a true story written so that it takes the reader from a materialistic view on life to a deeper reality.

The aim of this book is to open your mind, and with an open mind, you then attract that which you need to know into your life. Just like when I entered the present moment, I asked and received papers on that reality. If we do not know, we can't ask or attract the information until our minds are open to a world of possibilities. Once our minds are open, we let in the information, and due to the law of energy attraction, we even attract more information to us; the world is full of information, and that you may see.

Based on my theories on life, our lives are mapped out in a sense, and our choices are to fulfil that life or to make some lesser version of ourselves. The life is our choice for starters, so from a spirit level of choice, we have it all. From a mind perspective of choice, we have the choice to fulfil the spirit's choice. And our choice now is to be the mind or the spirit, and the latter giving all choice in the world.

> ***Life is a game.***
> ***I honestly believe we have two choices in life:***
> ***to be unconsciously played or to be consciously a player.***
> ***To be played or to be a player.***
> ***That is the question. This is my gift to you, and the choice is yours.***

My father sent me a message as I was finishing this book.

Arthur: Happy birthday, D.J. Don't dive too deeply into new water, lest there be rocks.

D.J.: Gotcha, wise words. Is you becoming a wizard?

Arthur: No, you is the wizard of Oz.

D.J.: Ha ha!